D1809905

ARCHITECTURAL
THEORY

ARCHITECTURAL THEORY VOLUME ONE

THE VITRUVIAN FALLACY

A History of the Categories in
Architecture and Philosophy

David Smith Capon

JOHN WILEY & SONS

Chichester • New York • Weinheim • Brisbane • Singapore • Toronto

61125

THE LIBRARY

THE SURREY INSTITUTE OF ART & DESIGN

Copyright © 1999 by D.S. Capon.

Published by John Wiley & Sons Ltd, Baffins Lane, Chichester, West Sussex
PO19 1UD, England

National 01243 779777. International (+44) 1243 779777

e-mail (for orders and customer service enquiries): cs-books@wiley.co.uk

Visit our Home Page on http://www.wiley.co.uk or http://www.wiley.com

David Smith Capon has asserted his right under the Copyright, Designs and Patents Act, 1988, to
be identified as the author of this work.

All rights reserved. No part of this publication may be reproduced, stored in a retrieval system,
or transmitted, in any form or by any means, electronic, mechanical, photocopying, recording,
scanning or otherwise, except under the terms of the Copyright, Designs and Patents Act 1988 or
under the terms of a licence issued by the Copyright Licensing Agency, 90 Tottenham Court Road,
London, UK W1P 9HE, without the permission in writing of John Wiley and Sons Ltd., Baffins
Lane, Chichester, West Sussex, UK PO19 1UD.

OTHER WILEY EDITORIAL OFFICES

John Wiley & Sons, Inc., 605 Third Avenue, New York, NY 10158-0012, USA

WILEY-VCH Verlag GmbH, Pappelallee 3, D-69469 Weinheim, Germany

Jacaranda Wiley Ltd, 33 Park Road, Milton, Queensland 4064, Australia

John Wiley & Sons (Canada) Ltd, 22 Worcester Road, Rexdale, Ontario M9W 1L1, Canada

John Wiley & Sons (Asia) Pte Ltd, 2 Clementi Loop #02-01, Jin Xing Distripark, Singapore 129809

LIBRARY OF CONGRESS CATALOGING-IN-PUBLICATION DATA

Capon, David Smith
  Architectural theory / David Smith Capon.
    p. cm.
  Contents: v. 1. The Vitruvian fallacy : a history of the
categories in architectural philosophy – v. 2. Le Corbusier's
legacy : principles of twentieth century architectural theory
arranged by category.
  Includes bibliographical references and index.
    ISBN 0-471-97946-5 (set : alk. paper). – ISBN 0-471-98588-0 (v.
1. : alk. paper). – ISBN 0-471-985899 (v. 2. : alk. paper)
    1. Architecture. I. Title.
NA2500.C3146 1999
720–dc21
                                     98–30281
                                           CIP

720 CAP

BRITISH LIBRARY CATALOGUING IN PUBLICATION DATA

A catalogue record for this book is available from the British Library

ISBN 0 471 98588 0 (Volume One)   0 471 98589 9 (Volume Two)
0 471 97946 5 (2 Volume Set)

Typeset in 9/12pt Caslon 224 from author's disks by Mayhew Typesetting, Rhayader, Powys
Printed and bound in Great Britain by Bookcraft (Bath) Ltd, Midsomer Norton

This book is printed on acid-free paper responsibly manufactured from sustainable forestry, in which at
least two trees are planted for each one used for paper production.

This book is dedicated
to
Catherine Christina
and
Emma Catherine

CONTENTS

PREFACE

The original purpose of this book was to search for and set out the principles and doctrines that have governed twentieth-century architectural theory in the Western world. The results of this investigation constitute Volume Two of the work.

In order to structure the subject in a logical manner it has been necessary to consider the notion of categorization itself as it has developed both in architectural theory and in Western philosophy. The results of this exercise constitute this present volume.

Volume Two discusses architectural theory in terms of Form, Function, Meaning, Construction, Context and Will. Volume One provides the reasons for using these six categories and describes the extent of each.

There are two ways of defining architectural theory, each with its own methodology. The first definition is that architectural theory consists primarily of what people have said or written about the subject. An appropriate methodology would, in this case, consist of collecting and studying the literature, interpreting the various statements in relation to the context in which they were written, and coming to an informed conclusion on the relative value of the statements that have been made. This would constitute a historical approach to architectural theory.

The second way of defining architectural theory is that it consists primarily of the way in which the various principles and doctrines of the subject are inter-related. The appropriate methodology here would be that of arguing the case for a particular structure through a series of rational arguments, and establishing a hierarchy of concepts through which the subject can be understood. This would constitute a philosophical approach to architectural theory.

A work on architectural theory can, however, be neither entirely one nor entirely the other, neither wholly a history nor wholly a philosophy. The two approaches reflect two aspects of the same subject, which are, in the final analysis, inextricable. They are, if you like, form and content of the same thing. It is as impossible to discuss the history of architectural theory without considering the structuring of the concepts as it is to discuss the structuring of the concepts without considering how the concepts have been used.

It has been decided therefore to take a dualistic approach to the work, not by way of a clear-cut separation between history and philsosophy but by a methodology in which there will be a continual interplay between these two aspects. This approach will be apparent not only in the decision to produce the work in two volumes but also in the way the individual chapters have been structured. Each chapter, excluding the introductory and concluding chapters, will be composed of a short historical section followed by a longer typological section. The historical section will set the context for the ideas which follow and will introduce the general structuring principles involved. The typological section will look at the ideas in turn and, in particular, the way in which these ideas have been used by various writers on the subjects concerned. A concluding section to each chapter (in Volume One at least) will look in more detail at particular structuring problems that may have arisen.

Three points need to be emphasized:

- First, this is not a history of architectural theory in the sense of providing a list, in chronological order, of those who have written about architecture with a summary of concepts discussed under each. Rather it is about the origin and development of the concepts themselves, where the omission of a concept will be considered a greater failing than the omission of a reference to any particular author.
- Second, in relation to these concepts, and the doctrines which proceed from them, no personal preferences will be expressed. If there is a single theme to this book, it lies in the ordering and classification of concepts and doctrines – a theme that was likened by M. H. Abrams to a survey of the "common ground" on which the various critical theories "meet and clash".
- Third, in relation to the ordering of these concepts a careful distinction will need to be made between classification and categorization. The book will classify nothing except elementary concepts and the doctrines arising from them, and will argue like many others against the simple pigeon-holing of architects and their buildings.

Reflecting the approach outlined above, we may note that the arguments put forward in this work also fall into two distinct types. There are arguments of induction, by which it is proposed that sufficient well-considered examples will be found to give credit to any point of view being put forward. There are also arguments of deduction by which it is hoped that logical clarity will be given to the conclusions being drawn. Arguments for the nature and number of the categories, for example, are of both types, and naturally the conclusions afforded by induction should be in agreement with the conclusions gained from deduction. Constant vigilance will be maintained, however, against other examples and arguments which may lead to alternative conclusions.

There is another problem to be faced. If the content of architectural theory belongs to the field of history, then, as we have said, its form belongs to the field of philosophy. There was a preface written by Bertrand Russell for a general work of his that began by apologizing to the specialists of the various schools in his field. It continued:

"If, however, books covering a wide field are to be writtten at all, it is inevitable, since we are not immortal, that those who write such books should spend less time on any one part than can be spent by a man who concentrates on a single author or a brief period."

This must be even more true for those who attempt to bring together such diverse disciplines as philosophy and architecture. If there is a mitigating factor in my own work it must be that it concentrates on one small, shared aspect of both

disciplines, that of the nature, number and correlation of the primary categories.
As these are commonly used, whether knowingly or unknowingly, in the works of
architects and critics alike, it is hoped that the following pages will be of some
interest in furthering an understanding of the different approaches available in the
subject of architecture.

The study arose from a thesis prepared as part of the degree course in Architecture at the University of Edinburgh. One reason for choosing Edinburgh was
that it offered the opportunity of studying Philosophy and Literature for two years.
The idea that I should write a book was suggested, after I graduated in 1974, by the
head of the School of Architecture, Professor Guy Oddie. Some initial ideas were
published in 1983 in an essay entitled *Categories in Architectural Theory and
Design*, after which it was again suggested that I write a book, by the late Professor
Barrie Wilson, a Vice-Principal of the University. More recently, Professor Robert
Tavernor, for a while Forbes Professor of Architecture at the University of
Edinburgh, and at the time of writing, Director of Studies at the School of Architecture at Bath, has written, "there is undoubtedly a need for a book, especially as
a teaching aid for architectural history and theory courses, which covers the
categories of Western philosophy".

I thank them all for the encouragement that they have given in this enterprise.

LEGEND

Besides the notes and references, bibliography and index to be found at the end of
both volumes, there are three further aids to understanding the work which we
shall describe here, namely a brief glossary of terms, a mini-thesaurus, and an
explanation of the diagrams which will appear throughout the book.

The book is composed for the most part of words. It is intended that the most
important of these words will represent the kinds of things we can say about
architecture. Conversely, they also represent the kinds of thing an architect
should be considering when designing a building. The book is concerned with an
understanding of architecture, and in turn with the design and criticism of
buildings, through the medium of words.

Words do not exist in isolation from the world but should be considered as the
closest representation of the world that the mind can make in order to judge, to
reason about, and to understand the world. The structure of the world is reflected,
in varying degrees of imperfection, in the structure of our words and language.

The arrangement of words into categories constitutes the structure or framework for a comprehensive understanding of architecture. A thesaurus provides
such a classification of words, but thesauri arranged arbitrarily should be distinguished from schemes like Roget's (described in Chapter 7), which attempt to
reflect the structuring of the world. A similar, if much simpler, framework is shown
in Table 1 and serves as a useful adjunct to the Index in discovering in which
chapter of Volume Two a particular topic will be discussed.

It is recognized that words are often imprecise in their meaning, and it is for
this reason that an understanding of the structuring principles underlying the
categories should be clearly understood. In addition to words, therefore, diagrams

will also be used as an aid to understanding the subject. It is important to understand how these diagrams work, and the following is intended as an initial explanation.

Each diagram consists of a centre, a circle around that centre, and a number of radii extending out from the centre to intersect the circle.

- The centre represents the object or thing under discussion. It may, for example, be a particular building, or the subject of architecture itself.
- The circle represents the sum of knowledge possible regarding that thing. It may be thought of as a series of points, where each point represents something we can say about the thing.
- The radii represent the relations linking the thing to the surrounding concepts. In fact, the radii shown generally represent not specific relations but kinds of relation each pointing to a particular range, or category, of concepts.

It will be useful to look at each of these ideas in a little more detail:

- *The centre*: The centre will not generally be annotated on these diagrams. The reason for this is the simple one that without reference to the surrounding concepts the object is unknowable. For example, a building cannot be known without reference to its location, its size, its date, its physicality, etc. Lack of identification will help to concentrate the mind on the kinds of concept by which an object may be known, and facilitate comparison between the diagrams.
- *The circle*: The circle of knowledge about an object consists of a spectrum of concepts which can be classified by the way in which they relate to the object. These concepts may be specific to the object, or by a process of further generalization they may be general concepts that apply to many objects. The highest concepts, which apply to all objects, are few in number and are known in philosophy as "categories". These categories may be labelled on the diagrams, but more often than not, because of their general nature, a slightly lower concept will be labelled instead as a substitute (e.g. the concept of Form instead of the category of Disjunction).
- *The radii*: The kinds of relation linking the concepts to the object are similarly few in number, and indeed correspond directly to the highest general concepts or categories. This volume concludes that there are three kinds of relation – Disjunctive, Causal or Inherent (or formal, causal and classificatory relations respectively). The number of relations linking a concept to the object is a different matter and each concept may be linked to the object in many different ways. Concepts are classified according to the dominant relationship to the object, although in some cases, what constitutes the dominant relationship may be far from clear. (If two relationship types are equally dominant we arrive at a notion of secondary categories, a notion which will become clearer in the text.)

The diagrams indicate some general points which are worth bearing in mind.

First, they indicate a general way of looking at the world which can be traced back to the ancient Greeks. Each object in the world can be seen as being linked to

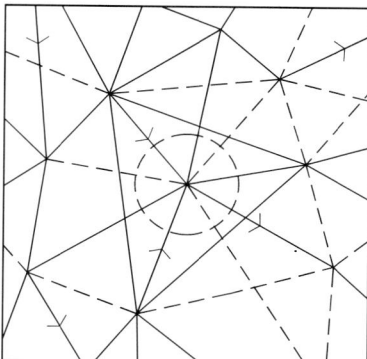

Step One: Each object in the world can be seen as being linked to other objects in the world by various relationships

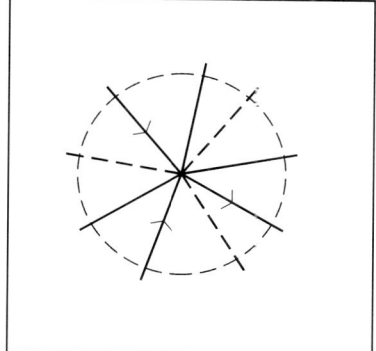

Step Two: Our awareness of a particular object may be represented by a circle around that object

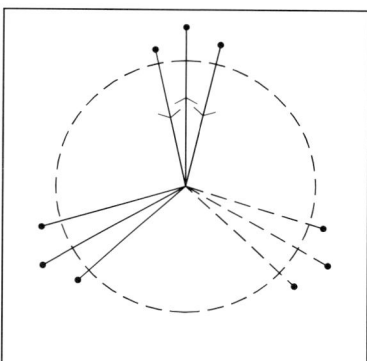

Step Three: Each object may be analysed, by categorizing the surrounding objects according to dominant relationship type

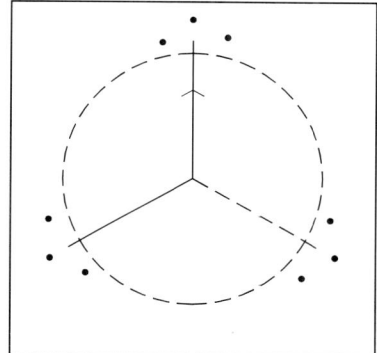

Step Four: We may then simplify the resulting diagram by reducing the number of relationship lines in each category to one

Figure 1 *Generation of a diagram to illustrate the theoretical principles that will be used throughout this book*

other objects in the world by various types of relationship (Figure 1: Step One). Our awareness of a particular object may be represented by a circle around that object which we can then look at in isolation (Step Two). Each object may be analysed, consciously or unconsciously, by categorizing, or grouping together, the surrounding objects according to dominant relationship type (Step Three). We may then simplify the resulting diagram by reducing the number of relationship lines to one, to arrive at a clearer picture of the cluster of concepts which comprise each category (Step Four).

Second, every object shown in Figure 1 may be subjected to the same analytical technique by switching the focus of attention to that object. This would entail drawing a second circle around the second object of attention. It can be seen that analysis according to the same set of categories can be carried out. In one diagram there may be several circles linked to a main circle showing an elaboration of subconcepts in relation to one of the main categories of analysis.

Third, following from the above, the same diagram may be used to show not only different aspects, or facets, of the object but also the different points of view taken by any enquiring subject. The orientation would depend on the main concepts upon which such a point of view was based. Each point of view can also be seen as the centre of its own subcircle, indicating that each one of us can see the object in many different ways by, for example, circling around it. Often, however, one view tends to be dominant according to our own particular bias.

It is clear from the above that we must deal not only with the "content" of architectural theory through the medium of words but also with the "structure" of architectural theory, not only in diagrammatic form but also through the medium of words. Words used in this latter sense belong more to the realm of general theory rather than architecture itself, and it will be useful to define here the ways in which some of these words have been used throughout these two volumes:

(1) *Element*: An element we shall take to be the simplest unit of understanding, of which there are two kinds – things and relations. As things can only be known through their relations, it has been assumed that only relations, in the final analysis, exist.

(2) *Thing*: A thing is anything which appears to have an individual existence and of which we can have a mental representation. It may be described as "object" or "subject" depending on whether it appears to exist outside or inside the mind.

(3) *Relation*: A relation is a connection between two or more things which can be understood to exist either naturally or in the mind, but which cannot be conceived of as having any individual existence. There are three kinds of relation recognized in this work:
  • Disjunctive or Spatial Relations (e.g. contiguity)
  • Causal Relations (e.g. cause and effect)
  • Inherent or Classificatory Relations (e.g. resemblance or association).
  The term "relationship" is a wider term than "relation" and it includes, or connotes, the two or more things so related.

(4) *Representation*: A representation is an image or reproduction of a thing placed before the mind, and consists of a matrix of relationships to which we may give a single name. It may be either immediate, in which case we call it an "intuition", or it may be subject to a degree of analysis, in which case it becomes a "concept".

(5) *Concept*: A concept is a generalization or abstraction made from a mental representation. Kinds of concept differ according to the degree of mental analysis which has taken place, and may be divided into notions and ideas.

(6) *Notion*: A notion is an unformulated, or only partially analysed, concept, clearer than an intuition but not as clear as an idea.

(7) *Idea*: An idea is a formulated concept, clearer than a notion, and connoting a degree of mental analysis of its subject matter in accordance with the categories of pure reason, or kinds of relation, described above.

(8) *Category*: The categories are the highest concepts under which all ideas can be systematically arranged. The term "category" may also be applied to the group of ideas so arranged. There are three primary categories (Disjunction, Causality and Inherence), and these correspond to the three types of relation listed above. Within these categories may be found concepts whose dominant relationship to the subject corresponds to one of these three types of relation. Examples include the concepts of Form, Function and Meaning respectively. There are three secondary categories (Modality, Community and Will), and these include concepts each of which is related to the subject by two equally dominant relationship types. Examples include the concepts of Construction, Context and Will.

(9) *Principle*: Principles are among the highest ideas, and may represent either a particular category or a relation between the categories. They may be distinguished from other ideas through an underlying suggestion of the relation of causality, and in consequence, through the way they may be seen as a source for further action.

(10) *Doctrine*: A doctrine is a body of notions, ideas and principles which focus on one or more distinct categories, e.g. formalism, functionalism etc. Each doctrine has both a historical and a theoretical aspect, the former consisting of what people have actually written, and the latter of an elaboration of the structuring of such ideas in relation to architectural theory as a whole.

Table 1 *A tabulation of the kinds of thing we can talk about in architecture according to category. A discussion of each concept may be found in the corresponding chapter of Volume Two.*

MINI-THESAURUS

PRIMARY CATEGORIES

Category One: Words relating to Form
form, shape, volume, surface, line, pattern, boundary;
quantity, size, dimension, unity, plurality, simplicity, complexity;
number, mathematics, geometry, structure, ratio, proportion;
harmony, symmetry, rhythm, axes, grids, syntax;
sense, colour, beauty, awareness, contemplation, perception, aesthetics;
objectivity, impartiality, justice, judgement, balance;
disjunction, opposition, contrast, articulation, juxtaposition, adjacency;
existence, space, being;
formalism, minimalism, mannerism, structuralism.

Category Two: Words relating to Function
function, purpose, reason, cause;
use, utility, practicality, pragmatics, work, activity, motion;
need, requirements, ability, means, ends;
effect, satisfaction, conveniency, comfort, pleasure;
exchange, interaction, efficiency, economics, costs, values;
systems, planning, services, heating, ventilation, energy;
psychology, sociology, behaviour, response;
morality, goodness, ethics, principles, aims;
functionalism, utilitarianism, brutalism, rationalism, systems theory.

Table 1 *(continued)*

Category Three: Words relating to Meaning
resemblance, imitation, likeness, difference, comparison, association;
classification, typology, category, doctrine, theory, knowledge;
style, fashion, taste, propriety, dreams, fantasies;
history, historic styles, periods, references, descriptions, criticism;
culture, customs, beliefs, religion, philosophy, myths, anthropology;
meaning, signification, signs, symbols, semantics, codes, analogy, metaphor;
quality, properties, attributes, characteristics, essence, perfection;
integrity, truth, honesty, sincerity;
historicism, academicism, postmodernism, symbolism, semiology, surrealism.

SECONDARY CATEGORIES

Category Four: Words relating to Modality
materials, substance, content, purity, homogeneity;
process, change, growth, flexibility, adaptability;
construction, craftsmanship, technology, manufacture, production, machines;
maintenance, life-cycle analysis, recycling, cleaning, corrosion, demolition;
modules, coordination, standardization, joints, detailing;
design, methodology, creativity, imagination, art, drawing, expression;
education, experience, wisdom, teaching, research;
property, wealth, identity, pride, responsibility, duty, self-respect;
constructivism, arts and crafts, organic theory, neo-gothic, metabolism, high-tech.

Category Five: Words relating to Context
context, site, surroundings, region, environment;
composition, townscape, landscape, place, movement, mass, space;
nature, communion, internal/external, ground, sky, plants, trees;
communication, light, sun, views, vision, sound, privacy;
ornament, decoration, poetry, music, dance;
scale, humanism, anthropomorphism, animism, bodily states;
feeling, community, sympathy, empathy, regard, love, sentiment;
age, nostalgia, past, memories, olde-worlde, quaintness;
contextualism, regionalism, neovernacular, picturesque.

Category Six: Words relating to Will
will, motivation, ambition, overcoming, persuasion;
politics, government, legislation, radicalism, professionalism;
power, strength, energy levels, intensity, grandeur, vastness;
emotion, sublime, spirit, enthusiasm, excitement, passion;
attitude, mood, humour, audacity, shockingness, optimism, nihilism;
confidence, conviction, courage, strength of purpose;
choice, freedom, partiality, likes, dislikes, prejudices, decisions;
originality, novelty, newness, future, modern, utopia;
modernism, futurism, utopianism, radicalism, avant-garde.

Note: The arrangement into six categories can be compared with that of *Roget's Thesaurus*, discussed in more detail in Chapter 7.

LIST OF PLATES

Picture Credits

Rheinisches Bildarchiv, Cologne	p. 60
Photo Scala, Florence	p. 36
Galleria dell'Academia, Venice	p. 2
British Architectural Library, RIBA, London	pp. 18, 96, 160, 178
National Trust Photographic Library	p. 124

SECTION 1

CATEGORIES IN ARCHITECTURE

A RETURN TO VITRUVIUS

CHAPTER 1

INTRODUCTION

One of the more curious notions of architectural theory which developed from Vitruvius was that the principles of architecture and the laws of the cosmos were somehow identical. What Vitruvius said in translation was this:

> "Our ancestors took their models from nature and by imitating them were led on by divine facts. . . . All machinery is derived from nature and is founded on the teaching and constructions of the revolution of the firmament, the sun, the moon, and the five planets."[1]

While it is engineering and not architecture that is mentioned here, Vitruvius remarked elsewhere that all such disciplines "have a common bond of union and intercourse with one another".[2] A building was seen as an assembly of elements, just as the universe itself was defined as "the general assemblage of all nature", and the creation of each entailed a necessary conformity to the simple precepts of geometry and proportion.

It is curious to us now because of the overriding concern with mathematics that developed, when we might have expected ideas from other disciplines to have been taken into account among the principles of architecture. The Greek philosopher Pythagoras was responsible to some extent as it was a tenet of his doctrine, or that of his followers, that everything in the final analysis could be reduced to number. Even Plato conceived of a material world composed of triangles, where the material elements, earth, air, fire and water could be analysed into cubes, tetrahedrons, octahedrons and icosahedrons respectively.[3]

Every natural form approximated to an ideal of perfection which could be analysed in terms of its shape and proportion, and nowhere was this more the case than with the human form. "Without symmetry and proportion", wrote Vitruvius, "there can be no principle in the design of any temple, that is, if there is no precise relation between its members, as in the case of a well-shaped man".[4]

Not only was there a vertical analogy between architecture and the cosmos, there also developed an important horizontal analogy between architecture and the human form. An architect should consider the geometry by which a man had been designed, where ". . . with hands and feet extended, and a pair of compasses centred at his navel, the fingers and toes of his two hands and feet will touch the circumference of a circle described therefrom".[5]

This was an image which seemed to haunt architecture in the late Middle Ages and the early Renaissance periods. We may think, for example, of the thirteenth-

---

Plate 1   *Leonardo da Vinci, "Uomo vitruviano" (Vitruvian Man) (Galleria dell'Academia)*

". . . this threefold nature, these three masses, Memmius, these three forms so different, these three textures so interwoven"

Lucretius

FUNCTION
(Commodity)

(1) The diagram on the right represents the typical view that the three Vitruvian categories constitute the three main aspects of good building, and that together they form a well balanced and comprehensive group.

CONSTRUCTION
(Firmness)

FORM
(Delight)

FUNCTION

CONSTRUCTION

(2) The purpose of this book is to show that the above interpretation is a false one; that these three aspects are neither well balanced nor comprehensive; and that their relationship to one another is more like that shown on the left.

FORM

CAUSALITY
(Function)

(3) The method will entail a consideration of the higher categories of philosophy under which these three concepts may be classified. It results in the discovery of two sets of three categories closely interlinked with one another and concludes with the consequences that this may have for architectural theory.

WILL

MODALITY
(Construction)

DISJUNCTION
(Form)

INHERENCE

COMMUNICATION

Note: For the sake of consistency all the diagrams that follow will accord with the following terminology and order:

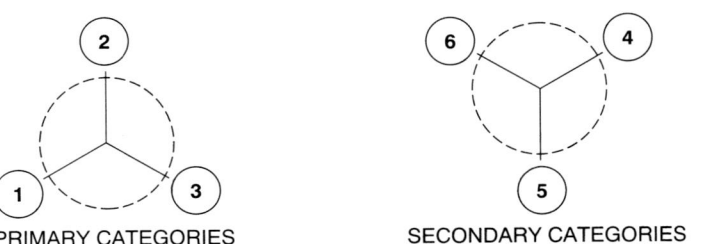

PRIMARY CATEGORIES

SECONDARY CATEGORIES

Figure 2   *The Vitruvian Fallacy*

century edition of the works of Hildegard von Bingen where an almost Christ-like figure was inserted in a circle which represented the macrocosm; or the late fifteenth-century drawing by Leonardo da Vinci where a stern figure with limbs outstretched seems to command adherence to the virtues of the square and the circle in which he is inscribed.

A third analogy that should be taken into account is the one between man and the cosmos, or between man and God. Wittkower gave an example of the mediaeval view from around the year 1303:

> "L'homme est un microcosm. Il est rond comme le monde car il doit autant de hauteur que d'envergure en étendant les bras."[*6]

The emphasis on geometry in this context is all the more surprising when we consider the importance of Church doctrine at the time, and the view that man was supposedly created in "the image of God". Augustine of Hippo many years before, had stated that this entailed not a single principle but a triple principle reflecting the Trinitarian nature of the godhead, and that this triple principle was reflected throughout creation.

However, the geometrical interpretation prevailed. The Gothic cathedral in the analysis of its facades into a series of square, triangles and circles could be seen as "a model of the mediaeval universe". Thierry of Chartres even conceived of the Holy Trinity in terms of an equilateral triangle, and the relation of Father to Son in terms of a square.[7]

Alberti in a "survey of desirable shapes for temples [churches] . . . began with a eulogy of the circle . . . a form where all the parts are harmoniously related like the members of a body",[8] and where divinity can most importantly reveal itself: "For Alberti – as for other Renaissance artists – this man-created harmony was a visible echo of a celestial and universally valid harmony."[9]

Alberti, in writing of the design of private houses suggested: "Let them be led from square rooms into round ones, and again from round into square."[10] He advocated[11] an architecture based on "the imitation of nature", remarking that "most things generated by nature are round . . . stars, trees, animals, the nests of birds. . . . We find too that nature is sometimes delighted with figures of six sides",[12] and here we may think perhaps of snowflakes and honeycombs used much later as examples by Gottfried Semper and Frank Lloyd Wright respectively. Above all, we should note the importance that Alberti attached to the concept of analogy: "Indeed, I am everyday more and more convinced of the Truth of Pythagoras's saying that Nature is sure to act consistently, and with constant analogy in all her operations."[13]

Francesco di Giorgio, a contemporary and acquaintance of Leonardo da Vinci, was one of the first to distinguish between the analogies of man and architecture, and man and the cosmos. He not only reaffirmed the idea that a circle formed the most perfect basic plan, but also concluded that the proportions of the classical entablature were a direct reflection of the proportions of the human face, the

---

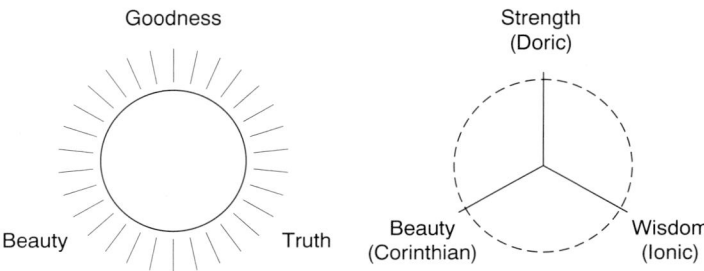

Figure 3 *A typical analogy between the Divine Mind and the concept of architecture, showing a mismatch between three of the "transcendentals" on the left and Langley's interpretation of the the three Classical Orders on the right*

various courses corresponding directly to the different levels of eyes, nose and mouth. "Man, called a little world", he wrote, "contains in himself all the general perfection of the whole world".[14]

Palladio, according to Wittkower, made an important "statement on the macrocosm–microcosm relation between the universe and the temple".[15] The centrally planned church of the Renaissance was an image of God's universe, and the circular form, in Palladio's words, made visible the "Oneness, the Infinite Essence, the Uniformity and Justice of God".[16] We might ask why these four particular concepts were chosen. The implication is that they constitute four different aspects of the godhead which could be symbolized by this particular form of temple. The term "Oneness", however, is more typically associated with the *unum, verum, bonum* formula of Scholastic theology, which in Renaissance thought evolved into the more familiar grouping, Beauty, Truth and Goodness (Figure 3). These too were among the "divine names" of early Christianity, and we might wonder by what shapes they too should be symbolized.

Returning to analogy, we may note that the architectural commentator, Barbaro, like Augustine, suggested that there was a likeness between the structuring of human intelligence and the divine intelligence seen behind natural phenomena: "The principle of art which is the human intellect, closely resembles the principle that moves Nature, which is an intelligence."[17]

For Scamozzi, the chief principles of art, or indeed science, were those of architecture for "architecture is the most worthiest and most important of the sciences. . . . It gives order to all things". This order . . . "is the rational, working principle of the world and nature, to which the architectural Orders are also subject".[18] We may note that Scamozzi, according to Kruft, wrote the most comprehensive work on "pure architectural theory" of the late Renaissance. Yet it too did not "offer a really coherent system of architecture" because Scamozzi also, in confirming "the analogy of the human body with architecture . . . found only geometrical laws".[19]

It will be worth while here, in relation to the concept of analogy, to briefly discuss the Orders which Scamozzi mentioned. Earlier descriptions of the Orders, particularly by Serlio and Vignola, constituted one of the prime subjects of architectural literature in the Renaissance and following periods. Filarete, for example, writing shortly after Alberti, recorded that Adam had been made in the image of God and that he became the builder of the first primitive hut.[20] The columns of this hut, he suggested, were the prototype of the Doric Order, analogous to the human form in their proportions, the capital of the column representing the human head. John Shute in the sixteenth century, following Serlio's definitive classification of the five orders, Doric, Ionic, Corinthian, Tuscan and Composite, depicted a caryatid variant for each of them – rather missing the point perhaps of the difference between analogy and imitation with regard to the human form.[21] Fréart de Chambray, in the seventeenth century, began to advocate a return to the models of ancient Greece, and recognized only the three Greek Orders, Doric, Ionic and Corinthian. These were to be seen not only as visible symbols of *la solide*, *la moyenne* and *la délicate*, an idea that can be traced back to Vitruvius, but also as a reflection of a fundamental threefold division within creation itself, a concept found in Greek philosophy as well as Christian theology. "For the excellence and perfection of an art", he wrote, "does not consist in the multiplicity of its principles; on the contrary, the simpler and fewer these are, the more is art to be admired".[22]

The abbé Laugier continued the search for rational principles in the eighteenth century, taking as the basis for his analogy a consideration of the primitive hut itself. Like de Chambray he tended to concentrate on geometrical and structural aspects, and he emphasized that it was an imitation of processes and not an imitation of forms that was at issue.[23]

In England, John Wood the Elder, like de Chambray, identified the three Orders with "the Strong, the Mean and the Delicate",[24] and Batty Langley, also in the eighteenth century, interpreted them in Masonic terms reflecting respectively the virtues of Strength, Wisdom and Beauty.[25]

An analogy which began solely as a geometrical one between a building and the cosmos can be seen to be developing into a wider structural analogy where the three higher principles attributable to the divine intelligence find their reflection in the three Vitruvian principles of *Firmitas*, *Utilitas* and *Venustas* (Figure 4). If the second term gives some difficulty we may note for the time being that Fréart de Chambray associated the term *Utilitas* with reason if not with wisdom itself.

However, let us stop here for a while. This is not primarily a work on the history of architectural theory, although the need is recognized to establish a context for the ideas that follow. There are questions beginning to be raised in the above summary to which we should direct particular attention, notably that of the relevance of analogy to the architectural debate, and above all, that of the number and nature of the principles of architecture, whether or not these are to be thought of as analogous to cosmic laws or to the structure of divine intelligence.

Regarding analogy, we should have to be very careful to distinguish not only between imitation and analogy but also between analogy and homology. For example, Alberti in one place wrote that Nature acts "with constant analogy in all her operations", yet in another he suggested that her law "runs through every Part and Action of Man's life and every Production of Nature herself, which are all directed by the Law of Congruity".[26]

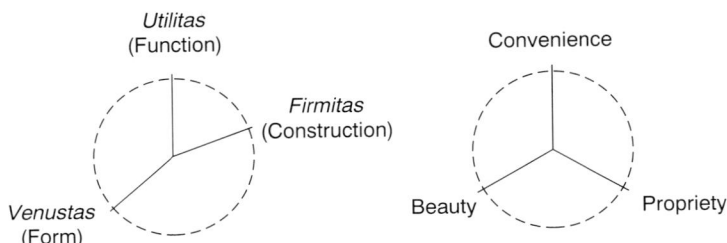

Figure 4 *Two sets of categories to be found in Vitruvius. On the left is the more traditional one interpreted by Wotton as Commodity, Firmness and Delight. On the right is one which reflects a more symmetrical arrangement of concepts*

It is clear that some knowledge of philosophy will be required to understand Classical theory, just as some knowledge of literature will be required to understand Romantic theory. Alberti in the fifteenth century had been schooled in Aristotelian logic at the University of Bologna, while Palladio, in the sixteenth century, had the benefit of new translations of and commentaries on Plato, undertaken by the Florentine Academy. A knowledge of philosophy will tell us, for example, that the particular grouping, Beauty, Goodness and Truth, which Palladio introduced to architecture (possibly through Barbaro) belongs to these commentaries, and is not to be found as such in the works of Plato who had adopted other formulations.

Some of Alberti's key ideas may be traced directly to Aristotle. For example, in Alberti we read "I shall define Beauty to be a harmony of all the parts, in whatsoever subject is appears, fitted together with such proportion and connection that nothing could be added, diminished or altered but for the worse".[27] Wittkower, rather misleadingly, suggested that this passage was "based on Vitruvius", but we find that Aristotle in one place wrote: "the mean is intermediate between excess and defect (so that often we say of a good work of art that it is not possible to take away or add anything)",[28] and in another place he described "a complete whole with its several incidents so closely connected so that the transposal or withdrawal of any one of them will disjoin and dislocate the whole".[29] Plato also spoke of "the principle of the mean" and warned us that in the arts we should be "on the watch against excess and defect".[30]

The lesson would seem to be this. While a study of architectural writers may be useful in understanding the application of general ideas to a particular subject, the source of these ideas and their relation to other general ideas should properly be sought in philosophy. Laugier, for example, proposed that the subject of proportion should be dealt with first by the philosophers and only then by architects. Because the subject of philosophy is so vast it will be necessary to define very carefully our particular areas of interest and investigate these thoroughly rather than concentrate on one particular book or one particular author.

Let us give another example. Later in the same work, Alberti extended the above definition of beauty as follows:

"We may conclude Beauty to be such a Consent and Agreement of the Parts
of a Whole in which it is found, as to Number, Finishing and Collocation, as
Congruity, that is to say, the principal Law of Nature requires."[3]

"*Concinnitas*", translated as congruity or harmony, and a term "clearly borrowed
from Cicero", was in Kruft's words "the governing principle of creation". It brought
things into relation with one another in three ways, through the number of parts,
through the proportioning of each part, and through the geometrical relation of the
parts to each other. However, these ideas too may be traced back to ancient
Greece. The three concepts may be compared either with the three differentiating
characteristics of the atom which Democritus had described, namely Order, Shape
and Position; or, as Rykwert suggested, to three of the ten logical categories of
Aristotle, namely Quantity, Quality and Relation.[32]

The structuring of the macrocosm, and the important distinction between
elements, categories and principles, is the province of the philosopher. The
structuring of the microcosm, in this case architecture, is the province of the
architectural theorist. If there is an analogy between the two, it may be supposed
that the one can learn from the other.

Two particular areas that we shall investigate more thoroughly in philosophy
are those of relation and categorization, but before we do so let us return briefly to
the history of architectural theory and summarize the development of the
categories in that field in order to see what further questions may be usefully
referred to the higher discipline.

The three categories of Vitruvius in their original order were *Firmitas, Utilitas*
and *Venustas*. (We shall term these categories rather than principles, as first, we
are concerned with the families of ideas which are represented by each term, and
second, the term "principle" has specific causal connotations which we should
wish to avoid at this stage.) The first two questions we may ask therefore are why
there should be three and what in fact did these terms mean. In Morgan's
translation they appear as Durability, Convenience and Beauty.[33] Yet in Latin
there would seem to be an important distinction between *Venustas* and
Pulchritudo which is the more familiar term for beauty. Granger had translated
the terms as Strength, Utility and Grace.[34]

Regarding the number of categories, we should note that Vitruvius also listed
six "fundamental principles of architecture", namely, Order, Arrangement,
Eurhythmy, Symmetry, Propriety and Economy.[35] How do these relate to the
three listed above? Are they, for example a subdivision of the category of
Venustas? If there is, as Alberti suggested, a "law of congruity" that runs through
every part and production of nature, we should expect to find the same number of
subdivisions to each category as there were number of original categories. Either
the first three categories were an insufficient number to give a properly balanced
account of architecture, or among the six "principles" there are some sub-
principles which could more usefully be considered under a single category.

If such questions appear to be too abstract we could ask how it was conceived
that these categories were grounded in reality. Isidore of Seville for example,
writing around AD 600, supposed that the three principles corresponded to three
basic operations of building: first, *Dispositio*, setting out the plan of the building to

THE LIBRARY

 THE SURREY INSTITUTE OF ART & DESIGN

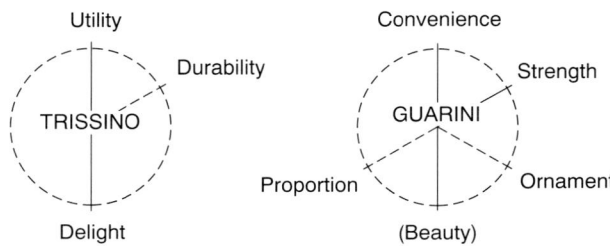

Figure 5 *Trissino (left) thought that there were two major concepts, Utility and Delight. Durability was a subsidiary category to Utility. Guarini (right) proposed four categories, Convenience, Strength, Proportion and Ornament, of which the latter two, Kruft assumed, were merely two subconcepts of Vitruvius's original category of Beauty*

accommodate the various activities and rooms required; second, *Constructio*, building up the walls, floors and roof of the building; and third, *Venustas*, adding whatever is required "for the sake of ornament".[36]

Closely connected with the question of reality is the question of order. Alberti, for example, reversed the order of the first two terms and spoke instead of "Conveniency . . . Stability . . . Beauty". Yet curiously, the sequence in which the subject of architecture is considered in the ten books of *De re aedificatoria*, as Kruft pointed out, maintains the original Vitruvian order:

Book I: Definitions
Books II & III: *Firmitas* (materials and construction)
Books IV & V: *Utilitas* (building types and their uses)
Books VI to IX: *Venustas* (ornament; theory of proportion)
Book X: General Conclusions

If architectural principles are indeed a reflection of cosmic laws then it could be of considerable significance which is first and which is second, or whether all three principles are of equal value.

Palladio in the sixteenth century followed Alberti's order and spoke of "*Commodità . . . Perpetuità . . . Belleza*".[37] An interesting question, however, is raised in a consideration of the ideas of his patron, Trissino – that of whether some of the categories are not secondary to others in a way differing from that of order. Like Alberti, Trissino considered *Utilità* to be the most important category, but followed it with *Dilettazione*, or pleasure. The category of *Durabilità* was however, in Kruft's words, entirely "dependent on and subordinated to *Utilità*,[38] an important notion and one which may point the way towards Construction being considered as the first of a set of secondary categories in some way "dependent on" the primary categories (Figure 5).

If we are to differentiate between types of category, we must also be careful to distinguish between categories and the concepts we might place under them. Guarini, a Theatine father, suggested in 1674 that the six principles of Vitruvius

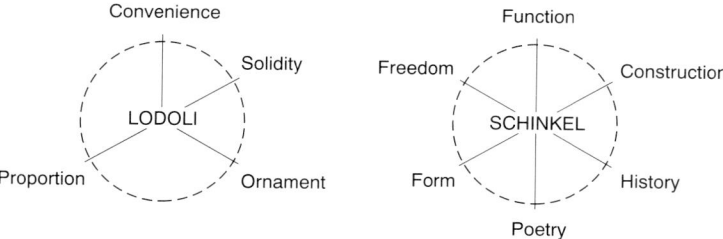

Figure 6 *The progress from Lodoli's four categories on the left to six categories present in Schinkel's work on the right. It is interesting to see "poetry" appearing in the position where Venustas occurred in Figure 5*

could be reduced to four: *Sodezza* (strength); *Eurhythmia* (or *Ornamento*); *Simmetria* (proportion); and *Distribuzione* (convenient arrangement of rooms), an ordering of which Kruft noted: "It is striking that Guarini mixes fundamental categories such as *Sodezza* with aesthetic concepts."[39]

The point that Kruft appears to be making is that if *Sodezza* belongs to a category that can be identified with *Firmitas*, then *Eurhythmia* and *Simmetria* are concepts which should be placed under a category identifiable with *Venustas*. We may liken the difference between categories and concepts in this respect to that between form and content. Whereas the categories structure our knowledge into groups of ideas, the concepts provide the ideas to fill out the structure. However, Guarini may perhaps have been suggesting that Venustas is a confusing term which has obscured the existence of two primary categories, namely that of Form, which includes the concept of proportion, and that of Meaning, which includes the concepts of style and ornament.

The ideas of Lodoli in the eighteenth century, according to his biographer Memmo, would tend to support this latter view. While singling out the concept of function for particular attention, Lodoli, like Guarini, listed four categories, namely Solidity, Proportion, Convenience and Ornament[40] (Figure 6). If Solidity represents a secondary category as Trissino had begun to suggest we have here grounds for a different alignment of the three primary categories and a different interpretation for the Vitruvian categories of *Firmitas*, *Utilitas* and *Venustas* from that traditionally given.

The history of the architectural categories in England began in the early seventeenth century with Henry Wotton's celebrated "elements", Commodity, Firmness and Delight.[41] Balthazar Gerbier and John Evelyn both gave a different order to the Vitruvian concepts, and Christopher Wren, following Evelyn's order, noted of "Beauty, Firmness and Convenience" that "the first two depend upon geometrical Reasons of Opticks and Staticks".[42] A question that arises here is, if we can analyse architectural concepts into even more fundamental elements like those of number and geometry, what other fundamental elements may be found through analysis, and what is their nature? There is no reason to suppose that they will be architectural in character, but such elements will certainly form the basis for a proper understanding of the categories. It would be interesting, for example, to analyse William Chambers' ideas on the subject written in the eighteenth

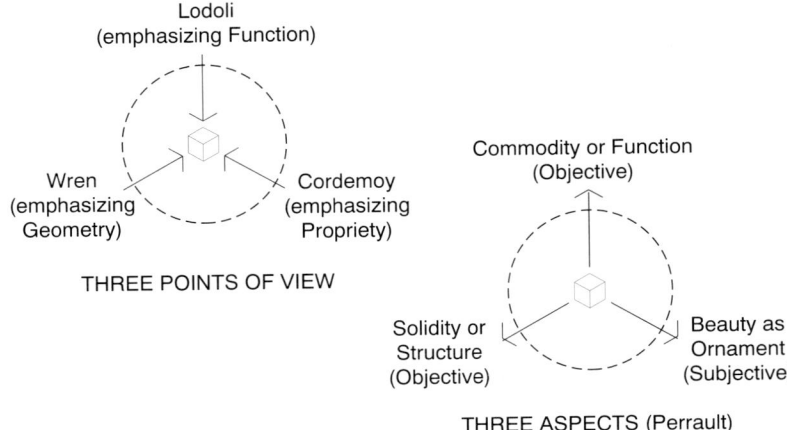

Figure 7 *Comparing three points of view taken by Wren, Lodoli and Cordemoy in generating their concepts, and three aspects of the subject discussed by Claude Perrault*

century, where "strength and duration" should be combined with "beauty, convenience and salubrity . . . and economy".[43]

In France, the history of architectural categories began slightly earlier than in England. Philibert Delorme in the sixteenth century suggested that "the use of geometric form . . . almost automatically brings with it 'convenience'"[44] a statement that raises questions concerning the interrelation of the categories. Does good Form always imply efficient Function, or are the two categories not autonomous in their respective spheres of action? The emphasis on *Utilitas*, or Convenience, was continued through the seventeenth century by writers like Le Muet and Fréart de Chambray, although we may note that François Blondel and Claude Perrault both commenced their Vitruvian groupings with *Solide* and *Solidité* respectively.

In the seventeenth century we see for the first time the application of modern philosophical ideas to the architectural categories. Following the introduction by Descartes of the idea that there is an essential distinction in the universe between the elements of Mind and Matter, the principle of dualism soon began to influence the course of architectural theory. Claude Perrault notably divided the categories into those which were "positive" and those which were "arbitrary".[45] *Solidité* and *Commodité* were objective categories and therefore positive, while *Beauté* tended to be subjective and therefore arbitrary (Figure 7). Fremin used the terms "*objet*" and "*sujet*" in 1702, but whether the distinction between objective and subjective should be applied only to concepts rather than categories, let alone be a distinction that reflects in some way cosmic laws, is a question that will need to be addressed. Kruft wrote of Fremin, perhaps not recognizing the Aristotelian formulation: "He gives the following portentous definition of architecture: 'Architecture is an art of building having regard to the thing itself [*objet*], the person for whom it is built [*sujet*], and the site [*lieu*]'."[46]

There is an underlying concept of appropriateness here which a few years later Cordemoy was to develop. If Wren tended to see the categories from the point of view of geometry, and Lodoli from the point of view of function, Cordemoy, appropriately for the beginning of the eighteenth century, interpreted them in the light of propriety. *Ordonnance* determined which of the Orders were appropriate for a particular use; *Disposition* was defined as "suitable arrangement"; and *Bienséance* represented the aesthetic aspect where "nothing will be found that is contrary to Nature, to custom, or to the use of things".[47] The notion that use or function was also implied under all these categories illustrates the confusion that was beginning to appear.

There was also the question of relativity that began to arise around this time. Boffrand, for example, declared in 1734, that the principles were not to be thought of as constants.[48] Viollet-le-Duc writing in the nineteenth century differentiated between those principles which were constant, for example the laws governing the properties of materials, and principles which were variable, for example those concerned with our interpretation of proportions, historical and social factors.[49] Again, there appears to be little distinction made between categories and concepts. A category established to include historical and social factors may itself be a constant, whilst the concepts included under the category will vary from age to age.

J. N. L. Durand, at the beginning of the nineteenth century, attempted the process of radical simplification. The sole object of architecture, he wrote, was "the most fitting and the most economic disposition".[50] He advocated two categories only: *Convenance* (propriety) which included the concepts of *solidité*, *salubrité* and *commodité*; and *Economie* (economy) which included *symétrie*, and *régularité*; which if added to his category of *Disposition* again approximates to the Vitruvian triad.

However, it is to Germany that we must turn for some of the most interesting developments of the nineteenth century. We may note that the development of the architectural categories in Germany commenced with Nicolaus Goldmann in the late seventeenth century, who identified the Vitruvian terms "*Starck . . . Bequem . . . Zierlich*" (Strong, Convenient and Ornamental) with similar terms found in the Bible.[51] Izzo, in the eighteenth century listed the categories "*Festigkeit . . . Bequemlichkeit . . . Schönheit*",[52] and under the second included not only hygienic but also psychological factors, an arrangement which would raise further questions on the proposed subjective/objective distinction noted above.

Weinbrenner, writing in 1819, attempted, in Kruft's words, "to link Kant's aesthetics to Durand's functionalism". Introducing the categories of Form, Function and Meaning, he "came to understand the principles underlying the works of the Ancients". There should be a "complete union of form and functional purpose", he said, and all ornamentation should "have meaning in itself which is in harmony with the meaning of that to which it belongs".[53]

Karl Friedrich Schinkel, who wrote "the most important theoretical works on architecture in Germany in the first half of the nineteenth century", extended even these categories. As a student of both the Classical and Romantic traditions he began with a consideration of what we shall call the Classical or analytical categories. In Kruft's words, Schinkel "evolved a complex theory of architecture

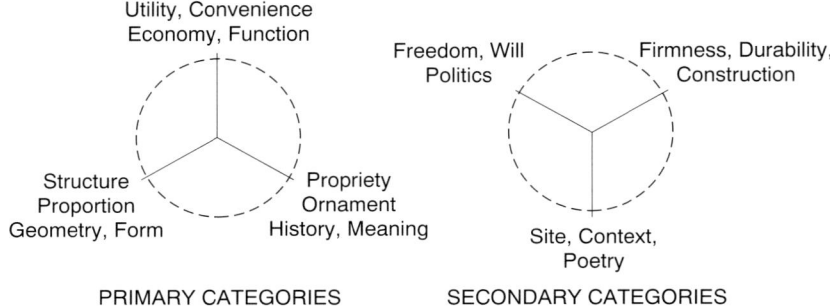

PRIMARY CATEGORIES   SECONDARY CATEGORIES

Figure 8 *The types of concept emerging which can be grouped under primary and secondary categories respectively*

taking into account functional, formal, social and historical factors".[54] Later in his life, however, Schinkel confessed:

> "Very early I fell victim to pure abstraction, which led me to evolve the entire concept of a work of architecture from the most immediate, trivial purpose and from the construction; the result was a rigid, lifeless design utterly devoid of freedom and lacking two vital elements – the historical and the poetic."[55]

The notion of freedom may be associated with the concept of the Will, and with Fichte whose lectures Schinkel had attended. The poetical element may be associated with Context and the Romantic movement which had been developing since the turn of the century. If we add these to Construction, which we have, with Trissino, already begun to consider as a secondary category, the following two sets may be tabulated (Figure 8):

Primary categories
(1) FORM, developed from the Vitruvian category of *Venustas*, and representing not only geometry but also those aspects of beauty concerned with symmetry and proportion.
(2) FUNCTION, developed from *Utilitas*, translated also as Commodity or Convenience, but including much of the "social" element mentioned by Schinkel. Durand's notion of Economy also belongs here.
(3) MEANING, also developed from *Venustas*, but represented those aspects of beauty concerned with taste, propriety and ornament. Schinkel's "historical" element belongs here too as we shall see.

Secondary categories
(4) CONSTRUCTION, developed from *Firmitas* and was translated variously as strength, durability and solidity. The fact that Vitruvius listed it first may be due to its association with form, or simply because it is the chief concern of building.

(5) CONTEXT. This is a complex category, hinted at by Fremin's *"lieu"*, but including also the "poetical" element of Schinkel. The two concepts of place and feeling were linked, for example, in the doctrine of the Picturesque.

(6) WILL, a category that was to become more important in the nineteenth century, as we shall see, but one that includes Schinkel's concept of freedom as well as other concepts of a more political nature.

The distinction between Classicism and Romanticism is probably the most important formulation that has occurred in the history of architectural categorization since Vitruvius. It will be one of the objectives of this book to explore the complexities of the two doctrines and discover how they might relate to the above two sets of categories.

Other theories of architecture of the nineteenthth century that we may mention range from Pugin's interpretation of Vitruvius in the grouping, Construction, Convenience and Propriety,[56] to Ruskin's more complicated *Seven Lamps of Architecture*[57] which will require some analysis. Kruft wrote of Fergusson that he was "a thinker who had a system of schemas, categories and tables to hand with which he could absorb any concept", and we may note that his "technical, sensuous and phonetic" categories were developed further by Ruskin who wrote: "We have thus . . . three great branches of architectural virtue, and we require of any building . . . that it act well [cf Function] . . . that it speak well [cf Meaning] . . . that it look well [cf Form]."[58]

Fergusson distinguished, in a way, between analogy and imitation when he advocated that "we ought always to copy the processes, never the forms of Nature". "In short", he wrote, "there is no principle involved in the structure of man which may not be taken as the most absolute standard of excellence in architecture".[59]

If the analogy between man and architecture was still alive in the nineteenth century, then so was that between macrocosm and microcosm. We read, for example, in the works of Ralph Waldo Emerson: "Although no diligence can rebuild the universe in a model, by the best accumulation or disposition of details, yet does the world reappear in miniature in every event, so that all the laws of nature may be read in the smallest fact."[60]

As it is the main purpose of this work to investigate the categories of architectural theory in the twentieth century we need say little further here of their development. While the Vitruvian categories have retained a central position in theory, from Geoffrey Scott writing in 1914 to the New Classicists of the 1980s, there have been many other interesting formulations worthy of study.

There is, however, one further question that has arisen in the twentieth century in addition to those described above, and it concerns the problem of whether categories should be considered as discrete or continuous. Connected with this is the recognition of a general negative attitude based on the erroneous premise that categories are by their nature discrete and divisive. While we shall investigate further the difference between categorization and classification in this respect, the truth that lies behind a proper conception of the categories would appear to be more akin to a continuous spectrum where individual concepts are clearly recognizable, yet where each merges with its neighbours at their common boundaries. Scott conceived of architecture as "a focus where three principles have converged

. . . blended in a single method",[61] and Eisenman, writing at the end of the century, has talked of the "blurring" of categories, and that architecture should "begin an exploration of the 'between' within these categories".[62]

The investigation of architectural theory in the twentieth century will, however, form the second and larger volume of the book. It will be mainly discursive in nature, consisting of the analysis of key texts and the setting out of examples of the kinds of concepts to be found under each particular category.

The first volume of the book will concentrate on establishing a framework of categories by which such an analysis can most effectively be undertaken. It will be more polemical in character, drawing not only on architectural texts but also on those works of philosophy which have dealt specifically with the problems of categorization.

Section One will conclude with an attempt to trace the Vitruvian categories to their source. In order to introduce the subject we shall begin with the earliest book written in the English language which deals with these categories, namely Henry Wotton's *The Elements of Architecture*. This is not a particularly profound work but it will give us an idea of the kinds of concept with which we shall be concerned. Also we shall look at the work of Alberti, from whom Wotton took many of his ideas, and who affords a prime example of the application of philosophy to architectural theory. And finally Vitruvius himself who, with Cicero, provides a link between the architectural theory that came after him, and the philosophers of ancient Greece, from whom many of his ideas were derived.

Section 2 will investigate the notion of categories in their philosophical context and attempt to follow the history of their development to the present day. We shall first turn our attention to the ideas of Plato and Aristotle in whose works we find the first written statements on the subject of categories in the history of Western thought. Interestingly, many of their own illustrations refer to Greek art and building, and we too may find these useful where relevant to the discussion.

The categories were an important concept in the thinking of the Dark and Middle Ages, and our investigation will entail a brief look at the history of Church doctrine with regard to them. Again examples will be drawn from the period, from the decline of the Roman Empire and early Christianity to the cathedrals of the high Gothic when Scholasticism and church architecture finally reached their apotheosis.

In the last two chapters of Section 2 we shall take a more intensive look at the categories of modern philosophy – a period generally held to have begun with Descartes in the early seventeenth century. These chapters will be two of the most difficult in the book, but essential if we are to understand first, that the categories of architecture are a reflection of higher categories, and second, how they are ordered and how they interrelate with one another.

In Section 3 we shall, after looking at some more general aspects of architectural theory in the nineteenth century, return to the discipline of architecture through a consideration of the links between architecture and philosophy in terms of architectural values and principles.

We may note that many of those who have written about architecture in the twentieth century have interested themselves in the general ideas of philosophy. We may mention Roger Scruton, a philosopher by training, who commenced his own work on the subject with the ideas of Immanuel Kant;[63] N. L. Prak who worked his way back through the philosophical works of Suzanne Langer to the ideas of Ernst Cassirer;[64] and Colin St John Wilson who has explored in his work the thoughts of Ludwig Wittgenstein, as philosopher and architect.[65] But little attention has been paid to the relation between the structuring of architectural theory and the categories of philosophy.

Now that we are nearing the end of the twentieth century, a slight stirring of interest may be discerned. The Deconstructionists, for example, with whom the names of Peter Eisenman and Bernard Tschumi have been associated, have taken ideas concerning the categories from the French philosopher Jacques Derrida. Hanno-Walter Kruft, who in the year of this introduction being written, published a definitive work on the history of architectural theory, defined architectural theory in terms of its aesthetic categories.[66] It is only by following such leads that we can hope to understand the immensely complicated subject of architecture in a balanced and comprehensive way, and only by developing a rigorous theoretical framework can we hope to come to any worthwhile conclusions regarding the principles of architecture, not only in terms of aesthetics, but also in terms of any moral or ethical implications that they may have for us at the end of the twentieth century.

Chapter 2
Vitruvian Categories

Wotton

The inner courtyard at Stirling Castle is little different today from the way it would have appeared at the beginning of the seventeenth century. Adjacent and at right angles to the Great Hall which Defoe described as one of the noblest mediaeval halls in Europe stands the Palace, built between 1539 and 1542, which with Falkland Palace represents one of the earliest works of the Renaissance in Scotland. The courtyard would have been approached obliquely as it is now, passing up and across a sloping outer court to enter under the enclosed bridge which still links the Hall to the Presence Chamber in the Palace.

In 1601, when James VI and his court were in residence, Henry Wotton, travelling under the assumed name of Octavio Baldi, sailed from Norway to Scotland with the news of a plot against the King's life. He had begun his journey in Florence, and the news he carried not only helped to ensure the Protestant succession in England but also led to the advancement of his own career and an early return to Italy as ambassador to Venice.[1]

Henry Wotton was born in Kent in 1568, four years after the birth of Shakespeare and five years before the birth of Inigo Jones. He studied at Oxford, with John Donne among others, and developed an early taste for politics and the arts in his travels to Italy. The Earl of Essex employed him as his secretary but the intrigues against Elizabeth which lost the Earl his head caused Wotton to make a prudent and hasty escape to Florence. There he entered the services of the Duke of Tuscany who, on intercepting certain letters from Rome, sent Wotton on his mission to Scotland. Upon James's accession to the English throne in 1603 Wotton was knighted and made ambassador to Venice where he remained intermittently for the next twenty-one years.

The English embassy was noted in the journals of the travellers of the time for the elevated level of conversation particularly with regard to Venetian glass, tapestry and painting, but where architecture also was "a matter for serious discussion".[2] At the end of his career as a diplomat, Wotton retired to England to spend the last fifteen years of his life as the Provost at Eton. The first task that he undertook before entering Holy Orders was to complete his best-known work, *The Elements of Architecture*, which was published in 1624.

In the Preface to *The Elements of Architecture*, Wotton admitted to being a "gatherer and disposer of other men's stuffe"[3] and that his principal sources were

---

Plate 2 *Alberti, Pallazo Rucellai (1446–1451) (British Architectural Library, RIBA, London)*

"I am very proud, revengeful, ambitious; with more offences at my beck than I have thoughts to put them in, imagination to give them shape, or time to act them in."

Hamlet

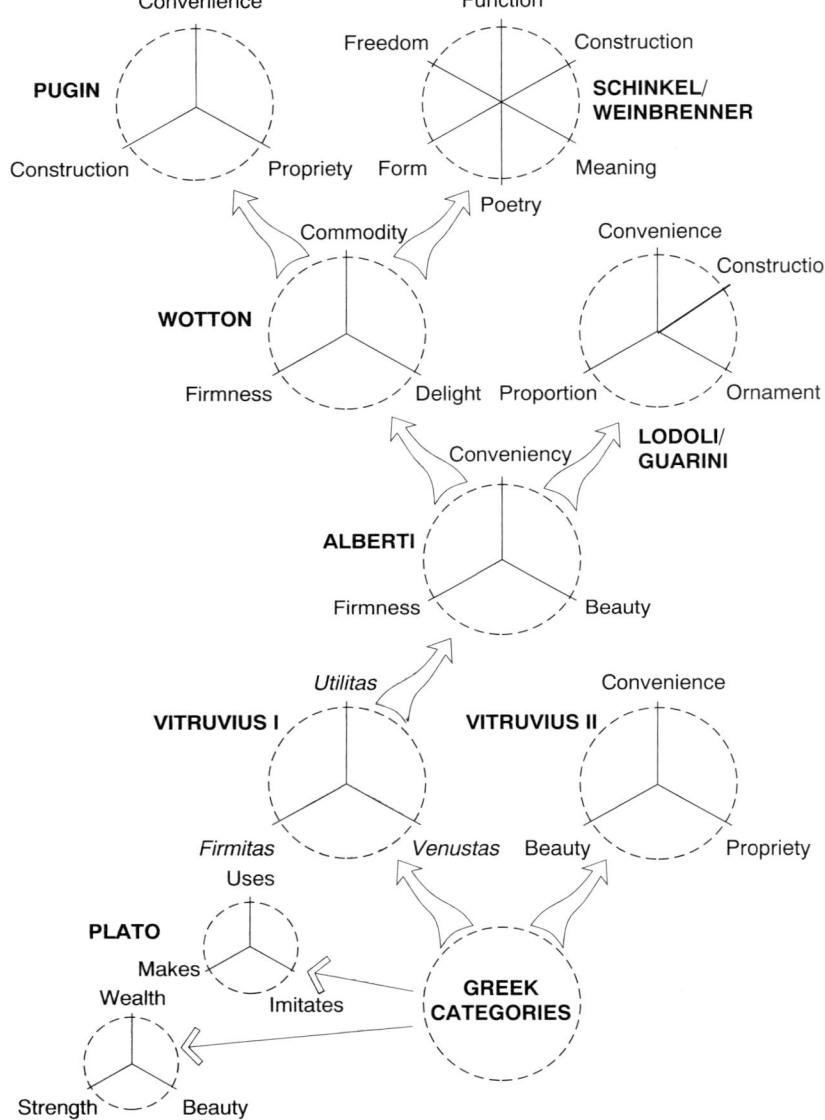

Figure 9 *The Vitruvian categories*

the works of Alberti and Vitruvius. It should be remembered that the first printing press had been introduced into England a little over one hundred years previously, and that works on architecture were still a novelty. The only serious exception was John Shute's *First and Chief Grounds of Architecture*, published in 1563, which again was derived from Alberti and was little more than a handbook describing the five Classical Orders.[4]

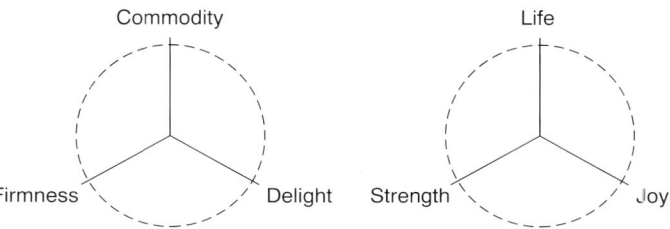

Figure 10 *Wotton's three elements of architecture (left) taken from Vitruvius can be compared with one of his poems which referred to the Creator as "my life, my strength, my joy, my all" (right)*

Wotton's work is remembered today almost entirely for its opening passage where the three conditions first outlined by Vitruvius, and by which all good architecture should be assessed, were translated into the English of the time as "Commodity, Firmness and Delight" (Figure 10).

"In Architecture as in all other Operative Arts, the End must direct the Operation. The End is to build well. Well building hath three conditions, Commodity, Firmness and Delight."[5]

Apart perhaps from Commodity the three terms would appear to need little further elaboration. A building should work, it should stand up, and, especially if it is to be considered as architecture, it should be pleasing. The chief virtue of Wotton lies in the quaintness of the terminology which has lent an air of authority to a statement that seems to be little more than a truism. Yet, one suspects that there must be something more. The idea has lasted for two millennia virtually unchanged and remains, as we shall see, the keystone to architectural theory. "All art", wrote Wotton, "is in truest perfection when it might be reduced to some natural principle".[6] But is there a natural principle behind these three seemingly arbitrary aspects? Are these the only three conditions for good building? How does Delight relate to Commodity and Firmness? How many kinds of Delight are there and to what natural principles may they be reduced?

Wotton gives no clear answers to these questions, nor does he define the terms he uses. He is a disposer of other men's stuff and it is to these others that we should turn. However, before we attempt to find the source of these ideas, it will serve as a useful introduction to sift through Wotton's text to gain what understanding we can of the way the terms are used:

- *Commodity*: The term Commodity is mentioned, albeit only in the negative, in two areas relating respectively to the external situation of a building and its internal arrangement. We learn first, of "incommodious access",[7] and second, of the "incommodity" of smoke entering rooms from the open fires used to heat the buildings.[8] Another way to look at the two uses of the term lies in the distinction between the convenience provided by the general arrangement of the building and the comfort afforded by its servicing and heating facilities. He added that the general layout of a house should conform to a preferred orientation, studies and libraries to the east, kitchens to the south, cellars to the north,[9] and noted that "the place of every part is to be determined by its use".[10] Like the parts of a body it is prudent to have rooms of all sizes to achieve a "graceful and useful distribution".[11] Inigo Jones, writing around the same time, spoke of a building as being a "Bautifull and Commodios thing": "This building hath on the sides places to maak wine, and stables, porticoes and other Commodities of a villa."[12] Such commodities may be likened in a sense to merchandise, factors that would be used in buying or selling the property, and we should take into account this second meaning, that of advantage or economic gain, that we see used, for example, by Shakespeare in his play *King John*.[13]

- *Firmness*: Under Firmness we might place all Wotton's references to good foundations and the bearing capacity of the soil.[14] Regarding the super-structure, "firs, cypresses and cedars", he wrote, "should be used for posts whereas oak and the like are more fit for crosse and traverse work".[15] Walls should be vertical with their corners firmly bound, and doors and windows should be as few and as small as possible for all openings are weakenings. Ledges should be of more strength for, "like bones",[16] they tie the building together. Columns should be placed precisely over one another, "as well for beauty as strength of the fabric",[17] and we may note in passing this connection between strength and beauty for future reference. It is also interesting to note that "Pillars or Pylasters" may be "considered as ornaments"[18] and not necessarily as the structural members they resemble.

- *Delight*: The term Delight occurs as infrequently as the other two. There is a telling reference to "chambers of delight"[19] which for Wotton meant studies and libraries, but it is clear that the proper source of delight in architecture should lie in the proportions "where the materials being but ordinary stone do yet ravish the beholder by a secret harmony in the proportions . . . form should triumph over matter".[20] He later revealed that the secret was to be found in those mathematical ratios discovered by the school of Pythagoras and evident in simple musical harmony, for example, the fifth (2 : 3) and the octave (1 : 2).[21] Where the length, width and height of a chamber met these proportions then there a similar beauty would be found. In striving for "coherence without distraction, without confusion, gracefulness will be achieved through recognizing a double analogy between the parts and the whole and between the parts themselves".[22] The twin concepts of uniformity and variety should be recognized as in the human body for "Man himself is the prototype of all exact symmetrie".[23] Art should imitate nature, and the most judicious artisans, he wrote, should be the "Mimiques of nature".[24]

Apart from the opening passage of *The Elements of Architecture*, the only other reference to the three conditions taken together occurred following the pronouncement that the circle is the most perfect form, although "in truth", a very unprofitable figure":[25]

- "in its fitness for commoditie and receipt being the most capable";
- "in its fitness for strength and duration being the most united in its parts";
- "and in its fitness for beauty and delight as imitating the celestrial orbes and the universal form".

It is curious that having discussed Delight in terms of coherence and the relationship of the parts to one another we now find that the concept of such a unity is classed under Firmness. One would have hoped that each of what should be fundamental categories would have possessed its own distinct vocabulary. The concept of Delight in fact does begin to take on a dual aspect, the contemplation of form and proportion, on the one hand, and the recognition of imitation and analogy, on the other – whether it is to celestial orbs or to human bodies. To give another example of this duality we need only turn to Wotton's contemporary, Inigo Jones.

Inigo Jones had visited Italy in the retinue of the Earl and Countess of Arundel between 1613 and 1614 and discussed architectural topics with Scamozzi, a pupil of Palladio.[26] His notes on Palladio make some reference to Henry Wotton,[27] although the latter was away from Venice at the time of his visit, and Jones returned to England to criticize Italian Mannerism as follows:

"These composed ornaments . . . brought in by Michell Angell and his followers in my opinion do not well in solid architecture and the facades of buildings, but in garden loggias, stucco or ornaments of chimney pieces or in the inner parts of houses . . . So in architecture ye outward ornaments ought to be sollid, proportionable according to the rules, masculine and unaffected."[28]

Here again, we see two distinct strands to Delight: the sculptural or painterly treatment of Michelangelo, often rather illogical structurally, and belonging, according to Inigo Jones, to the world of interior designers and landscape architects; and architecture proper, solid, unaffected and, remembering Wotton's words, "in truest perfection when it might be reduced to some natural principle".[29]

The Elements of Architecture concluded with a notice of intent by Wotton to embark on a further work entitled *A Philosophical Survey of Education or Moral Architecture*. Its subject, how through education one "could build a man", recalls the analogy between architecture and man which we noted in our introduction. The idea that there may be a set of categories applicable to both is suggested by a religious poem he wrote towards the end of his life, whose last line reflects the three Vitruvian concepts:

"But to me now, on thee I call,
My life, my strength, my joy, my all."[30]

The proposed work on moral architecture was never completed although some interesting notes regarding it appear in a collection of his miscellaneous writings, *Reliquiae Wottonianae*, and we shall return to them briefly in our concluding chapter.

ALBERTI

To understand one of the major influences acting upon Wotton we must return to Alberti and the beginning of the Italian Renaissance. In the fifteenth century the power of the church in Italy was in a period of decline following the schism between Rome and Avignon, and the ways of mediaeval Scholasticism, for which Florence had never been a centre, were being replaced by a fresh look at the works of classical Rome. Florence was an independent city-state in control of most of Tuscany, and its wealthy families, who had made their money in the cloth trade and banking, could afford to give patronage not only to new sculpture and building but also to the scholarship that was the central task of the Humanist movement. The "*Studia Humanitatis*", or study of the classics, was even beginning to infiltrate the curriculum of Scholastic theology and Aristotelian logic at the older schools and universities of Padua and Bologna where Alberti was to be educated.

Leon Battista Alberti was born in 1404 in Genoa to an old Florentine family who were at the time living in exile. He graduated from the University of Bologna, where he met as a fellow student the future Pope Nicholas V, and in 1432 he became attached to the papal court in Rome. Two years later the court moved to Florence where it lodged at the monastery of Santa Maria Novella, and also in Florence he became acquainted with Cosimo de Medici who was at the time its leading citizen.

In 1439, a visit by the Greek Byzantine legation from Constantinople prompted Cosimo to establish an academy at Florence, and as one of its central objectives he engaged Marsilio Ficino to translate the complete works of Plato. It may be noted that it was Alberti who was considered to be the greatest literary genius of his age even, as it was recorded by a contemporary, outshining Ficino at a gathering arranged by Lorenzo de Medici, Cosimo's grandson.[31] The most enduring of his talents, however, lay in the field of architecture, and besides his rebuilding the churches at Rimini and Mantua, he also designed a palace for Lorenzo's brother-in-law's family, the Palazzo Rucellai in Florence, which was built between 1446 and 1451.

It was during these years that he wrote the *De re aedificatoria* which was dedicated to Pope Nicholas in 1452. It was not finally published until 1485, fourteen years after the introduction of the printing press to Florence, and thirteen years after Alberti's death in 1472.

The book is of interest to us primarily for the various tripartite groupings that are presented to us, not surprisingly perhaps given Alberti's background in theology and philosophy (Figure 11). "All philosophers affirm", he wrote, "that nature consists in a ternary principle".[32] In the Preface, for example, he divided the arts into three: "Some arts we follow from necessity, some we approve for their usefulness, and some we esteem because they lead us to the knowledge of things that are delightful."[33]

In Book I of the ten books that constitute *De re aedificatoria* he introduced the three Vitruvian categories, but curiously he transposed the first two terms, referring to *Utilitas, Firmitas, Venustas*, and not the *Firmitas, Utilitas, Venustas* of the original. After listing the major elements of building that the architect should consider, namely the region, the site, the internal layout, the external walls, the roof and the apertures, he wrote:

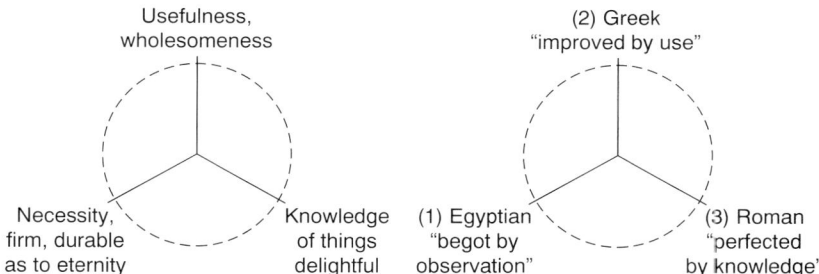

Figure 11 *Alberti utilized his interpretation of the Vitruvian categories (left) to structure three important phases in the development of architectural history (right). Note the sequence, which was probably influenced by mediaeval theology*

"Having considered whether there was anything that might concern any of these parts enumerated we found three:
- that each of them be adapted to some certain and determinate con-venience and above all be wholesome;
- that they be firm, solid, durable and in a manner eternal as to stability;
- and as to gracefulness and beauty, delicately and justly adorned and set off in all their parts."[34]

In Book VI he divided the history of architecture into three distinct phases: an Egyptian or Asian phase where architecture began and was "begot by chance and observation"; a Greek phase which was "nursed by use and experience" and was marked in particular by the skill of its workmen; and a Roman phase where perfection was finally achieved through knowledge gained from past examples and from rules "filed and perfected by the principles of philosophy".[35]

It would seem from first glance that Alberti, ignoring any historical incon-sistencies, ordered the categories arbitrarily for usefulness appears here in second place. A look in turn at the way Alberti approached each of the three categories of Vitruvius may go some way to dispelling this criticism, but for a deeper under-standing it will be necessary in the next chapter to investigate the works of Plato and Aristotle from where Alberti's ordering principles ultimately derive.

- *Utilitas*: The reason why *Utilitas* was placed first in his interpretation of Vitruvius may well have been due to the emphasis placed on causality in both Aristotelian and Scholastic logic. A building is born out of "necessity", Alberti wrote, to shelter us from the elements.[36] The first property of buildings is that they should be "accommodated for their respective purposes",[37] and that their value is measured by their "conveniency" in use.[38] Indeed, when we refer to a building it is its function that gives us our first idea of what it is, whether it is a palace to house the nobility, a basilica for the judiciary, or a church for worship. The first words of Book I, in fact, seem to advocate an early functional view of the arts in general: "Our ancestors have left us many and various arts tending to the pleasure and conveniency of life, acquired with the greatest industry or diligence . . . which arts have in view the great end of being serviceable to mankind".[39]

A link between function and economy is made in that a building should avoid "extravagant intemperance".[40] A balance should be achieved ". . . not less than dignity requires, nor greater than conveniency demands".[41] Rykwert, in his editorial footnotes,[42] commented that economy for Alberti was not only a moral but also an artistic principle, for, following Aristotle, Alberti had defined beauty as "a harmony of all the parts fitted together with such proportion and connection that nothing could be added, diminished or altered but for the worse".[43]

It was not the economy of plain utility that Alberti advocated for besides wisdom and virtue he also enjoyed and encouraged what he called the "lesser comforts",[44] but an economy or balance that required beauty and ornament as necessities for the creation of a thoroughly "wholesome" building.[45]

• *Firmitas*: If for Alberti utility was to be placed under the first category then the physical reality of the building was surely to be placed under the second. The subject of structure may be included under *Firmitas*, and through the concept of durability he introduced the concept of eternity: "firm, solid, durable in a manner eternal as to stability".[46] Materials were fully discussed in Book II, and constructional techniques in Book III, and it is notable that under this second category he mentioned "the skill of the workman"[47] and the "hand of the artificer".[48]

It is a curiosity of Book VI that after a discussion of the nature of beauty, he proceeded to elaborate on the more complicated constructional techniques connected with moving stones, including wheels, levers, pulleys, worms, screws, etc.[49] This dual aspect to Book VI may be seen as a reflection of the Aristotelian distinction between form and matter or, in Alberti's words, design and structure. "The whole art of building", he wrote, "consists in the design and the structure".[50] There is, in a sense, a parallel between relating the parts in the mind, whether in the contemplation of beauty or in the process of designing, and physically relating, "joining and uniting", to form a structure on site.[51] Instead of putting the mathematics of these techniques in a chapter that starts with delight, it may have made more sense to extend the category of *Firmitas* to incorporate mathematical aspects of beauty. That there is a link between the two concepts of firmness and beauty may be deduced from the following passage:

> "It is the property and business of the design to appoint to the edifice, and all its parts, their proper places, determinate numbers, just proportion and beautiful order so that the whole is proportionable. . . . We shall call the design a firm and graceful pre-ordering of the lines and angles conceived in the mind."[52]

It is of little surprise that Alberti later reduced the conditions of beauty to three, saying "The beauty of the edifice arises principally from three things, namely the number, figure and collocation of the several members".[53] It is of particular interest that Rykwert supposed that these corresponded to the three mediaeval categories of Quantity, Quality and Relation that derive ultimately from Aristotle.[54] We shall look in more detail at these categories in later chapters.

- *Venustas*: Some illumination is shed on Alberti's third category if we remember that in the third phase of historical development architecture was supposedly brought to perfection in Rome through the application of knowledge.[55] In the preface to *De re aedificatoria* it is important to note that the third of the arts is esteemed not because it is delightful in itself but because it leads us "to the knowledge of things that are delightful."[56]

In Book VI, Alberti substituted for "*venustas*" the word "*amoenitas*" meaning pleasure.[57] This he divided into two kinds, "*pulchritudo*" meaning beauty,[58] which he discussed in terms of harmony and proportion and which we suggested might be included under *Firmitas*, and "*ornamentum*" or ornament, which he defined in vague terms as an "auxiliary brightness . . . something added or fastened on",[59] and which should be included here. The link between ornament and knowledge is the clue to this third category and belonged, for Alberti, to the rules of propriety[60] which govern the type of ornament, style or classical order appropriate for a particular building. For instance, he suggested that if arches are suitable for theatres and basilicas, then columns and their entablature are more appropriate for churches and temples.[61] If the Corinthian Order is suitable for window surrounds, then the main door should be ornamented in the Ionic style.[62]

The link between ornament and delight is a more obvious one and introduces the concepts of imitation and resemblance. In Book VI, for example, Alberti allocated the effigies of noble statesmen to hallways, the representation of beautiful and comely faces to bedchambers, and for murals elsewhere he advised that "our minds are delighted in particular with the pictures of landscapes, harbours, flowery fields and thick groves".[63] In Book VII, he attempted to divide Delight itself into three depending on whether it proceeded from "the contrivance and invention of the mind . . . the hand of the artificer . . . or from nature herself",[64] and again we may see the concept of imitation or analogy connected with the third of these.

Throughout Alberti's work the impression is given of an attempt to structure all aspects of the subject into analogous sequences of three. After remarking on the philosophers' "ternary principle",[65] he developed the theme saying, " . . indeed, I am everyday more and more convinced of the truth of Pythagoras's saying that nature is sure to act consistently and with a constant analogy in all her operations".[66] Although the remark was made in the context of relating visual proportions to the harmonies of music it reflected a general way of thinking at the time. Some passages remind us of Aristotle's threefold division of general subjects into Ethics, Physics and Theology.[67] Other passages remind us of Thomas Aquinas's reduction of types of cause to three, Efficient, Formal and Final,[68] where the first cause clearly represents the necessity of building in the first place. We shall need to look more closely at mediaeval thought to understand the development of these categories, but we may note that W. Lotz in *Architecture in Italy 1400–1600* remarked that "the identity of aesthetic and theological categories was a peculiarity of the Renaissance conception of architecture",[69] this in connection with Palladio whose own contribution we might briefly consider.

The Florentine Academy was little more than an informal gathering that met notably at Lorenzo de Medici's country villa at Carregi. Under the initial direction of Ficino, who had been Lorenzo's tutor, the Academy continued to exert influence on the literary circles of Florence, with whom Gian Giorgio Trissino later came to be associated. It was Trissino who was to have such an influence on Palladio's architectural career and many of the ideas contained in Palladio's literary work may have derived from this fruitful association. In 1570, Palladio's *I quattro libri dell'architettura* were published and, unlike Alberti's architectural work, they received almost immediate widespread acclaim.

Like Alberti, Palladio sought to establish architecture on natural principles and, undoubtedly through either Trissino or Barbaro's teaching, he introduced into architectural theory the Platonic ideas of Beauty, Goodness and Truth that Ficino had first formulated:

> "That manner of building cannot but be blamed which departs from that which the nature of things teacheth and from that simplicity which appears in the things produced by her, framing as it were another nature, and deviating from the true, good and beautiful method of building."[70]

More than Alberti's work, however, Palladio's books are directed towards individual buildings, and the descriptions of his own buildings were to be a source of information for the following centuries. Again, the importance of Vitruvius was stressed, *I quattro libri* beginning, like Wotton's, with a reference to the three categories:

> "Great care ought to be taken before a building is begun of the several parts of the plan and the elevation of the whole building intended to be raised: For three things according to Vitruvius ought to be considered in every fabric, without which no edifice will deserve to be commended: and these are utility or convenience, duration and beauty."[71]

In the original Italian, according to Kruft,[72] the terms are "*utilità* (which he sees as a synonym for *commodità*), *perpetuità* and *bellezza*", and it is interesting to note that the term *Utilitas* has been replaced here with the two words translated as utility and convenience.

VITRUVIUS

There has been much speculation on the dates of Vitruvius, but it would appear that the *De architectura libri decem* were written shortly after the start of the reign of the Emperor Augustus in 31 BC.[73] The Roman Republic had come to a close after some 500 years of existence. The first 250 years, from 510 BC, had been spent in the conquest of Italy during which time Rome absorbed much of both the Etruscan culture to the north and the culture of the Greek colonies to the south.

The second 250 years witnessed the conversion of the Western world into a patchwork of Roman provinces, among which Greece had become a Roman dependency in 146 BC. During the period of the Republic, Rome had established those strengths upon which Western civilization was founded: power through military might, an efficient communications network through which the ideas of Greeks, Egyptians and Jews could be assimilated, and an extraordinary constructional and engineering ability to which the Rome of Vitruvius's time bore witness.

Little is known of Vitruvius's life except for the few facts that can be deduced from the Ten Books. In the introductory dedication we learn that he was known to the Emperor's father and that he had been engaged in military engineering works. He designed and supervised the construction of the new basilica at Fano, and played an important role in the refurbishment of 82 temples in Rome. In this he was influenced by his knowledge of Greek temples, listed and described in detail in the Ten Books.

While he acknowledged the writings of Greek architects, notably Pytheos and Hermogenes,[74] in formulating his own views on architecture, Vitruvius also stressed the importance for architects of an education in history, philosophy and music.[75] He mentioned his own acquaintance with the works of Cicero, Lucretius and Varro,[76] and noted that these Roman writers openly modelled their work on the literature of the Greeks. Pythagoras, Democritus, Plato and Aristotle are referred to throughout Vitruvius's work.[77]

The De architectura libri decem were probably published over a period of time, and in their final form would have existed as ten scrolls kept together in a canister. Vitruvius recorded that ten was thought by some, including Plato, to be the perfect number.[78] The first three chapters of Book I, however, suggested various divisions of the subject matter, not into ten, but into two, six and three respectively:

1. Chapter One states that an architect should be knowledgeable, and that "knowledge is the child of practice and theory".[79]
2. Chapter Two describes six factors upon which good architecture depends, namely: Order (Greek "taxis"), Arrangement (Greek "diathesis"), Eurhythmy, Symmetry, Propriety and Distribution (Greek "oeconomica"), which we discussed to some extent in our introduction[80] (see Figure 14).
3. Chapter Three begins by classifying buildings into private and public, and the latter into buildings used for religious, utilitarian and defensive purposes.[81] This has an interesting parallel in the structuring of early peoples into the priest, peasant and soldier classes[82] (Figure 12).

Vitruvius continued in Chapter Three with the words: "All buildings must be built with due reference to durability, convenience and beauty".[83] ("Haec autem ita fieri debent, ut habeatur ratio firmitatis, utilitatis, venustatis".[84])

Durability related to foundations and materials; convenience to the arrangement of apartments so that they present no hindrance to use; and beauty to ". . . when the appearance of the work is pleasing and in good taste, and when its members are in due proportion according to correct principles of symmetry".[85] We shall look at each of these three principles in turn (Figure 13), and note in passing that beauty itself is here described according to three different aspects.

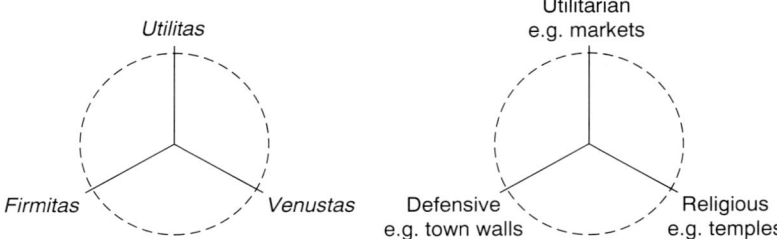

Figure 12 *The traditional Vitruvian categories (left), corresponding to Wotton's Firmness, Commodity and Delight, can be compared with Vitruvius's three classes of public building (right)*

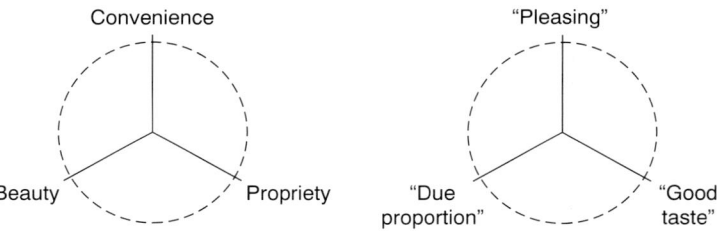

Figure 13 *Another of Vitruvius's threefold grouping of concepts is shown (left) and compared (right) with the three ideas he used to explain his category of "Venustas". The three concepts may also be compared with Pugin's Construction, Convenience and Propriety*

- *Firmitas*: Vitruvius, as we have seen, divided his first category into two parts, the first dealing with structure and the second with materials.[86] There were no structural calculations then as we know them today and dimensions were determined by general rules of proportion. In the case of foundations, arches and roof timbers, Vitruvius used vague phrases such as "to a height commensurate with the requirements of the size of the building",[87] or "as far as magnitude shall seem to require".[88] However, to ensure that the entablature or lintel above did not crack, the thickness and spacing of the columns were governed by more exacting rules, and these gradually became incorporated into the more general rules of proportion that came to govern the ornamental profiles of base, capital and entablature.[89]

  In the discussion of building materials in Book II there is a similar concern with ratios – those by which individual elements were mixed to form bricks and mortar, and upon which depended their durability.[90] Whereas good stone was thought to be virtually indestructible, and charred olive wood was also recommended for its long life, it was admitted by Vitruvius that the only materials that endure for eternity were the indivisible "atoms" of Democritus.[91]

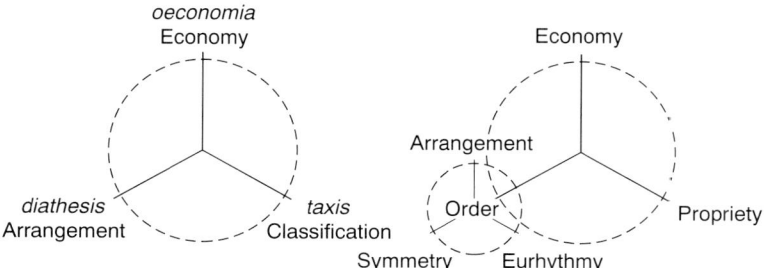

Figure 14 *The six categories of Vitruvius give some problems. He translated three of them from the Greek which we may arrange as shown (left). Alternatively, we may see three of them as subcategories of the concept of "Order" (right)*

Granger, in a footnote to his translation of Vitruvius, compared the three differentiae of the atom – shape, order and position – with the three principles of architecture which Vitruvius had specifically translated from the Greek,[92] namely, *diathesis*, *oeconomia* and *taxis*. The resulting correspondence between physics and aesthetics in this respect would certainly bear out Vitruvius's view that all studies "have a common bond of union and intercourse with one another"[93] (Figure 14).

- *Utilitas*: Vitruvius's second category dealt primarily with how convenient a building was in use, from the arrangement of rooms within a house, to the location of the building in the city. He discussed the relationship between public and private rooms,[94] the orientation of rooms in relation to sunlight,[95] and the "special needs" of the various classes of citizen, whether noblemen, businessmen, lawyers or farmers.[96] All aspects were worthy of attention. For example, in discussing the width left between the columns of a temple he advised that if they were too close then "when the matrons mount the steps for public prayer or thanksgiving they cannot pass through the intercolumnation with their arms about one another".[97]

In describing the origin of the house, Vitruvius, following Lucretius to some extent, speculated on how men first banded together.[98] There were social and practical advantages to be gained from a division of labour, and he listed the various trades involved in building: stonemasons, carpenters, plasterers, painters, plumbers, etc.[99] In his section on utilitarian buildings, Vitruvius began with a discussion of the Forum, the traditional meeting place of the Roman people, and continued with the Basilica where the business of the day was transacted.[100]

Another aspect that should be included under *utilitas* is that of economy. In linking utility with economy Vitruvius spoke of practical requirements and the need for a "thrifty balancing of cost and common sense in the construction of the works".[101] We may also note that "*utilis*", as opposed to "*usus*", had wider connotations than simple use, and in the writings of Cicero the word had clear social and moral implications.[102]

- *Venustas*: The Latin term *venustas* with its suggestion of the goddess Venus, corresponds to Wotton's category of delight. Cicero, in expounding on the notion of propriety discussed two orders of beauty: that appropriate to Roman women – *venustas* – and that appropriate to Roman men – *dignitas*.[103] Ornamentation, whether of dress or building, clearly belonged under the former category.

The concept of propriety, or "*decor*", was one of Vitruvius's six principles of architecture,[104] and defined by him as that "perfection of style which comes when a work is authoritatively constructed on approved principles".[105] Such authority could only derive from an architect's thorough knowledge of history and those socially prescribed rules which governed, for example, which style of ornamentation was appropriate for the temple of which god. The Doric Order was associated with "manly beauty, naked and unadorned",[106] and was suitable for the temples of Mars and, strangely, Minerva. The Ionic, with the volutes of its columns hanging down "like curly ringlets" had the "delicacy, adornment and proportion appropriate to a woman",[107] and was suitable for the temples of Juno and Diana. The Corinthian, in "imitating the slenderness of a maiden" afforded a style that was suitable for the temple of Venus and Flora.[108]

Roman partiality for the Corinthian Order reveals a general feeling for nature present in the Augustan age, reflected both in Virgil's pastoral eclogues and the floral decorations and festoons of flowers and fruit which decorated its buildings. Similarly, frescos showing landscapes, rivers, groves and mountains were advocated by Vitruvius.[109] "The ancients required realistic pictures of real things" he wrote, and he deplored the bad taste of his day where murals owed more to fantasy than strict observation.[110]

✻

Although Book I set out the three categories of Strength, Utility and Beauty in their most quoted form there are other groupings in Vitruvius's work which refer to the various kinds of delight to be found in architecture. At the end of Book VI for instance, we find the passage: "The layman cannot tell what it is to be like without seeing it finished, whereas the architect as soon as he has formed the conception . . . has a definite idea of the beauty, the convenience and the propriety that will distinguish it."[111]

It does not surprise us to learn that beauty may be listed separately from propriety (Figure 13). If we turn back to Book I we recall that Vitruvius offered three shades of meaning for the term *venustas*, ". . . when the appearance of the work is pleasing and in good taste, and when its members are in due proportion according to the correct principles of symmetry".[112] Comparing the two passages we may begin to identify beauty with the concept of proportion, and propriety with the concept of good taste. Elsewhere in Book VI, however, we find Vitruvius distancing beauty from proportion:

"There is nothing to which an architect should devote more attention than to the exact proportions of his building. . . . It is the next part of wisdom to consider the nature of the site . . . or the questions of use or beauty."[113]

Either beauty here is standing in for ornamentation and propriety, or "proportions" here refer only to those necessary for structural firmness. Vitruvius, in fact, suggested a distinction between the proportions necessary for setting out a building, and the subsequent adaptation of these proportions either by "science" or by "flashes of genius" to please the eye.[114] Either way, the simple division into strength, utility and beauty is misleading in not giving due recognition to the fact that the important concept of proportion is shared between the two categories of strength and beauty.

In order to understand the underlying concepts on which these ideas are based it is necessary to return to the thoughts of the ancient Greeks, but before we do so we might briefly consider the work of Cicero in this context.

Cicero was born in 103 BC and led an active public life before becoming a consul in 64 BC. He had received some education at the Academy in Athens and was nicknamed "the Greek"[115] by his contemporaries for his translation and adaptation of many Greek works. His copious treatises on morals, philosophy and oratory, as well as numerous speeches and letters, became standard material for the education of Roman youth.

The derivation of Cicero's ideas from Plato and Aristotle is indicated by the titles of his works, *Republic*, *Laws*, *Topics*, etc.[116] His "threefold scheme of philosophy", for example, is inherited directly from Plato, and we may note particularly the order in which the three subjects appeared in the *Tusculan Disputations*:

> "The threefold progeny of the soul . . . one centred in the knowledge of the universe and the disentanglement of the secrets of nature; the second in distinguishing things that should be sought out or avoided and in framing a rule of life; the third in judging what is the consequence to every premise, what is incompatible with it, and in this lies all of refinement of argument and truth of judgement."[117]

This pattern recurs in Cicero's work and may well have provided the inspiration for the Vitruvian categories, where Physics may be seen to correspond with Firmness, Ethics with Utility, and Judgement with Beauty.

There are many other threefold groupings to be found in Cicero's works, and because of the important role these works played in introducing Greek ideas into mediaeval thought, we may usefully note the following (Figure 15):

1. In *De Natura Deorum* he listed three aspects of divinity worthy of investigation, namely, the Form of God, the nature of his Activity, and the operation of his Intelligence.[118]
2. In discussing the four cardinal virtues, Wisdom, Justice, Courage and Temperance, he described the last three as being "parts of wisdom", concerned with social utility, strength of mind and propriety of character respectively.[119]
3. In a passage, that at first glance reminds us directly of Vitruvius, he wrote that houses should be characterized by their serviceableness (*usus*), convenience (*commoditas*), and distinction (*dignitas*), the feminine of which we have already seen was *venustas*.[120]
4. In a work on oratory, he divided the subject into three sections: divisions of speech, functions of the orator, and different sorts of speech.[121] Regarding the orator's ability to speak well, he suggested that three factors were important,

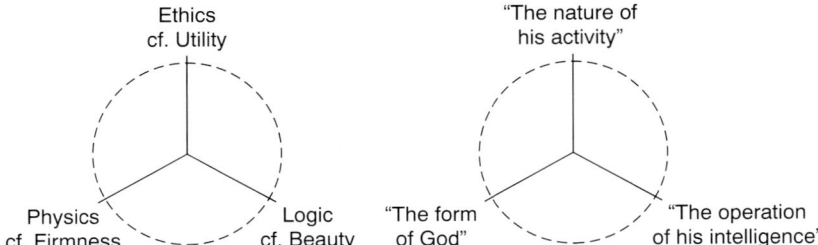

Figure 15 *One influence on Vitruvius's thought may have been Cicero who took many of his own ideas from the Greeks. Cicero followed the Greek division of philosophy into Physics, Ethics and Logic (left), and suggested a similar threefold structure for the nature of God (right)*

namely, elegance, clearness and propriety;[122] and regarding the constitution of propriety itself, he listed three elements, beauty, tact and taste.[123]

Although some glimmering of similarity may be observed in the way these various sets of terms are grouped together, we are, with Cicero, still a long way from discovering any natural principles upon which such categories may have been formulated. Their very similarity suggests that any solution to our problem will be found earlier rather than later in the development of philosophical thought, and it is to the ancient Greeks that we must now turn our attention.

SECTION 2

CATEGORIES IN PHILOSOPHY AND LITERATURE

FROM ANCIENT GREECE TO THE NINETEENTH CENTURY

CHAPTER 3
GREEK CATEGORIES

We left the previous chapter looking for natural principles upon wh.ch the architectural categories of firmness, commodity and delight, or any other convincing set of categories, might be based. It seems clear that we should be looking for these principles in the world of general ideas, and it makes sense to begin our search with the thoughts of the ancient Greeks.

There are two figures in Greek philosophy of importance here, namely Plato and Aristotle, and we shall in this chapter look at their ideas in turn. Although there are broad similarities between the work of the two philosophers, they have a difference of approach which should be noted. At its simplest, Plato's approach was more holistic, concerned with major concepts like beauty, goodness and truth, and in the first section of the chapter we shall see how these and similar broad-based ideas can be related back to our architectural categories.

Aristotle's approach, on the other hand, was more analytical. He introduced the term "category", and through his ideas we begin to see how terms like quantity, quality, substance and relation can be linked to architectural theory. More importantly we see how various kinds of logical statement, or proposition, which relate to the kinds of thing we can say about architecture, were developed.

Both Plato and Aristotle had something to say on the number of basic principles – whether two, three or four – and the ways in which these can be interrelated. These ideas too will have some bearing on the formulation of our own architectural categories.

PLATO

Plato wrote his dialogues, of which there are about thirty, between 399 BC and 347 BC. The brief age of Athenian political supremacy in Greece had passed. The Peloponnesian wars, ending in 404 BC with the victory of the Spartans under Lysander, had marked the end of the golden age of Pericles which had witnessed the erection of the Parthenon.

While rivalry between the city-states had promoted a spirit of competition in their public works, it reflected too a division between peoples that reached back for more than a thousand years to the waves of settlers who had migrated there from the north. First came the Ionians, generally thought of as an artistic and industrious people, who settled throughout the peninsula, in Athens, Corinth and

---

Plate 3 *Acropolis, Athens (Photo Scala, Florence)*
"Any young man and much more any old one, when he sees or hears anything strange, stands considering . . . like a person who is at a place where three ways meet . . . and he will say to himself . . . which is the way"

Plato

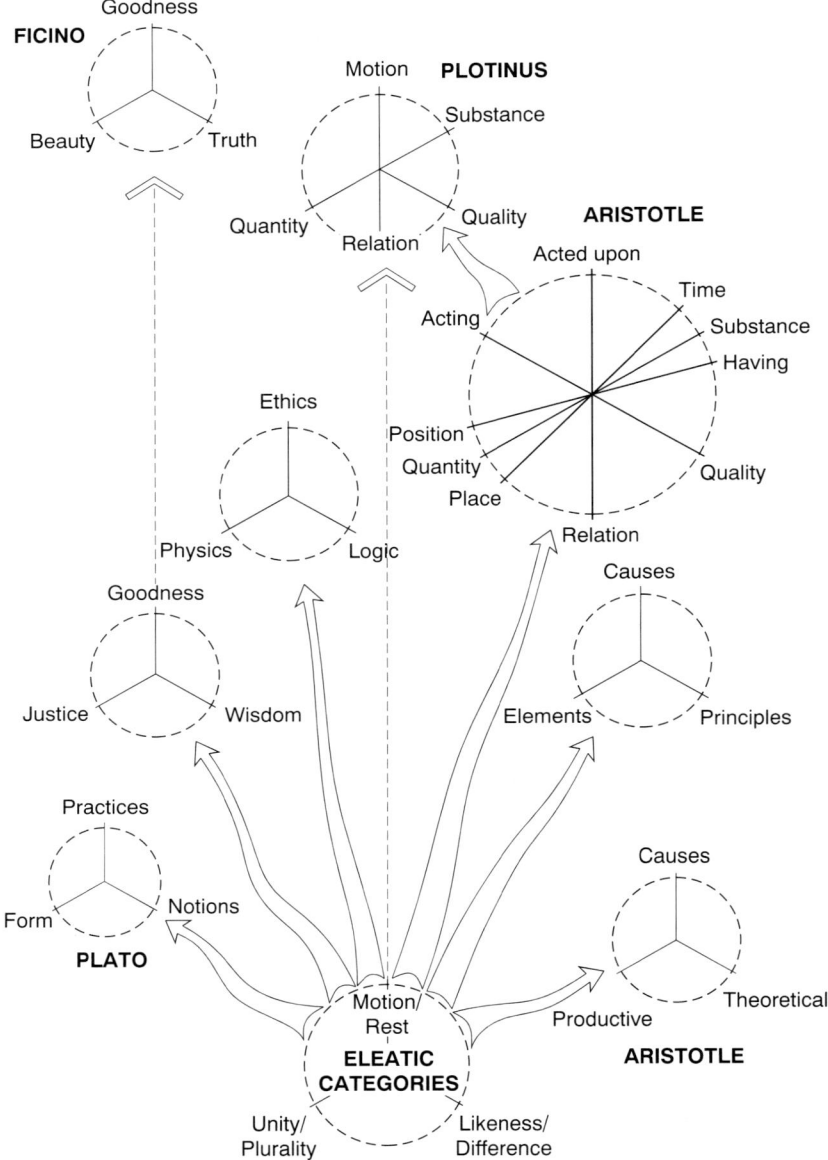

Figure 16 *The Greek categories*

as far afield as Troy in Asia Minor; second, the Achaeans from about 1580 BC, the subject of Homer's *Iliad* and *Odyssey*, a great trading nation who established links throughout the Mediterranean and formed what we know as the Mycenaean civilization; and third, the Dorians from 1100 BC, who introduced the Iron Age and the more spartan elements of Greek life with their gymnasia and the games they established at Olympia.

With this influx and the subsequent growth of wealthy, autonomous city-states, a colonizing movement began outwards from Greece: eastwards to the coast of Asia Minor where the Ionians established their twelve cities, the Dodecapolis, including Miletus, Ephesus and the island cities of Samos and Chios; and westwards to Sicily and the southern coast of Italy, where cities like Syracuse and Tarentum were established by Corinth and Sparta respectively.

The wealth and influence of these colonies were more than equal to that of the Greek mainland and were reflected in their buildings and their schools of thought. The temples of Sicily and Italy exemplify the best of the Doric style of architecture which was developing simultaneously in the West, from about 560 BC, although the earlier Doric temple of Hera at Olympia of 590 BC gives an interesting illustration of the transition from timber to stone construction. The temple of Artemis at Ephesus, also built around 560 BC, was, according to Vitruvius, one of the wonders of the world, and it is thought that its Ionic volutes and friezes were brought to Greece through Ionia's trading links with Egypt and Asia Minor. The Corinthian style was only fully developed by the Romans, although it had appeared internally in Greece as early as about 450 BC. Its supposed invention by the Corinthian craftsman, Callimachus, reminds us that Corinth was until about 550 BC second in prosperity only to the cities of Ionia, and that its trade in oil, wine, ceramics, metalwork and perfume represent the art and industry upon which the wealth of Greece was founded.

In 387 BC when Plato was forty, he visited the western colonies in Italy, first seeing his friend Archytas in Tarentum. Archytas was a leading figure of the city, like Pericles had been in Athens, and was not only a military commander but also a mathematician and a Pythagorean. There were three essential qualities of an administrator, Archytas is noted as saying: authority, wisdom and love of mankind.[1]

As Plato travelled along the southern coast he would have passed through the city of Croton where Pythagoras had emigrated from his native island of Samos approximately 150 years earlier. The earliest recorded Greek thinkers had in fact lived in these eastern and western colonies. The school of Miletus in the east had given rise to Thales, Anaximenes and Heraclitus who had respectively proposed that the world was composed of either water, air or fire. Heraclitus had also stated that all things come out of "the One", and that opposite concepts such as heat and cold give rise to constant movement and flux.

The school of Elea in the west, led by Parmenides and Zeno, had proposed, on the other hand, an eternal, unchanging "One" and concerned itself with mental rather than material concepts. From them derive the famous "Eleatic dilemmas"[2] where there appeared to be no logical contradiction in identifying the nature of the world with either the following concepts or their contraries: unity or plurality, motion or rest, and likeness or difference (Figure 17). The world could be thought of as one, a single existence, or many separate existences. The things in the world could be seen as constantly moving or changing, or the ideas of movement and change themselves could be seen as eternal, unchanging principles. Or the things in the world could be seen as all being comparable in terms of their properties such as size and shape, yet at the same time they are all different. No two objects are alike. Cornford suggested that these concepts, presented to us in Plato's dialogues, constitute one of the earliest forms of meaningful categorization.[3]

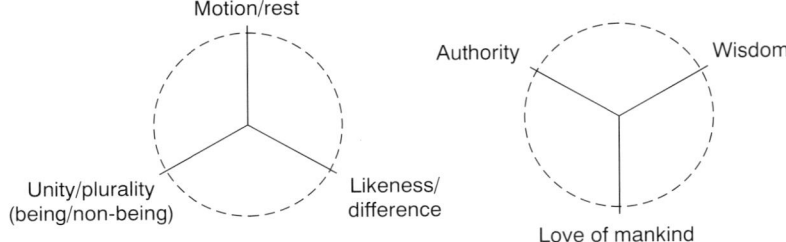

Figure 17 *Two of the earliest forms of categorization in the West. The Eleatic dilemmas on the left recorded by Plato, and the three essential qualities of a good administrator (right) recorded by the Neopythagorean, Archytas.*

Travelling across to Sicily, Plato is said to have visited the volcano, Mount Etna, into which Empedocles had thrown himself, thinking erroneously that he was a god. Empedocles originated the idea that there were four elements: air, fire, earth and water, and that all things were composed of a mix of these in different proportions.[4] Anaxagoras, an Ionian, invited to Athens by Pericles, developed this idea and suggested that even the smallest particle of matter contained some of each element, and that things differed only in the proportion of their mix.[5]

Eventually, Plato arrived at Syracuse, the largest and wealthiest city of the western colonies, where he was to instruct the younger Dionysius in philosophy. The first meeting was rather stormy. The elder Dionysius claimed that Plato's speech was like that of a "doddering greybeard", and Plato replied that "his in turn was like that of a despot".[6] Plato, according to the story, was deported to the island of Aegina, and after Anniceris of Cyrene liberated him from prison, "they visited, next morning, the temple of Aphaia on its grey rock above the terraces of pines. . . . They saw to the south the mountain which supported the temple of Panhellenic Zeus . . . and northwards the hills of Attica across the strait", to where Plato was to return to found his Academy.[7]

✲

The facts we know of Plato's life are recorded in his letters and in the works of Aristotle, Cicero and Plutarch. He was born in either 427 or 428 BC, into a wealthy Athenian family where two of his uncles were friends of Socrates. It is thought that he commenced writing his dialogues after the trial and death of Socrates in 399 BC, and that not only the dialogue form of question and answer but also his concern with the concepts of virtue and goodness followed from Socrates' teaching. Socrates wrote nothing down, teaching mainly out of doors in the agora or at the gymnasia situated outside the city walls. These were the places where the youth of Athens exercised and were educated, and included those by the sanctuary of the hero Academus to the west, and of Apollo Lyceis to the east, later to become the Academy and Lyceum respectively. The dialogue *Lysis*, for example, began:

"I was going from the Academy straight to the Lyceum intending to take the outer road which is close under the wall when I came to the postern gate of the city which is by the fountain of Panops. . . ."[8]

Apart from this brief passage there is little description of Athens in Plato's work. Ion, in the dialogue of the same name, was described as having come from the theatre at Epidaurus to perform at the Panathenaia, the four-yearly festival that culminated in the famous procession depicted on the sculptured frieze of the Parthenon. The Acropolis had been redesigned after the devastation of the Persian wars and the Parthenon rebuilt between 447 and 438 BC by Pericles under the direction of the sculptor, Phidias, and the architects, Ictinus and Callicrates. Not as large as the temples of the eastern colonies, it combined the styles of the Doric and the Ionic, and besides the statue of Athena it housed in the rear the treasury of the Delian League.

Cimon, who had organized the League as a defence against the Persians, had also set out the gardens around the grove of Academus, and it was here that Plato, approximately one hundred years later, established his Academy. Plato's country house lay to the north along the river Cephissus, and we are told that here, in the early morning, he would write with a stylus on a wax tablet before walking down to the Academy, praying at the shrine of the muses and, after ablutions, beginning the day's lectures to his pupils.[9]

Architecture as the science or art of building was referred to as such in the dialogue *Charmides*,[10] and although never discussed in great detail by Plato it appeared regularly in his writing with the other arts and crafts which were part of Athenian life. The closest approximation to the Vitruvian categories that may be found in his work occurs in a passage which has nothing to do with art or architecture and instead describes three goods of the body: Strength, Wealth and Beauty.[11] However, before searching for any natural principles that might underlie such categories let us first look at some threefold divisions relating to the arts in general which appear in the *Republic* and *Laws*.

First, in the *Republic*, he asked in connection with the painters' craft:

"Does the painter know the right form of the bridle and reins? Nay, hardly even the maker, only the horseman who knows how to use them, he knows their right form. . . . There are three arts which are concerned with all things: one which uses, another which makes, a third which imitates them."[12]

Commodity may be seen to correspond with the "one which uses"; Firmness with the one "which makes"; and Delight with the painters' art "which imitates" (Figure 18). A similar version is found in the *Sophist* which also described different kinds of art.[13]

Second, in *Laws*, he discussed the importance of the Greek chorus in the education of the young. Musical competitions were regularly held in the Odeon of Pericles, which was built around 435 BC and situated below the Acropolis (adjacent to the older theatre of Dionysos), and he gave this advice to the judges:

"In drawing, music or any other art, he who is a competent judge must possess three things: he must know in the first place of what the imitation is;

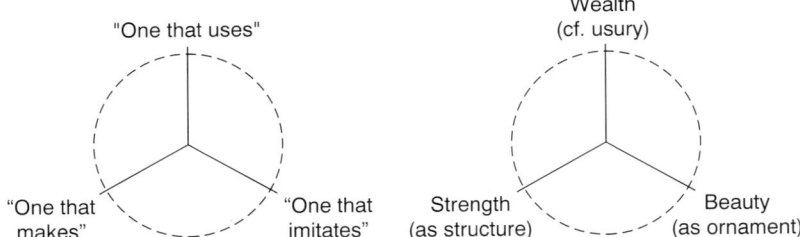

Figure 18 *Plato's three kinds of art (left), and his three goods of the body (right). Both may be compared with the Vitruvian categories shown in Figure 12*

secondly he must know that it is true; and thirdly that it has been well-executed in words and melodies and rhythms."[14]

There are three aspects here, each of which requires some explanation:

1. ". . . of what the imitation is". All these arts were seen to consist primarily in imitation, but the only value of their subject-matter for Plato lay in the utilitarian one of how well it promoted virtue and goodness.[15]
2. ". . . that it is true". Although delight may certainly be derived from such imitations, Plato wrote of the arts that "imitation is not to be judged by pleasure but by the standard of truth and by no other whatsoever".[16]
3. ". . . that it has been well-executed in words and melodies and rhythms". This referred to both the construction of the piece and to its performance, through which the beauty of its melodies and rhythm will be judged.

We see emerging here the three Classical ideals of Goodness, Truth and Beauty,[17] which while not being natural principles in themselves, offer an alternative base from which to commence our investigations (Figure 19). Although Plato discussed each of these three concepts in some depth, he did not refer to them once as a composite set. The more common formulations in the dialogues were Beauty, Goodness and Justice of which there are ten mentions,[18] and Justice, Goodness and Wisdom (or Nobility) of which there are eight mentions.[19] As with the Vitruvian categories we shall look at each in turn, in what we propose will be their correct order, before proceeding to investigate the structuring principles which lie underneath.

- *Beauty*: We have noted before the link between beauty and firmness when considering the proportions of structural members, and this conjunction is nowhere more apparent than in the columns and lintels of the Greek temple. Plato not only asserted the importance of mathematical proportion to music, but also "the observance of measure to the excellence or beauty of every work of art".[20] In *Philebus* he wrote that the art of building is superior even to the art of music in considering that "the dominant elements of knowledge required are arithmetic and mensuration".[21]

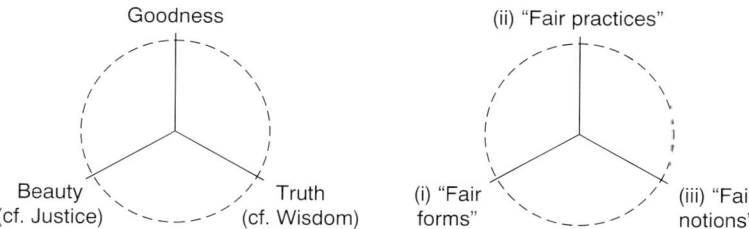

Figure 19 *Plato did not refer specifically to the grouping Beauty, Goodness and Truth in his work. The commonest formulation was Justice, Goodness and Wisdom (left). In his* Symposium, *however, we read "The true order of going is to use the beauties of the earth as steps along the way . . . from fair forms to fair practices, and from fair practices to fair notions" (right). Note the order*

This link between beauty and mathematics may be approached through either arithmetic or geometry. Archytas, whom Plato had visited in Tarentum, was not only the first to have written on mechanics but was also the first to have distinguished between the arithmetic, the geometric and the harmonic mean in the study of proportions.[22] In the *Republic* Plato distinguished three principles of rhythm out of which all metrical systems in poetry, for example, could be framed, 1 : 1, 1 : 2 and 2 : 3,[23] and from Pythagoreans like Archytas he would have learned of the importance of such numerical systems to the laws of symmetry and harmony which framed the universe. "Geometrical equality", he proclaimed, "is mighty both among gods and men".[24] With regard to the beauty of pure geometry, he wrote in *Philebus*:

"True pleasures are those which are given by the beauty of colour and form . . . straight lines and circles and the plane or solid forms which are formed out of them by turning lathes and rulers and measurers of angles, for these I affirm to be not only relatively beautiful like other things, but they are eternally and absolutely beautiful".[25]

He added that "colours, too" may be "of the same character. and sounds when smooth and clear and utter a single pure tone". All depended on simplicity, "the simplicity of a truly and nobly ordered mind".[26]

We should need to distinguish here between the beauty to be found in a "pure tone" and the kind of beauty found in the more complex harmonies and proportions mentioned above. Harmony for Plato involved the "reconciliation of opposites" where the resulting oneness, as Heraclitus said, is "united by disunion".[27] We are reminded of the Eleatic dilemmas when we read in the *Republic* that first, "the beautiful is the diverse", and second, that "the beautiful is the one".[28]

Beauty for the Greeks encompassed not only the geometry of the temple in architecture but also the grace of the human body in sculpture. In *Gorgias* Plato remarked that the beauty of the body was a matter for the trainers at the gymnasium; bodily grace was linked with bodily fitness, and beauty once again was linked with strength and firmness.[29]

- *Goodness*: The notion that a good building should be valued as such primarily according to its usefulness was implied by Plato in the *Republic*. "The excellency of every structure", he wrote, "is relative to the use for which nature or the artist has intended it".[30] However, in considering the idea of a good building we should perhaps look first at the concept of goodness itself.

  Goodness was discussed by Plato in terms of the ends which moved men in their daily affairs. The chief end of human life, "*eudaimonia*", was defined as being if not exactly happiness, then a very similar condition. The first seeds of utilitarianism were sown when Plato wrote "our object in the construction of the state is the greatest happiness of the whole".[31]

  Another and more dubious end was that of pleasure, and Callicles in *Gorgias*, for example, argued that luxury and pleasure were the goods which men strive after.[32] Elsewhere, Plato advised against such excesses as the Sicilian banquet, Athenian confectionery and Corinthian women.[33]

  There were for Plato two kinds of good:

  1. First, there were the goods of the body: health, wealth, strength, beauty, etc. Pleasure in relation to these was described as the effect following "the return of things to their own nature".[34] If the body lacked food, then its intake would give pleasure. If the body was cold, then warmth and shelter would give pleasure. Buildings were seen as "a shield against heat and cold",[35] and as shelter against "the rains from heaven".[36] A building, like the state, arose out of the needs of mankind, and housed those services which every state may be said to need: "food, art, revenue, religion and government".[37]

  2. Second, there were the goods of the soul: courage, temperance, justice and wisdom.[38] We have previously compared the first three of these with Strength, Utility and Beauty, and we might note regarding temperance that Plato introduced "the principle of the mean"[39] by which all our affairs, including the arts, should be on the watch against excess and defect. The fourth virtue, wisdom, was described in *Laws* as being the guide of the others.[40]

  It should be mentioned that Plato's own opinion was that the beauty implicit in a well-ordered work of art will itself encourage virtue in those who contemplate it: "Beauty, the effluence of fair works, will visit the eye and ear, like a healthful breeze from a purer region, and insensibly draw the soul, even in childhood, into harmony with the beauty of reason."[41]

  A work of art should instil the virtues of courage, temperance, justice and wisdom, and we may suppose on a more prosaic level that in architecture this would have proceeded through size and grandeur, the efficiency of the building's functioning, the harmony of its parts or the nature of the subject being imitated.

- *Truth*: The last of Plato's three kinds of art was "that which imitates", and even music was seen to consist in "imitation and representation".[42] There are two aspects of imitation that we should consider, and these are, first, the delight that works of imitation give, and second, the notion of truth implicit in the correspondence of the copy to the original. In the first case we are considering a "liking for" or agreeableness of the work to the subject, and in the second its "likeness to" or agreement with an original object or prototype.

With regard to delight, Plato noted differences in taste not only between male and female but between young and old in their natural liking for, for example, puppet shows, or the poetry of Hesiod and Homer.[43] Commonly, the delights were those of association or recollection, but in *Laws*[44] and *Philebus*[45] he discussed the higher pleasures of discerning meaning in the complexities of style and taste. The excellence of music may be measured by the pleasure given, but "only in so far as it delighted the best-educated".[46] A degree of knowledge was accepted as a necessary requirement, and the ability to discern truth from falsehood was viewed as an important faculty of the critic.

Turning to the concept of truth itself we should note that only the correspondence theory of truth was fully considered by Plato. Truth consisted not only in the conformity of the work to an original but also in the correspondence of the original with its supposedly perfected form in the world of ideas. Although we tend to think of architecture as non-representational, Plato would have thought that if a carpenter "makes a shuttle according to the true form of the shuttle" so too the builder should build a house according to the "true form" of the house.[47]

The art of the painter, on the other hand, was "thrice removed from the truth"[48] in imitating only the appearance of things and not their reality. A painting of a bed, for example, was the representation of an imperfect copy: "Beds are of three kinds and there are three artists who superintend them: God, the maker of the bed, and the painter."[49] We might compare beds to buildings . . . and buildings to the state itself. "A state can only be happy", wrote Plato, "which is planned by artists who make use of heavenly patterns";[50] and similarly in *Laws* we read that "there is said to have been, in the time of Cronos, a blessed state and way of life of which the best ordered of existing states is a copy".[51]

*

Having looked briefly at some ideas in Plato's dialogues that relate most closely to those of Firmness, Commodity and Delight, and having introduced three ways of understanding art, relating to the contemplation of beauty, the instilling of goodness, or a reflection upon truth, we should now recall a question raised earlier: whether there is a natural principle behind this seemingly arbitrary division into three.

Plato did not concern himself with the problem of "well building" as such, but he was concerned with the similar question of what the virtues were in a good man. In the *Statesman*, for example, there is reference to a "divine bond" or "divine principle" which: "heals and unites dissimilar parts of virtue, which principle consists in the honourable, the just and the good".[52]

If not with one idea, "then with three we may take our prey",[53] he wrote in *Philebus* in attempting to define goodness, and the idea was reflected in a general principle by which, "the same process of division and subdivision"[54] may be applied to all classes of enquiry.

The same principle of division results, as may be expected, in broadly similar concepts being applied to very different subject-matter. From more than a hundred tripartite groupings found throughout the dialogues, three broad categories, each containing an, as yet, unrelated range of loosely connected words, can be identified:

1. Beauty, harmony, symmetry, number, strength, body, form, being, existence
2. Goodness, goodwill, deeds, practice, process, utility, usefulness, agent/patient, motion, cause
3. Truth, wisdom, knowledge, mind, dream, resemblance, likeness, quality, nobility, class.

The division is not as clear-cut as would appear from the above list, for example Plato identified beauty with usefulness in one passage[55] and both goodness and wisdom with symmetry and harmony in others,[56] but, as we shall see, there were good reasons for this.

We are reminded too, in looking at these three categories, of the Eleatic dilemmas mentioned previously.[57] These appeared in several forms throughout the dialogues, and if they were thought of as being in some way the natural principles underlying the above categories, then we may suppose that the correspondence would have been that of Unity/Plurality (or Being/Non-Being) with category (1); Motion/Rest with category (2); and Likeness/Difference with category (3).

The question of the number of differentiating principles had been raised before Plato's time: ". . . at one time one said that there were three principles, another two principles . . . others said that things were many in name but in nature one."[58]

Plato suggested that in the structuring of a supposedly unified subject, in our case the subject of architecture, one did not progress immediately to a myriad unrelated topics but through an initial differentiation into a definite number of categories:

"This unity we find in everything, and having found we may next proceed to look for two or if not then for three or for some other number, subdividing each of these units until at last the unity with which we began is seen not only as one and many and infinite but also as a definite number."[59]

He used as an analogy the Egyptian legend of the god, Theuth, the ibis-headed god of writing, who on observing that the range of possible sounds was infinite, realized that an arbitrary decision was required to limit the number of vowels that should be used to a definite number.[60] That, for Plato, the definite number should be three was implied in various passages, the three principles of the soul in *Republic*,[61] the three natures described in the *Timaeus*,[62] or the threefold knowledge of things in *Laws*.[63]

Two different explanations were given as to why there should be three:

(1) The first is found in *Parmenides* and takes almost the form of a riddle: "if one is, then number must also be . . . the whole becomes three." There is a subject,

"one", a verb, "is", and, third, a relation "the whole" between them.[54] The idea of "one" can be included under the category of unity/plurality; the idea of "is" or "must" under motion/rest as patient or cause; and the idea of "whole" under likeness/difference as in a class of similar or different things.

(2) The second explanation is given in *Timaeus* and states that if there is to be a differentiation into parts, then, "two things cannot be held together without a third".[65] He supposed, for example, that the natural world was composed of a mixture of fire and earth held together by the concept of proportion which governs their mix,[66] again, two different elements and a relation between them.

Two questions immediately raise themselves. First, if, for instance, the Egyptian vowels were to be considered as three kinds of sound, then our categories would be three kinds of what? Surely not two kinds of one thing and one kind of another as this would presuppose a prior differentiation into, say, objects and relations. Second, the question of why only three still remains unclear. ". . . As children say entreatingly, 'give us both' . . .",[67] we should perhaps be looking for an analogy that accepts the possibility of two and three, and many and infinite, to explain why the subject can be seen in the number of ways it so obviously has been.

There is a an analogy used variously throughout Plato's works which may be of interest here, and it is that of the circle. In Epistle 7, for example, he wrote: "For everything that exists there are three classes of object through which knowledge about it must come, firstly a name, secondly a description, and thirdly an image."[68]

A circle has a name; its description is the "thing which has everywhere equal distances between its extremities and its centre"; and its image is of "the circle which is drawn and erased, turned on a lathe and destroyed, processes which do not affect the real circle. . . . The same doctrine holds good in relation to shapes and surfaces both straight and curved, in regard to the good, the beautiful and the just, and in regard to all bodies, natural and artificial".[69]

In *Laws*, Plato declared that the city itself should be built in a circle, on the heights for defence, an "acropolis" in fact, or high town.[70] The walls should be formed by a ring of private houses, and in the centre, an *agora*, or market place, should be separated off, with around it temples placed to Hestia and Zeus and Athena.

In *Phaedrus*, the circle is used for the shape of knowledge itself: "Now, of the heaven which is above the heavens, no earthly poet has ever sung . . . the colourless and formless and intangible essence and only reality dwells encircled by true knowledge."[71]

To gain any understanding at all of this intangible essence one could only circle around it taking each aspect in turn: "This roundabout progress through all things", said Zeno in *Parmenides*, "is the only way in which the mind can attain truth".[72]

A similar picture is brought to mind by the *Symposium*, where the idea of circular progress may be combined with that of an ascent, to reach an intangible essence which was now also that of absolute beauty:

"The true order of going is to use the beauties of the earth as steps along which to mount upwards for the sake of that other beauty . . . from fair forms to fair practices, and from fair practices to fair notions until he arrives at the notion of absolute beauty."[73]

The analogy we should take with us is of a central notion of architecture with around it, in a circle, something approaching these three concepts of fair forms, good practices and true notions, through which we should view our subject. While these three viewpoints give us a well-balanced notion of the whole, the circular analogy allows, on the one hand for an infinite number of viewpoints around the circumference or, on the other, for two diametrically opposed viewpoints along any "definite number" of diameters we may choose.

There is no direct and obvious source for Commodity, Firmness and Delight in the philosophical texts that have been handed down to us. In fact, the earlier groups of ideas from which the Vitruvian ideas may have sprung, developed through Aristotle, the mediaeval schoolmen and the philosophers of the enlightenment into something very different.

We have seen that Plato was beginning to be aware of the importance of categorization. In *Philebus* he referred to it as "a gift from heaven, to be tossed among men by the hand of a new Prometheus".[74] It does not surprise us to learn that it was at about this time that Aristotle came down from Macedonia to begin his studies at the Academy.

ARISTOTLE

The influence of Hellenism was at its most potent in the period between the death of Alexander and the birth of Christ. With the spread of Greek culture, the centres of trade and learning shifted from Athens to newly developing towns like Alexandria, Pergamum and the city of Rhodes. The beginning of an almost pedantic spirit of analysis and classification in literature and art criticism can be discerned which began with Aristotle and lasted until the end of the Classical era.

Alexander, who at the age of thirteen had been tutored by Aristotle, left Greece with his army in 334 BC and in only eleven years, before he died in Babylon, exchanged the concept of city-states for one of world dominion that Rome was later to emulate. He took on his campaign scientists and philosophers, sending back natural species for examination, and encountering in India the gymnosophists,[75] or naked wise men, an encounter which was to encourage an interesting cross-fertilization of ideas with the East.

It is said that thirty-four towns were named after him, the most well-known being in Egypt:

"On reaching the coast he sailed westwards and passing Canobus came to the ancient fishing village of Rhacotis. There, between Lake Mareotis and the island of Pharos, he marked out the ground plan of the city which he called Alexandria."[76]

Alexander's empire became fragmented after his death into three separate realms: Antipater attempted to hold Macedonia and Greece, Athens remaining as a centre for philosophy for another 600 years. Ptolemy took Egypt, and Alexandria quickly rose to become the leading city in the Mediterranean for trade and for the arts and sciences. The "Museum", based around the Temple to the Muses, developed the air of a university, and with its vast library became known for its schools of poetry and mathematics. From among the mathematicians we know of Euclid who formulated the elements of geometry, and Hero who it is said also lectured on building construction (and invented an early steam engine).

The largest share of the empire fell to Seleucus who, like Ptolemy, had accompanied Alexander eastwards and who, as the first of the Seleucid dynasty, founded Antioch as its capital. Pergamum in Asia Minor broke away in 262 BC and King Attalus created a hill-top city to rival Athens, close to Halicarnassus where King Mausolus, 100 years earlier, had removed his own capital.

The two great trading cities, Rhodes and Alexandria, commanded the eastern Mediterranean, and boats would ply their trade between the gigantic bronze Colossus on one shore, across the sea to pass the lighthouse of the Pharos on the other. A tour of the seven wonders of the world, mentioned by Vitruvius,[77] provides an interesting itinerary of the Hellenistic world: from the pyramids in the south to the temple of Artemis at Ephesus; and from the statue of Zeus at Olympia in the west, to the fabled hanging gardens of Babylon. One wonders what the secret of these wonders was. Was it their size, or the quality of their construction? Was it the beauty of their forms, the beauty of the gardens or the lifelikeness of the imagery? Even utility as a possible factor is represented in the wondrous functioning of the lighthouse.

It is not recorded what Aristotle taught Alexander during their three years together. No doubt Alexander took away with him some of the ideas on cities that Aristotle was later to set down in *Politics*. In this work he ascribed the invention of the art of planning cities to Hippodamus of Miletus, "an eccentric with flowing hair and love of ornament",[78] who had been invited to Athens 150 years earlier to lay out the Piraeus.

In *Oeconomica*, he specifically referred to King Alexander and the problems he had in decanting the inhabitants of Canobus into the new city of Alexandria.[79] Otherwise, Aristotle, like Plato, has little to say on architecture although referring often to the art of building in making more general points.

His powers of observation on which his more scientific approach to philosophy was based derived from an early interest in biology and medicine. His father was a physician and friend to Amyntas II, Philip's father, in the Macedonian court. Stagyra, the modern Stavro, on the northern shores of the Aegean Sea, where Aristotle was born in 384 BC, had recently fallen under Macedonian influence. Early in the fifth century at the Olympic Games, Macedonia had been recognized as a Greek state, and not being entirely a cultural backwater had attracted artists like Zeuxis the painter and Euripides the dramatist who had written *The Bacchae* there.

However, the centre for Greek education was Athens, and at the age of eighteen Aristotle went to study at the Academy under Plato. Here he remained until Plato's death nineteen years later, and was well thought of, being called by Plato "the mind of the school".[80] Philip was by this time harassing Athens, finally defeating its army in 338 BC at Chaeoronea. Aristotle was obliged to leave. With Xenocrates he travelled to Assos in the Troad, an interesting city in that it possessed the only Doric temple in Asia Minor, and after three years there stayed another year and a half on the island of Lesbos where Terpander had supposedly invented Greek classical music and where Sappho had written her poetry. He remarked in *Ethics* on an ancient way of building stone walls peculiar to the island, where the stones are cut in undulating lines to fit closely into one another for their greater strength.[81]

It was during his stay at Lesbos that Aristotle was called to Pella, the Macedonian capital, to take up employment as tutor to the young Alexander. In 335 BC he returned to Athens, rented some buildings near the Lyceum and "every morning walked up and down with his pupils in the stoa or among the trees and discussed the more abstruse questions of philosophy".[82] It is thought that the peripatetic school which he founded lay in the vicinity of the present National Gardens and that his colleague and successor, Theophrastus, had a garden adjacent, where Syntagma Square is now situated.

Alexander's death in 323 BC obliged Aristotle once more to leave Athens and he died a year later on the island of Euboea, in Chalcis, his mother's home town. He had a wife, Pythias, who bore him a daughter, and when she died, Herpyllis, also of Stagyra, bore him a son, Nichomachus.

It is clear that Aristotle owed much to Plato in all areas of thought except perhaps that of the natural sciences. "Now all things are ordered in some way, water-animals and birds and plants", he wrote, "for all things are ordered in relation to one another [and] must come together if they are to be distinguished".[83]

His early interest in the natural sciences led to a full attempt at the classification of the animal kingdom, and developed into the view that all our knowledge can be seen as classification or categorization:

> "We should first examine definitions according to the way in which the subject is divided. For example, the first genus may be 'animal', the next 'two-footed animal', then again, 'wingless two-footed animal'."[84]

Following this passage from *Metaphysics*, Aristotle suggested that we can define a house in three ways, either as "bricks and timbers in a particular configuration, a receptacle for sheltering animals and goods",[85] or as the composite of matter and form which constitutes the idea of the house.[86] If we think of building as an art we can begin to compare this with the three kinds of art that were described by Plato, the one which makes, the one which uses, and the one which imitates. Certainly, there appears to be a close similarity between Plato's subdivision of art and Aristotle's subdivision of the types of knowledge, to be found in *Topics* (Figure 20):

> "The differentiae of relative terms are themselves relative as is the case also of knowledge. This is classed as theoretical, practical and productive, and each of these denotes a relation for it speculates upon something, and produces something and does something."[87]

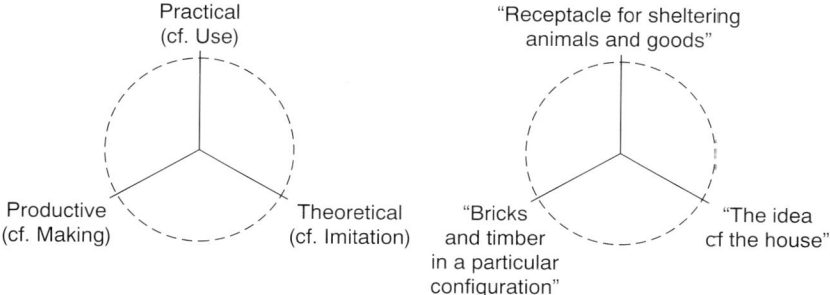

Figure 20 *Aristotle's three kinds of knowledge (left) can be compared with Plato's three kinds of art (see Figure 18). Aristotle also considered the different ways in which a building might be defined (right)*

The end of productive knowledge is in the making of the utensil; the end of practical knowledge lies in its use; and the "end of theoretical knowledge is truth",[88] discerning appearance from reality, or the genuine article from the imitation.

Aristotle seems also to have been aware of Plato's three concepts of beauty, goodness and truth, and, in *Physics*, after proclaiming that "All excellencies depend upon particular relations"[89] he discussed each one in terms of his developing interest in relations:

- Beauty and strength were seen in terms of "the blending of elements in due proportion"[90]
- Moral excellence was concerned with performance or conduct in relation to pleasure and pain[91]
- The excellence of the soul, or at least its intellectual part, was seen as a striving for "the perfection of its nature"[92] through the relations which constitute knowledge and truth.

We shall return to the fundamental concept of relation in due course, although, in passing, we might just note a possible link between Aristotle's "particular relations" fragmenting into three, and Plato's "divine bond" which as we saw previously also fragmented into three.

Taking Aristotle's interest in classification a stage further we come to perhaps his greatest achievement, the development of those logical ideas set out in the works known collectively as the *Organon*. These include *Topics*, *De Interpretatione*, the *Prior and Posterior Analytics*, and the *Categories*.

One important example of classification is to be found in *Topics* where Aristotle divided the realm of philosophy into three areas: Natural Philosophy dealing with the physical world; Ethics dealing with human action and conduct; and Logic dealing with the structure of knowledge.[93]

Another example of classification, and perhaps the most important from our point of view, were his various proposals for classifying the basic elements of our thoughts. He investigated terms and their definitions, the way terms are combined into propositions and judgements, and how these as premises could be formulated

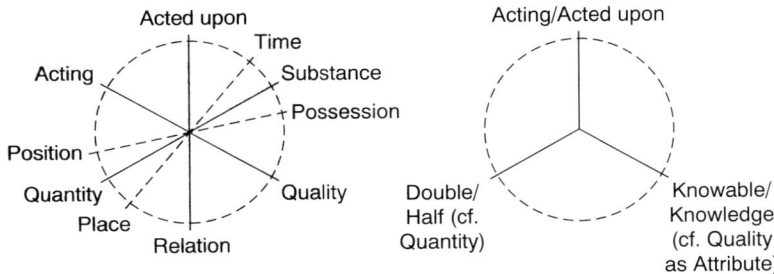

Figure 21 *Aristotle's ten categories (left) were an odd assortment later reduced in number by Plotinus (see Figure 25). Aristotle did, however, note three kinds of relation (right) which may be compared with Plotinus's and also Aquinas's later work*

into reasoned lines of thought.[94] What concerns us primarily are propositions and judgements: the kinds of proposition that we can make about architecture (statements that start "architecture is . . ."); and the kinds of judgement we can make about buildings (statements that start "that particular building is . . ."). Both consist of a subject and a predicate. Given a particular subject it is the range of predicates that we can make that defines our field of enquiry. The Greek for predicate was *kategorien* and Aristotle's ten categories were the first attempt to set out the types of predicate that could be attributed to any subject (Figure 21): ". . . each signifies either substance or quantity or quality or relation or where or when or being-in-a-position or having or acting or being acted upon."[95]

Aristotle gave no reason why there should be ten and it is thought that they may have derived from a study of parts of speech undertaken at the Academy.[96] It was not until the Neo-Platonists of the third century AD that a tentative structure was given. Plotinus reduced the list to five, first, two, Substance and Relation, and second, a set of three, Quantity, Quality and Motion (which included acting and being acted upon), all three of which could be subsumed under the category of Relation.[97]

Again we are returned to the important concept of relation, and it will be useful to look at these three concepts, Quantity, Quality and Motion in turn as a precursor to the more rigorous formulation of relationship types that will develop as the book proceeds. We should at the same time attempt to discover how these three concepts might be connected with the Vitruvian categories, or notions of Beauty, Goodness and Truth, which we have discussed previously.

Before discussing these three terms in detail, we might note that in a parallel development, the kinds of judgement similarly became three, each of which was also to be based on a relationship type. Aristotle's propositions were the simple ones of subject and predicate linked together by the "categoric" or inherent relation.[98] Within fifty years of Aristotle's death, there arose in Athens a new school of thought, the Stoic school, founded by another Zeno and named after the *Stoa Poikile*, or "painted colonnade" which lay on the north side of the Agora. It is from one of his followers, Chrysippus, that we first learn of two non-simple propositions named after the types of relationship that link the terms, the "disjunctive" and the

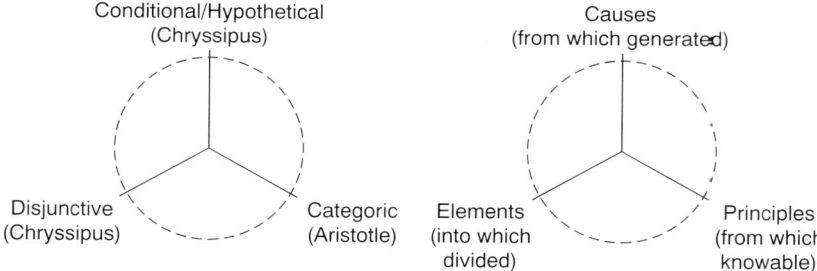

Figure 22 *Aristotle's logic developed one kind of proposition to which Chryssipus added two more (left). This structure may be compared with Kant's later categories (see Figure 29). "The object of an enquiry in any department," wrote Aristotle, "has principles, causes and elements" (right)*

"hypothetical"[99] respectively (Figure 22). To determine the meaning of these we shall compare each with one of the three categories referred to above, Quantity with the Disjunctive, Quality with the Inherent, and Motion with the Hypothetical, taking each one in its proper order.

- *Quantity*: The disjunctive judgement as such was not referred to by Aristotle. He noted the disjunctive phrase, "whether white or black",[100] and recorded that the Greek word for judge, *dikastes*, meant "one who bisects".[101] In a sense, the word judgement does mean the separating out of confused issues and weighing them in the balance. One thinks of the scales of justice; the two kinds of justice that Aristotle related back to arithmetic or geometric ratios;[102] or his definition of justice as "a species of the proportionate".[103] This act of disjoining or separating out was asserted by Anaxagoras to constitute the first action of the mind.[104] Aristotle reformulated the notion by stating that it is the particular function of the senses to carry out this initial act of separation, saying that the object of perception "has no actual parts until it is separated".[105] If we think of the perception of a field of colour, for example, we can see that there must be a disjunctive action of the mind and eye involved in separating out the colours, reminiscent of Plato's description of Theuth separating out the vowels from a continuum of sound. In fact, Aristotle introduced an early notion of the spectrum where "if one were to pass from white to black one would come to crimson or grey before coming to black, and similarly with other colours".[106]

  A study of perception, the Greek for which was *aesthesis*, is necessary in any consideration of aesthetics and it is unfortunate that a work linking beauty and mathematics mentioned by Aristotle has now long been lost.[107] We might note, however, that Xenocrates, who had studied at the Academy with Aristotle, claimed that form and number had the same nature, for the reason given that the boundaries of form are limited by three dimensions,[108] each of which is an extension of magnitude.

  The connection between disjunction and the category of quantity is clear. Quantity was "that which is divisible",[109] and "that which is composed of parts which have position in relation to one another".[110] In *Categories*, Aristotle confirmed that the relations of "time also and place are of this kind",[111] and in *Metaphysics* he even added that "the musical and the white are said to be quantities"[112] also.

From these ideas, two aspects of disjunction can be distinguished: first, the act of disjunction and its corollary, the bringing together of parts in relation to one another, (which Aristotle identified with Production); and, second, the state of disjunction which, in lending itself to such concepts as place, time and mathematics, would allow later philosophers to consider the concept of existence itself under this primary category. We may make an initial supposition that Firmness belongs to this category, having something to do with mathematical structure and production. We may also suppose that Beauty, or at least important aspects of beauty, belong under this category, not only through the concept of mathematical proportion but also through the idea of aesthetics being itself a term derived from the Greek for sensory perception.

- *Motion*: The second kind of logical proposition was the hypothetical or, as Chrysippus called it, the conditional proposition.[113] It formed the basis for rational thought where, for Aristotle, "certain things being laid down, something other than these comes about through them".[114] The following of consequences from antecedent propositions may be included under a more general law of cause and effect if, first, we understand that the Greek for cause, *aition*, had a wider meaning, "that which is responsible for",[115] and second, we accept Aristotle's assertion that premises are in fact the "causes" of their conclusions. He referred to the hypothetical in *Physics* where he gave an example of the reasoning behind the material specification for a saw:

> "For instance, why is a saw such as it is? To effect so and so . . . This end however cannot be realized unless it is made of iron. It is therefore necessary for it to be of iron if we are to have a saw . . . what is necessary then is necessary on a hypothesis."[116]

The material cause was one of four kinds of cause described by Aristotle:

- the efficient or first cause, "the source which begins motion"[117]
- the final cause, "that for the sake of which something is done"[118]
- the material cause, "that from which as a constituent something is generated"[119]
- the formal cause, "this being a formula of the essence, for example, in the case of the octave, the ratio 2 : 1".[120]

His illustration, in *Metaphysics*, was that of a house: "The same thing may have all the kinds of causes, for example, in the case of a house, the source of motion is the art of the builder, the final cause is its function, the matter is earth and stones, the form is its structure."[121]

While it is difficult to conceive of form being a cause, the idea of function being a cause of a building was developed further by Aristotle to show that both function and final cause are connected with the concept of goodness. His book, *Nichomachean Ethics*, begins by suggesting that the good is "that at which all things aim", and later continues: ". . . just as for a flute player, a sculptor, or any artist, and in general all things that have a function or activity, the good and the "well" is thought to reside in the function, so would it seem to be for a man if he has a function."[122]

Not only does goodness belong here but also pleasure. A human being, as he pointed out, has many functions, the highest being that of reason,[123] and it is the active exercising of these functions that give rise to pleasure. Aristotle described pleasure as a kind of motion, ". . . a movement by which the soul as a whole is consciously brought into its natural state of being".[124] Similarly, the good was also seen to be derived from an initial lack or privation, and a good house, for example, was described as being "desirable and lacking in nothing . . . where everything has its proper place and so be ready for use".[125]

If Beauty belonged under the previous category of Quantity, then Goodness belongs under this category, a category which contains Motion, and more importantly the underlying relation of cause and effect. From among the Vitruvian categories, we may suppose that Commodity belongs here under this category, also being connected with cause and "the sake for which something is done".

- *Quality*: The third type of proposition, the categorical, is based on the relationship type of inherence. This relation is the one which links the subject to its predicate. If we were to say that "a house is made of bricks and timber", or that "a house is a receptacle for sheltering animals and goods", then both these ideas or attributes could be said to inhere within the substance of the subject, the house. Aristotle described the relationship itself in *Metaphysics* where he wrote: "By thinking things together or apart I do not mean thinking them in succession but so thinking them that they become a unity of sorts."[126]

From the simpler unity of the subject–predicate statement Aristotle moved on to consider first, the idea of several subjects sharing the same predicate, and, second, the idea of several predicates inhering in the one subject.

(1) The first aspect introduces the category of Quality, a term which, notably under Epicurus, expanded to cover all attributes and properties.[127] It is where a quality is shared among several things that "these things are called similar or dissimilar",[128] (cf the Eleatic categories of likeness and difference). The association of similar things through their common attributes was developed through his interest in classification. It also introduces Aristotle's concept of "the universal . . . whose nature is such that it belongs to many, and without which it is impossible to acquire knowledge",[129] for "knowledge is of universals".[130] This was a peculiarly Aristotelian concept which was to tax the minds of some of the most important of mediaeval thinkers as we shall see.

(2) In order to consider the converse, where several predicates inhere in the one subject, Aristotle introduced the concepts of definition and meaning. The attributes that belonged to a subject are, he said, either "essential" or "accidental".[131] The essential attributes contributed towards the defini-tion or essence of the subject: the accidental attributes towards any wider

meanings or associations it has. Whatever the difference between the two may have been, such attributes were used to classify works as Aristotle classified "species" of poetry saying they differ from one another in three ways, "either by a difference in their means, or by a difference in their objects, or in the manner of their representation".[132]

From a consideration of the relation between the several predicates of a single subject, the concept of integrity was developed. With it came what was to become known as the coherence theory of truth, where as Aristotle said: "With a true view all the data harmonize, but with a false one the facts soon clash."[133]

With integrity came a notion of taste based on propriety, or what was "fitting in relation to the agent, the circumstances and the object".[134] Appropriateness due to the object lay, for example, in the symbolism behind the siting of a temple, "to give due elevation to virtue".[135] Appropriateness due to circumstances required a knowledge of both history and contemporary ideas, where, as Plato had said, such a taste could be measured "only in so far as it delighted the best educated".[136] Appropriateness due to the agent lay in the variety of styles open to him and that "each class of men, each type of disposition will have its own appropriate way of letting the truth appear".[137] To each style belonged its own peculiar qualities, its own scale of perfection, like a "correctness of language"[138] which involved not only "clarity of delivery" but also the avoidance of "strange words" and "inappropriate metaphors".[139]

✳

The importance to architecture of the categories is illustrated in *Metaphysics*. For Aristotle, architecture was an art, "a reasoned state or capacity to make",[140] and as such consisted of bringing together, in the intellect, predicates drawn from each of the categories until the proposed subject was fully defined. The example given was that of a bronze sphere where it was not the bronze or the sphere that was generated but the bringing of the attributes of a sphere to those of the bronze: ". . . so also in the case of whatness and of quality and of quantity and of the other categories the situation is similar, for it is not a certain quality that is generated, but wood with that quality, and it is not a certain quantity but the wood with that quantity."[141]

If we consider the Aristotelian categories as developed by Plotinus, we can begin to discern in a more recognizable form those predicates which will serve to define the final building:

- Substance, for example the materials and construction of the building
- Relation, for example how the building relates to its context and surroundings
- Quantity, for example the spatial configuration, dimensions and proportions of the structure
- Quality, for example the type, style or period of the building
- Motion, for example the function or activities that the building will contain.

The problems arising from bringing such differing ideas together was illustrated in *Politics*; where concepts of form, style and use were brought to bear on the planning of cities:

> "The arrangement of private houses is considered to be more agreeable and generally more convenient [use] if the street are regularly laid out [form] after the modern fashion [style] which Hippodamus introduced, but for security in war, the antiquated mode of building which made it difficult for assailants to find their way in is preferable. . . . A city should therefore adopt both plans of building: it is possible to arrange the houses irregularly as husbandmen plant their vines in clumps. The whole town should not be laid out in straight lines, but only certain quarters and regions, thus security and beauty will be combined."[142]

Another example of bringing different ideas together was his view that not only should cities have walls but "care should be taken to make them ornamental".[143]

A good building (like the good man described in *Politics*),[144] will be such through its nature, its habits and its reason, which we may interpret as what it is, what it does and what ideas it contains. These, he said, "must be in harmony with one another".[145] They should form a unity which "must not only present a certain order in the arrangement of its parts"[146] but which should also be "a complete whole with its several incidents so closely connected that the transposal or withdrawal of any one of them will disjoin and dislocate the whole".[147]

The natural principles governing generation or creation were internal, like those governing the organic unity of living creatures, "for those things are natural which by a continuous movement from an internal principle arrive at some completion".[148]

The search for principles introduces again the question of their number. How many ultimate principles are there, or, logically, how many ultimate principles should there be?

The question was tackled from the premise that there is one existence, a unity, a whole, which must become subdivided or disjoined in some way in order to arrive at the plurality we see around us. The very first division should lead to the formation of a set of principles through which all subsequent subdivisions will be based.

Aristotle, in surveying previous views on the subject, concluded that the initial subdivision should be into two or into three parts, although in *Physics* he concluded "that whether there are two or three is a matter of considerable difficulty".[149]

(1) Regarding division into two he stated that "all thinkers posit the principles as being contraries . . . which we call opposites, contradictories, contraries, relatives, extremes".[150] From the idea of two could be developed the idea of four, as, for example, in *De Generatione* where he argued for the existence of four elements: "Since however the elements are seen to be more than two, the contrarieties must be at least two. But the contrarieties being two, the elements must be four (as they evidently are) and cannot be three."[151] The

four elements were fire (hot and dry), air (hot and moist), water (cold and moist) and earth (cold and dry).[152] Similarly, there were four causes, which may also be seen as two sets of contraries: first and final, and formal and material.[153]

While it is important to distinguish elements from principles, the problem with this method would be the same in both cases. No reason can be given for the contents of such divisions. For example, where do the notions of hotness, coldness, moistness, dryness come from in the first place?

(2) Divisions into three were also discussed in *De Generatione*. The sequence of reasoning progresses in two stages. The first stage is an argument against Monism, and introduces action or motion as a second principle of existence: "For not only those who postulate a plurality of elements employ their reciprocal action and passion to generate the compound: those who derive things from a single element are equally compelled to introduce acting".[154] The second stage recognizes that acting can "only occur between things which are such as to touch one another". There is a "relation" between the two things, not only in that they have relative position, but also that they are different from one another.[155] They are different according to their attributes, and in *De Caelo* he gave a similar argument against Monism in that there must be a prior relationship type of differentiation: "Now those who decide for a single element . . . and proceed to generate other things out of it by the use of [for example] the attributes of density and rarity . . . deprive the element of its priority".[156] Like most scientists, however, he could understand spatial relations and causal relations belonging to the physical world, but he had difficulty with this differentiating relationship. Is it something only "relative to perception" he asked?[157] He was not happy with the idea of introducing a divine mind as Anaxagoras, for example, had done: "All things are at rest until the mind introduced motion and separated them".[158] Yet when discussing mental phenomena in *De Anima* he talked of the three principles Unity, Activity and Discrimination, as though linked in some way with the three characteristics of the soul, Sense, Will and Thought: "That which discriminates, though both numerically one and indivisible is at the same time divided in its being. . . . It must lose its unity by being put into activity."[159]

It should be said, however, that the trinitarian principle did not seem to be as important to Aristotle as the principle of contraries. In *Metaphysics* he even tried to derive the one from the other, stating that there must be three principles: two contraries and a medium in which they inhere, for example white, black and surface; or light, dark and air,[160] and this again was to have some importance in Scholastic thought. He recognized, however, the importance of the trinitarian principle to others:

"For as the Pythagoreans say, the world and all that is in it is determined by the number three since beginning and middle and end give the number of an all and the number they give is a triad. And so having taken these three from nature as (so to speak) laws of it we make further use of the number three in the worship of the Gods."[161]

Here Aristotle appears to be referring to common oaths made to three gods, as in the Homeric appeal to Zeus, Athene and Apollo.

＊

The idea that categories are based in some way on types of relationship is an important one. Aristotle gave a clear example of three types of relation in *Metaphysics* when he said: "Things are called relative as the double to the half . . . as that which can act to that which can be acted upon . . . as the knowable to knowledge."[162]

It is surely becoming apparent that not only is there a link between these and the three categories of Quantity, Motion and Quality, and the three concepts of Beauty, Goodness and Truth, but also perhaps with the three Vitruvian categories of Firmness, Commodity and Delight. We shall continue this investigation in the ensuing chapters.

This section on Aristotle may be usefully concluded with a look at the developing concept of relation itself. Relation was more than just one of ten equal categories and it was Aristotle who was the first to emphasize the fundamental opposition between Substance and Relation.[163] The ideas that he introduced which are central to aesthetics such as unity, harmony and the concept of the imagination all owe more to relation than to substance.[164] Yet, almost perversely, Aristotle concluded *Metaphysics* arguing against the superiority of relations over substance, an act occasioned it seems by rivalry between the Lyceum and the Academy. Speussipus, nephew and successor of Plato, maintained the view that "a thing cannot be known apart from the knowledge of other things, for to know what a thing is, we must know how it differs from other things".[165] This view had its negative side and soon fell under the influence of the scepticism that Pyrrho had brought back from the East, where he had accompanied Alexander on his Indian expedition. "All things are relative",[166] the Sceptics declared, and from such a viewpoint the discovery of any absolute first principles would be an impossibility.

In the last two centuries before Christ, these ideas were investigated further. Polystratus in Athens introduced the notion of the subjectivity of observer-dependent attributes.[167] Aenesidemus in Alexandria categorized ten types of subjectivity including conditioning by culture, familiarity or unfamiliarity with an object, and the effect of mood and associations on perception.[168] Perhaps, in a sense, these ideas received their initial inspiration from Aristotle. He realized that there must be a self or subject perceiving the perception, "a sense which is aware of itself".[169] Although beauty for Aristotle was couched in the objective language of "symmetry, order and limitation",[170] he admitted to there being a special pleasure in the perception of one's own existence, the pleasures of "being awake, sensing and thinking",[171] and these in relation to our perception of the outside world:

"If life itself is good and pleasant and if he who sees perceives that he sees, then to perceive that we perceive is to perceive that we exist, itself one of the things that is most pleasant."[172]

CHAPTER 4
MEDIAEVAL CATEGORIES

HISTORICAL INTRODUCTION

Throughout the Dark and Middle Ages, the Ten Books of Vitruvius were religiously copied by the monasteries of the Western world, and consulted as virtually the only available text on building matters. Manuscripts dating from the tenth and fourteenth centuries, for example, have survived from St Augustine's Abbey in Canterbury,[1] and in the choir of the nearby cathedral their influence may still be seen in the proportions of the columns and capitals.

To understand the development of the three categories it is important to consider this period as a continuation of, and not a break with, the Classical traditions of Greece and Rome. In many ways it represented the next step, a more complex phase of development, which in order to facilitate comprehension, clothed the same basic concepts in a different set of ideas. Just as the problem of the Incarnation was in a general sense that of the relation between the material world and the ideal world, so too many of the questions regarding the Holy Trinity were a development of questions previously raised on the ultimate differentiation of being, the number and content of its basic categories, and their relation to one another and the world.

Apart from the Gospels, there were two traditions on which the early writers drew, namely the Greek and the Hebrew. Fragments of Greek ideas are found in the Epistles of Paul, alongside references to the Old Testament, and St John's Gospel has been clearly influenced by Hellenic thought. The idea of the "Word" or "*Logos*" found in John's Gospel was at the same time being developed by Philo of Alexandria (c. 15 BC–AD 50), and it was in Alexandria in the third century that the Christian Platonists, Clement and Origen, and the Neoplatonists, notably Plotinus, co-existed.

Plotinus spent the latter part of his life teaching in Rome, where Tertullian and Novatian had taught before him, and it was here, around AD 250 that his *Enneads* were being collated by his pupil, Porphyry. This was the time of the great persecutions of Decius and Valerian, and later, around 300 by Diocletian, whose palaces and public baths may represent for us the grander Roman architecture of the period. In 305, Diocletian abdicated, and Constantine, his successor, in 313, proclaimed religious toleration throughout the empire. Church building flourished;

Plate 4 *Cologne Cathedral, nineteenth-century proposals for completing the building (Rheinische Bildarchiv, Cologne)*

"*This was how I saw the horses and their riders in my vision: They wore breastplates, fiery red, blue and sulphur yellow; the horses had heads like lions' heads, and out of their mouths came fire, smoke and sulphur*"

Book of Revelation

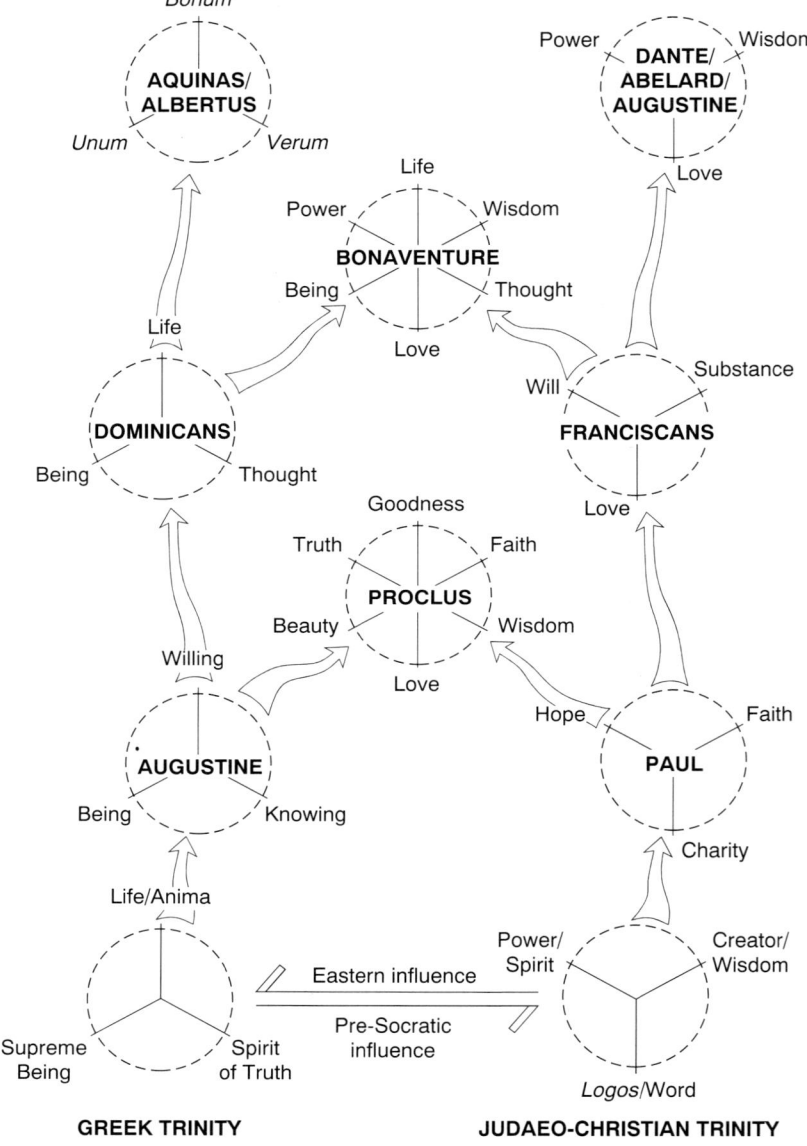

Figure 23 *Mediaeval categories*

Eusebius described, in a unique example of the time, the consecration in 316 of the new church at Tyre;[2] and in 326 Constantinople was founded on the old city of Byzantium.

The events of the fourth century were critical to the development of the concept of the Trinity, and began with the Council of Nicaea which Constantine convened in 325. Athanasius was present, and it was mainly due to his efforts, and

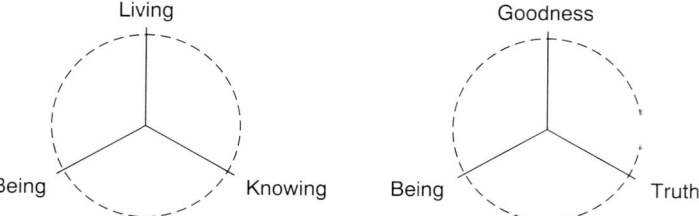

Figure 24 *Augustine used the trinitarian formula in many groupings of concepts, two of which are shown above. These may be compared with the Way, the Life and the Truth of the Gospels, and the Unum, Bonum, Verum of mediaeval logic*

those of the Cappadocians – Basil and the two Gregories, of Nyssa and Nazianzus – that in 381 the Nicene doctrine was accepted by the church. This stated:

- That there were three Persons in one Substance
- That the two heresies lying to either side were to be avoided, namely the Arian heresy, that there were three distinct Persons unrelated by substance; and the Sabellian heresy, that the three Persons were only three aspects of the one God
- That the three Persons were co-equal.[3]

The Goths crossed the Danube in 376, and in 410, under Alaric, entered Rome. Ambrose had consecrated the Church of the Holy Apostles, now S. Ambrogio, in Milan, and in the Baptistery there, was to baptize Augustine who was to become, from his bishopric in Hippo in North Africa, the most influential of the "Doctors" of the Western church. Three centuries earlier, the third Bishop of Rome, Clement I, had proposed the idea that the nature of God is reflected in his works,[4] and now Augustine, thoroughly educated in Classical and Neoplatonic ideas, proposed the notion that it was the Trinity itself that was so reflected, through the three divine concepts of Being, Willing and Knowing[5] (Figure 24).

Neoplatonism was continued into the fifth century by Proclus, one of the last heads of the Academy in Athens before the school was closed down by Justinian in 529. Coincidentally this was the same year that Benedict founded his monastery at Monte Cassino, and three years before building work began on the Hagia Sophia in Constantinople. The ideas of Proclus were introduced into Christianity in the sixth century by a shadowy figure, possibly Syrian, who signed himself "Dionysius the Areopagite" and who, through his mysticism, was to have an influential effect on the writing and building works of Suger in the twelfth century.

There was a growing interest in the classification of knowledge. This resulted in one of the first encyclopedias, which was compiled by Isidore, Bishop of Seville (560–637): "In building", he said, "there are three elements – plan, construction and decoration (*dispositio, constructio, venustas*). The plan is the marking out of the ground or site and of the foundations. The construction is the building of the walls and elevations . . . the decoration is all that is added to buildings for the sake of adornment and beauty, such as gilded vaults, incrustations of precious marbles, and coloured paintings".[6]

Education was generally confined to cathedral and abbey schools (*scholae*) where it was particularly encouraged by Charlemagne around 800, and his Carolingian successors. The birth of modern Europe – France, Germany and Italy – can be said to date from this time, as does the incursion of the Normans, who besieged Paris in 888, and who from their bases at Caen and Bayeux were to affect both the course of mediaeval thought and the Romanesque and Gothic styles of building.

The first wave of Scholasticism began to gather momentum around 1066 when Berengar from the Cathedral School of Tours insisted on a place for reason alongside the growing authoritarianism of the church. Anselm of Canterbury (1033–1109) attempted a rational approach to the understanding of God; and Abelard who arrived at the Notre Dame School in Paris in the year 1100 began to formulate a meaning for the Trinity in terms of Love, Power and Wisdom.[7] This period was the high point of the Romanesque: the Crusades had commenced in 1096; the abbeys of the Cistercian Order were spreading under Bernard of Clairvaux; and the influential schools of Chartres and St Victor, outside Paris, were generating a wealth of new and interesting ideas.

The second wave of Scholasticism gained impetus from the formal institution of the Universities of Paris (1150–1170), Bologna (c. 1158) and Oxford (c. 1168), and the foundation of the two Orders of friars by Dominic and Francis respectively. There was a renewed interest in the works of Aristotle, stimulated by contact with a highly articulate Arabic culture. Gilbert of Poitiers, at Chartres, for example, had divided the categories into two sets, primary and secondary, according to whether they inhered in the object or not:

- Primary Categories: Substance, Relation, Quantity, Quality
- Secondary Categories: Place, Time, Situation, Condition, Action and Passion.[8]

Such terms were to be distinguished from concepts like Beauty, Goodness and Truth which, influenced by Arabic philosophy, were now to be called "transcendentals".

With chairs of theology at Paris, the two most famous Dominicans, Albertus Magnus and Thomas Aquinas, asserted the twin principles of reason and faith, Aquinas in particular developing the transcendental notion of *Unum, Bonum, Verum* as the *Ens realissimum*.[9] There is a story that the two were present at the inception of the rebuilding of Cologne Cathedral in 1248 (which, however, was not completed until the nineteenth century). The Franciscans, Bonaventure and Duns Scotus, on the other hand, moved towards a position of asserting the power of Love and the Will over those of the Intellect; and it was through another Franciscan, William of Occam in the fourteenth century, that the links between science and theology eventually began to be severed.

THE TRINITY: CLASSICAL GREEK VERSION

The feature that most distinguished the Christian religion from the Jewish and Moslem religions was the central concept of the Trinity. For theologians it was and

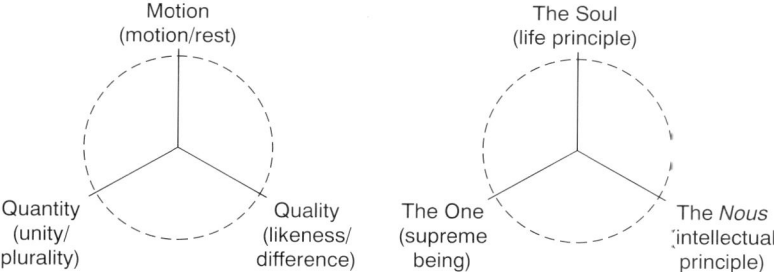

Figure 25 *Plotinus reduced Aristotle's categories to three kinds of relation (left) which can be compared with the Eleatic categories. He also developed the idea of a threefold godhead (right) which was influential in early Christian doctrine*

remains a difficult conceptual problem; and we may perhaps best introduce the subject of the Trinity through Basil, who suggested that the resolution of the problem may lie more in the types of relation existing between the three members of the Godhead than in the nature of the Persons themselves.[10]

With regard to Classical development, Plotinus, as we have seen, had reduced Aristotle's categories to five: Substance, Relation, Quantity, Quality and Action, and stated that there were grounds for the latter three "to be considered as relations"[11] (Figure 25). Thomas Aquinas amplified this saying that in God "relations are real"[12] and that there were indeed three types of relation which give a natural order to the world:

- Quantity, as in double and half
- Activity, as in acting and being acted upon
- Understanding, through likenesses of Quality, as found in the concepts of Genus and Species.[13]

We should compare this with Aristotle's three types of relation with which we concluded our previous chapter.

It is also interesting to compare this subdivision of concepts with three aspects of the mediaeval church which, in Aquinas's view, required consideration:

(1) Its beauty, which should be enough to "dispirit the Queen of Sheba"
(2) Its activities, which should be "orderly and expeditiously arranged"
(3) Its integrity, which should consist in its "essential perfection".[14]

Isidore had similarly distinguished between Beauty, Utility and Appropriateness (*pulchro, utile, apto*),[15] and elsewhere between form, movement and species.

Both Tertullian, in the earliest surviving discourse on the Trinity[16] (c. 210), and Abelard in the twelfth century[17] used a similar format to explain the ways in which the members of the Trinity may be distinguished:

- In terms of Quantity, as a three-in-one, the first step in deriving plurality from unity

- In terms of Order, that the Son is begotten by the Father, and that the Spirit proceeds from the Father and the Son
- In terms of the individual Qualities and attributes of the Persons within the Godhead.

The last was a problem in that the nature of one was held to be the nature of them all. The solution put forward by Augustine lay in finding attributes that were convertible into one another (an essential characteristic of transcendentals), and he determined upon three ". . . to know, to live and to be, are one and the same".[18] The idea undoubtedly came to him while at Rome from Victorinus who had used the threefold division Being, Life and Thought to signify the Godhead, but it was also taken from an idea found in the Gospels: "I embraced the mediator between God and Man, Jesus Christ. He was calling to me and saying: I am the Way, I am the Truth and I am the Life."[19]

The other powerful influence, as Augustine admitted, was the Classical Greek tradition. In particular, there was Plotinus who had also developed the concept of a threefold God composed of the following three ideas:

(1) The One (the "Supreme Being")
(2) The Nous (the "Intellectual Principle")
(3) The Soul (the "Life Principle").[20]

Although Theodoret at the beginning of the fifth century identified this directly with the concept of Father, Son and Spirit,[21] there remained doubts, not the least of which concerned the order. One view which maintained the above order was that of Hilary, Bishop of Poitiers (300–367), who adapted the Eleatic categories as follows:

- Father as Eternal Being
- Son as Image of the Father (*"Species in Imagine"*)
- Spirit as Active in the World (*"Usus in Munere"*).[22]

The more integrated view, as we shall see, tends to reverse the main attributes of the last two in line with various direct scriptural readings (Figure 26):

- Father as Being-Principle, as the "I AM" of Moses
- Son as Life-Principle, as in "I am the bread of Life"
- Spirit as Truth-Principle, as the "Spirit of Truth".[23]

Whatever the order, the fundamental notion introduced by Augustine was that the structuring of the Trinity was reflected in the structuring of the world. Not only was Man, or Woman, made in the image of God, through the concepts of Being, Life and Mind, but so were his or her aspirations, those highest categories, or "transcendentals" which have come down to us as Beauty, Goodness and Truth. It is

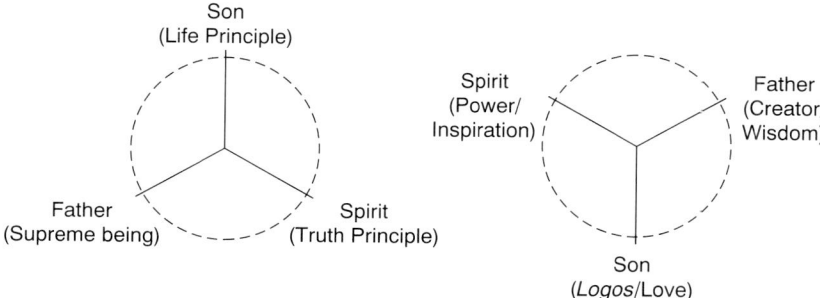

Figure 26 *Two versions of the Trinity. In the Classical Greek version (left) Hilary reversed the positions of Son and Spirit. In the Judaeo-Christian version (right), influenced by Philo, we see the three Old Testament concepts of Wisdom, Word and Spirit*

curious that the these latter three concepts were never mentioned together as such although many similar threefold groups were recorded by Augustine including Being, Goodness and Truth,[24] and Beauty, Pleasure and Truth.[25]

The concept of the transcendentals is, in its Scholastic sense, thought to be of Arabic origin as previously mentioned. Besides signifying an interconvertibility of meaning between the terms which comprised the transcendentals, it also signified a series of universal predicates which could be attributed to the humblest building just as much as to God. We may compare the list of transcendentals with the list of "Divine Names" which Pseudo-Dionysius had compiled in the sixth century and which attributed to God the concepts of the One, the Good, Light, Love, Beauty, Truth, etc. The common transcendentals introduced in the twelfth century were four in number: *Ens, Unum, Bonum, Verum*[26] (Being, One, Goodness and Truth). Bonaventure added *Pulchrum* (Beauty) to replace, or to be equivalent to *Ens* (Being),[27] an equivalence which we shall discuss in more detail in our next section. Given that Pseudo-Dionysus had elevated the concept of the One to be above all others[28], we find here a precedent for the three transcendentals, Beauty, Goodness and Truth, which were finally established as a group by Ficino in the fourteenth century to reflect the attributes of the Holy Trinity.

CATEGORY ONE: BEAUTY AND BEING

There was a Greek term *Pankalia* that referred to a belief commonly held that all things, all being, could be seen as beautiful. Plotinus, for example, had equated Beauty and Being in many passages, for instance "Being is desirable because it is identical with Beauty, and Beauty is loved because it is Being".[29] What distinguished Beauty in one sense from Being was the requirement for the former to have a perceiving subject. This led to the definition of Beauty by Aquinas as "that which pleases when seen",[30] and a reaffirmation of the central notion of perception to aesthetics in its facility for "grasping a thing's existence more firmly".[31]

Around 1270, Witelo in *De Perspectiva* described two kinds of perception:

(1) Simple sensory perception through which we are aware of colour and light
(2) Complex judgemental perception through which we are aware of form and proportion.[32]

This is an important distinction in aesthetics and one to which we shall return.

A similar twofold conception of beauty had been prevalent throughout the Middle Ages, stemming in part from Augustine's transcription of a statement in Cicero that "All bodily beauty consists in the proportion of parts together with a certain agreeableness of colour".[33]

Plotinus had asked if there were not some one principle underlying these two aspects of beauty. It could not be a "symmetry of parts" because "the loveliness of colour and even the light of the sun are devoid of parts".[34] For Plotinus it was the mere "unity that is beautiful", either the unity of part touching part in the outer world or the "unison" of an isolated part touching one's soul in the inner world.[35]

To these two aspects, which he termed Proportion and Clarity, Aquinas added a third, Integrity, the three as a whole constituting a reflection of the Godhead which could be contemplated in all things:

"Whether the Holy Doctors have correctly assigned essential attributes to the three Persons . . . three things are necessary for beauty: first, Integrity or perfection, for things that are lacking in something are for this reason ugly; also due Proportion or consonance; and again Clarity for we call things beautiful when they are highly coloured."[36]

It will be useful to look at these three concepts, Proportion, Clarity and Integrity, in turn.

- *Proportion*: In the writings of Augustine we find reference to the typical aesthetic concepts of symmetry, geometry, contrast, harmony and unity. Beautiful things possess a "geometrical regularity" and "please by proportion"; they are "composed of contrarieties"; and like a choir, or army, consist of a "harmony . . . unifying many souls into one".[37] Classical proportions were generally rejected in this period, although certain theorists like Grosseteste, Bishop of Lincoln, continued the notion that "harmony derives only from the five proportions to be found between the numbers, one, two, three and four".[38]

  Proportions were important to the structure of buildings as we see in the records of the construction of Milan cathedral. In these records we also note a way of setting out the works by methods known as *ad triangulum* or *ad quadratum* where the elements of the section, for example, were made to align with either a series of equilateral triangles, or a series of mathematically proportioned rectangles.[39] Intellectual satisfaction we can assume was achieved in knowing that the disposition of the work corresponded to some unseen geometrical order, whether or not such shapes symbolized anything in the divine realm.

- *Clarity*: The concept of light was introduced into the subject of aesthetics by the Neoplatonists, and passed into the Christian tradition chiefly through the writings of Pseudo-Dionysius. It became one of the main features of the emerging Gothic style after Suger, Abbot of St Denis, enlarged the choir there in 1144, and described the result as "pervaded by the wonderful and uninterrupted light of the most luminous windows".[40] For Suger, spiritual regeneration could be effected through the provision of such windows, but also through the contemplation of the colours in paintings, hangings and jewellery, and "the many-coloured stones that glowed".[41] We might note that the earliest stained glass windows still surviving are found at Augsburg and date from the eleventh century. Albertus Magnus later saw form itself as an intellectual light, and suggested that it was the clarity of form shining out from matter and impressing itself upon the observer that gave a thing its beauty.[42]

- *Integrity*: Duns Scotus perhaps gave the best summing up of the concept of integrity when he likened it to some sort of wholeness, writing: "Beauty is not some kind of absolute quality in beautiful objects. It is rather the aggregate of all the properties of such objects, for example, magnitude, shape and colour, and the sum of all the connections among themselves and between themselves and the objects."[43] It was in the seeing of all these connections or relations that the difficulty lay; and in order to grasp the beauty of the whole, the spiritual exercises of meditation and contemplation were developed. Richard of St Victor, in fact, described three mental stages prescribed to attain heightened perception, namely, concentration, meditation and contemplation.[44] The final stage, "contemplation", he noted, "has an aesthetic character . . . where the soul expands and is uplifted by the beauty it perceives".[45] To the mystic, such contemplation marked the final stage in the soul's journey towards God – a God described as "pure existence, in which all others partake"[46] – and in whose contemplation even one's own soul becomes united or integrated. Through such concepts, we can begin to understand the mediaeval church, its interior spaces, stained glass and rose windows, as objects of contemplation, even seeing in the height and spire a symbol of the mystical ascent itself.[47]

CATEGORY TWO: GOODNESS AND LIFE

In the same way that God could be defined as the "Supreme Being" under the first category, here he was seen as "the first Cause", by Anselm for example, and the "first Good" by Aquinas.[48] Since Aristotle, goodness had been linked with causality, as we have seen. We think, for example of the phrase, "good causes".

Albertus Magnus reduced Aristotle's types of cause from four to three, and in this he was followed by Aquinas who wrote: "God works throughout all activity after the manner of three causes: the formal, the efficient and the final"[49] (Figure 27).

Figure 27 *Aquinas reduced Aristotle's four kinds of cause to three (left) which can be compared with three things necessary for beauty. He also described three kinds of virtue (right), theological, moral, and intellectual, each of which he further subdivided into three*

If these represented three types of good, and if, as Aquinas said, "Everything is good according to its function"[50] we should be able to extract three kinds of function against which a building's performance might be judged. For example:

- Under formal cause we might consider one function of the building to be pleasing to the eye through its form and colour.
- Under efficient cause a second function could lie in the building housing a particular set of activities in a convenient and efficient manner,
- Under final cause we should consider the purpose or ultimate ends of human life in general, and how a building could best function in order to promote these higher ends.

All these notions contributed to the idea of the good in the Middle Ages, and it will be useful to look at each in turn.

FORMAL CAUSE

While for Duns Scotus it was Love that moved the first cause, for Aquinas it was Beauty: "All things are caused by beauty . . .", he said, ". . . No-one takes the trouble to build an effigy except for its beauty".[51] Beauty had been equated with Goodness since the Neoplatonists, but there was another influential, if somewhat heretical, view expressed by the Gnostics that it was the devil who was responsible for the material world, and that physical beauty should therefore be abhorred. Even Augustine warned his flock to "resist the allurement of the eye" and to be wary of "the snares and temptations"[52] of this world.

A distinction came to be drawn between material beauty and spiritual beauty, reflected, for example, in the austerity of the Cistercians who prohibited excess and ornamentation in their churches, and instead used only simple materials and forms. The difference might be compared to that which Aquinas drew between

Goodness, which is "the object of our desiring faculties", and Beauty which he defined as the object of our impartial cognitive powers.[53]

Efficient Cause

The second function of the building lies in housing a particular set of activities in a convenient and efficient manner. Types of building differ according to social function, and we are reminded of Paul who likened the social division of the people to the limbs and organs of the body of Christ where "the whole frame grows through the due activity of each part".[54] The concept of barter, or exchange, was important in this activity, as it was for Augustine, who interestingly referred to money as "a term of relation".[55] Augustine's book, *The City of God*, it may be noted, was an important influence on Charlemagne and the ideals he brought to establishing a working empire in the ninth century.

Aquinas noted that all such systems as the mediaeval economy and way of trading could be "defined with reference to a particular set of causes and effects".[56] The primary causes were the people's needs, which he referred to in terms of material goods such as "food, drink, clothing, shelter" etc. The social system required to effect the satisfaction of these needs, however, has grown more complex as society has developed.

The earliest division of tribal society into king, priest and people was reflected in the later concept of the three estates: nobility, church and bourgeoisie. Such a division was recorded by Philip of Vitry, secretary to Philip VI, who wrote as plague and war were breaking out in the fourteenth century:

"In order to escape the evils which they saw coming, the people divided themselves into three parts. One was to pray to God; for trading and ploughing the second; and later to guard these two parts from wrong or injury, knights were created."[57]

The division of the French people in this way was symbolized in their *fleur-de-lys* and was clearly trinitarian, the knights representing the body, the church the mind and the people the soul of the nation.

The building types that arose are reminiscent of Vitruvius's "three classes of public building, the first for defensive, the second for religious and the third for utilitarian purposes".[58] The mediaeval castles and manor houses were the centre of local judiciary power; the merchant's houses often included shops or counting houses at ground-floor level; and from the monasteries and cathedrals developed the libraries, schools and universities as centres of learning.

Final Cause

The third function of the building lies in promoting those higher values of human life which were more properly the subject of ethics or morality. Aquinas, with the classificatory mind of the Scholastic, divided the virtues into three types: the

Theological, the Moral and the Intellectual, corresponding to soul, body and mind respectively,[59] and it will be useful to discuss these, in turn, in relation to the church architecture of the time.

- *The theological virtues*: Faith, Hope and Charity, denoted knowledge of, movement towards, and union with God respectively. As in music where Augustine, for example, approved of singing in order that "weaker spirits may be inspired with feelings of devotion"[60] so it was thought that churches could inspire both love of God, and love of neighbour. Love of God might be inspired by providing objects of sublimity and contemplation; and love of neighbour by filling the church with light, as described by Eusebius at Tyre, where "men formerly downcast looked at each other with smiling countenances and beaming eyes".[61]
- *The moral virtues*: Justice, Temperance, Fortitude and Prudence, regulated respectively the will, the two bodily appetites of pleasure and fear, and the reasoning faculty. For example, with regard to justice and temperance, luxury and wasteful extravagance were to be rejected if a building were to be considered in relation to society as a whole. "The walls of the church are indeed resplendent", Bernard said of a church of the Cluniac Order, "but her poor go in need. She clothes her stones with gold, and leaves her children to go naked. The eyes of the rich are flattered at the expense of the poor."[62] Aquinas, however, with regard to prudence, did not entirely exclude appropriate show and visual pleasure, but said "Austerity, in so far as it is a virtue, does not exclude all pleasures, but only those which are excessive and disordered".[63]
- *The intellectual virtues*: Wisdom, Science and Understanding, dealt with divine, practical and theoretical knowledge respectively. One function of the mediaeval church was to communicate historical and scriptural knowledge through its sculptures, paintings and stained glass windows. Aquinas emphasized the didactic nature of such features and asked how can a man have faith and live a good life "unless the truth is first proposed to him"?[64]

CATEGORY THREE: TRUTH AND KNOWLEDGE

"Truth" was for Augustine another one of the "Divine Names"[65] for God, and the concept of truth had been a problem for Christianity since Pilate had first queried its nature. It was related to the divine mind and the world of ideas by Aquinas who said "Everything is said to be true in the absolute sense because of its relation to a mind on which it depends".[66] Whether or not this is the case, the relationship type behind truth or knowledge had been stated by Plotinus to be one of likeness: "All knowing comes by likeness" and "truth is the identity of the knowing act with its object".[67] Likeness in turn depended on shared qualities, so that when Aquinas said that "A house, for example, is true if it turns out like the plan in an architect's mind"[68] it was the qualities inherent in the house and the idea that were to be compared.

Three theories of truth have been handed down from the Greeks: the Correspondence theory from Plato, the Pragmatic theory from Epicurus, and the Coherence theory from Chrysippus.[69] These theories differed according to whether the criterion of truth was the accordance of the object with the idea (correspondence), the accordance of desired effect to actual effect (pragmatic), or the accordance of part to whole (coherence). All three have a bearing on the notion of meaning in architecture, particularly important to the church architecture of the time, and it will be useful to look at each one in turn.

CORRESPONDENCE THEORY

Meaning under this theory is derived from associating a building with an idea, either through formal resemblance or through other shared qualities. There were degrees by which an object might correspond to an idea in the mind depending on the number of qualities shared between the two.[70] On the one hand, if the number of shared qualities was many, and included such formal qualities as shape and proportion, then the relationship would be that of resemblance and we could speak of a "true likeness". Augustine, for example, wrote "The senses relay the finished product to the mind, so that by referring it to the truth that presides there as arbiter, it may decide whether it is well or badly made".[71]

Plotinus called it "beautiful . . . when he found the house standing before him correspondent with his inner ideal of a house". Aquinas remarked that "an image is called beautiful if it represents even an ugly thing faithfully",[72] and here we might think, for example, of the carved heads and gargoyles that decorate mediaeval stonework.

The concept of perfection is an interesting one in this context as it may refer solely to an exact likeness between an object and the picture in one's mind, or it may connote something more, a correspondence with an ideal of beauty, not perhaps to be found in ugly things or gargoyles.

On the other hand, where the number of shared qualities are fewer, we speak not so much of resemblance but more of suggestion or association. Silentarius, for example, described the coloured marbles of the Hagia Sophia as evocative of landscapes, of fruit, and of images of undescribed sensuality.[73] The clusters of colonettes in church interiors have been likened to fountains, and the ribs of the high stone vaults to the branches of trees arching over the nave.[74]

The meaning that buildings have for us may depend on personal associations which in turn depend on memory. Augustine referred to "the vast cloisters of the memory . . . a storehouse for countless images . . . where everything is preserved separately according to its category".[75]

Meaning may also depend on more institutionalized associations, and there was often a perceived reality to these associative relationships which it is hard to understand today. For example, Augustine conceived of beauty as a window through which to see the divine.[76] Beauty was not only associated with God, but the qualities of beauty in the object were held to be the actual qualities of God shared out upon the earth. A beautiful building actually partook of the divine.

Similarly, in holy icons, there were qualities attributed to the physical icon which partook of the actual qualities of the original saint depicted. The icon could thus be seen as a true fragment of the saint[77] . . . a view which led to charges of idolatry and the iconoclast controversy which raged between 726 and 843.

PRAGMATIC THEORY

Meaning under this theory is derived from the effect the building, or part of a building, has on the mind or spirit of the spectator. Church architecture, for example, was used to communicate religious truth, either pictorially or through the use of symbols, and could therefore be judged according to the effectiveness of such communication.

Although Gregory I in the sixth century had encouraged the use of pictures in churches for those who could not read,[78] it was not until 1025 that the Synod of Arras concluded that "whatever people could not grasp through the scriptures should be learnt by means of images".[79] This led to the development of pictorial stained glass windows, the earliest, as we have seen, dating from the eleventh century in Augsburg; and sculptured groups on external facades, first in Catalonia and then at Cluny in 1095.

The purpose of theological teaching was threefold according to Aquinas, "to refute error, to teach morals and to contemplate truth",[80] a division which corresponded to the literal, moral and spiritual interpretations that Jerome had earlier read into holy scripture.[81] Philo, long before Jerome, had differentiated between literal and non-literal meanings, the latter including allegory and symbolism as alternative means of communicating truth.[82]

Symbolism also played an important part in church architecture, and there were many different types. Besides colour symbolism, which we shall discuss later, there was number symbolism, where, for example, three doors, four pedentives or twelve columns, might represent the Trinity, the Evangelists or the Apostles respectively. There was also a more conceptual symbolism at work where, for example, the walls might represent the *vita activa* (active life), and the ceiling the *vita contemplativa* (contemplative life) respectively.[83]

Heraldry too was symbolic and lent its patterns to church furnishings, ceiling bosses and floor tiles. Again, the symbolism was intended to communicate meaning at several levels, and it is important to distinguish, for example, between the emblematic function of, say, a lion for England and its symbolic connotation of strength.

Beasts, herbs and even stones were endowed with symbolic significance.[84] All nature, according to Eriugena, was "one vast store of symbols",[85] and as we saw in our previous section, a physical relationship was often supposed to exist between an object and what it signified, in some instances assuming the nature of cause and effect. Although we should say today that this is a prime example of a category mistake, we should note that by the same token, according to Proclus, elements from the world of ideas, like saints and angels, could similarly be imbued with powers and a reality all of their own.[86]

COHERENCE THEORY

From the coherence theory of truth is derived the notion that meaning comes from the relation between a building and its historical context – the ideas and influences of the time, the prevailing technology, and other such determining factors.

We say, for example, that a building is "true to its age", and it will be useful to look here briefly at the nature of the Gothic style and how it developed in different countries.

The development of the Gothic from its Romanesque and Early Christian origins makes an interesting study in this respect. Influences on style have been seen to reside not only in a country's available technology and economic situation but also in its general beliefs and patterns of thought.[87] There was a shift in interest from Platonism to Aristotelianism during this period, and this has been compared to the development from the simpler Platonic forms of the Early Christian period and the Romanesque to the more organic and dynamic forms of the Gothic.[88] The analytic methods of Scholasticism have also been seen to be reflected in the hierarchical arrangements, and the divisions and subdivisions, of the typical cathedral facade.[89]

However, just as no system is entirely self-contained, so the borrowing of stylistic features from other cultures reflected a wider trade in knowledge and ideas. The Romanesque, for example, took much of its vocabulary from fifth-century Syrian architecture,[90] while the Gothic, according to Wren, incorporated pointed windows for their associations with the Holy Land.[91]

This borrowing of forms from other cultures may be compared to the adoption of ideas to form an integrated and coherent theology. Ammonias held this notion of borrowing ideas from other cultures to be flawed. The syncretistic view of the Gnostics, with their amalgam of Persian, Jewish and Christian ideas, was wrong, he said: better to stick to a single system which has been organically developed over time, whichever system it may be for "every system contains the whole truth in various levels of perfection".[92]

Whatever the merits of such a view, it naturally led to religious dogma, which was then opposed in turn by free-thinkers like Abelard who stated that "every age must have its own answers".[93] The uniqueness of a style to its age was promoted by Duns Scotus who in saying that perfection comes from uniqueness ". . . the more general a thing is, the less it exists",[94] led the way to a more contemporary view of artistic truth. In this context, we may also note Alan of Lille who said that "a new art turns the shadow of things into reality and changes all lies into truth".[95]

PRIMARY AND SECONDARY CATEGORIES

Plotinus recorded that "philosophy at a very early age investigated the number and character of the existents . . . some found ten, others less . . . to some the genera are the first principles, to others only a generic classification of existents".[96] He realized that some sets were reducible, or posterior, to others: "Why are not Beauty, Goodness and the virtues, Knowledge and Intelligence included among the primary genera?"[97] he asked. He came to the conclusion that both the transcendental categories of Beauty, Goodness and Truth and the Aristotelian categories of Quantity, Quality, Activity, etc. were in some way posterior to the Eleatic categories of Plato:

Unity/Plurality   Motion/Stability   Identity/Difference[98]

Plotinus called these "the hearth of reality" and from them evolved what has been called "the three moments of the Neoplatonic world process":[99]

- First, the "One", and his view that "the origin of things is a contemplation"
- "The second is certainly an activity . . . a secondary phase . . . life streaming from life . . . energy running through the universe"[100]
- Third, Intelligence ". . . Activity is prior to Intellection . . . and self-knowledge"[101]

Similar ideas were introduced into Early Christian thought. Gregory of Nazianus for instance, summed it up saying "Therefore Unity having from all eternity arrived by motion at duality, came to rest in trinity".[102]

Augustine compared the threefold process with the act of creation described in Genesis where first, the Father spake, second, the Word set the world in motion, and third, the Spirit "saw that it was good".[103] According to Proclus, his predecessor, Iamblichus, coined the term "reversion" for the final phase: "Iamblichus called the monad, the cause of identity; the dyad, the introduction of procession and difference; and the triad, the origin of reversion."[104] In another, more telling image, Plotinus likened the three moments to the centre, the radii and the circumference of a circle:

"How is this unity also a plurality . . . it is like a circle which in projection becomes a circumference, a centre, a system of radii. . . . From the One arises a circumradiation . . . the Intellection circles in its multiple unity around the Supreme which stands to it as archetype to image."[105]

Let us pause here a while. One of the principles of the categoric method which we can take from Plotinus is that "all things are in all things", by which we take to mean that each of the three moments, or highest categories, are in all things. We could say, for example, that there should be three types of centre, three types of radii, and three types of circumference, each set reflecting the initial process of division.

Let us concentrate on the three types of radii circumradiating, or "overflowing" from the One. Plotinus tells us not to think of individual or "separated radii"[106] but to imagine each of them branching out from the One like the foliage of a tree. We may think of each one resullting in its own distinctive kind of network, as described below:

"Particular things push forth as from a single root . . . branching into multiplicity . . . until we have in our metaphor, bough and crest, foliage and fruit."[107]

- First, Being divides and subdivides to become a "plurality in unity", "space . . .", as Philo said, ". . . that embraceth all things".[108]
- Second, regarding Motion, Plotinus borrowed from the Stoics the notion of "the interconnection of the causative forces and their linked descent".[109]
- Third, Knowledge itself was seen by Porphyry as a "tree",[110] branching out from the highest genera, down through intermediate species, to individuals themselves. Such classification was based on likeness and difference and the inherent qualities within individuals.

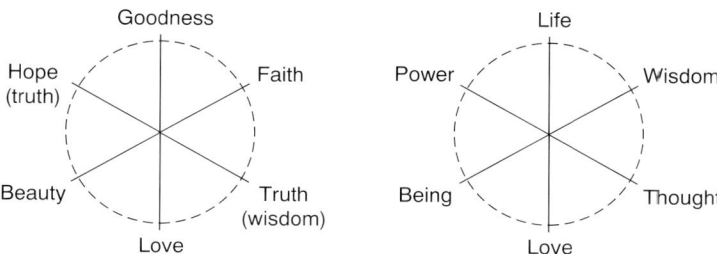

Figure 28 *On the left we see how Proclus attempted to reconcile Classical (Beauty, Goodness and Truth) and Christian (Faith, Hope and Charity) traditions. In Bonaventura's "Soul's Journey towards God" (right) the contemplative stages involving Being, Life and Thought are followed by a consideration of the Power, Wisdom and Love of God*

Just as for Plotinus a stone could be subjected to the categories of substance, quantity, quality, motion etc.,[111] so here we see an individual being, a building for example, lying within and defined by these three overlapping networks of relationships, a reflection of "the one, first centre". Our minds tend to see the elements thus formed rather than the relations. As Plotinus said: "we ignore the radial lines and think only of their terminals."[112] But in contrast to the associated idea of relativity, here it is the relations that absolutely define the thing: "Within our nature is such a centre by which we grasp and are linked and held."[113]

Reversion may be likened to standing anywhere on the circumference of this "outward streaming of life" and looking back at the One in contemplation. Plotinus introduced the concept of points of view where any point on the circumference gives only a partial aspect of the whole: "Looking outwards we see many faces; look inward and all is one head."[114] The faces or aspects on the circumference differ according to the predominance of relationship types. According to Proclus: "Iamblichus said all are in each but one of them predominates more in one than another."[115]

In each of the primary categories discussed so far, Beauty, Goodness and Truth, there is a single predominant relationship type which Proclus referred to as the "monad". However, there are secondary categories falling between these three where two relationship types are almost equally predominant, the "dyads" arising from the "biformed principle".[116] Proclus concluded that "There are not only three monads, but also three dyads".[117] In a passage in the Platonic Theology written while he was head of the Academy at Athens, Proclus illustrated the possibility of three primary and three secondary categories (Figure 28):

> "In short there are three things which replenish divine natures . . . viz Goodness, Wisdom and Beauty. And again there are three things which collect together the natures that are to be filled, being secondary indeed to the former . . . and these are Faith, Truth and Love."[118]

The latter grouping clearly resembles Paul's Faith, Hope and Charity[119] and it seems almost as though Proclus were attempting a last-minute reconciliation between the Classical and Christian traditions. While Aquinas thought that Faith, Hope and Charity derived ultimately from a passage in Ecclesiasticus 2.8–18,[120] there is another tradition from which secondary categories can be derived, which although loosely termed Judaeo-Christian reached back to a common mythology that predated the Eleatic categories of Classical Greece.

THE TRINITY: JUDAEO-CHRISTIAN VERSION

From the baptismal formula given at the end of Matthew's Gospel: "Go ye therefore baptising in the name of the Father, Son and Holy Spirit"[121] and from various references in Scripture the following general interpretation can be developed:

- Father as Creator, "Maker of Heaven and Earth"
- Son as Word (*Logos*) or Love "of which we all partake"
- Spirit as Power and Inspiration "like flames of fire"[122]

In Abelard,[123] and later, Dante,[124] it should be noted that it is the Father who represents Power, the Son, Wisdom, and the Spirit, Love.

If the Greek view had developed through analysis and reason, then the Judaeo-Christian view developed more through revelation and intuition. In the circle analogy of Plotinus we can liken reason to the "separated radii" and intuition to the fused radii which can grasp two or more aspects simultaneously. Aquinas was to assert that both feeling and reason, both the body and the mind, were equally important, saying "Science shines only on the mind; Faith enlightens the mind and also warms the affections".[125] The Franciscans went further and in demoting the status of the human intellect, asserted substance over form, love over reason, and a will for living over the understanding of life.[126]

To understand the historical development of these three secondary categories, Substance, Love and Will, we might begin in the eighth century BC with Hesiod who stated three similar principles near the beginning of his *Theogony*:

"In truth, then foremost sprang Chaos, and next broad-bosomed Earth, ever secure seat of all the immortals, who inhabit the peaks of snow-capt Olympus . . . and Love, who is most beautiful among immortal Gods".[127]

Substance may be compared with "Earth", Love of course with "Love", which leaves the Will to be compared with "Chaos".

Three centuries later, Empedocles incorporated Love as one of his six principles, introduced Strife to replace the Chaos of Hesiod, and increased the number of material elements to four: earth, air, fire and water.[128] The notion that the Greek divinities reflected such principles was recorded by Plutarch who said "All religions are fundamentally one . . . the gods are symbolic . . . attributes of an unknowable God."[129] Proclus, who saw the male gods as monadic in character and the female gods as dyadic,[130] rationalized the twelve Olympians into sets of three,

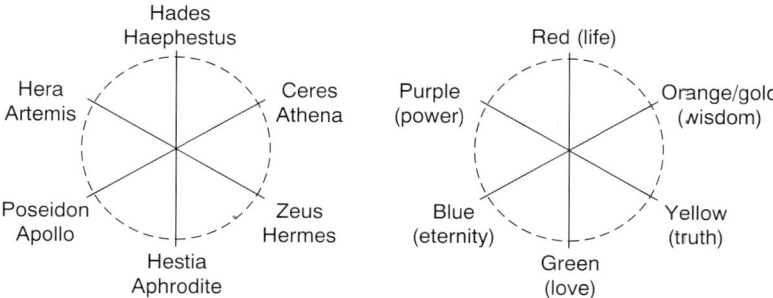

Figure 29 *The Greek pantheon of twelve gods was divided by Proclus into six male and six female gods according to "monadic" or "dyadic" relations (left). Some clearly represent concepts shown in Figure 28 (Athena wisdom, Aphrodite love, etc.). Other kinds of symbolism, like the colour symbolism shown on the right, have less clear historical warrant (see text)*

and we may see, for example, in the statues of Athena, Aphrodite and Artemis that ornament the palaces of the Renaissance, the three principles of Wisdom, Love and Strife respectively[131] (Figure 29).

Christianity, it was said by Gregory of Nyssa, steered a middle course between Greek polytheism and Judaic monotheism.[132] But just as a trinitarian structure could be imposed on Greek plurality, as described above, so there were three concepts in the Old Testament which could be endowed with divine characteristics, namely Wisdom, Word and Spirit.[133] Philo Judaeus at the time of Christ saw in the *Logos* "the cement and bond of union by which the several parts of the universe are kept together".[134] It linked together two other powers, the creative power by which the world was formed and the legal power by which the world was governed.[135] Tertullian followed Justin Martyr in linking Creation with Wisdom, and saw the three in terms of Creative Wisdom, Existence and Power of Authority.[136] Augustine in his *De Trinitate* gave the Middle Ages its most potent formulation in the three concepts Wisdom, Love and Power.[137] Abelard linked the three directly to the Holy Trinity and was accused of heresy,[138] while Dante in one passage, amending Power to moral strength, gave the order as "*sapienza, amore e virtute*".[139]

The idea that these secondary categories were somehow higher or nearer to God than the primary categories of the Greeks was proposed by Bonaventura. In the *Soul's Journey towards God*[140] he described six ascending levels of illumination which were developed from those of Richard of St Victor.[141] Only after passing through the contemplative stages involving Being, Life and Thought could the soul rise to consider the Power, Wisdom and Love of God.[142] He even suggested that such secondary categories might be a result of "joining" concepts together as Proclus had suggested. After reminding us of the Gospel injunction to "Love the Lord your God with all your heart, all your soul and all your mind" he said "Any one of these ways can be doubled according to whether we consider God as the alpha and omega . . . or we can consider each way independently or joined together".[143]

Before investigating each of the three categories in turn, we should note that there is no inherent reason why the circle of knowledge should not be divided into any number of compartments. Proclus, for example, divided each of the three primary categories into three subcategories,[144] and the resulting "mystical" number nine was reflected in the lists and circular diagrams of the Majorcan missionary Ramon Lull (c. 1235–1315).[145] Basil, who, according to Aquinas, had introduced the idea of relation into the Godhead, likened the problem to that of discerning the boundaries of the colours in the rainbow:

> "There is found in them a certain inexpressible and incomprehensible union and distinction, since neither the differences of the Persons breaks the continuity of nature, nor the common attributes of substance dissolves the individual character of their distinctive marks. . . . In Spring at various times you have beheld the brilliance of the . . . rainbow . . . being of many colours it is imperceptibly mingled with the varied hues of the dyes . . . between the blue-green and the flame colour, or the flame colour and the purple, or that and the amber, the space which both mixes and separates the two colours cannot be discerned . . . it is possible to reason that the specific qualities of the persons, like any one of the brilliant colours which appear in the rainbow, flash in each of those persons which we believe to be in the Holy Trinity."[146]

Following the principle known as Occam's razor,[147] that there is no reason to multiply the number of existents without necessity, we may take six categories as being perhaps the most expedient for our understanding. Six was the perfect number for Augustine in combining one, two and three together,[148] and we may now, following this passage from Basil, liken our secondary categories to secondary colours, seeing in each the joining of two primaries taken in turn:

Primary categories
(1) Blue: the colour of eternity and supreme being "Under his feet there was, as it were, a pavement of sapphire, clear blue as the very heavens".[149]
(2) Red: the colour of divine goodness and life, also their opposites: "though your sins be as scarlet they shall be as white as snow".[150]
(3) Yellow: the colour of light and truth, "as the wings of a dove covered with silver and her feathers with yellow-gold".[151]

Secondary categories
(1) Orange (Gold): the colour of wisdom and mutable substance "On the throne sat one whose appearance was like the gleam of jasper and cornelian".[152]
(2) Green: the colour of love and communion "and around the throne was a rainbow bright as an emerald".[153]
(3) Purple: the colour of regal power and passion "the purple raiment that was on the kings of Midian".[154]

Although Dante referred to red as the colour of divine goodness and the angel of temperance,[155] and some precedent may be found in Classical mythology, gold as the colour of Athena, green as the colour of Aphrodite etc.,[156] there appears to have been no agreed colour symbolism in the Middle Ages.[157] The colours that "flash" forth from the stained glass windows of the time reflect more the fact that the Persons of the Godhead were to be seen equally in all things.

CATEGORY FOUR: CREATION AND SUBSTANCE

There are two things we need to look at under each of the secondary categories. The first consists of the kinds of concept found under each category, paying particular attention to how the double nature of their concepts was conceived from the Early Christian to the mediaeval periods. The second consists of a discussion of some of the more important concepts of the time in a more general way and the particular implications these may have for architectural theory.

"One characteristic of Faith" . . . said Aquinas, is that man ". . . is engaged by the Good and the True".[158] Our fourth category, while not linking in any obvious way the Good and the True, does bring together the underlying concepts of Motion and Quality.

Concepts that were seen to have this double nature comprise a family of ideas which include Substance, Process, Creation, Wisdom and Craftsmanship. Substance, for example, for Plotinus, was a "composite of matter and quality" where matter was seen as ". . . relative to something which acts".[159] Process was seen as a motion involving changes in quality, in the accumulation of qualities, or in the accumulation of ideas, there being for Plotinus three kinds:

- Natural processes, e.g. growth and decay
- Artificial processes, e.g. architecture and ship-building
- Purposive processes, e.g. enquiry and learning.[160]

Both Philo and Aquinas likened the process of creation to that of architecture and the stamping of ideas on matter.[161] For Philo, Wisdom was the "artificer of all things" and was part "eternal activity" and part "eternal archetype"[162] (Figure 30). Again we see concepts from the two categories of Motion and Quality coming together.

With reference to wisdom, Paul distinguished wisdom from science;[163] and Aquinas was to emphasize its wider, more practical nature: "Divine Wisdom's next function was to create. God's wisdom is that of an artist whose knowledge of what he makes is practical as well as theoretical . . . ascribing meaning and cause to the going forth of creation."[164] Here, most importantly, we see the introduction of two other concepts used to represent our primary categories, namely 'cause' and "meaning", from which the secondary categories are derived.

Like wisdom, knowledge was similarly an important aspect of the skill of the mediaeval craftsman. "The perfect artisan", said Duns Scotus, "has a distinct knowledge of everything to be done before he does it".[165] Again, we see the double nature of craftsmanship in, first, the knowledge required, and, second the activity required, to produce any worthwhile artefact.

In order to develop these concepts in relation to architecture and design, we might usefully look more closely, for example, at the concepts of imagination,

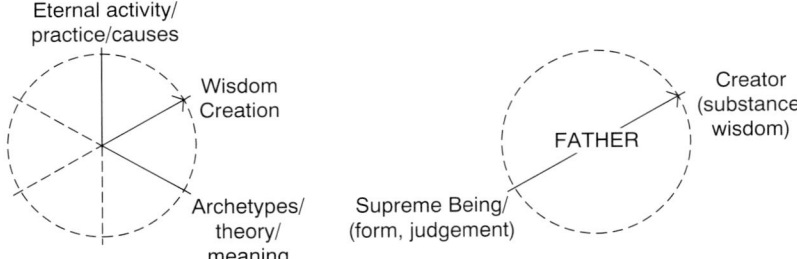

Figure 30 *In the next three figures we concentrate on the three secondary categories, which draw on the Franciscan assertions, of substance over form (above right), of love over reason (Figure 31), and of the will to live over abstract knowledge (Figure 32). Above left illustrates an idea of Philo's which explains Wisdom in terms of a combination of activity and archetypes*

purity of material and the notion of the organic, as they relate to creativity, substance and process respectively. The importance of the imagination was noted by Philostratus who had said "Great works of art are produced not by imitation but by imagination".[166] Aquinas referred the concept of imagination to the twin concepts of knowledge and activity. Knowledge was placed in a "kind of storehouse of forms"[167] upon which the process of imagination could then set to work, as "an activity which by separating and joining, forms different images of things, even of things not received by sense."[168] Plotinus before him noted the difference between such a mechanical imagination and a more organic conception of creation:

"All that comes to be, work of nature or craft, some wisdom has made . . . it converts and shapes the matter of things not by push and pull and lever work but by the bestowal of ideas . . . the relation may be illustrated by the powers in a seed, all lie indistinguished in the unit, the formative ideas gathered in one kernel, yet in the unit there is eye principle and hand principle."[169]

He contrasts reason which "must seize first one element of truth and then another"[170] with what he calls a kind of "spiritual intuition". Pseudo-Dionysius extended the analogy, comparing reason with a straight line, and intuition, which "directly apprehends" to a circle. A spiral approach to the problem, he continued, combines both "the rational and the discursive".[171]

The intuition, as Duns Scotus pointed out, may produce nothing more than a "confused sense image",[172] and in the third stage, that of perfecting the work "the object is to separate the essences from the many incidental features associated with them".[173] "Act as does the creator of a statue!" Plotinus had said, ". . . he cuts away here, smoothes there, to make this line lighter, this other purer, until a lovely face has grown on the work".[174]

It was this process of stripping away extraneous material that linked the idea of creation with that of purity. As Plotinus said, "Gold is degraded when mixed with earthly particles",[175] and for him the perception of beauty as a spiritual union with God demanded a purity in the perceiver as well as in the object perceived.[176] It was the sacrament of baptism which provided this symbolic cleansing.

For Christianity, the body was an integral part of the idea of the Resurrection, and the material world was seen as beautiful in itself, as being part of God's creation. There was a "love of life"[177] that Augustine noted, expressed later in the exuberance of mediaeval carving, where life showed itself in all its variety and vitality, "knowledge and movement".[178] For Aquinas the world of creation was one of material substance, and even wealth could be respected and displayed, if it could be shown to have a general beneficial effect.[179]

However, there was also an "inward beauty" to the body, which for John Chrysostom was reflected in the "shining cheeks and clear eyes of women who refuse to adorn themselves with cosmetics".[180] This Platonic view of beauty was recalled by Aquinas who saw beauty in the simple disposition of the body and its limbs, of Christ and his church,[181] a view perhaps nowhere better reflected than in the unconcealed construction of the Gothic cathedral.

To our consideration of the mediaeval cathedral, there are two principles we might bring which we may broadly describe as organic, and which we may borrow from Aquinas's description of bodily life. The first principle is that of constant activity, change or flux, where, for example, he could say that "All our life is in a condition of flux".[182] The first thing we may note about Gothic cathedrals, particularly English ones, are the changes that have been made to the building through history, the additions, the extensions, the side-chapels, the outbuildings, which have all contributed to the growth of the building over time. Even the pointed vaulting was developed according to some theorists to accommodate changes in height and width that would have been difficult to achieve satisfactorily with the more Classical, semi-circular vaulting. This vaulting which arches upwards and outwards from the piers remind us also of the metaphors that Plotinus used, "the overflowing of creation",[183] and "the tree of rational life giving reasoned being to the growth into which it enters".[184] Form ". . . becomes beautiful by sharing in the creative power", Inge said in his work on Plotinus.[185]

A second principle which we can describe as organic and which we can apply to the mediaeval cathedral is that of integrity, where, for example, Aquinas could write that "however complex the parts they all make up the integrity of the single body".[186] Here we might think of the great French cathedrals of Rheims or Amiens where the overall form would appear more unified than the typically disjointed nature of English cathedrals. However, there is an integrity of purpose to consider over and above that of pure form, and if this purpose changes and grows as human understanding grows and develops then so the church building should change and develop.

"God's creatures can be called his words", said Aquinas, "for they manifest his mind as effects manifest their cause".[187] Beauty was empty without seeing the mind of the creator behind it,[188] a view initiated by Augustine but taken up by Aquinas: "Accordingly let us consider creatures in order to view and marvel at divine wisdom".[189] Even in a work of art, where one is drawn to admire the skill of the craftsman, one should proceed behind and beyond to "the God who gave him his mind . . . created his materials . . . and created the craftsman's body and limbs".[190]

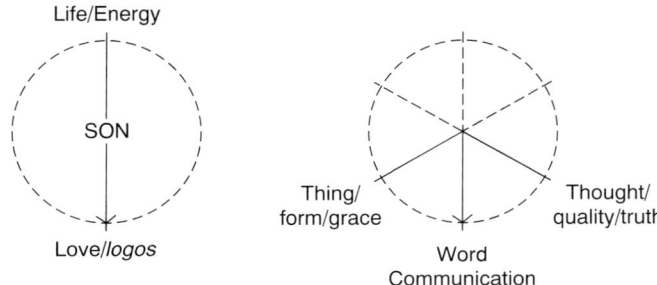

Figure 31 *In Christian theology the Son represents not only life and love (left), but also the logos or word (right). Clement of Alexandria said "If we look upward he is energy, if we look downward he is high priest". John referred to "the word, full of grace and truth", and Boethius distinguished communication from both the thing and the thought*

CATEGORY FIVE: LOVE AND COMMUNICATION

Our method here will be the same as in the previous section consisting of discussing, first, the more general concepts that belong under this category, and, second, particular concepts which have a bearing on architectural theory. The relevant general concepts in which the "biformed principle" can be traced include Communication, Word and Love, and from these we shall progress to a discussion of Feeling in architectural theory.

The central concept in this category is that of communication. Its importance to the subject of architecture can be inferred from a statement made by Plotinus: "Some things, material shapes for instance, are gracious not by anything inherent, but by something communicated."[191]

Not only must a gracious object have form, but it must also have an idea which can be communicated. Boethius (480–524) was particularly concerned with the concept of communication, and he clearly linked together the two primary realms of Being and Thought in what came to be known as the Boethian triplet (Figure 31): "There are three things out of which all communication arises: the thing itself, the thought of the thing, and the communication."[192]

Now, all communication takes place through a medium. This may be through language (verbal communication) or, in another sense, through light (visual communication). Regarding verbal communication, the *logos* or "word" was an important concept in Early Christian thought. In John's Gospel, both aspects of communication, verbal and visual, are apparent, when after writing "In the beginning was the Word . . ." he continues "and the light shineth in darkness". In this version of the Trinity, the Word was the Second Person, and, according to John, participated in two realms: "The Word . . . dwelt among us . . . full of Grace and Truth."[193] Again, these two concepts may be compared with Form and Knowledge. Paul spoke of the *logos* as a "double-edged sword",[194] capable of dividing asunder not only the joints of the body but also the thoughts of the heart.

Regarding visual communication, it required, as Witelo was to point out,[195] a certain "relation between the features of the object and their suitability in respect of the subject". If there was no common language in which both subject and object, or for Augustine, two subjects could participate,[196] then there could be no communication. Here we are talking about not so much Form and Thought but more about Form and a certain shared Quality through which a sense of communion could be realized. Plotinus referred to the idea of community as "form and quality".[197]

Eusebius, as we have seen, described somewhat symbolically, the communion engendered by light as it flooded through the new church at Tyre, where men and women could now "look at each other with smiling countenances and beaming eyes." A number of people were participating in something held in common between them. Athanasius ascribed the Platonic function of participation to the *logos*, and Pseudo-Dionysius later defined participation as a "sharing in the properties of another being".[198]

Here the concept of love may be introduced. The connection between verbal communication and the concept of love is not at first sight an obvious one. It is clear that both form a part of social intercourse and bring people together for the good of society as a whole. We might say that whereas verbal communication represents the analytical aspects of this present category, love and feeling represent the more synthetic or diffuse aspects.

Aquinas certainly admitted that "there are close parallels between the communication of words and between lover and beloved".[199] Love went further than communication however, by forging a union between lover and beloved through the perception of shared properties of humanity: "Love is the effective cause of real union; by knowledge is the beloved said to be in the lover, because embraced in mind."[200] Love therefore participates in the two realms of Unity and Knowledge.

Turning now to consider some of the concepts of this category in relation to architectural theory, we shall look in particular at the concept of feeling in architecture as it was developing at this time. The connection of beauty and love was recognized, for example, by Pseudo-Dionysius who said "if beauty moves . . . the movement itself is love".[201] Bonaventure went further and said: "the greatest pleasure is not contemplation of form, but love . . . without love there is no delight".[202] The importance of feelings, in this case the sympathetic affection on which this kind of love was based, was known to Epicurus in a much earlier age: ". . . feelings are the criteria of truth . . . the soul contains elements of co-affection (*sympatheia*) in sharing colour and shape."[203]

For Plotinus, these feelings were "an unreasoned consciousness of friendly relations".[204] There was a "sympathy of unchained forces"[205] in the universe from which arose not only the powers of charm and magic but because of our "belonging integrally to that unity" our very "amenability to experience".[206] "Why is the living ugly more attractive than the sculpted handsome?" Plotinus asked, ". . . because there is soul there . . . beauty is that which truly calls out our love . . . the intense love called out by life".[207]

Aquinas described the soul as "that through which we have communion with animals"[208] and if we extend this idea as Francis had done to include communion with the whole of nature,[209] we begin to see a link with the growing importance of sunlight, gardens and even places like the open courtyard that Eusebius described "where men can see the sky".[210] Aquinas explained such beauty as a sympathetic correlation between subject and object: "The senses delight in rightly proportioned things as similar to themselves . . . as smiling applied to a field means only that the field in the beauty of its smiling is like to the beauty of the human smile by proportionate likeness."[211]

Plotinus made an analogy with the strings of a lyre where "the sounding of one string awakens what might pass for perception in another . . . the vibration in a lyre affects another by virtue of the sympathy existing between them".[212] The idea that "the human soul might be moved in various ways by different sounds" as Aquinas put it, had been noted by Boethius:

> "Both body and soul are subject to the laws of music. The human soul modulates its feelings in the manner of the musical modes . . . the union of our soul with our body is held together by the binding force of music."[213]

With musical theory we are getting closer to architectural theory, the rhythm of piers in a church, for example, or the rising and falling cadences of roof and spires. For Augustine, rhythm was directly related by the psyche to bodily movement,[214] whereas musical modes were more akin to the movements ascribed by the Stoics to particular feelings. For example:

- Joy, was likened to swelling.
- Fear was likened to shrinking.
- Appetite was likened to stretching.[215]

Desire, for Augustine, was seen as movement towards a thing,[216] and in church architecture there was not only the physical movement of pilgrims and processions to be considered around the aisles and ambulatories but also a perceived spiritual movement, "the soul's journey towards God" symbolized in the verticality of the piers, the smaller shafts and the spires. This upward movement might be contrasted with the claims of the Milanese architects, regarding the structural thickness of members, that "the weight of the pier ought to follow its own reason in a downward direction".[217] The concept of tension between upward and downward forces was noted by Galen, a physician in the second century, who observed in the hovering bird the opposition generated between the force of gravity and the muscular exertions of the bird itself.[218]

From movement we pass to rest, and in Aquinas we read: "The beautiful is that in which the appetite comes to rest through contemplation and knowledge".[219] The closest idea to our modern notion of empathy, or the projection of self into these patterns of movement and rest, is perhaps given by Longinus when he said of the Classical writer Herodotus that he "makes the hearer feel that he himself is moving".[220] Longinus listed many figures of speech designed to move the feelings, emphasizing that subtlety was required in their use ". . . for art is perfect when it seems to be nature".[221] He compared the immediacy of feeling in a painting with its light and shade "which lie near to our minds through a sort of natural kinship".[222] Indeed, one of his figures, *periphrasis*, has been translated in English as "picturesqueness of speech".[223] The informal layout of the mediaeval town might be pictured through figures that add "accumulation . . . variation . . . climax";[224] or alternatively a sense of context might be introduced through figures which are "inspired by occasion".[225] Feelings aroused by past ages may also be introduced through "changes of tense",[226] and we might picture the vaulting of a mediaeval cathedral when we read John Chrysostom's words:

"Look at the sky, how beautiful it is and how vast, all crowned with a diadem of stars . . . like some young creature full of sap it preserves all the shining and freshness of an earlier age."[227]

Category Six: Spirit and The Will

As in our previous two sections, we shall look first at general "biformed" concepts that belong under this category, for example the concepts of Spirit, Power and the Will as they entered Scholastic thought. Second, we shall consider some of their more general applications to architectural theory, in particular, with reference to the concept of the Sublime.

The spirit was an important concept in Early Christian thought. Indeed, the term occurs in the first few sentences of the book of Genesis as "the spirit moving over the face of the water". Augustine identified the spirit with the divine Will, existing "before any creation takes place".[228]

The concept of the spirit, or will, brings together two concepts from our primary categories, namely Being and Activity. In the beginning there was Being "without form, and void", and, somehow, by some mysterious process, life and activity were created through the medium of the divine Will. Plotinus, in discussing the Will, spoke of a similar duality:

"Will and Essence in the Supreme must be identical . . . there is a certain duality, act against essence . . . Existence carries with it either acting or answering to action . . . How can we allow power to colour and none to configuration . . . It is surely untenable that an entity should have existence and yet no power to effect."[229]

One of the chief characteristics of the Spirit was that it was unknowable. As Aquinas said, "The Holy Ghost is well nigh anonymous . . . we speak of spirits when we see movement springing from a hidden source".[230] Plotinus explained this, saying "We know the unknowable because in our deepest ground we are the unknowable . . . there is a mystery in ourselves."[231]

When we turn to look at the concept of the Will, we may note that Aquinas spoke of a twofold will: "a will to communicate" and a "will to create"[232] Although linking the three secondary categories – creation, communication, will – this subdivision does little to explain the Will in relation to its two adjacent primary categories, Being and Activity. In order to address this we need to look at two other aspects of the Will that were developing at this time, namely, freedom and necessity. Both Clement and Augustine had introduced the concepts of the freedom of the will and Christian liberty, to counteract older ideas of Stoic determinism, where:

- Freedom, or liberty, rests on the concept underlying Being, namely that of Disjunction. Freedom requires the choice of either–or.
- Necessity, or determinism, rests on the concept underlying Activity, namely that of Cause and Effect. This supplies a motive force to the will.

These two concepts struggled against one another then as always. Longinus, for example, while allowing the use of precedent, and condemning the "pursuit of novelty as the fashionable craze of the day"[233] also praised freedom: "For freedom it is said, has the power to feed the imagination of the lofty-minded and inspire hope; and where it prevails there spreads abroad the eagerness of mutual rivalry and the emulous pursuit of the foremost place."[234]

Opposing the traditional dogma of the church in the twelfth century, Abelard in his pursuit of freedom was condemned by Bernard for writing about "new things".[235] The attitude of the Church remained that some regulation and guidance was required: Law was thought "necessary due to the uncertainty of human judgements"[236] as Aquinas said, ". . . Man should seek to emulate God as an artist who sets to work through an exemplar in his mind and love in his will".[237]

The concept of the will in the individual had been seen since Aristotle as "inclination to action" induced by a lack of something in the subject.[238] The idea of Will as motivation was extended by Aquinas who said that "Everything seeks after its own perfection. . . . Will has not for its only act to seek what it does not possess, but also to love and delight in what it does possess".[239]

Our third concept, the concept of power, may be introduced through Plotinus, for whom the spirit (*Nous*) "repeated the act of the One in pouring forth a great power".[240] For Aquinas, this power was "twofold, active and passive"[241] and borrowed from the categories of Motion and Quantity respectively. If we compare power with energy in physics, we might think of the more modern notions of kinetic and potential energy in relation to Motion and Quantity respectively.

When we turn to look at these concepts in architecture, we could begin with the concept of power, and ask in what ways can the power of architecture affect the human spirit. The answer from the above analysis would be in two ways:

- In terms of Quantity, through size and grandeur
- In terms of Motion, through moving the emotions in some way.

These two aspects relate to two aspects of the Sublime that were developed much later, namely the mathematical and the dynamical. Both aspects are to be found in embryo in a work entitled *On the Sublime*, thought to have been written by Longinus in the second century (Figure 32).

Regarding quantity and size, Longinus spoke of examples of the Sublime which were "independent of passion" but relied instead on "grandeur of conception" and "elevated composition",[242] where "our imaginations often pass beyond the bounds

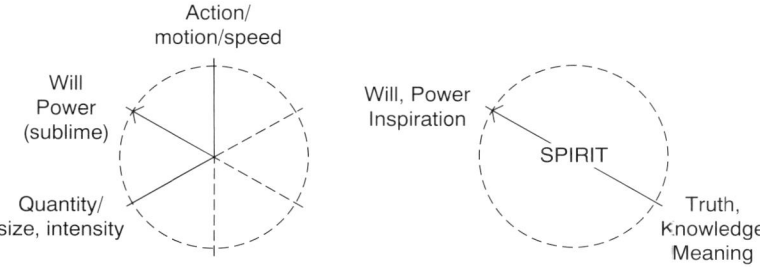

Figure 32 *In Christian theology the Spirit represents not only will and inspiration, but he is also the "spirit of truth". Tillich referred to the Spirit as "the unity of power and meaning" (right). The concept of power was also important to Longinus's deliberations on the Sublime (left) concerning which he referred to "speed, power and intensity"*

of space". Greatness, tending towards the infinite, had always been one of the divine names, and it is its reflection in the vast size and internal spaces of the mediaeval cathedrals that belongs in this final category. Eusebius, in the fourth century, described the church at Tyre as "lofty and large" with a "single mighty gateway flanked by two others".

Quantity also related the Will to strength. To paraphrase Augustine, not only was "music recommended, so that weaker spirits may be inspired with devotion"[243] but also architecture, through its size and grandeur could ". . . confer on the Will, strength to do the good".[244]

The expression of power was naturally of importance to the ambitions of architects and their patrons. We might think of Justinian, and his architects Anthemius of Tralles and Isidorus of Miletus, who attempted to "outdo Solomon"[245] with the Church of Hagia Sophia; or Constantine whose new churches were said to be "expressive of his power and dignity" and who attempted, with the Church of the Holy Sepulchre, "to build a basilica more beautiful than any on earth".[246] Even more visionary was Charlemagne under whom the new Europe was to become a *"Respublica Christiana"*,[247] based on Augustine's *City of God*. This latter work was itself inspired by the Stoics' utopian ideal of "Cosmopolis",[248] or the city of "Platonopolis" that Plotinus himself had proposed, in collusion with the Emperor Gallienus, to be established in the Campania.[249]

Regarding Motion and the moving of the emotions, Longinus in *On the Sublime* noted that one of the main characteristics of sublimity lay in the "expression" of "vehement emotions", the aim of which was to "transport" one, through ecstasy "nearer the majesty of God".[250] It was to be found particularly in literary styles noted for their "speed, power and intensity", where "passion sets order at defiance",[251] and was recognized by a "leaping from subject to subject . . . as by a veering wind" and by "striking words" and "exaggeration".[252]

In Plotinus, who was writing at about the same time, we can begin to see the distinction growing between a gentle beauty, on the one hand, and a sublime beauty, on the other, which was connected with violence and distortion:

"The good is gentle, and friendly and tender. Beauty is all violence and stupefaction, its pleasure is spoiled with pain."[253]

Motion related the Will not only to desire, which Augustine identified with the will,[254] but also to the turbulence of the emotions and passions, where he was to say, for example, that "Love is but an intense Will".[255] It is important to distinguish here between two aspects of love, the "twofold Venus"[256] as Plotinus called it:

- First, love as feeling or sympathy, in the unification of the realms of Being and Thought, described by Aquinas as "Love . . . the effective cause of real union because embraced in mind", which we discussed in the previous section
- Second, love as emotion or passion, in the unification of the realms of Being and Activity, the "longing to be molten into one" as Plotinus described it, where "the soul, by affiliation to the noblest existents in the hierarchy of being . . . thrills with an immediate delight".[257] According to Plotinus "Beauty is the motive of attraction".[258]

Aquinas had seen in love the fusion of the "awareness of the beloved" with the "power of loving"[259] and it is this awareness of an internal power, whether of passion, suffering or even pain, that led to both the tortured forms of Romanesque sculpture and the expression of vehement emotions dscribed in literature by Longinus.

CATEGORIES AND RELATIONS

Now that we have considered all six categories in turn, we need to return to something we said at the beginning of this chapter, namely that the questions regarding the Holy Trinity were a development of questions previously raised on the ultimate differentiation of Being – the number and content of its basic categories, and their relation to one another and to the world.

The importance to architecture of resolving these questions should now be clear, and for the next few pages we shall therefore concentrate on a particular aspect of the concept of the Trinity in order that in the next chapter we may return to the subject of architecture with a clearer understanding of one of its most important underlying principles. This particular aspect is the principle of types of relation.

In order to introduce the subject of relation with respect to the Trinity, we need first to look at the notion of universals with respect to our categories. The Aristotelian categories, as we have seen, had been reduced to types of relation by Plotinus.[260] The original ten categories had been reduced to five: Substance, Relation, Quantity, Quality and Activity,[261] and the latter three identified with modes of relating, and the Eleatic categories of Unity, Motion and Differentiation as shown below:[262]

(1) Substance
(2) Relation
(3) Quantity (cf. Unity/Plurality)
(4) Activity (cf. Motion/Stability)
(5) Quality (cf. Similarity/Difference)

Porphyry, a pupil of Plotinus, concentrating on the categories of Substance and Quality, established from other ideas found in Aristotle, the five predicables of Genus, Species, Specific Difference, Property and Accident:

Substance   { Genus
(*in quid*)   { Species
(*in quale quid*) Specific Difference
Quality   { Property
(*in quale*)   { Accident[263]

From the identification of Genus and Species with Substance arose the peculiarly Scholastic problem of the "universal", which Aristotle had differentiated from the "individual":

- The Individual: that which is predicated of a single subject
- The Universal: that which is predicated of many subjects.[264]

Categories, and their underlying relations, have similar problems to those of the universal in that both may be described as "that which is predicated of many subjects". Porphyry raised the question of the reality of universals, but in clearly distinguishing between the classificatory interests of logic and the speculative curiosity of metaphysicians left the question to be answered by the metaphysicians.[265] These fell into two broad camps:

(1) Nominalists, who thought universals were mental labels and existed only as names in the mind
(2) Realists, who thought that universals existed in the real world.

Virtually all the major schoolmen were "Realists" and one of their interests lay in the identification of the highest categories of existence with what might be properly predicated of God.[266] Eriugena, following Boethius, confirmed that none of Aristotle's categories, with the single exception of Relation, could be predicated of God,[267] and the idea that relations were real was most clearly stated by Aquinas:

"Those who subscribe to the proposition that there are three persons in one nature must thereby hold that in God, relations are real . . ."[268]
"Some have said that relation is not a reality but only an idea. But this is plainly seen to be false from the very fact that things themselves have a mutual natural order and relation. . . . There are three conditions that make a relation to be real or logical . . . genus and species . . . quantity . . . action and passion."[269]

We should note two points here. First, that relations were considered by Aquinas to be real, whether existing in God or not. The notion that relations might not be real in any sense of the word was illogical and destroyed all possibility of thought. Even substance could only in the final analysis be known through its relations, either through logical relations or through its relations to an observer. Second, we should note that the three conditions listed by Aquinas approximate very closely to the three types of relation suggested by Plotinus, and ultimately Aristotle, namely Quantity, Activity and Quality.

The secondary categories too were important in defining the personal nature of God. While Plotinus, long before, had suggested that we take a stone as an example, saying that it too has "substance, quantity, quality, motion",[270] Duns Scotus saw the danger of applying such categories to God, saying instead that we attribute Wisdom and Will to God "otherwise we may as well say God is a stone".[271] A distinction had to be drawn between such impersonal and analytical relations, on the one hand, and, on the other, the idea of more personal relations which Tertullian and Novatian had introduced to counteract the older Stoical idea of God as impersonal nature.[272]

Eriugena's notion that "Relation appeared to be the only category which is properly predicable of God"[273] was thought to solve the anomaly between unity and plurality, and the respective heresies of Sabellianism and Arianism.[274] Athenagoras,[275] and later Augustine,[276] in answer to the question of why there should be three Persons, developed the notion that if God was both Love and self-contained, then the Holy Spirit could be represented as the bond of love between the Father and the Son. This was an idea that had its roots in Philo's interpretation of the *logos*, but also in the much earlier idea of Empedocles that Love was the relating principle of the world.

However, the notion that the Trinity consisted of two Persons and a bond between them was inadequate. Tertullian emphasized the idea that the Holy Spirit was a Person, co-equal with the other two in the formula *"tres personae, una substantia"*.[277] To maintain the idea of relation, his pupil, Novatian, introduced the idea of a mutual interpenetration of the Persons.[278] This idea progressed through Hilary and Augustine, until in Abelard we see the concepts of Wisdom and Power being added to Love to represent respectively the three relations between the three Persons.[279] Basil cautioned that Substance should also be represented by the first term in the series, otherwise there was the danger that four divine Persons might arise.[280]

Yet still this was unsatisfactory. There remained the fundamental difference between the Persons and the relations between them, which Duns Scotus pointed out: "Unless the terms of a relation are known, the relation itself cannot be known."[281] Interestingly, Kirk more recently reversed this by saying that as we know empirically the three ways in which we can relate to God, this must surely point to three Persons, or "terminals" in a loving and personal God.[282]

William of Occam, after Duns Scotus, said that "he could as readily assume that one essence equals three absolutes as to assume that one essence in reality equals three relations".[283] Augustine had confirmed that there was no distribution of functions in the Trinity,[284] and Abelard finally agreed with what Jerome had said, that what is said about one of them is said about them all.[285] Basil's conclusion was that "These are not three in relation to each other, so that we can as it were count them, one, two, three, but the Father one, the Son one, the Spirit one".[286]

In his rainbow analogy we saw how each of the primaries could be seen to merge to form a secondary or a two-in-one. It was becoming clear that each was to be seen as a three-in-one, and we must now look at how the third primary was brought to bear on each Person so that, as Gregory of Nyssa said, we can see how "the whole Godhead operates on each of them".[287]

COLOUR AND WHEEL SYMBOLISM

In order to explain these complex ideas, the Neoplatonists of Alexandria turned to symbolic diagrams for help. "The wise men of Egypt", according to Plotinus, "left aside the writing form of words . . . and drew pictures instead . . . they exhibited the absence of discursiveness in the intellectual realm".[288] God and the heavens, as we have seen, were depicted by him in circular form: "God . . . as within, at the innermost depth, the outer circling round him".[289] The symbolism of the circle is seen in the splendour of the Gothic rose windows; in the floor tile patterns known as "labrynths", one of the most well-known examples centring on a six-cusped rose at Chartres Cathedral;[290] and perhaps most famously in the wheeling circles of heaven and hell described in the *Divine Comedy* of Dante Alighieri.[291]

Clement of Alexandria, perhaps recalling the passage in Revelation which described a "rainbow round the throne, in sight like unto an emerald", likened the Son to "a circle, all the powers orbed and united in Him".[292] Through the circle vertically he almost draws a diameter: "if we look upwards, he is energy, if we look downwards, he is high priest."[293] By such a diametric coordination of abstract quality and person, we begin to see a way of bringing the third primary category to bear on the merging of the other two, and elevating the meaning of each of the secondary categories to the status of a three-in-one.

In our own diagram we simply draw three equally spaced diameters each of which connects a primary category with a secondary category. The resulting six-spoked wheel may be compared with the *chi–rho* symbol that Constantine introduced into early Christianity.[294] It is thought to have derived from an earlier Roman symbol which represented the sun. It is notable that all churches were to become orientated towards the rising sun, itself a symbol of the risen Christ, in the fifth century.

If to such figurative symbolism is added colour symbolism, of Dante for instance, where the white, green and red of Beatrice's garments represented Faith, Hope and Charity respectively,[295] we may begin to see a source for the "colour-wheel" analogy that has been used by more recent theologians. In *Trinity in Reformation Theology* Loeschen wrote "Luther almost begins working with a pair, or axis, of oppositely related colours on the wheel";[296] and in Tillich's work we see a clearer example of the combining of primary and secondary categories in the Person of the Spirit who is said to reflect ". . . the unity of Power and Meaning".[297]

The notion of colour symbolism is very old, and we may think of the colours of the Hebrew ephod, the upper garment of the priests: white, blue, purple and red representing the four elements, earth, air, water and fire respectively.[298] The twelve tribes of Israel, represented, for example, in Chagall's abstract stained glass windows at the Hadassah Synagogue in Jerusalem, each had for its emblem a coloured stone, according to Exodus:

> "Make the breast-plate of judgement; it shall be made like the ephod, by a seamster in gold with blue, purple and scarlet yarns and finely woven linen . . . set in it four rows of precious stones . . . the stones shall correspond to the twelve sons of Israel name by name."[299]

Richard of St Victor in his *Benjamin Minor*, discussed the virtues and attributes symbolized by the twelve sons; and it is certainly curious that in the supposed three-by-four format we may see not only the three primary categories in the three concepts of Firstness, Strife and Law of the three eldest brothers, Ruben, Simeon and Levi, but also reading diagonally a suggestion of Vitruvius in the Strength, Commerce and Happiness of Ruben, Zebulun and Asher.[300]

More recently, Paul Frankl in his book, *The Gothic*, used a circular analogy to describe personality, where the spokes of the wheel served to connect the various categories of subject together:

> "One can distribute the various subjects such as economics, technology, politics, science, philosophy, art, as individual points on a circle . . . all these points are firmly united with each other across the centre. . . . In universal minds such as Albertus Magnus or Thomas Aquinas the whole circle is included in the personality . . . in the case of architects, the majority of the periphery lies outside them."[301]

He introduced to this concept the notion of colour, suggesting that each pattern may be seen as "a personally coloured unity" where "in this colourfulness there is a dominant shade".[302]

The end of the Scholastic period marked the beginning of a decline in symbolism as a method of explaining complex concepts to the laity. William of Occam's opinion that universals could not be real was based on an Aquinian concept of understanding in which objects and meaning were linked not by a relationship of inherence which lay behind the concept of symbolism but by a relationship of cause and effect that lay behind the very act of understanding.[303] This perceived demarcation between two realms, one which contained symbol, and one which contained activity, contributed to the final separation of science and theology.

Occam borrowed from Avicenna the distinction in language between "terms of first intention" that denote things in the real world and "terms of second intention" which only say something about the terms themselves.[304] The results were twofold. First, the emphasis was shifted back from the second-intention predicables of Porphyry: genus, species, essence, accident, etc. to the categories of Aristotle: quantity, quality, cause and effect, upon which the developing interest in science was to be based.[305] Second, it was realized that classification itself could be seen in two ways: first, as a logical and scientific device which gave order to the act of understanding[306] (first intention), and second, as a metaphysical or theological reality (second intention), the intricacies of which were to evaporate with the disappearance of the last of the mediaeval schoolmen. For Occam, reason and belief were irreconcilable issues, and the subject matter of faith was to be returned to only that which had been revealed, a movement culminating in the sixteenth century with Michael Servetus[307] and the denial that even the existence of the Trinity could be deduced from the pages of Scripture.

ct : sir christopher wren
9 : 1675 - 1710
about £750.000 -

ELEVATION OF WEST FRONT.

· SCALE OF FEET ·

CHAPTER 5
MODERN CATEGORIES: I

The three Vitruvian categories were to reappear in the seventeenth century in a work by a Dutchman, Sir Balthazar Gerbier, practising in England, entitled *A Brief Discourse concerning the Three Chief Principles of Building viz Solidity, Convenience and Ornament.*[1] A few years later they appeared in John Evelyn's *Account of Architects and Architecture* where they were given the Scholastic appellation of transcendencies: "Thus accomplished, an Architect is perfectly qualified to answer all the transcendencies of this Noble Art which is to build handsomely, solidly and usefully."[2]

However, apart from changes in order, it is difficult to see any development of the three ideas here, and we must again turn our attention away for a while from architecture to literature to understand their further progress. Just as architectural critics borrowed their ideas from Vitruvius so the early literary critics tended to borrow from Horace, and we find, for example, Sir Philip Sidney as early as 1594 reinterpreting one of Horace's maxims on poetry when he said "Poesie therefore is an arte of imitation . . . with this end, to teach and to delight".[3] In 1674, Nicolas Boileau, the French poet and critic, wrote down the following thoughts in *L'Art Poetique*:

"Would you in this great art acquire Renown?
Authors observe the Rules, I here lay down,
In prudent lessons, everywhere abound,
With pleasant, joyn the useful and the sound."[4]

If any parallels can be drawn between architecture and poetry they might surely be taken from this last line where Firmness can be compared with soundness, Commodity with usefulness, and Delight with pleasantness. Further parallels might be discovered in literature and philosophy by first, tracing the continuing development of Classical and mediaeval patterns of subdivision of the subject matter, and second, by investigating the new spirit of rationalism and scientific enquiry that was beginning to appear in the seventeenth and eighteenth centuries.

One line of development traceable back through Aquinas to Aristotle, and which bears comparison with Vitruvius, emerged in the *Leviathan* of Thomas Hobbes who, as a notable free-thinker at the time of the English Civil War and the subsequent Commonwealth, stands at the forefront of modern philosophy:

Plate 5 *St Paul's Cathedral, London, elevation of west front, measured and drawn by A. F. E. Poley, 1927 (British Architectural Library, RIBA, London)*

"*This is a gift that I have, simple, simple; a foolish extravagant spirit full of forms, figures, shapes, objects, ideas, apprehensions, motions, revolutions*"

Love's Labour's Lost

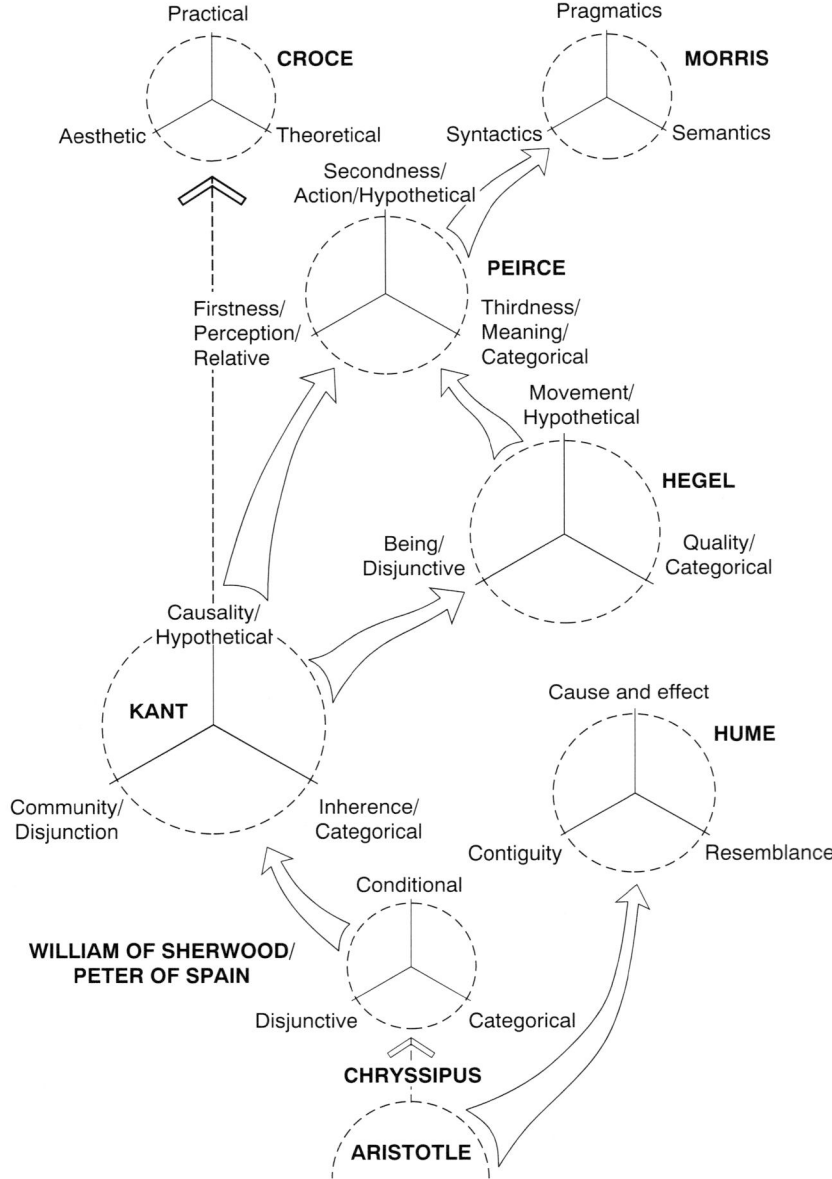

Figure 33 Modern categories I

"Of good, there may be three kinds: Good in the Promise (final cause), that is *'Pulchrum'*, Beauty; Good in Effect as the end desired which is called *'Jucundum'*, Delightful; and Good in the Means which is called *'Utile'*, Profitable."[5]

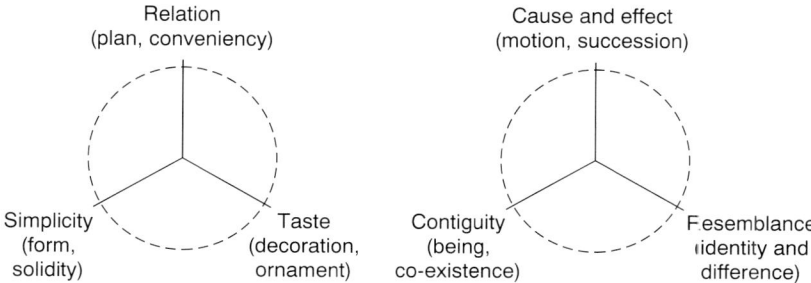

Figure 34 *Sulzer's article on architecture in the* Encyclopédie *introduced three concepts (left) which are compared with Goldman and Gerbier's earlier interpretations of Vitruvius. Meanwhile, in philosophy, David Hume introduced his three principles of association among ideas (right), which are here compared with the Eleatic categories, and those of Locke and Comte*

Elsewhere, he linked Beauty in building with "Commodity" and "Civility" saying that all three should be the "workmanship of Fancy but guided by the precepts of true philosophy".[6]

Another line of development resulted from the publication of Aristotle's *Poetics* in 1498, and consisted of the notion that good works of literature should conform to certain rules. Gian Giorgio Trissino, the Italian playwright and patron of Palladio, wrote poems and plays early in the sixteenth century according to the "rules"; and another Italian, Julius Caesar Scaliger, in 1561, formulated the three unities of Aristotle, namely that all works should be unified in Place, Time and Action.[7] The idea was taken up in the French theatre of the seventeenth century by Corneille and Racine, and we may note the disputes in French architecture between rules and taste, around 1670, of François Blondel and Claude Perrault respectively.[8]

Perhaps the most potent line of development, however, was the Platonic one which had culminated in the three Scholastic transcendentals of *Unum, Verum, Bonum*. In the closing decade of the fifteenth century, Marsilio Ficino at the Florentine Academy introduced the three concepts of Beauty, Goodness and Truth in his *Commentaries* on Plato's dialogues;[9] and as we have seen, Palladio brought these three principles into architecture in the *I Quattro Libri* of 1570.

In the eighteenth century, J. G. Sulzer, in the Supplement to the great French *Encyclopédie*, began to link these ideas to the Vitruvian group (Figure 34), previously interpreted by N. Goldmann in 1696 as Form, Plan and Decoration. We can tabulate these ideas as follows:

Palladio 1570	*Goldmann 1696*	*Sulzer 1776*	
Beauty	Form	Aesthetic	"Noble Simplicity"
Goodness	Plan	Moral	"Considered Relation"
Truth	Decoration	Intellectual	"Sure Taste"

For architectural form to be beautiful "noble simplicity" was demanded; for the plan or layout of a building to be good, "considered relations" between the rooms were required; and for the decoration to be intellectually satisfying, a "sure taste" was necessary. These were the three criteria of building for J. G. Sulzer.[10]

The linked principles of Beauty, Goodness and Truth reappeared from time to time, for example in the works of Muratori (1706), Diderot (1750) and Shelley (1821),[11] and although Nietzsche later rejected the grouping of the three concepts as being "unworthy of a philosopher",[12] they were popularized by Victor Cousin, French philosopher and virtual head of the Sorbonne for a time, in his book *Du Vrai, du Beau et du Bien* which was published in 1854.[13]

SCIENTIFIC ENQUIRY

Following the Reformation, there developed a period of philosophical enquiry and scientific investigation known as the Enlightenment, or the Age of Reason. Two distinct trends may be noted based on deductive and inductive reasoning respectively.

The first, the Rationalist school, is generally said to have begun in 1637 with the publication of the *Discourse on Method* by René Descartes. The correct method according to Descartes was to work from first principles, "seeking first things that are simple and then little by little and by degrees passing to others more difficult".[14] We might think of Laugier's *Essai sur l'architecture* of 1753 where it was argued that the idea of a Greek temple could be deduced from the principles of a primitive hut.

The second, the Empirical school, was associated more with British philosophy. It developed under Sir Isaac Newton in the field of science, and John Locke in philosophy, and its method consisted of reasoning from practical experience and scientific experiment in order to build up a pattern of more general truths. The Royal Society had been founded in 1660, the year of the Restoration of Charles II; John Evelyn, the diarist who later presided over the committee considering schemes for rebuilding St Paul's Cathedral, gave the society its name; and Sir Christopher Wren, then Gresham Professor of Astronomy, gave the Society's first lecture. While Newton, who was elected a Fellow of the Royal Society in 1672, was working on the *Principia Mathematica*, which was to be published in 1687, John Locke, living for a while under the assumed name of Dr Van der Linden in Holland, was working on his *Essay concerning Human Understanding*, which appeared in 1690.

Influenced by Newton's study of the elements, forces and laws of motion of the physical world, Locke developed a mechanically deterministic view of the mind, and in the fourth edition of his *Essay*, published in 1700, he included a chapter entitled the "Association of Ideas".[15] This principle, to which we shall return, was developed more fully in the eighteenth century by David Hume, and the doctrine of associationism remained a dominant one for the next two centuries.

The Irishman, George Berkeley, should also be mentioned as an immediate successor to the ideas of Locke, and it was Hume's attacks on Berkeley that were to awaken from his "dogmatic slumbers" perhaps the greatest philosopher of the eighteenth century, Immanuel Kant. It might be noted that Kant, from his chair of philosophy at the University of Königsberg, published a series of three great books which in a sense, dealt in turn with the True, the Good and the Beautiful

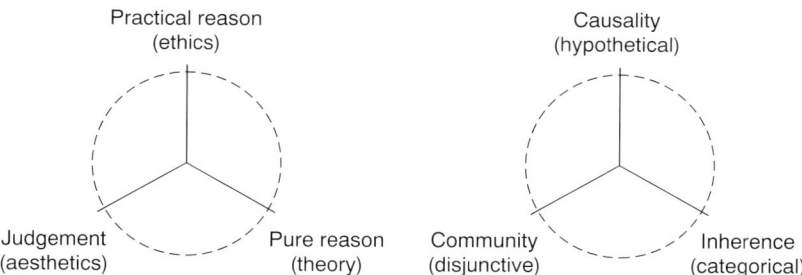

Figure 35 *Kant's three* Critiques, *and their subject matter, are shown on the left. They may be compared with Aristotle's three kinds of knowledge (Figure 20). Kant's three categories of relation (right) may be compared with his three kinds of predicate shown in parentheses (cf. Aristotle, Figure 22) and also Hume's three principles of association (Figure 34)*

respectively (Figure 35): *The Critique of Pure Reason* (1781), *The Critique of Practical Reason* (1786) and *The Critique of Judgement* (1790).[16]

PRIMARY CATEGORIES

Apart from his geometry, the ideas of Descartes are of particular significance to us in two ways. First, there was an idea which came to be known as Cartesian doubt. This required that the ultimate principle from which any rational system could be deduced should be a certain and self-evident truth which, for Descartes, was the now-famous *cogito ergo sum*: "I think, therefore I am". "But what then am I? A thing which thinks . . . a thing which doubts, understands, affirms, denies, wills, refuses, which also imagines and feels."[17]

Second, there was Cartesian dualism which proposed that there were two distinct realms, the physical and the mental. This idea was to become extremely influential, but it should be noted in passing that it had evolved from a scholastic training and the particular grasping of ideas: God, Mind and Matter.

The ideas of Locke were not so systematic. The mind, he thought, was initially empty, a *tabula rasa*, into which all our ideas arrive from the material world through experience. Knowledge consisted of the perception of relations among ideas and these included mathematical relations, scientific relations such as co-existence and succession, and the analytic relations of identity and difference.[18] While it is clear that he developed the principle of the association of ideas from Hobbes's earlier "trains" of thought,[19] it was left to David Hume, from suggestions in Aristotle's *Parva Naturalia*,[20] to formulate the three ways by which our ideas connect together:

> "To me, there appears to be only three principles of connexion among ideas, namely Resemblance, Contiguity in time or place, and Cause or Effect. . . . A picture naturally leads our thoughts to the original; the mention of one apartment in a building naturally introduces an enquiry or discourse

concerning the others; and if we think of a wound we can scarcely forbear reflecting on the pain which follows it."[21]

Hume's *Treatise of Human Nature*, which in his own words "fell dead-born from the press", appeared in 1739, and the revised *Enquiry concerning Human Understanding* in 1758. He died in Edinburgh in 1776, nine years after the building of the New Town had commenced.

THE CATEGORIES OF KANT

The problem that had troubled Hume, of being able to establish these principles of connection, in particular that of cause and effect, from experience, was solved by Kant who took the view that our knowledge is only partly derived from the external world. Part of our knowledge, he argued, must also be due to the modifying nature of our own minds, which far from being a *tabula rasa*, imposed on our perception not only the forms of Space and Time but also the Categories, which he understood to be *a priori* concepts contained within the understanding.

> "Everything in our knowledge which belongs to intuition – feelings of pleasure and pain, and the will, not being knowledge are excluded – contains nothing but mere relations; namely of location . . . change of location . . . and of laws according to which the change is determined."[22]

Kant's categories of relation are three, namely Community, Causality and Inherence, and may be compared with Hume's three principles of connection, and also the oldest categories of all, the Eleatic categories of Plato:

Kant's categories of relation	Hume's principles of association	Eleatic categories of Plato
Community	Contiguity	Unity/Plurality
Causality	Cause and Effect	Motion/Rest
Inherence	Resemblance	Identity/Difference

The table of the twelve categories which give form to our concepts is preceded in the *Critique of Pure Reason* by the table of twelve judgements which give similar form to types of proposition.[23] Both tables are arranged in sets of three arranged in four main groups: Quantity, Quality, Relation and Modality of which, Kant said, only the first three constitute the content of a proposition.[24] These three groups may be compared with the three types of proposition listed under Relation in the first table, and the corresponding categories of Relation in the second table:

Main headings	Types of proposition	Categories of relation
Quantity	Disjunctive	Community
Relation	Hypothetical	Causality
Quality	Categorical	Inherence

The reason for generating the fourth category heading, Modality, appears to have been an attempt to rationalize, like Aristotle, the initial division of unity into two, saying that "all *a priori* division of concepts must be by dichotomy".[25] The first division was therefore into two, the Mathematical (Quantity and Quality) and the Dynamical (Relation and Modality), and Kant explained the subsequent groups of three by saying that "the third category in each class always arises from the combination of the second category with the first",[26] an idea which was to have a profound influence on Hegel's dialectic. In fact, W. T. Stace in *The Philosophy of Hegel* tells us that to make Kant's "architectonic" structure completely symmetrical, a third category would need to be added to the Mathematical and the Dynamical, and this Hegel proposed with his idea of Notion.[27]

THE CATEGORIES OF HEGEL

When Kant died in 1804, Georg Wilhelm Friedrich Hegel was 34, and an unknown lecturer at Jena. His *Science of Logic* appeared in 1812 and his *Lectures on Aesthetics* was put together posthumously from notes written during his professorship at Berlin from 1818 to 1831, the same period that the architect Karl Friedrich Schinkel was designing Berlin's theatre and museum in Grecian style.

Hegel attempted to provide a more comprehensive system than Kant, and his results can be seen in a large fold-out diagram of concepts that in structure was almost entirely triadic.[28] An initial unity, which he termed the "Absolute", was divided first into three: Logic, Nature and Spirit, and each of these was divided into three, for example Logic was divided into Being, Essence and Notion, and so on. Some of Kant's triads are found here in amended form, e.g. Space, Time and Motion instead of Space, Time and Matter; Quantity, Quality and Measure instead of Quantity, Quality and Relation; but perhaps the most important difference was that while Kant had seen the categories as "subjective mental processes", Hegel saw them as "objective ontological entities" existing in the world:[29] "The first principle of the world, the Absolute, is a system of categories . . . the categories must be the reason of which the world is a consequent."[30]

In typical Cartesian manner, Hegel's dialectic began from a principle of which he could be absolutely certain, the principle that "There is Being". From this thesis he found that the antithesis, "There is Nothing", could be equally valid, and from the two taken together he arrived at a synthesis, "There is Becoming". The synthesis became in turn a new thesis, "There is Movement", with a corresponding antithesis, "There is Rest", and a consequent synthesis, "There is determinate being" or "Quality".[31] By a continuation of this method, Hegel arrived at his table of some 270 "categories" of which two underlying patterns should be distinguished:

- First, there is the dialectic proper: Thesis–Antithesis–Synthesis in which the differentia that move a genus towards its species is always the negative, or antithesis.
- Second, there is the sequence, Thesis–First Synthesis–Second Synthesis which in the above example was Being, Motion and Quality, and which sets the pattern for the higher categories such as Being, Essence and Notion (Figure 36).

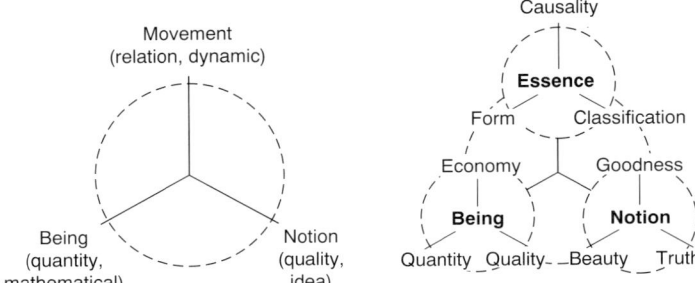

Figure 36 *Hegel's derivation of categories by dialectic method (left) are compared with Kant's main headings in his tables of categories. Hegel developed a series of 270 categories some of which are shown on the right*

(1) *Being* was differentiated from Nothing by containing within it the principle of "Other",[32] and may thus be compared with Kant's category of Disjunction. Stace called the category of Being the sphere of common sense, containing the concepts of consciousness, sensation, quantity, quality and measure, the latter which was seen as a kind of "economy".[33]

(2) *Essence*: "Other" separated itself from the "One" by a motion or a "passing over into another", and its essence is reflected in Hegel's first synthesis of "Becoming".[34] For Stace, the category of Essence was the sphere of Science, containing within it first, the thing, its form and its properties; second, cause, effect and reciprocity; and third, the principles of classification, identity and difference.[35]

(3) *Notion*: Having passed over into "Other", there is an almost Neoplatonic return into a higher unity that in embracing the "One" and the "Other" enables them to be considered together through their common qualities.[36] This, according to Stace, is the sphere of philosophy proper where we find, for instance, not only the three types of judgement: Disjunctive, Hypothetical and Categorical, but also the concepts of Goodness, Truth and Beauty.[37]

In order to compare these three categories with those of Kant, whose nomenclature describes more clearly the underlying relationships involved, we might tabulate, in a simplified manner, the concepts described above. We find, in a way that reminds us of Proclus, and for reasons that will be investigated later, that the same threefold pattern may be read horizontally as well as vertically:

Hegelian orientation

(A)	Being:	(AA)	Quantity	(BA)	Economy	(CA)	Quality
(B)	Essence:	(AB)	Form	(BB)	Causality	(CB)	Classification
(C)	Notion:	(AC)	Beauty	(BC)	Goodness	(CC)	Truth

Kantian orientation

(A)	Disjunction:	(AA)	Quantity	(AB)	Form	(AC)	Beauty
(B)	Causality:	(BA)	Economy	(BB)	Causality	(BC)	Goodness
(C)	Inherence:	(CA)	Quality	(CB)	Classification	(CC)	Truth

The three categories will be explored here according to the latter orientation. It should also be noted that we have substituted the term "Disjunction" for the term "Community" in answer to certain objections raised by Schopenhauer.[38] The term, "Community", as we shall see, will play an important part in the formation of the secondary, or what Kant called "derivative", categories.

The Categories of Peirce

Eight years after Hegel died in 1831, Charles Sanders Peirce was born at Cambridge in Massachusetts. He was to become perhaps the greatest American philosopher of modern times. Both William James and Bertrand Russell professed an indebtedness to his ideas, and although he wrote little on art, we might like to think that by the time he died, in 1914, the pioneering days of the Chicago school and Louis Sullivan were over, and the Modern Movement in architecture was well under way.

Like Descartes and Hegel, Peirce developed a system of categories from a single indisputable principle of knowledge, in his case it was the awareness of his own ideas.[39] He referred to Hegel as being "in some respects the greatest philosopher that ever lived", but nonetheless recorded that his own categories "grew originally out of a study of Kant", and like Kant's categories, his own had their origin in the mind: "It seems that the true categories of consciousness are first, feeling . . . second, a sense of resistance . . . and third, synthetic consciousness . . . . or thought."[40]

Elsewhere, he called the three primary categories: Quality, Reaction and Meaning,[41] and even: Firstness, Secondness and Thirdness,[42] names which both gave them an unambiguous order and lent them an abstract quality appropriate to the highest transcendentals (Figure 37): "Perhaps it is not right to call these categories conceptions, they are so intangible that they are rather tones or tints upon conceptions."[43]

(1) *Firstness (Quality)*: "The first is predominant in feeling . . . we must think of a quality without parts, e.g. the colour of magenta . . . When I say it is a quality I do not mean that it 'inheres' in a subject . . . The whole content of consciousness is made up of qualities of feeling, as truly as the whole of space is made up of points, or the whole of time by instants."[44]

(2) *Secondness (Reaction)*: "This is present even in such a rudimentary fragment of experience as a simple feeling . . . an action and reaction between our soul and the stimulus . . . The idea of second is predominant in the ideas of causation and of statical force . . . the real is active; we acknowledge it by calling it the actual."[45]

(3) *Thirdness (Meaning)*: "Thirdness is essentially of a general nature . . . ideas in which thirdness predominate [include] the idea of a sign or representation . . . Every genuine triadic relation involves meaning . . . the idea of meaning is irreducible to those of quality and reaction . . . synthetical consciousness is the consciousness of a third or medium."[46]

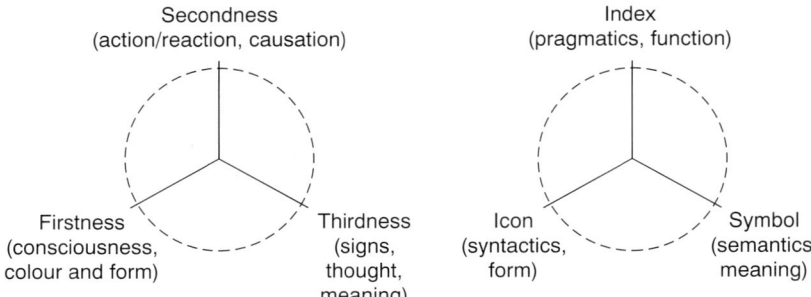

Figure 37 *Peirce in his* Logic of Relatives *utilized many triadic groupings of concepts including one establishing an initial order (left), and one describing types of sign (right), which is here compared with Morris's three branches of Semiotics*

These categories formed a part of Peirce's "Logic of Relatives" and derive partly from a feeling for the "spirit of scholasticism" and partly from an interest in the work of De Morgan at Cambridge who had introduced types of relation in his 'Formal Logic' of 1849. The reason why there are only three kinds of relation seems to be the mathematical one that although the above monadic, dyadic and triadic "nodes" are irreducible to one another, every node of higher valency is reducible to a "compound of triadic relations".[47]

＊

It seems clear from a reading of Hume, Kant and Peirce that a case can now be made for the view that our three categories have developed into three types of relation through which we understand the world, or by which the elements and ideas of the world might be connected together. If these three relationship types underlie in some way the more familiar groupings of Firmness, Commodity and Delight, or Beauty, Goodness and Truth, it will be useful to look at each in turn, and attempt to understand the concepts that were developing within each category over this period.

CATEGORY ONE: DISJUNCTION AND FORM

The relationship type of Disjunction which we have derived from Kant's tables may be explored in three ways:

- First, as constituting in some way the basis of Being which was Hegel's first category
- Second, as constituting in some way the basis of Perception which represents Peirce's first category
- Third, as constituting in some way the basis of Aesthetics which, we might note, was placed before the Practical and Theoretical categories by Benedetto

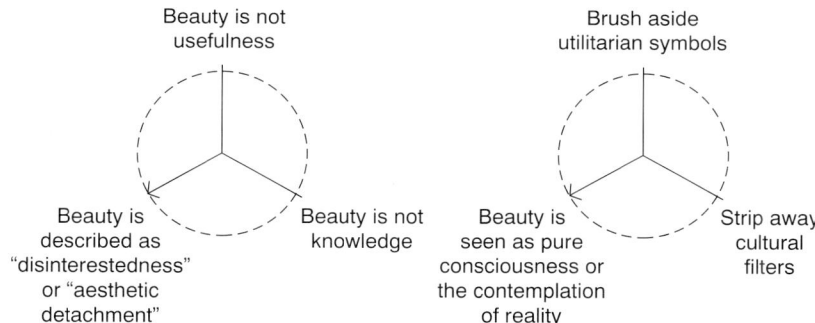

Figure 38 *Two views of beauty. First, that of Hutcheson (left) who distinguished the beauty of a thing from its use, or from any knowledge or associations we may have of the thing. Second, that of Bergson (right) who saw beauty as the pure contemplation of reality*

Croce in 1902.[48] As Aesthetics, in a sense, introduces the other two we shall begin with that subject.

One of the first essays on aesthetics as we understand the term was written by Francis Hutcheson in Dublin in 1725, and it was entitled *An Inquiry into the Original of our Ideas of Beauty and Virtue*. He was a disciple of the third Earl of Shaftesbury, who incidentally had introduced the idea that beauty lay in the form and not the matter of a work,[49] and we may note in Hutcheson's essay two themes:

(1) The realm of aesthetics should be distinguished from the realms of utility and knowledge (Figure 38): "The capacity to perceive beauty may correctly be called a sense because the pleasure it produces does not arise from any knowledge of principles, proportions, causes, or of the usefulness of the object."[50] Following Baumgarten's coining of the term "aesthetics"[51] in 1735, Kant, in emphasizing the notion of "disinterestedness"[52] in art, similarly distinguished the "keen awareness"[53] of aesthetic detachment from purposiveness, on the one hand, and conceptualization on the other.[54]

(2) Hutcheson's second theme consisted of drawing a distinction between "absolute beauty" and "relative beauty". Although he considered the first in terms of intrinsic harmony and variety, and the second in terms of imitation or resemblance, thus reflecting two of our primary categories, there is another way of looking at the distinction.[55] Kant, for example, contrasted the pleasure which colour may give to the sense, and the satisfaction that a design may give by its form:

> "A mere colour, for instance the green of a lawn, or a mere tone, for instance that of a violin, are by most people called beautiful in themselves . . . In painting, sculpture, and indeed all the arts of form such as architecture and gardening, the essential thing is the design. And herein it is not what pleases the senses, but what satisfies us by its form."[56]

If aesthetics can be based in some sense on the relationship of disjunction we might expect to be able to trace the development of the distinction in the following terms:

- Aesthetics based on Perception, the disjunction of subject/object and its leading to the contemplation of the Absolute (cf. "absolute beauty")
- Aesthetics based on Form, the disjunction within objects themselves, and its leading to the contemplation of Relations (cf. "relative beauty")

We shall discuss these two ideas in turn.

PERCEPTION

The notion of perception was the subject of much discussion at the beginning of the eighteenth century. Berkeley's view was perhaps the most radical and was summed up by Sartre as "to exist is to be perceived".[57] Hume in his essay, *The Standard of Taste* linked beauty to perception saying that "Beauty is no quality of things in themselves: It exists merely in the mind which contemplates them; and each mind perceives a different beauty".[58]

He distinguished between Impressions which entered the mind through the internal senses, and Ideas, fainter copies of these, which were able to be associated and cross-related in the mind.[59] Just as the external senses could be compared to a gateway separating the body from the external world, so a second gateway was conceived, Locke's "Internal Sense",[60] which separated the thinking subject from the thoughts perceived. In Kant, this "inner sense" developed into the notion of "consciousness"[61] which was to play an important part in the development of aesthetics in the nineteenth and twentieth centuries.

There were two elements in perception according to Kant: representation and consciousness.[62] Consciousness itself could be either clear or diffuse, and at the beginning of the nineteenth century it was compared to a lamp which could illuminate either a smaller or a larger area of our thoughts. "The light of poetry," wrote William Hazlitt, "while it shows us the object, throws a sparkling radiance all around";[63] and Artur Schopenhauer, who had studied the transcendentalism of the East, noted that as the area of consciousness expands, so the separation between self and object tended to disappear:

> "Where a man . . . gives the whole power of his mind to perception and lets his whole consciousness be filled with the quiet contemplation of the natural object actually present . . . he loses himself in the object . . . and he can no longer separate the perceiver from the perception, but both become one."[64]

Schopenhauer soon realized that if perception were to be the only criterion then with an open mind everything might be seen as beautiful: "Since every given thing may be observed in a purely objective manner, it follows that everything is also beautiful . . . one thing is only taken as more beautiful than another because it makes this pure objective contemplation easier."[65]

Following Schopenhauer, we might mention Kierkegaard, whose views were to promote the consciousness of our own existence over the detached abstraction of thought;[66] and in a similar vein, Nietzsche who was to proclaim art as "the affirmation of existence"[67] through its ability to heighten consciousness. As a contrast to Schopenhauer's view that beauty lay in those objects which make contemplation easier, we might place Bergson's view of art of 1900, that it should strip away our cultural filters from even the most difficult of subjects:

"Our normal way of experiencing is responding to things as members of classes (not as individuals) noting only the labels fixed to them . . . Art has no other object than to brush aside the utilitarian symbols, the conventional and socially accepted generalities, in short, everything that veils reality from us in order to bring us face to face with reality itself."[68]

John Dewey, at the beginning of the twentieth century, similarly spoke of art as the "outcome of dealing with natural things for the sake of intensifying, purifying, prolonging and deepening the satisfaction which they spontaneously afford",[69] and the idea of art as something which should increase or intensify our awareness in some way has been a commonplace in twentieth-century thought.[70]

FORM AND BEING

In order to understand the development of a theory of aesthetics based on the contemplation of formal relations, it will be useful in the first instance, to understand how form and being were conceived.

From the seventeenth century, Space and Time had been commonly distinguished through their differing, underlying modes of relation which Locke had termed Co-existence and Succession respectively.[71] David Hume realized that behind these two was a simpler relation that encompassed both space and time, that of Contiguity, where two things or events may be juxtaposed either spatially or sequentially.[72] In the work of Kant, we see a further regress, beyond the notion of Co-existence implied in the term Community, to the corresponding category of Disjunction where we can visualize not only the continua of space and time being broken down into juxtaposed elements but also any continuum that there might be in the conceptual world. We think of the disjunctive in grammar, or its equivalent in the mathematical conception of the universe that was to succeed Newton's interpretation of space and time.[73]

Being was seen not as an additive phenomenon piece upon piece like Frankl's view of Romanesque architecture but as a whole to be divided, part relating to part, like some French cathedral of the High Gothic.[74] Form too could be seen not as the addition of lines and surfaces to one another but as the cutting out of shape from a continuum:[75]

"Spinoza formulated the profoundly important principle that all determination is negation," said Hegel, "To determine a thing is to cut it off from some sphere of being. To define it is to set boundaries. To say that a thing is green limits it by cutting it off from the sphere of pink or blue".[76] The continuum of Being from which forms were created was called by Hegel the "Absolute", and he defined beauty as "the shining of the Absolute through the veils of the sense world".[77] Art approached this "most comprehensive spiritual truth" by "counterfeiting the spatial co-existence of inorganically connected parts", by "balancing opposite or discordant qualities", and by generally reconciling diversity within an overall scheme of unity.[78]

Denis Didérot, who with Jean d'Alembert was one of the chief editors of the *Encyclopédie* which began to appear from 1750 onwards, held that beauty lay in the number of relationships or "rapports" that could be contemplated in a work of art: "We are glad to perceive in great art, the consequence of multiple relationships all at once, and the more 'rapports' the more beautiful the work."[79]

The types of relation he mentioned included connection, mutual fitness and conformity.[80] While it may be noted that things other than art exhibit formal relations, an aestheticism developed in the nineteenth century that distinguished between "productions in which an aesthetic value is, or is supposed to be prominent",[81] and lesser objects which merely emphasized utilitarian or academic values. The phrase *L'art pour l'art* can be traced back to 1804,[82] and in 1856, Théophile Gautier, editor of *L'Artiste*, voiced the "autonomy of art",[83] encouraging the secession of art from the utilitarian and academic realms. F. H. Bradley in his Oxford lecture of 1901, entitled "Poetry for Poetry's sake", stated that:

> "Poetry is not imitation but an end in itself . . . For its nature is not to be a part, nor yet a copy of the real world . . . but to be a world by itself, independent, complete, autonomous, and to possess it fully, you must enter that world and conform to its laws."[84]

He rejected, however, the aesthete's view that "art is the whole or supreme end of human life" just as he rejected the doctrine of "form for form's sake" saying ". . . it is possible to abstract this nearly formal element of style [from a work]. . . but you could not read with pleasure for an hour a composition which had no other merit". John Ruskin too, rejected *aesthesis* or "animal consciousness",[85] for the more critical and intellectually rigorous realm of *theoria*,[86] and we may conclude with John Dewey that although perceptual satisfaction may well lie in the formal relations of the work of art, this does not preclude a cognitive satisfaction being required from the meaningful relations that might also be found in the work.[87]

CATEGORY TWO: CAUSALITY AND FUNCTION

Kant placed the category of Cause and Effect in second place, and Peirce confirmed the order saying, "The idea of second is predominant in the ideas of causation".[88] If sensation is first, said Peirce, then practical reaction is naturally second, and here he improved on Kant and the mediaeval tradition in placing ethics (or "practics") as the second of the "normative sciences", which now take the order: Aesthetics, Ethics, and Logic.[89]

The second half of the nineteenth century, when Peirce was formulating his views, was above all the period when the concept of morality was reintroduced into art. Tolstoy, for example, stated that beauty alone could not serve as a definition of art, for "art, unlike beauty is not judged by the pleasure it affords but whether it is good".[90] In asking the question "What is the function of art?" he answered that "Art should be defined like a shoe or a typewriter . . . and how they connect up causally with other things".[91] The purpose of good art lay in "the movement of humanity towards perfection, and that through art, love and trust can help replace the evils of society".[92] John Ruskin was also noted for his moral views, saying, for example, that "Art is moral in its causes and effects", and that "Architecture expresses the moral qualities of those who build, affecting in turn those who use".[93]

In order to understand the development of the relation between ethics and art, we must return to the seventeenth century when Scholasticism was beginning to give way to the more materialistic views of the Enlightenment. For Hobbes, for example, "life was nothing but a motion of the limbs", and the Good consisted of the object of a body's desire, and the body's movement towards gaining this object.[94] The scholastic language of efficient and final causes was translated into the concept of means and ends, the end desired according to Hobbes consisted of delight, and "good in the means" consisted of utility or profitability. Among the many views which followed, of what should be considered means and what ends, we might note the view of Lowth who reversed Hobbes's order to suggest that pleasure was only the means for which utility was the end.[95] In the eighteenth century it seemed clear that reason and the advance of science were to be considered means, and we shall therefore discuss reason first, followed by function and utility, which were considered among the ends of art.

REASON AND THE RULES

Hegel's conclusion that "reason is the substance of the universe"[96] had its roots in the seventeenth century when Gottfried Leibniz, in developing the field of logic, was beginning to substitute the notion of "sufficient reason" for the older notion of cause.[97] (It might be noted that in the twentieth century too, reason and cause were being compared by philosophers: George Santayana, for example, stated that, like cause and effect, reason proceeds from data to conclusions;[98] and George Stout remarked that "a cause is a reason . . . an intelligible ground of an effect").[99]

However, regarding the end of mediaeval superstition, Thomas Spratt, one of the founders of the Royal Society, wrote in 1667 ". . . from the time in which the real philosophy has appeared, there is scarce any whisper of such horrors . . . The course of things goes quietly along in its own true channel of natural causes and effects".[100] Galileo, working at the beginning of the century, had not only contributed to Newton's three Laws of Motion, published in 1687, but also to the general idea that all things could be explained mechanistically in terms of cause and effect.[101]

A parallel was soon drawn between the laws of science and the rules of art in that if a particular effect, or end, was required then so there must be an ascertainable means for attaining such an end. These means, John Dennis wrote in 1701, "are otherwise called the Rules",[102] and the idea that good art could be subject to such rules was typical of the Neoclassical period. Shaftesbury, for

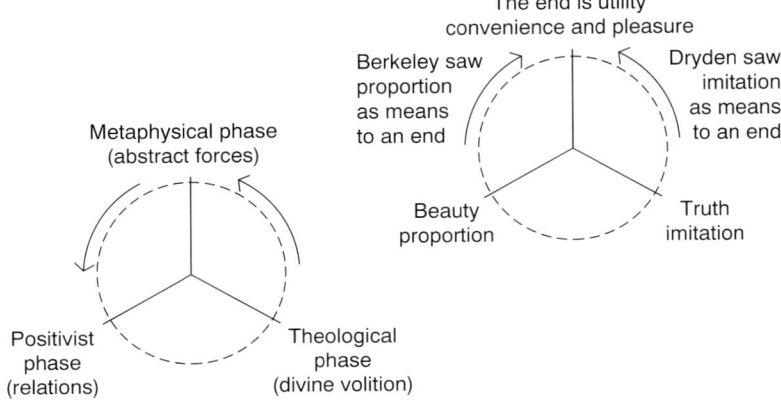

Figure 39 *Two very different diagrams. The first (left) shows Comte's "Law of the Three States" describing cultural development in terms of how things are explained. The second (right) shows eighteenth-century concern with means and ends, where Shaftesbury could say, for example, "Beauty and truth are clearly joined with the notions of utility and convenience"*

example, in his book, *Characteristics* published in 1711, emphasized the need for rules and alluded to such Aristotelian principles as "the real beauty of composition, the unity of design, the truth of character and the just imitation of nature in each particular".[103] In architecture, James Gibbs produced *Rules for Drawing the Several Parts of Architecture* in 1732, a work which had influence not only in Britain but in the American colonies also.

Perhaps the chief exponent of this view was the painter Sir Joshua Reynolds who gave a series of "Discourses" to mark the foundation of the Royal Academy in 1768. "Reason determines everything," he said, ". . . even works of genius, like any other effect, as they must have their causes, must likewise have their rules".[104]

However, the scepticism which Hume had expressed, arising from the inability to observe causal forces actually at work, resulted in the nineteenth century in a shift of scientific thinking away from the metaphysics of causal explanation. We see this clearly, for example, in the ideas of Ernst Mach, whose work was to influence Albert Einstein, and for whom causal links and abstract forces were replaced by the "functional relationships" of mathematics.[105]

Another opponent to the explanation of things solely by the action of physical forces was Auguste Comte who, around 1826, introduced the idea of Positivism. He developed the idea that there were "Three States" (Figure 39) through which mankind has developed . . .[106]

(1) A theological phase where phenomena were explained by divine volition
(2) A metaphysical phase where phenomena were explained by abstract forces
(3) A positivist phase where phenomena were to be explained through a description of their relations, which, following Locke and Hume, he saw as being three, namely: Co-existence, Succession and Resemblance.

Comte established an order in the sciences: Mathematics, Astronomy, Physics, Chemistry and Biology, and he introduced the new science of Sociology In this, he was in correspondence with John Stuart Mill in England, whose own argument against the rationale of cause and effect lay in the fact that there was no simple way, for example, of estimating the complex effect of social tendencies.[107]

Function and Utility

For John Dryden, and for Neoclassical poetry in general, pleasure was the end for which imitation was the means.[108] Although this may very well have been applicable to the architecture of the time, there was, following Hobbes, the suggestion that utility also could be considered in terms of means and ends. Shaftesbury, in recognizing that the beauty of nature lay in "the adaptation of every limb and proportion" to some activity and purpose, concluded that, "beauty and truth are plainly joined with the notion of utility and convenience".[109] Berkeley added that even the proportions of architecture could be esteemed "only as they are relative to some certain use or end";[110] and Hume a little later said:

"A great part of beauty . . . is derived from the idea of convenience or utility . . . The order and convenience of a palace are no less essential to its beauty than its mere figure and appearance."[111]

In the nineteenth century an early form of functionalism was beginning to develop in architecture. Pugin (for whom the Vitruvian categories had evolved to become Construction, Convenience and Propriety) was particularly concerned that the ground plan should evolve from the purpose of the building;[112] Viollet-le-Duc in France proposed the view that the beauty of a Gothic cathedral lay in the fact that its buttresses and vaulting clearly expressed a structural purpose;[113] and in 1851, Horatio Greenough wrote to Ralph Waldo Emerson, saying that he found in the principle that beauty follows from function a theory that "will do for all structures from a bedstead to a cathedral . . . [seeing] in the ships, the carriages and the engines a partial illustration of the doctrine, and a glorious foretaste of what structure can be in this country".[114] Emerson, in turn, in 1860, wrote:

"Beauty rests on necessities. The line of beauty is the result of perfect economy. The cell of the bee is built at that angle which gives the most strength with the least wax."[115]

Herbert Spencer, in England, took a similar view, that "Beauty follows the principle of economy".[116]

Such was the persuasiveness of the notion that beauty was derived from an adaptation to purpose that Kant, in attempting to maintain his view that beauty lay in an essential "disinterestedness", suggested that an object, to be truly beautiful, required a sense of "purposiveness without purpose".[117] Interestingly, Pol Abraham pointed out much later that many of the ribs and colonettes in Gothic cathedrals, while looking purposeful, serve no structural function whatsoever.[118]

Regarding the higher ends that architecture might serve, we might note the views of Jeremy Bentham in the eighteenth century who developed the doctrine of Utilitarianism, or the principle of "the greatest happiness of the greatest number". Bentham's opinion was that the arts could only be justified in so far as they were conducive to pleasure or profit, and he was not at all convinced that much pleasure, let alone profit, could be afforded for instance by poetry.[119] He and his successor, James Mill, were more interested in social problems, homelessness and the Poor Laws, although it should be said that the latter's son, John Stuart Mill, who published *Utilitarianism* in 1861, recognized the importance of feelings, and even poetry, in being among the essential comforts of life that utilitarianism could foster.[120]

We might also mention Matthew Arnold and William Morris in England, who at about this time were beginning to promote their own brands of humanism and socialism respectively against the more brutalizing influences of industrial society; and Gautier in France, who, in defending art against plain utility, said that works of art "have done more to lift the soul than all the treatises of the moralists".[121] We shall return to the subject of morality in architecture in our concluding chapter.

CATEGORY THREE: INHERENCE AND MEANING

The two ways in which Kant's concept of Inherence might be approached are reflected in his two tables, and correspond, in a sense, to matter and mind respectively. In the table of categories, Inherence is viewed as the relation between substance and accident, or a thing and its qualities, and it is through the comparison of the qualities of one thing with another that the notion of Resemblance, Hume's corresponding category, can be derived. In the table of judgements, it is the inherence of a predicate within a subject that forms the basis of Categorical propositions, and it is on such propositions, as Russell was to agree, that all philosophy has been founded, all knowledge and all truth.[122] In Peirce, the "ideas in which thirdness is predominant" include those of thought, meaning, sign and representation, and to explore these ideas further we might draw out the following headings:

(1) Association and Taste, ideas developing in the eighteenth century based on resemblance, discernment and propriety
(2) Classification and Style, ideas of particular concern in the nineteenth century with its interests in science and history
(3) Meaning and Truth. In the twentieth century, the quest for knowledge returned to the subject of knowledge itself, resulting in such works as *The Meaning of Meaning*, and the viewing of architecture as a referential sign or symbol system.

ASSOCIATION AND TASTE

John Locke, who as we have seen initiated the doctrine of associationism, introduced an important distinction between primary and secondary qualities. The primary qualities, shape, form, dimension, etc. were in his opinion inseparable from a body; the secondary qualities, colour, taste, smell, etc. were subjective and dependent on the percipient.[123] Later, the notion of tertiary qualities, mentioned by S. Alexander, for instance, were introduced, and P. Leon listed such typical qualities as serenity, majesty, mysteriousness, gloom, etc.[124] Whether these qualities belonged in some sense to the object, as Dewey supposed,[125] or whether all qualities including primary qualities were subjective as Berkeley had thought,[126] it was through a consideration of such inherent properties that, in the eighteenth century, the concepts of association and taste began to develop.

Good taste depended on discernment, the freeing of the mind from "all prejudices" as Hume said, and the ability of the mind to judge the relative merits and qualities of the ideas being brought together. John Dennis, writing in 1701, had said that, "Taste . . . is nothing but a fine discernment for truth",[127] and Joseph Addison writing some ten years later in the *Spectator* said:

> "A man of fine taste in writing will discern, not only the general beauties and imperfections of an author, but discover the several ways of thinking and expressing himself, which diversify him from all other authors, with the several other infusions of thought and language, and the particular authors from whom they borrowed."[128]

It is from this period, which we associate with the London coffee houses and the fashionable world of the *beau monde*, that there arose the notion of criticism in literature and the arts. Shaftesbury, for example, "defended the cause of critics against indolent and supine authors" saying that "a legitimate and just taste cannot be made . . . without the antecedent labour and pain of criticism". Accordingly he emphasized the "force of good education" in forming good taste.[129] Hutcheson said that "knowledge . . . may superadd a distinct rational pleasure", and he differentiated sensation from perception through the latter's "power of comparing objects . . . and observing their relations and proportions".[130] And a few years later, Hume in reinforcing the view that it was "rare to meet with a man who has a just taste without a sound understanding" also emphasized the underlying notion of comparison: "It is impossible to continue in the practice of contemplating any order of beauty, without being frequently obliged to form 'comparisons' between the several species and degrees of excellence, and estimating their proportion to each other."[131]

Hume, as we have seen, developed the concept of association, and it is important to distinguish, regarding the ideas being brought together, between those based on a common knowledge which inform criticism and those arising out of personal experience which help form our natural taste. Of this latter kind he said "we are more pleased . . . with pictures and characters that resemble objects which are found in our own age and country" or those things which we perceive to be similar to ourselves "from a conformity of humour or disposition".[132]

It was Hutcheson who pointed out that "the association of ideas makes objects pleasant and delightful", and accordingly he drew an important distinction between beauty on the one hand, and taste, on the other:

> "Associations of ideas give to objects a kind of agreeableness or disagreeableness that is easily confused with beauty and ugliness . . . if any colour or

fashion be commonly used by rustics or by men of any disagreeable pro-
fession, employment or temper . . . these additional ideas may cause a constant dislike to them . . . although the colour or form be no way disagreeable
of themselves."[133]

By the end of the century, however, the current of associationism was so strong
that beauty and taste were becoming thoroughly confused. Archibald Alison in
1790 formulated a theory of aesthetics in which all our perceptions could be
reduced to association;[134] and Francis Jeffrey, writing in the *Edinburgh Review* in
1806 said: "A beautiful object is one that is associated either in our past experience or by some universal analogy with pleasure, or emotions that upon the whole
are pleasant".[135]

Both Hutcheson and Schopenhauer suggested that the pleasures to be found in
the Gothic were based primarily on an association of ideas.

CLASSIFICATION AND STYLE

In 1762, the idea that all the arts were not necessarily imitative was proposed by
Lord Kames in his *Elements of Criticism*: "Of all the fine arts, painting only and
sculpture are in their nature imitative; music like architecture is productive of
originals, and copies not from nature."[136]

At about the same time, Edward Young in his *Conjectures* pointed out that all
the arts might be mimetic but in a different way. They may in fact be imitating
the styles of other artists,[137] and it is from this period that we see the whole
nineteenth-century debate about style commencing, albeit in an initially vague
form. Edward Gibbon, the historian, for example, defined style as the "image of
character";[138] and Thomas de Quincey later differentiated between style as
"separable ornament" and style as the "incarnation of thought".[139]

In order to understand style, it is useful to look at the process of classification,
and the manner in which, in order to gain knowledge, our understanding proceeds
in differentiating things according to various kinds of resemblance. Locke had said
that all knowledge consists in "the perception of the agreement or disagreement of
ideas",[140] and Hume was to say later that "When we have found a resemblance
among several objects we apply the same name".[141]

Names were required by historians, in particular those historians surveying the
building stocks of England, France and Germany at the beginning of the nineteenth
century, in order to distinguish one style of building from another. Such names
were generally based on three kinds of inherent attribute found in buildings, and to
illustrate this we may consider some examples taken from Rickman's *Styles of
English Architecture* of 1817[142] (Figure 40):

(1) Formal characteristics, e.g. Decorated, Pointed, Perpendicular, etc.
(2) Position in sequence of development, e.g. Early, Late, Modern, etc.
(3) Cultural associations, e.g. Saxon, Norman, Gothic, etc.

Associations became prominent in the "Battle of the Styles" of the nineteenth
century, between for example, those who preferred the Gothic style, like Pugin for

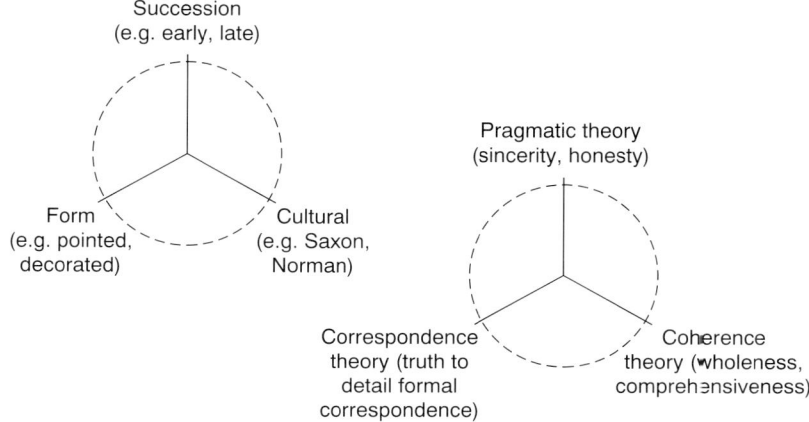

Figure 40 *Diagrams showing some common examples of historical style (left) given by Rickman; and the different theories of truth (right) introduced by Bradley. For a building to be "true" in any sense, it would need to take into account concepts from both diagrams*

its Christian associations, or those who preferred the Classical style, which Sebastiano Serlio, three centuries earlier, had suggested was "more appropriate for noblemen".[143]

Behind this interest in classification (an interest which was also taken in the sciences of the time, in botany by Carolus Linnaeus as early as 1738, and in chemistry by Dmitri Mendeleyev in 1869), there was an underlying philosophical trend. J. S. Mill for example, said that all logic concerned itself with the way information is organized;[144] Karl Pearson, that the only way of arriving at truth is by classifying facts and reasoning about them;[145] and Herbert Spencer that "knowing is classifying, or grasping the like and separating the unlike".[146] The structuring relationship of genus and species led, in the discussion of style, to two different points of view:

- That which emphasized the genus and the concept of similarity
- That which emphasized the species and the concept of individuality.

The first was the typically Neoclassical view, and we may think of Samuel Johnson's remark that "greatness consists in generalizing". Joshua Reynolds painted only the "general form of things", and the closeness of the finished work to some abstract Platonic ideal became the measure of its perfection: "From a reiterated experience and a close comparison of the objects in nature, an artist becomes possessed of the idea of that central form . . . from which every deviation is deformity."[147]

Against these views may be mentioned William Blake, who in response to Reynold's *Discourses* declared "To Generalize is to be an Idiot. To particularize is the Alone distinction of Merit".[148] A reviewer of Sir Walter Scott's *Lady of the Lake* in 1810, similarly stated:

"Whatever he represents has a character of individuality, and is drawn with an accuracy and minuteness of discrimination . . . He is able to discover characteristic differences where the eye of dullness sees nothing but uniformity."[149] William Hazlitt, writing around 1820, said "A thing is more perfect by being more itself . . . The ideal is not an abstraction of nature [nor] a mean or average proportion [but consists in] the singling out of some one thing or leading quality of an object and making it the pervading and regulating principle of all the rest".[150]

MEANING AND TRUTH

The notion of art or architecture as the carrier of meaning can be seen as a development from the theories of signs of the Middle Ages.[151] Gotthold Lessing, in his influential essay *Laocoön* of 1766, distinguished the "natural signs" of painting from the "conventional signs" of poetry;[152] A. W. Schlegel emphasized the central role of metaphor, myth and symbol in art;[153] and J.W. von Goethe, in his *Farbenlehre* of 1810 outlined the symbolic, allegorical and mystical meanings of colours.[154]

It was in the latter half of the nineteenth century, however, that our more modern notions of signification developed. Peirce, for example, extended the relationship type of Inherence, which had typically linked an object to its attribute, to encompass three elements: the sign itself or "ground", the attribute or "object signified", and an "interpretant" or language system which "fulfils the office of interpreter" through which the sign can be understood.[155] In Europe, Ferdinand de Saussure, in his *General Course on Linguistics* distinguished between the Signifier and the Signified,[156] to which Charles Ogden and Ivor Richards in *The Meaning of Meaning*, changing the names of these two terms, added a third to give: Symbol, Referent and Thought.[157]

According to Peirce, "A sign is anything which is related to a second thing, its object, in respect to a quality, in such a way as to bring a third thing, its interpretant, into relation to the same object".[158] He distinguished between three types of sign: the Icon, the Index and the Symbol:

"The first is the diagrammatic sign or Icon which exhibits a similarity or analogy to the subject of discourse; the second is the Index which like a pronoun, demonstrative or relative, forces the attention to the particular object without describing it; the third, or Symbol, is the general name or description which signifies its object by means of an association of ideas or habitual connection between the name and the character signified."[159]

Charles Morris, writing in 1938, and influenced by Peirce's work distinguished three realms in the field of "Semiotics", or study of signs – Syntactics, Pragmatics and Semantics – which we may liken to the form, function and meaning of signs respectively.[160] Of semiotics applied to art he said:

"It is the imitation theory given a more technical formulation and more scientific grounding . . . A picture signifies by similarity, even an abstract visual design is simply an extreme case of generality of reference."[161]

In the twentieth century, the common ground between meaning and truth was being explored with interest. P.F. Strawson, for example, distinguished between sentences, which were either significant or meaningless, and statements, which could be either true or false.[162] The idea that art and beauty might be connected with truth was one that was of interest to Shaftesbury in 1711:

> "For all beauty is truth. True features make the beauty of a face, and true proportions the beauty of architecture, a true measure that of harmony and music."[163]

Although Shaftesbury distinguished three kinds of truth: the Poetical (Graphical or Plastic); the Historical or Narrative (a part of Moral Truth): and the Critical;[164] the main division noted in the works of logic of the twentieth century, that of F.H. Bradley for instance, remained that of Correspondence Theory, Coherence Theory and Pragmatic Theory.[165] Peirce introduced the Pragmatic theory and named it as such,[166] but concepts from the two other theories were certainly distinguished in the eighteenth century, for instance, by Reynolds: "The natural appetite or task of the human mind is for truth; whether that truth results . . . from the agreement of the representation of any object with the thing represented; or from the correspondence of the several parts of any arrangement with each other."[167]

It will be useful to look at the three theories briefly in turn:

(1) Correspondence Theory: An example of this kind of truth would be the truth to detail required by Greek Revivalism, as inspired by both Winckelmann's studies of 1755, *Thoughts on the Imitation of Greek Works in Painting and Sculpture* and Stuart and Revett's *The Antiquities of Athens* which appeared in 1762.

(2) Pragmatic Theory: For Keats, the simple truth was that works of art existed and had their causes and effects.[168] For Wordsworth, poetry was to be "weighed in the balance of feeling",[169] and he introduced the virtue of sincerity in a work, just as Shaftesbury had introduced the virtue of honesty[170] to describe this kind of truth.

(3) Coherence Theory: Shaftesbury, reflecting on the necessity for the artist to maintain internal coherence in the work, wrote ". . . the piece, if it be beautiful and carries truth, must be a whole, by itself, complete, independent, and withal as great and comprehensive as he can make it".[171] Bodmer in 1740, spoke of a poem's "coherence within itself" saying that the poet "troubles himself not at all with rational truth but only with poetic truth".[172] We may think here of Dryden's artistic or "Poetic Licence" of 1677.[173]

Although in one sense such an "independent" or "autonomous" work may be seen to be cut off from the real world in terms of space and time, in another, in terms of sense and meaning, it must necessarily remain an inherent part of a culture. "The truth is the whole . . .", said Hegel ". . . and nothing partial is quite true".[174] For a work to be true in this sense, it must maintain some kind of coherence with the age in which it was created.

Johann Herder likened art and its various forms and styles to plants which "grow out of the soil of its own time and place . . .", the nature of the soil comprising ". . . history, tradition, customs and religion, the spirit of the time, of the people, of feeling, of language."[175] The difficulty of reconciling all these aspects of a culture has led to two different views of the incorporation of such cultural associations into a work of architecture. Both were mentioned by Ruskin. On the one hand, he used the argument to justify the reuse of styles from the past:

> "We want no new style of architecture . . . if we have good laws their age is of no importance . . . Noble architecture is in some sort the embodiment of the Polity, Life, History and Religious Faith of a Nation."[176]

On the other hand, there was the view, hinted at by Ruskin, and which developed the ideas of Hegel, that a style of architecture should reflect the ideas and technology of the day – the "spirit of the times".[177] Ruskin mentioned this in relation to the new architecture of iron and steel, and it was a view that was to result in the renunciation of any meaning a new building may have in terms of history and the past, and was to lead eventually to the architecture of the twentieth century.

SECONDARY CATEGORIES

So far, with regard to the philosophy of mind of the eighteenth century, we have dealt only with what Kant called the cognitive faculties, Judgement, Reason and Understanding,[178] and how they bear on the Aesthetic, Ethical and Theoretical aspects of building respectively. Now we need to turn our attention to the other mental faculties, the Imagination, Feelings and Will which Descartes, for example, had mentioned,[179] or the feelings of Pride, Love and Direct Passions which Hume had listed,[180] and see how they correspond with the secondary categories which we introduced in the previous chapter.

There are two relevant views which we may carry forward from the seventeenth century. First, there was that of Locke who had concluded that "there are differences in nature, but the differences proceed by continuous gradation".[181] The analogy that should be noted was the discovery in 1665, by Newton, that white sunlight on passing through a glass prism is refracted into a virtually continuous spectrum.[182] Second, there was the view of Gottfried Leibniz who, in his *Discourse on Metaphysics* of 1686, differentiated between individual ideas of which we can be distinctly aware, and the "blurred blending of infinite percepts" which can only be clearly comprehended by the intuitive faculties:

> "When I am able to recognize a thing without being able to say in what its differences or characteristics consist, the knowledge is confused . . . we may know clearly that a poem or picture is well or badly done only because there is in it a certain *'je ne sais quoi'*."[183]

Alexander Baumgarten developed the distinction as that between Logic, on the one hand, and Aesthetics (or *cognitio confusa*), on the other;[184] and Kant, who rejected Baumgarten's linking of aesthetics with taste, introduced a division between the Intellectual and the Intuitive faculties respectively[185] (Figure 41):

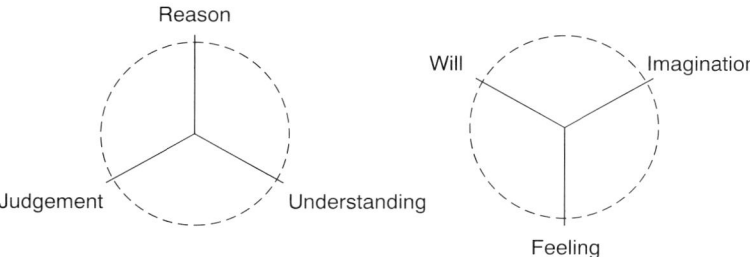

Figure 41 *Diagrams showing the cognitive faculties (left) and the intuitive faculties (right). The cognitive faculties are analytical and correspond to the primary categories; the intuitive faculties are synthetical and correspond to the secondary categories*

Intellectual faculties	Intuitive faculties
Judgement	Imagination
Reason	Feeling
Understanding	Will

Behind this division was one which Aristotle had introduced into science, namely that between analysis and synthesis.[186] For Kant, analysis belonged to the logical faculties and consisted of reducing complex representations into their constituent concepts and relations. Simplifying, we might say:

(1) Judgement analyses the representation into its Disjunctive relations, into "the divided knowledge and of the members of the division taken together".

(2) Reason analyses the representation into its Hypothetical relations, those "of the ground to its consequence".

(3) Understanding analyses the representation into its Categorical relations, those "of the predicate to the subject".[187]

Synthesis, on the other hand, belonged to the intuitive faculties: the Imagination in "the act of putting different representations together",[188] and Intuition itself in "grasping what is manifold in them in one act of knowledge".[189] Henri Bergson, much later, was to differentiate between the intellect, which circled step by step around its object taking each aspect in turn, and intuition which grasped its object from several sides simultaneously.[190]

It was Kant's view that we can only know such an object through the relationships it enters into, and that we can never know the "thing-in-itself": "Everything in our knowledge . . . contains nothing but mere relations . . . what objects may be in themselves remains completely unknown to us."[191] Schopenhauer gave an appropriate analogy when he said that we are like "a man who goes round a castle looking in vain for an entrance and sometimes sketching the façades".[192]

In considering the relations that constitute knowledge, Kant distinguished between form, on the one hand, and content, or matter, on the other. To construct the table of judgements he said "we abstract all content from a judgement and consider only the form of the understanding".[193] Elsewhere he said "In any judgement we can call the given concepts logical matter, and their relation the form of the judgement".[194] Given that all concepts are composed of relations, then the purest concepts will be composed of only one kind of relation and, given that there are only three kinds of relation, they may be arranged under three primary categories. Where, however, the concepts are composed of more than one kind of relation they become what Kant called "derivative concepts", mentioned, for example, when he complained of Aristotle and his ten categories, that ". . . he merely picked them up as they came his way . . . Aristotle's list also ennumerates among the original concepts some derivative concepts, and of the original concepts some are entirely lacking . . ."[195]

It should be noted that similar remarks have been addressed to Kant's categories, by Stace for example,[196] but it is, however, in Kant's work that we find the development of a method by which, through combination, such "derivative" or secondary categories can be derived from the primary categories: "All *a priori* division of concepts must be by dichotomy . . . the third category in each class always arises from the combination of the second category with the first."[197]

"Community" was an example he gave of a category so formed,[198] and Hegel was to show how "Modality" through the concept of Becoming could be seen as a synthetic category.[199] Hegel and Schopenhauer between them were to develop the third of our secondary categories which they termed "Spirit"[200] and "Will"[201] respectively.

In order to reach a clear understanding on how these categories relate to one another, we return to the analogy already made with colour. One of Goethe's many interests was that of colour, and in his *Farbenlehre* of 1810 he developed Newton's colour wheel into a chromatic circle which consisted of the three primary colours interspersed with the three secondary colours (Figure 42). He suggested that the two "triangles" or the one "hexagon" thus formed might symbolize "primordial relations",[202] and we can usefully extract two principles from what he called the "fundamental laws of colour harmony":

(1) The Principle of Combination: "Yellow, blue and red may be assumed as pure elementary colours already existing; from these, violet, orange and green are the simplest combined result".[203]

(2) The Principle of Complementation: "The eye especially demands completeness. . . yellow demands purple; orange demands blue; red demands green; and vice versa . . . Imagine a moveable diametrical index in the colorific circle. The index as it moves around the whole circle indicates at its two extremes the complementary colours".[204]

Hegel, a little later, was to say:

"In modern physical science, the opposition first observed to exist in magnetism as polarity, has come to be regarded as a universal law pervading the whole of nature . . . Thus at one time the colours are regarded as in polar opposition to one another and called complementary colours; and at another time they are looked at in their indifferent and merely quantitative difference of red, yellow, green etc."[205]

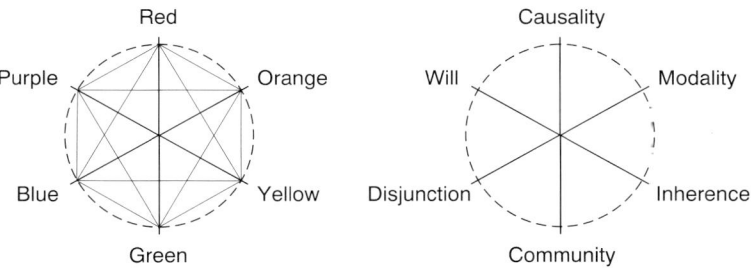

Figure 42 *Goethe's analogy to "primordial relations" (left) showing "a chromatic circle . . . forming two triangles or one hexagon" – illustrating the principles of combination and complementation. The corresponding primary and secondary categories taken from Kant are shown to the right*

In exploring the secondary categories which we shall term Modality, Community and Will respectively, we shall need to bear these two principles in mind, first, by showing how the concepts of each complement those of the opposite primary category, that is:

- That Modality (orange) complements Disjunction (blue)
- That Community (green) complements Causality (red)
- That Will (purple) complements Inherence (yellow)

and second, by showing how the concepts contained under each might result from the other two primary categories:

- That Modality (orange) derives from Causality (red) and Inherence (yellow)
- That Community (green) derives from Inherence (yellow) and Disjunction (blue)
- That Will (purple) derives from Disjunction (blue) and Causality (red).

These categories with their colour codings might be tabulated as follows to show how they complement one another:

Primary categories	Secondary categories
Disjunction (blue)	Modality (orange)
Causality (red)	Community (green)
Inherence (yellow)	Will (purple)

In our next chapter we shall look in more detail at each of the secondary categories in turn. Interestingly, many of the concepts that we shall discuss were nurtured by the Romantic Movement which was beginning to develop at the end of the eighteenth century. If the primary categories can be associated with the critical analyses of the Enlightenment, it is of little surprise that the secondary categories can be associated with Romanticism, itself a reaction to such rationalization.

Chapter 6

Modern Categories: II

The analogy that Goethe made with the colour circle recalls the ideas of microcosm and macrocosm which we discussed in our introduction:

> "Every diagram in which the variety of colours may be represented points to those primordial relations which belong both to nature and the organ of vision. . . . When we find the two separate principles producing green on the one hand and red in their intenser state, we can hardly refrain from thinking in the first case on the earthly, in the last on the heavenly, generation of the *Elohim*."

The analogy that we shall make is that of comparing the primary colours to the main concepts of Classicism, and the secondary colours to the main concepts of Romanticism, in order to help understand the complex interrelationship between these two doctrines. We may note that just as Goethe moved between a Romantic and Classical standpoint in the world of ideas, so too could Schinkel move between working in a Classical and Gothic style in architecture.

Both the Gothic and the Romantic movements had their roots in the Enlightenment that brought the Dark Ages to a close, the Gothic from the Romanesque, and the Romantic from the literature of the Romance languages themselves. Such tales as the *Chanson de Roland* and the Arthurian legends (influenced by the earlier *Lives of the Saints*) tended to deal with three main topics: religion, love and combat, which, while loosely reflecting Paul's faith, hope and charity, also lead to the three faculties of mind on which the secondary categories are based:

(1) The Imagination, conjuring up images of the miraculous and the supernatural
(2) The Feelings, responding to the charms of nature and to courtly love
(3) The Will, encouraging the knights in their quests and combats for life over death.

"We are creatures of imagination, passion and self-will" wrote the critic, William Hazlitt in 1818;[1] and Stieglitz, whose history of German architecture published in 1820 distinguished the rational Greeks from the romantic Germans, wrote of the great cathedrals inspiring us with thoughts of the Holy Trinity and the ideas of Creation, Love and Spirit.[2]

Plate 6 *The Pantheon at Stourhead seen across the lake (© National Trust Photographic Library/Nick Meers)*

"And when the woman saw that the tree was good for food, and that it was pleasant to the eyes, and a tree to be desired to make one wise, she took of the fruit thereof, and did eat"
Genesis

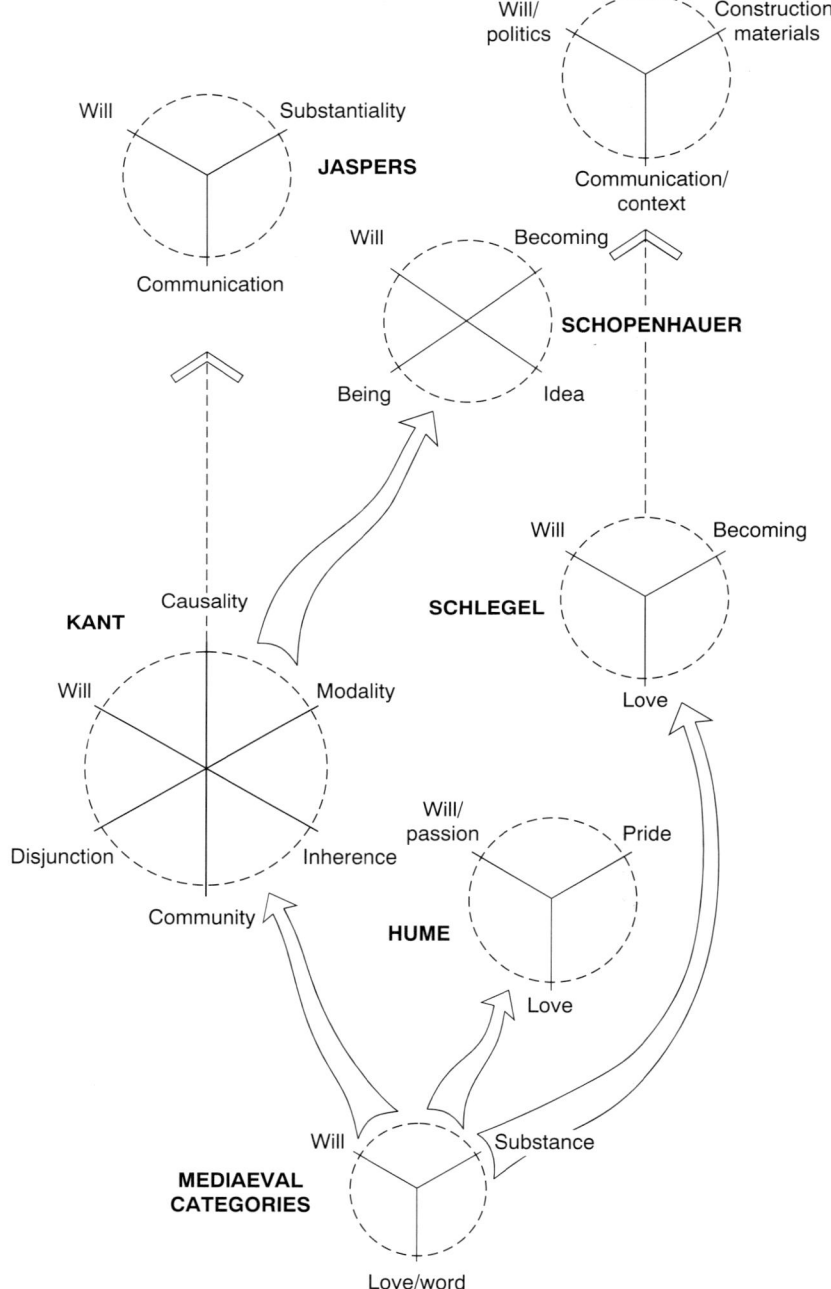

Figure 43 *Modern categories II*

The division of the subject finds confirmation in M.C. Beardsley's *Aesthetics from Classical Greece to the Present* which divided the chapter entitled "Romanticism" into three sections:[3] the first dealing with theories of imagination; the second with the aesthetics of feeling; and the third with the concept of the will as expounded by Schopenhauer and Nietzsche. A.O. Lovejoy in his essay *On the Discrimination of Romanticisms* suggested a similar division by country:[4] Germany and its concern for Organic theory and the imagination; England and its feeling for landscape and poetry; and France in its passionate involvement with revolution and liberty. As a simple introduction to the subject, it will be useful to look at each of these countries in turn to see how each reacted in its own way to the Neoclassicism of the eighteenth century.

GERMAN ROMANTICISM

There are three names connected with the *Sturm und Drang*[5] movement in German literature that we may mention, namely those of Herder, Goethe and Schiller. J.G. von Herder, who was from East Prussia, had attended Kant's lectures at Königsberg in 1762, before meeting the younger Goethe in Strasbourg in 1770. Both were repelled by Paul Holbach's idea of the brain as a machine and instead preferred to see man the artist as part of organic nature to be discussed in terms of his imagination and feelings. The poet, said Herder, "must express his feelings".[6] Goethe, writing *On German Architecture* in 1772, said of the Classicism of France and Italy that "these nations have measured rather than felt".[7] By 1794, the playwright J.C.F. Schiller had met both Herder and Goethe, and after lecturing on Aesthetics at Jena, published his essay *On Naïve and Sentimental Poetry*[8] in 1795 which, in explaining the differences between ancient and modern, laid the foundations for German Romanticism.

In philosophy, both J.G. Fichte and then Friedrich Schelling lectured at Jena. Fichte carried Kant's subjectivity further by querying the need for the thing-in-itself, and stressed the importance of the will.[9] Schelling, who published his *System of Transcendental Idealism* in 1800, developed the notion of the organic, and in following Herder's view that music was the proper language of feeling, suggested that architecture itself could be seen as "frozen music".[10]

In 1798, the journal *Athenäum* was first published, and in it Friedrich Schlegel defined *Romantische Poesie* in terms that might be compared with our three categories of modality, community and will:[11]

(1) "The romantic kind of poetry . . . should forever be becoming and never perfected"
(2) "Romantic poetry is to the arts what society and sociability, friendship and love are to life"
(3) ". . . It recognizes as its first commandment that the will of the poet can tolerate no law above itself."

He differentiated "poetical criticism" from the "analytic" method of Classicism, and in 1801, his brother A. W. Schlegel gave a series of lectures in Berlin which

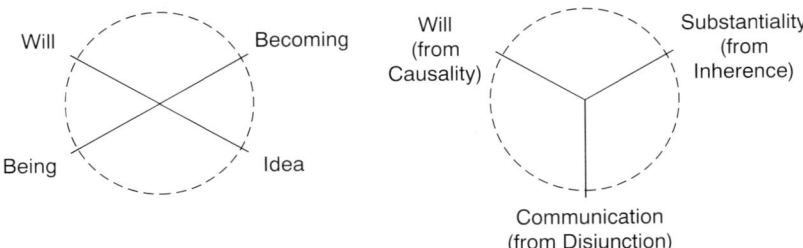

Figure 44 *The Romantic Movement's contribution to categorization consisted of opposing the primary categories with complementary concepts. Schopenhauer's "fourfold root of the principle of sufficient reason" is shown (left). Jasper's later rearrangement of Kant's categories is shown on the right*

introduced the important distinction between the Classical and the Romantic: "By an example taken from another art, that of architecture," he said, we see that ". . . the Pantheon is not more different from Westminster Abbey or the Church of St Stephen in Vienna, than the structure of a tragedy of Sophocles from a drama of Shakespeare . . . each is great and admirable in its kind."[12]

Hegel, arriving at Jena in 1801, collaborated with Schelling for a while. In suggesting that the difference between Classical and Romantic was that between space and time respectively,[13] he was building on an opposition that had first appeared in Lessing's *Laocoön* where the arts of painting and sculpture had been seen in spatial terms, and the arts of poetry and music were conceived in terms of time.[14] The related opposition between Being and Becoming was incorporated by Schopenhauer in 1813 into his *Fourfold Root of the Principle of Sufficient Reason*[15] (Figure 44). The other two types of "relatedness" consisted of the opposition between Will and Idea, concepts which were further developed in *The World as Will and Idea* published by Schopenhauer in 1818.[16]

ENGLISH ROMANTICISM

Romanticism began in England in the early eighteenth century by combining a taste for Neoclassical country houses with a feeling for irregularly formed, natural landscape. Shaftesbury, who it may be noted disliked the systematic thinking of the empiricists, wrote in 1711 of the "blissful mansions, known seats, delightful prospects" and their gardens of "cypresses, groves and wildernesses".[17] Those who sought woods, rivers and seashores were "deep in the romantic way". The introduction of Palladianism and its tendency towards the picturesque were developed in the gardens of William Kent and Capability Brown, while William Gilpin in 1792 added the term "Picturesque" as a third category to Edmund Burke's "Sublime and Beautiful".[18]

This sympathy with nature was reflected in the English poetry of the time, and at the beginning of the nineteenth century its two leading exponents, William Wordsworth and Samuel Taylor Coleridge, were also writing on matters of more

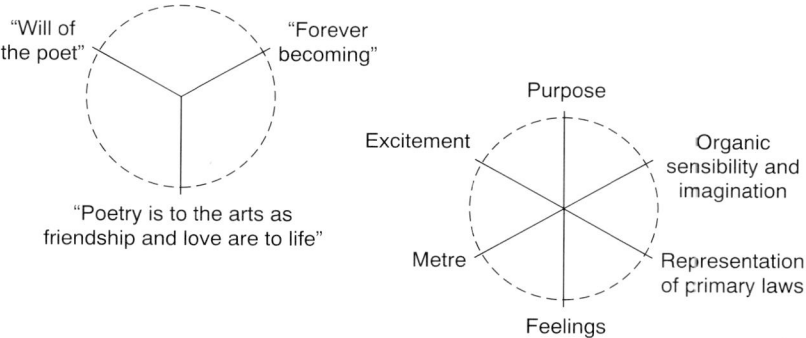

Figure 45 *Two different interpretations of Romantic poetry. An analysis of F. Schlegel's* Romantische Poesie *on the left, and Wordsworth's* Preface to Lyrical Ballads *on the right*

general significance. Coleridge, after a trip to Germany in 1798, began to set down his own ideas of the role of the imagination in his *Biographia Literaria* which finally appeared in 1817. Meanwhile, Wordsworth had published in 1800 the *Preface to Lyrical Ballads* which the critic M. H. Abrams has described as having "something of the aspect of a romantic manifesto".[19] Abrams extracted several points of note,[20] and with a reading of the original, we might list these points under our primary and secondary categories respectively (Figure 45):

By primary category:
(1) "Part of the pleasure given by poetry depends on the metre" (cf Form)
(2) "Each of the poems has a purpose, [in particular] the amelioration of the affections" (cf. Function)
(3) In each "the incidents of common life are made interesting by tracing in them the primary laws of our nature" (cf. Meaning)

By secondary category:
(4) The complex end proposed "requires an imagination or more than usual organic sensibility" (cf. Imagination)
(5) Poets should "convey their feelings and notions in simple and unelaborated expressions" (cf. Feelings)
(6) "The end of poetry is to produce excitement" although poetry itself may be described as "emotion recollected in tranquillity"[21] (cf. Will).

The well-known quotation from Wordsworth's *Prelude* that "Poetry is the spontaneous overflow of powerful feelings"[22] sums up the ideas of imagination, feeling and power which Romanticism required.

In opposing feeling and poetic truth to "analytical industry" and science, Wordsworth was reflecting a general opinion that countermeasures were required against the dehumanizing aspects of the Industrial Revolution. The Utilitarians, as we have seen, preferred political action to words in order to promote the general good, but there were those including Shelley and J. S. Mill who claimed that the expression of sympathetic feeling in itself could be an instrument for good. Matthew Arnold argued for a new Humanism where religion and poetry could be united; and A. W. Pugin in *True Principles of Pointed or Christian Architecture*, published in 1843, argued for a similar link between religion and architecture. John Ruskin, writing on architecture a few years later, contrasted the beauty of nature with the ugliness of industrial society; and William Morris, also around the middle of the century, began his opposition to mass production by promoting a return to fine craftsmanship in the vernacular tradition.

FRENCH ROMANTICISM

It was against the background of French Classicism, the Academies and the Beaux Arts tradition that French Romanticism began to emerge. We can see it stirring in the great *Encyclopédie* of 1750 to 1776, edited by Denis Didérot and Jean d'Alembert, where the subject "Architecture", although at first classified in the prospectus under the general category of Reason, and discussed in terms of mathematics, human need and *convenance* (propriety), was transferred in Volume I to the category of Imagination where the Fine Arts were to be found.[23] We may note that in relation to imagination, Diderot in his article on "Genius" contrasted the imagination and the will with the more "gentle emotions" into which genius sometimes lapses (Figure 46).

Jean-Jacques Rousseau, generally recognized as the first French Romantic, although born in Geneva, came to fame through a prize-winning essay which proclaimed the superiority of the "noble savage" over the civilized European.[24] In religious matters he argued for the supremacy of feeling over reason, and in politics he urged a free democracy over the monarchy of Louis XV and the excesses of his predecessors who had created the palace at Versailles. His *Contrat Social* of 1762 inspired both Robespierre and Chateaubriand, but it was eleven years after his death that, in 1789, the Bastille was stormed and the French Revolution began. Interestingly, the revolutionary cry of "*Liberté, Égalité, Fraternité*"[25] reappeared in another guise in 1855 when Martin, stressing the Frenchness of Gothic architecture and the pointed arch (*l'ogive*) proclaimed "*L'ogive, art national; l'ogive, l'art laïque, l'ogive, art libre*".[26] We should note the order in which this version of the secondary categories appeared: national pride, brotherhood and freedom, respectively.

François Chateaubriand, a reactionary to the Revolution, came to literary prominence under Napoleon Bonaparte and the First Empire. "His fertility of ideas, luxury of natural description and vehemence of expression"[27] influenced a generation of French writers including Victor Hugo, whose more extreme notions included that of "burning everything previously adored".[28] Viollet-le-Duc, who had himself refused a Beaux Arts education, was inspired by such works as Hugo's *Notre Dame de Paris* of 1831, and he worked under Prosper Mérimée before establishing himself as one of the foremost restorers of France's Gothic buildings.

Two complementary themes which recurred in French literature in the nineteenth century were the human passions, "*les passions du coeur humain*"[29]

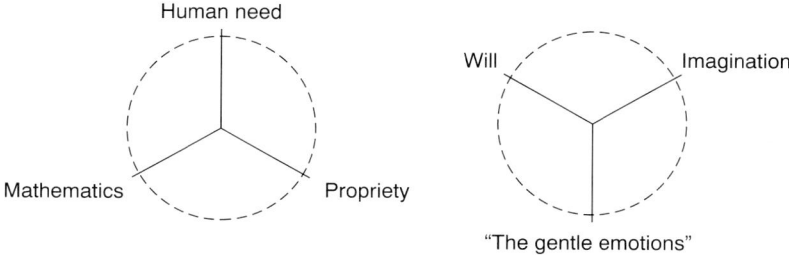

Figure 46 *The French* Encyclopédie, *edited by Diderot and D'Alembert, first classified architecture under Reason in terms of the above concepts (left), before transferring the subject to Imagination and the Arts where it was discussed in terms of "genius" (right)*

as described by Chateaubriand, and an intense realism, *"la vraie veritée"*.[30] This latter, and its intention to shock, was described by Hugo as a *"frisson nouveau"*,[31] a comment particularly directed towards the works of Baudelaire and Zola.

In painting, the desire for realism passed through Courbet to Manet and the "truth to appearance"[32] of the Impressionists. In the last decades of the nineteenth century arose the concept of *Art Nouveau* as a further reaction to Academicism and Historicism, and whose drive to rid architecture of all the cultural meaning of the past was to lead eventually to the Modern Movement.

✻

Now that we have traced in brief outline some of the relevant aspects of the development of Romanticism, we can turn our attention to the main concepts of the movement. In particular, we shall look at concepts drawn from our three main categories in turn, namely Modality, Communication and Will, and under each introduce some ideas of particular relevance to the theory of architecture.

CATEGORY FOUR: MODALITY AND CONSTRUCTION

The category of Modality arose out of the scholastic concept of Substance and denoted the changing state of being of a thing. We understand the category, said Kant "by placing under the predicament of modality, the predicables of coming to be, ceasing to be, change, etc."[33] In his table of judgements we see listed three "principles of modality . . . the concepts of possibility, actuality and necessity",[34] and it is not too difficult to see how they might be applied to the design and construction process:

- Necessity, in establishing the needs
- Possibility, in considering, through the imagination, what Leibniz called "com-possibles",[35] or the possible solutions that might work together
- Actuality, in the construction and realization of the building itself.

Substance, for Kant, would have been that which remained through the process of construction; Matter would be its manifestation in space; while Material would be that which undergoes a change, a distinction which he exemplified as follows:

> "A philosopher on being asked how much smoke weighs", made the reply, "Subtract from the weight of wood burnt the weight of the ashes which are left over, and you will have the weight of the smoke . . . even in fire the matter (substance) does not vanish but only suffers an alteration of form."[36]

Although the principle of the conservation of energy replaced the doctrine of substance in about 1850, the notion of change and maintenance remained as central concepts in the development of materialism. Adam Smith in the *Wealth of Nations*, published in 1776, stressed that in the consideration of fixed capital, such as machines or buildings, the concept of maintenance was of paramount import-ance.[37] Karl Marx in *Das Kapital* of 1873, in conceiving that the mode of pro-duction was the driving force of an economy, incorporated into his materialism the Hegelian dialectic of growth and change, saying that although "philosophers have interpreted the world in various ways, the real task is to change it".[38]

In order to see how the category of Modality fits into our system of categories, we need to check its conformity with the twin principles of complementation and combination, which we shall now take in turn.

PRINCIPLE OF COMPLEMENTATION (ORANGE VERSUS BLUE)

The category of Modality complements that of Disjunction and its typical concepts of Space, Form and Being with the concepts of Time, Matter and Becoming respectively (Figure 47):

(1) Time versus Space: Hume considered space and time as two kinds of con-tiguity; Kant as two forms of sensible intuition. Hegel saw space and time as thesis and antithesis for which matter was the resulting synthesis,[39] and we might compare these views with the more recent, and dubious, view of time as merely a "fourth dimension"[40] in the mathematical calculations of relativity theory. An interest in "space-time" has led to such books as Alexander's *Space, Time and Deity* of 1920 and Giedion's *Space, Time and Architecture* of 1941.

(2) Matter versus Form (or Content versus Form): Kant distinguished between "matter . . . . which corresponds to sensation" and "form . . . which allows of its being ordered in certain relations".[41] A few years later, Schiller saw art as a unity of form and content in its reconciliation of two basic drives: *Stofftrieb*, which would bind us in the stream of time to nature and reality; and *Formtrieb*, which in lifting us out of time would allow a contemplation of harmony in the diversity of perception.[42]

(3) Becoming versus Being: Friedrich Schlegel said of Romantic art that "it should forever be becoming and never perfected", and he saw in Gothic architecture a reflection of the profusion of nature and its ever continuing growth.[43] A. W. Schlegel too, saw everything as "an eternal becoming, an

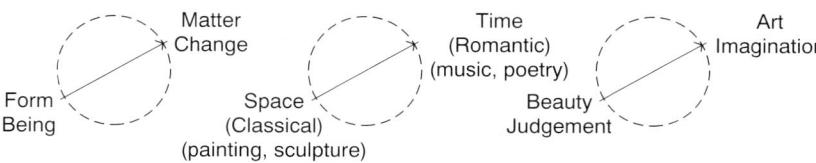

Figure 47 *Principle of complementation. Shows various concepts of the Romantic period and illustrates the shift of emphasis from the primary category of Disjunction to the secondary category of Modality. Music, however, also has a strong "spatial" element, and both painting and poetry rely heavily on the category of Inherence*

unintermitted process of creation".[44] If Being, for Hegel, could be "identified with matter, with what persists amid all change" then its complement was to be seen as a Becoming:

> "Becoming always contains Being and Nothing in such a way that these two are always changing into each other and reciprocally cancelling each other. . . . Even Becoming however, is an extremely poor term, it needs to grow in depth and weight of meaning. Such deepened force we find for example in Life. . . . All life is a becoming".[45]

PRINCIPLE OF COMBINATION (ORANGE (RED + YELLOW))

The category of Modality and its typical concepts of Time, Matter and Change can be seen as a combination of concepts drawn from both the category of Causality (motion, activity, action and reaction, etc.) and the category of Inherence (abstraction, qualification, idealization, etc.) (Figure 48).

(1) Time (succession + duration): Although architecture in the eighteenth century was seen with painting and sculpture as one of the static arts, there were aspects to it such as Blondel's sequences of spaces[46] that could be compared with the more time-based arts of music, poetry and drama. Our ideas of time, Kant said, come from our continually changing perceptions. "All such alterations," he said, "take place in conformity with the law of cause and effect" and consist of "contradictorily opposed predicates" meeting inherently "in one and the same object, one after the other".[47] Henri Bergson contrasted the idea of succession with that of duration where ". . . like experience, its phases melt into one another and form an organic whole".[48]

(2) Matter (properties + qualities): In the consideration of materials, two things are important: first, how it will perform in use; and second what quality will be appropriate in a particular situation. In Hegel's logical system the material essence of a thing was seen as a synthesis of its causal interrelation with other things, and its inherent relations of identity and difference. "Substance is," he said, ". . . the totality of accidents", and these are of two kinds: its properties which relate to the causal functioning of the material; and its qualities through which it can be compared with similar materials.[49] Peirce

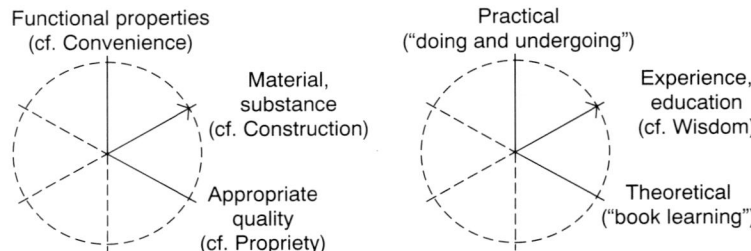

Figure 48 *Principle of combination: The diagram above-left indicates the Causal and Inherent aspects of matter (compared with Pugin's Convenience, Construction and Propriety). The diagram above-right indicates Dewey's practical and theoretical aspects of education*

confirmed the difference when he said ". . . mere qualities do not resist . . . we directly perceive matter through reaction".[50]

(3) Becoming (efficient + final cause): The coming into being of ideas in the imagination of the artist began to be likened in the eighteenth century to that of organic growth. Goethe, for example, inspired by Strasburg Cathedral saw "Gothic architecture as an organic product of growth in the mind of genius".[51] The idea of the organic in German thought can be traced back to Leibniz who explained the growth of plants through two causes borrowed from mediaeval philosophy: the Efficient Cause in the light, heat and moisture required; and the Final Cause in "the notion of the plant itself"[52] which is present even in the seed. The idea of an inherent unifying idea explained not only the initial growth of the plant but also its subsequent "self-maintenance" which Schelling referred to when he asked, "What is the perfection of an individual thing? Nothing but the creative life within it, its power of self-maintenance".[53] Less prosaically, we may see similar ideas beginning to emerge around 1850 in the new field of thermodynamics, and in particular, the concepts of entropy and homeostasis which were later to be incorporated into general systems theories.[54]

✻

Now that we have suggested a possible way of analysing the concepts included under the category of Modality, we can turn to some of its major concepts of relevance to architecture. These include the notions of imagination and expression which were developing at the time, and particular ideas concerning art and construction, and the materials and components, necessary to both.

THE IMAGINATION

John Foster, in 1805, in an essay entitled *Application of the Epithet Romantic*, concluded that the term "Romantic" was generally applied to works where "imagination was more in evidence than judgement".[55] The polarity between imagination and judgement can be traced back to Hobbes who had said that Judgement was the ability to discern differences, and Imagination (or "Fancy")[56] was the ability to discern similarities. Locke used the term "Wit" for the ability to bring ideas together, as opposed to Judgement which separated them from one another.[57] In Kant, the Judgement is mainly disjunctive and analytical whereas "the Imagination is the synthetic faculty" whose function lies in relating or bringing ideas together.[58]

Although the mind in the eighteenth century was generally thought of as operating through the association of ideas, Hume noted in addition, the requirement for a controlling design:

"In all compositions of genius therefore 'tis requisite that the writer have some plan or object . . . a production without a design would resemble more the ravings of a madman than the sober efforts of genius and learning . . . [ideas] must be related to each other in the imagination and form a kind of unity which may bring them under one plan or view."[59]

Such "genius" was generally held to "transcend known rules", and in the nineteenth century, particularly under Shelley and Thomas Carlyle, it became an unconscious organic activity outside the direction of the conscious will.[60]

Given association as efficient cause, and controlling ideas as final cause, the next stage in the development of the imagination was to differentiate between the mechanical and the organic conception of the mind. "What we need in philosophy", Coleridge wrote to Wordsworth in 1815, "is the substitution of life for the philosophy of mechanism",[61] and in his *Biographia Literaria* he distinguished accordingly between the Primary Imagination or Fancy, and the Secondary Imagination:[62]

(1) The Primary Imagination is mechanical, works through the laws of association and is the primary agent of perception.
(2) The Secondary Imagination is organic and "dissolves, diffuses and dissipates in order to recreate".

Influenced by Fichte's notion of an imagination which "gathered together opposites", Coleridge set down the twin principles of combination and polarity through which it worked:

"The poet diffuses a tone and spirit of unity that blends and (as it were) fuses each into each, by that synthetic and magical power, the imagination. This power reveals itself in the balance or reconciliation of opposite or discordant qualities."[63]

Benedetto Croce, a century later, also remarked on these twin principles, but in addition denoted the fields in which such a synthesis needs to be realized: "There is a double movement of the mind, the dialectical movement through opposites and the cyclical movement through distinct levels . . . aesthetic, practical, theoretical . . ."[64]

The difference between analysis and synthesis began to be compounded by a further difference between mechanical synthesis and organic synthesis, or the synthetic and the organic. I. A. Richards saw the difference as merely one of complexity between the number of "links" or "cross-connections" involved.[65] It was an "inadequate psychology" he said, that set up "thinking and feeling as being inimical to one another".[66] Reason as well as Imagination was needed in the design process and Peirce described three kinds of reason that might be brought to bear: namely, deduction from initial premises; induction based on experiment and observation; and abduction which lay in the recognition of general characteristics in order to limit the range of possibilities.[67] Regarding deduction he said:

> "We form in the imagination some sort of diagrammatic representation of the facts as skeletonized as possible . . . either geometrical, that is such that familiar spatial relations stand for relations asserted in the premises, or algebraical. . . . This diagram which has been constructed to represent the same relations which are abstractly expressed in the premises is then observed, and a hypothesis suggests itself that there is a certain relation between some of its parts. . . . In order to test this, various experiments are made upon the diagram which is changed in various ways . . . this is called diagrammatic or schematic reasoning."[68]

Through the principle of combination it should hardly surprise us that reasoning and the use of imagery should be linked together in the creative process. Samuel Johnson brought the two together when he said that "Poetry is the art of uniting pleasure with truth, by calling imagination to the help of reason";[69] and before him Thomas Hobbes had said that "All that is beautiful or defensible in building . . . is the workmanship of fancy but guided by the precepts of true philosophy".[70]

ART: MATERIAL AND CONSTRUCTION

Another important concept that can be discussed under the category of Modality is that of art, particularly in the sense of arts and crafts, and in this section we shall introduce the subjects of material, expression and construction.

At the beginning of the eighteenth century, art in general was seen as it had been from Classical times as a productive craft and a skill to be learned. Addison, for example, in contrasting nature and art, said that whereas nature could be viewed as a "wilderness of noble plants", art was more like a garden "shaped by the skill of a gardener".[71] However, Didérot in his article on "Art" in the *Encyclopédie* was beginning to notice a shift away from the idea of art as craftsmanship to the idea of art as the expression of genius.[72] He confirmed the view that art partook of both the practical and the theoretical spheres, and the development might therefore be seen as a shift in emphasis, from craftsmanship representing the practical side to genius representing the theoretical. E. L. Boullée, who succeeded J. F. Blondel at the Academy of Architecture, moved so far from the practical nature of building that he concluded that it was "sufficient activity for the architect merely to propose a design".[73]

Alexander Pope in his *Prefaces* of 1711 differentiated between natural and artful genius in his comparison of the works of Shakespeare and Homer. The originality of Shakespeare, in Pope's opinion, drew from "the fountains of nature", while the art of Homer "came to him not without some tincture of learning".[74] The analogy he made was that between "an ancient majestic piece of Gothic architecture" and a "neat modern building", presumably Neoclassical (and perhaps something like the prototypical Buckingham House of 1705).[75]

It should be noted that even in the works of the secondary imagination which may appear to be created out of nothing (like Shelley's "great statue or picture growing as a child in its mother's womb")[76] there was a content of ideas which in being "dissolved, diffused and dissipated" became expressed in some way in the finished work. Shelley talked of a poem as the "expression of imagination",[77] and A. W. Schlegel defined the word "expression" (*Ausdruck*) in this context as "being very strikingly chosen: the inner pressed out as though by a force alien to us".[78] Expression was becoming a central concept in the theory of art, and we should note here two distinct kinds, the expression of either mental or bodily attributes which corresponded to the theoretical and practical aspects of art respectively.

(1) *Expression of mind*: In considering the cognitive material, or content of the mind, out of which the work of art will arise, we may think in terms of either specific ideas, such as Coleridge's "expression of purpose",[79] or the more general "expression of personality" which Abrams described: "The primary qualities of a good poem are literally the attributes of the mind and temper of its composer: sincerity, integrity, benignity, shrewdness, etc."[80] John Keble in 1831 attempted to establish the personality of Homer from the *Iliad*,[81] and we might compare this with attempts to establish the personality of an architect from his buildings. Coleridge had said that the imagination echoes the creative principle of the universe,[82] and there was a religious analogy too when Albrecht Dürer said that "Man like a God . . . can pour forth that which he hath for a long time gathered into him from without".[83] The idea that what is expressed is dependent on what had previously been taken in, either through education or general experience, led, for example, to Auguste Comte's connection between art and education[84] and John Dewey's notion of "art as experience . . . a doing and an undergoing".[85]

(2) *Expression of body*: The expression of self in art was seen in a sense as stemming from the idea of pride. Pride was the first of Hume's three secondary categories, and he suggested that it was based on the "double relation"[86] of first, the inherent idea of self, and second, a particular subject, the "cause", which fell into three main types corresponding to mind, body and estate:

> "Pride or self-esteem may arise from either the qualities of the mind: wit, good sense, learning, courage, integrity; from those of the body: beauty, strength, agility, good mien, address in dancing, riding and fencing; or from external advantages: country, family, children, relations, riches, houses, gardens, horses, dogs, clothes."[87]

While expression of estate may be seen, for instance, in the patronage of the wealthy, the expression of bodily attributes is more clearly exemplified in the arts of singing and dancing. We might think of Schiller's expression of joy in the things of nature ". . . the tacitly creative life, the serene spontaneity of its activity",[88] or Shelley's "ineffable joy"[89] in poetic composition. Hume, in his list of bodily attributes, added after strength, agility and address in dancing, "dexterity in any manual business or manufacture".[90] Regarding the pride and skill of the craftsman, we may think of John Dewey's example of a sculptor chipping away at marble, and his view of the importance of the medium in expression: "Only where material is employed is there expression and art."[91]

*

The knowledge of materials and the ability of the craftsman to bring out the pure inner nature of the material, brings us back to the idea of art as a creative process. Shaftesbury, with an allusion that was to be borrowed by Herder and Schiller, stated that an artist or poet is ". . . a second maker, a just Prometheus under Jove . . . he forms a whole, coherent and proportioned in itself".[92] We can see here, as we saw in Addison earlier, the principle of complementation at work in bringing aesthetics into art, that art only becomes more than mere making when the beauty of form and shape are brought to bear on construction. Pugin's second principle of architecture suggested this also, that architecture should consist only of the embellishment of necessary construction, rather than in idle decoration for its own sake.[93]

It is clear that Pugin's first principle, that architecture lies in a consideration of Construction, Convenience and Propriety, reflects in its own way the Vitruvian triad of Firmness, Commodity and Delight. While in the new category of Propriety it goes some way towards indicating the requirement for a proper category of meaning, it does exemplify a common confusion between primary and secondary categories:

Vitruvius	Pugin	Category
Firmitas	Construction	A secondary category under Modality
Utilitas	Convenience	A primary category under Causality
Venustas	Propriety	A primary category under Inherence

If construction as such is to be included in a threefold grouping it should, strictly speaking, be placed with the other secondary categories. Jean Felibien, secretary of the French Academy of Architecture, for example, writing in 1699, wrote of the Gothic in terms of its construction, lightness and daring.[94] William Chambers, architect and treasurer of the English Royal Academy, similarly wrote in his *Treatise on Civil Architecture* of 1759 of the construction, lightness and boldness of Gothic architecture in reference to the constructive skills shown at Salisbury cathedral: "To those usually called Gothic architects we are indebted for the first considerable improvements in construction, there is a lightness in their works, an art and boldness of execution, to which the ancients never arrived."[95]

In order to understand Felibien's introduction of classifying buildings by their lightness, or aesthetic "weight", we need to turn to our next secondary category, that of Communication or Feeling.

CATEGORY FIVE: COMMUNICATION AND CONTEXT

The category of Communication may be compared in a general way with the corresponding mediaeval category which included the concepts of Love and the Word. Love, after Pride, was the second of Hume's three kinds of passion, and in Book II of his *Treatise* we see him developing the concept of "Sympathy, or the communication of the passions".[96] However, it is to Kant and his category of Community that we first turn for a preliminary understanding of the concepts involved, and we may note that the term is used in several senses:

(1) In any sphere of knowledge, Community results from the disjunction of parts within the whole, such parts remaining an inherent part of the whole and "reciprocally determining each other".[97]
(2) The concept of feeling may be seen to derive from a community of indistinct perceptions where "without community each appearance of a perception in space is broken off from every other".[98]
(3) The notion of communion with nature is suggested by the idea that "the light which plays between our eye and the celestial bodies produces a mediate community between us and them and shows us that they coexist".[99]
(4) Regarding communities of people, Kant regarded humanity's chief feature as "the faculty of being able to communicate", and fine art as involving the "reciprocal communication of ideas between the more cultured and ruder sections of the community".[100]

The idea of art as the "communication of feelings"[101] was continued in the nineteenth century, for example by J.F. Herbart, and perhaps most influentially by Leo Tolstoy.[102] The idea of "Communication" as a category was developed in the twentieth century by Karl Jaspers who, deriving it from Kant's Disjunction, placed it alongside his two other "existential categories": "Substantiality", which he derived from Inherence, and "Will" which he derived from Causality.[103]

PRINCIPLE OF COMPLEMENTATION (GREEN VERSUS RED)

The category of Communication complements that of Causality, and its typical concepts of Reason, Utility and Industry, with the concepts of Feeling, Poetry and Nature respectively (Figure 49).

(1) Feeling versus reason: The opposition between the cognitive and the intuitive, or the analytical and the synthetic, began to polarize in the eighteenth century

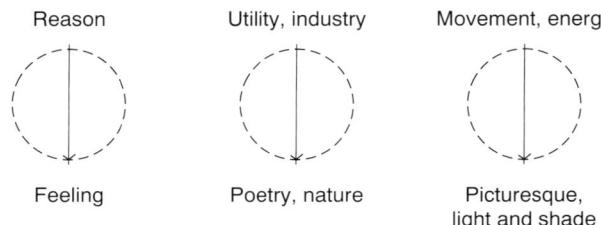

Reason   Utility, industry   Movement, energy

Feeling   Poetry, nature   Picturesque, light and shade

Figure 49 *Principle of complementation: The development of Romanticism was closely connected with Rousseau's opposition of feeling to reason (left). Other common complementary concepts of the period are shown above, centre and right*

into that between reason and feeling. Frankl, in his book on the Gothic, defined Romanticism as "the revolt of feeling against reason"[104] and we might think of Rousseau who contrasted feeling and reason in his book *Emile*.[105] Hume, in a similar way, had contrasted reason and sympathy, such "reasoning" he said, being "founded on the relations of cause and effect".[106] Hegel countered Rousseau's "appeal to heart and feelings" with reason as might be expected, but curiously conceived reason as being, in a sense, a more developed phase of feeling.[107]

(2) Poetry versus utility: The distinction between poetry and utility may be compared with the older polarity between words and deeds of which Emerson was to say "Words and deeds are quite indifferent modes of the divine energy. Words are also actions and actions are a kind of words."[108] The earlier Utilitarians derided poetry, Thomas Love Peacock, for instance saying, "Poetry cannot claim the slightest share in any one of the comforts and utilities of life . . . the poet is a waster of his own time and a robber of that of others".[109] J. S. Mill widened the scope of Utilitarianism to include feeling as a necessary complement of the good, and in saying that "Poetry is feeling"[110] joined Shelley who had described poetry as a "higher utility" and as a "great instrument of the moral good".[111] Ruskin contrasted architecture with plain utility, and said of ". . . Poetry and Architecture; the latter in some sort includes the former, and is mightier in reality".[112]

(3) Nature versus industry: The idea that reason could complement nature was typically Neoclassical and we might think of the "beautiful temples" set in woods full of "intricate thickets . . . embroideries of flowers . . . falls of water . . . rocky paths and pleasing grottoes"[113] that Addison described in 1709. As the Age of Reason became overshadowed by the Industrial Revolution, so a sense of alienation set in and we find, for example, Coleridge opposing the natural intellect to the "philosophy of mechanism",[114] and Wordsworth opposing the life of feeling to "analytical industry".[115] Auguste Comte and then Matthew Arnold[116] argued for a new Humanism to counteract the dehumanizing influence of industrial society, and William Morris in his desire "to preserve the natural beauty of the earth against the industrial age" suggested that "buildings should be fit substitutes for what they replace".[117]

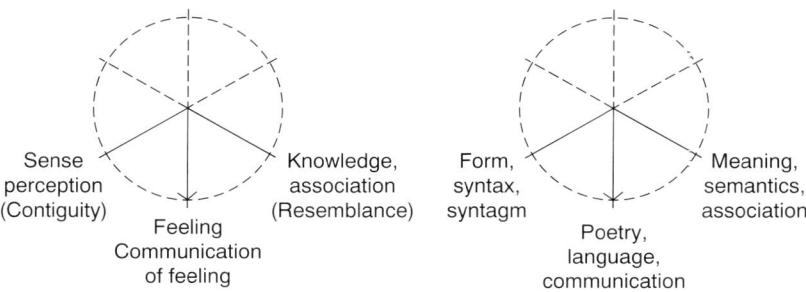

Figure 50 *Principle of combination. The Hegelian triad of sense perception, knowledge and feeling may be compared with Hume's linking of feeling with Contiguity and Resemblance (left). The two aspects of poetry, its form and meaning, may be compared with Saussure's analysis of language into "syntagm" and "association" (right)*

PRINCIPLE OF COMBINATION (GREEN (BLUE + YELLOW))

The category of Communication and its typical concepts of community, feeling and aspects of such art forms as poetry, music and dance can be seen as a combination of concepts drawn from both the category of Disjunction (e.g. number, form and perception) and the category of Inherence (e.g. participation, knowledge and meaning) (Figure 50):

(1) Community (number + participation): The co-existence of a number of things in space, said Kant, "cannot be known in experience save on the assumption of their mutual interaction . . . All substances, so far as they co-exist, stand in thorough-going community, that is in mutual interaction".[118] Community, he said, may be compared with "composition",[119] in the inherent relation of parts within a whole, and we might think of communicating doors, for instance, enabling participation in a larger space. Charles Morris defined such Communication as "the making common of some property to a number of things".[120] Hume combined two of his primary categories, "resemblance and contiguity", in explaining that the communication of feeling among peoples depended first, on "the great resemblance among human creatures" and second, on their "relation of contiguity".[121] We might compare this with the communication of buildings in a street, which buildings stand next to which, and in what respects they resemble one another.

(2) Feeling (sensation + knowledge): William Hazlitt at the beginning of the nineteenth century referred to the complex nature of feeling, distinguishing it from the more analytical parts of the mind by its indistinct nature: "In art, in taste, in life, in speech, you decide from feeling not from reason; that is from the impression of a number of things on the mind . . . though you may not be able to analyse or account for it in the several particulars."[122] According to Hegel, knowledge had a triadic movement: first, the sense perception which he termed objective; second, the mental analysis of this which he termed

subjective; and third, from the synthesis of sensation and cognition there arose self-knowledge, or feeling, in which subject and object become indistinct.[123] Kant had talked of feeling's "independence from concepts and sensations",[124] and Peirce, following Hegel, had instead combined "consciousness" and "quality" to describe, contrary to Hazlitt's view, the simplicity of feeling.[125] Hegel's merging of sensation and knowledge may be discerned perhaps in Walter Pater's description of music, "the ideal of all art . . . because in music it is impossible to distinguish the form from the substance, the subject from the expression".[126]

(3) Art (form + meaning): Albrecht Dürer, writing on painting at the beginning of the sixteenth century, described his art as arising from the twin principles of harmony and representation,[127] where harmony clearly belongs under the category of Form, and representation under the category of Meaning. As a means of communication, we may compare it with linguistics in the twentieth century, and Ferdinand de Saussure who discussed language in terms of syntagmic and associative relations,[128] or Rudolf Carnap who saw language as a combination of syntax and semantics.[129] The idea of art as a form of communication developed in the twentieth century and we may see the two aspects of form and meaning expressed in Bradley's concept of "significant form" introduced in 1901:

> "The style is here expressive also of a particular meaning, or rather is one aspect of that unity whose other aspect is meaning. So that what you apprehend may be called indifferently an expressed meaning or significant form."[130]

Clive Bell popularized the notion in his book *Art* which appeared in 1913:

> "These relations and combinations of lines and colours, these aesthetically moving forms I call 'significant form' . . . Significant form is the one quality common to all works of visual art."[131]

*

Now that we have looked at possible ways of analysing the concepts included under the category of Communication, we can turn to some of its major concepts of relevance to architecture. These include notions of feeling which were being explored at the time, including ideas of personification and anthropomorphism, and the notions of townscape and landscape.

FEELING: EMPATHY AND SYMPATHY

To understand the role of feeling in architecture we might best approach the subject through its development in poetry and music. Voltaire, writing before Rousseau, had described poetry as "almost nothing but feeling",[132] and both Herder and J. S. Mill, for example, were to define poetry as "expression of feeling".[133] A distinction was beginning to be drawn between:

- Feeling derived from the meaning of the words
- Feeling derived from their overall pattern.

Abrams described the analogy as that of poetry seen as painting, or poetry seen as music.[134] Adam Smith distinguished between the communication of information, on the one hand, and the communication of feeling, as in music, on the other, whose effect "has been called expression" and which "in fact signifies and suggests nothing".[135] Novalis went so far as to say that even "painting and the plastic arts are therefore nothing but a figuration of music"[136] and led the way for both Schelling who, as we have seen, likened architecture to "frozen music",[137] and Herbart who in 1808 said "Like the musician, the architect in designing a building, interlaces pattern with pattern . . . music should express feelings, as though the feelings aroused by it were the basis of those rules of double and single counterpoint in which its true essence lies".[138]

A correlation, or what T. S. Eliot was later to call an "objective correlative",[139] was beginning to be distinguished between the feelings expressed and the shape of the words or the musical pattern used to express the feeling. J. S. Mill said that poetry "embodies itself in symbols which are the nearest possible representation of the feeling in the exact shape in which it exists in the poet's mind".[140] Eduard Hanslick, the music critic, in 1854, limited the type of feeling that could be expressed by music to those relating to form and motion:

> "A certain class of ideas, however is quite susceptible of being adequately expressed by means which unquestionably belong to the sphere of music proper . . . those associated with strength, motion, ratio; the ideas of intensity, waxing and diminishing, of motion, hastening and lingering, of ingeniously complex and simple progression . . . that is, only their dynamic properties."[141]

Richard Wagner disagreed with such a limitation and declared that in his work the whole range of human feeling could be expressed.[142]

To understand one aspect of this difference of opinion we must return to our initial distinction between feelings based on meaning or significance, and feelings based on the form or the "dynamic properties" of the work, and see how this developed into the difference between feelings of sympathy and feelings of empathy respectively. Mitchell in 1907 gave the following formulation:[143]

- Sympathy: "having fellow-feeling with", the emphasis is on shared ideas between one person and another, or one building and another, through resemblance
- Empathy: "reading a feeling into others or into things", here the emphasis is on the form, shape or spatial configuration of the person or thing.

(1) *Sympathy*: According to Hume, sympathy depended on "the great resemblance among human creatures".[144] Our sympathies might lie in the story behind a figure carved in stone; in our knowledge of the artist who produced the work; in the imagined life of the inhabitants who lived in the building so many years ago; or even in the thoughts of our fellows whom we imagine experience the work in a similar way to ourselves. Wordsworth defined a poet as someone who ". . .

carrying everywhere relation and love, binds together by passion and knowledge, the vast empire of human society, as it spreads over the whole earth, and over all time . . . he utters feelings which by habitual and direct sympathy connect us with our fellow beings".[145] Jane Austen in 1813, in *Pride and Prejudice*, described a fashion for visiting country houses, Blenheim, Chatsworth and "Pemberley", and how the enjoyment of her heroine in the latter was increased by imagining herself as mistress of the house, and how in such rooms she would have entertained her family.[146] Sir Walter Scott introduced with *Waverley*, in 1814, the genre of the historic novel, and in speaking of art as "communication" invited sympathy between his readers and the historical characters of the past.[147] Ruskin too, talked of "a sense of strange companionship with past generations in seeing what they saw. . . . With the thought of them rose strange sympathies with all the unknown of human life."[148]

In *What is Art?*, Tolstoy published in 1896 perhaps the most comprehensive set of ideas relating to feeling, sympathy and communication. He defined art as ". . . a medium for communicating feelings . . . by means of movement, lines, colours, sounds or forms expressed in words: to transmit that feeling so that others may experience the same . . . this is the activity of art".[149] The aims of art were of the highest: ". . . a means of union among men, joining them together in the same feelings. . . . The subject matter of Christian art is such feeling as can unite man with God and with one another. . . . Each is glad that another feels what he feels, glad of the communion established".[150]

(2) *Empathy*: Although empathy is generally regarded as a twentieth-century concept, developed in particular by Theodor Lipps in his *Aesthetik* of 1903, the term *Einfühlung* was discussed by R. Vischer in 1873,[151] and even mentioned by Novalis who, in 1798, described it as ". . . merging himself with natural beings through the medium of sensuous perception, feeling himself, as it were, into them".[152] Lord Kames in 1762 wrote that "an elevated object makes the spectator stretch upwards . . . a great object makes the spectator endeavour to enlarge his bulk".[153] We might here begin to distinguish between feelings which we read into the mass of things and feelings which we read into the spaces between things. Felibien classified buildings according to their aesthetic "weight":[154] Romanesque was heavy; Gothic was light; and Classical was the mean between the two. Avril, on the other hand, writing in 1774, suggested a sense of movement upwards in describing a Gothic vault that "seemed to spring from the very foot of the piers that support it".[155] Hegel also described "the pointed arch continuing in a visual way the pier itself",[156] but went further, and in allowing for "movement of the soul" introduced a new significance for interior space.[157] Frankl reminds us of the image of the architect floating through a Gothic church in a picture painted by Moritz von Schwind, a close friend of Schubert.[158]

By the middle of the nineteenth century the imagery of perceived movement was fairly commonplace. In Germany in 1852 we find Kugler, for example, saying "The consciousness of the observer . . . ought as it were to identify itself with the life that inspires the organism, soar aloft with it, radiate out with it in the piers, curve upwards with it in the vaults".[159]

In England too, between 1851 and 1853, Ruskin was completing the *Stones of Venice* where, in a passage which also illustrates the principle of complementation, he said:

> "Gothic is not only the best, but the only rational architecture as being that which can fit itself most easily to all services vulgar or noble. . . . Undefined in its slope of roof, height of shaft, breadth of arch or disposition of ground plan, it can shrink into a turret, expand into a hall, coil into a staircase or spring into a spire".[160]

These statements might be compared with those of Lipps who described the feeling of empathy by saying:

> "I feel myself in the contemplated object . . . I am even spatially in its position. . . . So far as my consciousness goes I am absolutely identical with it. . ."[161]
>
> "I feel myself thus in the contemplated object . . . as though we actually made the movements we were watching. . . . This is what is meant by Empathy, that the distinction between the self and the object disappears, or rather does not yet exist."[162]

CONTEXT: TOWNSCAPE AND LANDSCAPE

From Kant's idea of a necessary community among our perceptions, without which we can have no knowledge, there arose the notion of context. Comte, for example, held that literature is only fully explicable in terms of context.[163] Hippolyte Taine, who succeeded Viollet-le-Duc at the Ecole des Beaux Arts, listed three categories that govern context, namely Surroundings (*Milieu*), Race and Epoch.[164] If we think of these as objective in some way, then to them we might bring those subjective elements that had been seen from Locke and Hume onwards as playing an important part of perception. Wordsworth reflected the view that there was a balance between informing the senses from both the object and the mind, ". . . what they half create, and what perceive".[165] The context surrounding our perceptions might therefore be seen as a combination of the two realms, subjective and objective, each drawing in turn from the Disjunctive and Inherent categories:

	Disjunctive	*Inherent*
Subjective:	Colour	Association
Objective:	Surroundings	Epoch

In architecture, the division of context into townscape (which is a twentieth-century term) and landscape follows in a way an older division between art and nature, with the difference that each begins, in the eighteenth century, to draw on elements from the other.

Townscape and the Picturesque

In contrast to the geometric planning of the new towns of the eighteenth century, such as Nancy from 1750, Bath from 1754 and Edinburgh from 1768, there was also developing in this period the notion of the Picturesque. Following Gilpin's publication of 1792, Uvedale Price in his *Essays on the Picturesque* of 1794 defined the term as follows: "The qualities which make objects picturesque are as distinct as those which make them beautiful or sublime . . . the two opposite qualities of roughness, and of sudden variation, joined to that of irregularity are the most efficient causes of the picturesque."[166]

A feeling for light and shade, which had been connected with the term since it was first mentioned as "*alla pittoresca*" by Giorgio Vasari in 1550,[167] was, with atmosphere, incorporated in the definition of the Picturesque by Kugler. Robert Adam, like Vanbrugh before him,[168] described the idea in terms of movement, ". . . the rise and fall, advance and recess. . .",[169] and we might think of the comparison that A. W. Schlegel made between architecture and dancing.[170] Price spoke of "age and decay" as important factors, an idea on which Ruskin elaborated in his *Lamp of Memory*: "For indeed the greatest glory of a building is not in its stones, nor in its gold. Its glory is in its age, and in that deep sense of voicefulness, of stern watching, of mysterious sympathy, nay even approval or condemnation, which we feel in walls that have long been washed by the passing waves of humanity."[171]

If the Picturesque elicits sympathy from the complex or affective side of human nature, then we may suppose that its opposite, the geometrical, must induce sympathy from the rational side of human nature. George Santayana, for example, said, "the very process of perception is made delightful by the object's fitness to be perceived . . . a symmetry and an individuation which helps us to distinguish objects".[172] Thomas Hulme, in discussing the preference for geometric patterns by some cultures because they rise above the "intransience of the organic", said "The disgust with the trivial and accidental characteristics of living shapes, the searching after an austerity, a perfection and a rigidity which vital things can never have . . . lead here to the geometrical".[173]

Here we find ourselves returning to the squares, the crescents and the circuses that typified the new towns of the eighteenth century. While there may be pleasure to be derived from contemplating the grid layout and axes that determine their overall form, a lot of the delight may, perhaps unconsciously, be coming from the trees, the weathered stone, the sense of age, and other elements which properly belong under the Picturesque.

Landscape and Nature

The change that was taking place at the beginning of the eighteenth century, away from formal gardens to a preference for more irregular landscaping, was recorded by Addison in his essay *Nature and Art*:

> "Our English gardens are not so entertaining to the fancy as those in France or Italy where we see a large extent of ground covered over with an agreeable mixture of gardens and forests . . . more charming than that neatness and elegance which we meet in our country. . . . Our trees rise in

cones, globes and pyramids. I would rather look upon a tree in all its luxuriancy and diffusion of boughs and branches than when it is trimmed into a mathematical figure."[174]

Yet if this reflected the preference for art to resemble nature, Addison elsewhere suggested that nature should also resemble art or at least that a garden should look like a picture. The following passage hints at this early interpretation of the Picturesque and ends with another allusion to the principle of combination:

> "We find the works of nature still more pleasant, the more they resemble those of art; for in this case our pleasure arises from a double principle, from the agreeableness of the object to the eye, and from their similitude to other objects."[175]

Schiller in his essay *On Naïve and Sentimental Poetry* written in 1795, emphasized the central theme of a love of nature about which these shifts take place, and he reminds us of the sufficiency of simple forms and meanings in folk art and decoration which were of interest in the eighteenth century:

> "There are moments in our lives when we dedicate a kind of love and tender respect to nature in plants, minerals, animals and landscapes; as well as to human nature in children, in the customs of country folk and to the primitive world . . . simply because it is nature."[176]

At a more complex level we might think of the imitation of nature in the ornamentation of the Rococo style, or F. Schlegel's description of Cologne Cathedral as a profusion of vegetable forms.[177] Ruskin too, saw beauty as being "derived chiefly from the external appearance of organic nature", the pointed arch resembling the profile of a leaf for example,[178] and it was not until R.G. Collingwood suggested that the essential nature of sympathy lay in "the love that life feels for life"[179] that a preference for real plants as opposed to their imitation can be seen to emerge.

Personification and Anthropomorphism

With regard to the connection between human nature and external nature, Wordsworth emphasized the "nature that connected him with the world".[180] Coleridge, in a similar way, described one of the poet's objectives as being to "make the external internal, the internal external, to make nature thought and thought nature".[181] For Coleridge, art was "the power of humanizing nature, or infusing the thoughts and passions of man into everything which is the object of his contemplation".[182] The personification that had been part of Neoclassicism, the attribution of human form to the virtues, for example, gave way to something based on feeling rather than intellect. Kant, for example, said: "We call trees and buildings majestic or dignified, and meadows smiling or gay; even colours are called pure, chaste, tender because they arouse feelings".[183] Hegel, with his concern for the spiritual, defended personification: "Personification and anthropomorphism have been freely blamed as a degradation of the spiritual; but art if it is to make mind apprehensible to sense must rise to such anthropomorphism, for it is only in body that mind is adequately manifest to the senses."[184]

There was an undercurrent of pantheism that passed from Shaftesbury to the German Romantic movement, and through Hegel was to influence Peirce:

> "Every scientific explanation of a natural phenomenon is a hypothesis that there is something in nature to which the human reason is analogous . . . there is a degree of baseness in denying our birthright as children of God and in shamefacedly slinking away from an anthropomorphic conception of the universe."[185]

In Volume Two we shall see how this theme develops in architecture, in particular through the works of Rudolf Steiner who founded the Anthroposophical Society in 1913,[186] and Geoffrey Scott, who in his book on Humanism was to describe architecture in terms of the "transcription of bodily states".[187]

CATEGORY SIX: WILL AND POLITICS

The development of the concept of the Will, which had been a feature of Augustine's thought, is of importance in our consideration of the freedom of expression of an artist or architect, and the political system under which he finds himself. Although Rousseau may be credited with an early consideration of the Will, particularly in relation to government and politics, we see it emerging as a separate category of thought most clearly in the thoughts of Hume, Kant and Schopenhauer:

(1) The third and final section of David Hume's treatment of the Passions was entitled "Will and the Direct Passions". Following Hobbes's view of the Will as being the strongest of all the natural desires,[188] Hume similarly linked the ideas of Will and Emotion. "Strength of mind," he said "implies the prevalence of calm passion above the violent".[189]

(2) Volition, or desire, was one of Kant's three faculties of the mind,[190] and, in introducing the concept of the freedom of the will, he said "When we are dealing with what happens there are only two kinds of causality conceivable by us; the causality is either according to nature or arises from freedom. . . . Freedom in the practical sense is the will's independence of coercion through sensuous impulses".[191] Kant also made the important distinction between feelings, which belong to our previous category, and emotions or "passions" which "belong to the faculty of desire".[192] Hobbes had also related emotions to motive power, saying that desires tend to be satisfied through "voluntary action whose motive power is emotion".[193]

(3) With Schopenhauer, and Nietzsche after him, the concept of the Will became of paramount importance. As one of his four categories of relatedness:[194] Being, Becoming, Will and Idea, it became the dominant theme in his book, *The World as Will and Idea*. Here Schopenhauer saw existence itself as "primal will", everywhere in restless conflict, the only escape from which were brief moments of "release and forgetting"[195] which could be enjoyed

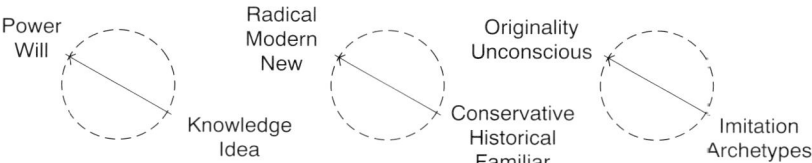

Figure 51 *Principle of complementation. The opposition of power and knowledge was known to the ancient Greeks. Schopenhauer contrasted will and idea (or representation). Other complementary ideas belonging to this group are shown above, centre and right*

through aesthetic contemplation. The ideas of Schopenhauer were overshadowed to some extent by those of Hegel, whose third category was Spirit. In fact we may compare in a general way his three highest categories, namely Idea, Nature and Spirit,[196] with Kant's three faculties of the mind: Cognition, Feeling and Will.[197]

PRINCIPLE OF COMPLEMENTATION (PURPLE VERSUS YELLOW)

The category of the Will complements that of Inherence, and its typical concepts of Idea, Knowledge, Imitation, with the concepts of Will, Power and Originality respectively (Figure 51).

(1) Will versus idea: In *Emile* published in 1762, Rousseau developed the two principles of Will and Intelligence: ". . . there is no real action without Will. This is my first principle . . . matter in motion according to fixed laws points me to an intelligence; that is the second article of my creed."[198] Fichte, in 1794, introduced the polarity between Will and Knowledge,[199] and it was his stress on the subjective "Ego" that influenced Coleridge and his subsequent description of the role of will in art as the "distinct power whose function is to control, determine and modify the phantasmal chaos of association".[200] Schopenhauer in *The World as Will and Idea* identified the two concepts with Kant's *Noumena* and *Phenomena*,[201] and it is the Will as *Noumenon*, as the unknown at the heart of self, that might be compared with the Spirit and the seat of our passions and emotions. In the twentieth century we think of the polarity between Jung's Unconscious and the Archetypes, and the power that he thought could be released from the "deepest springs of life" through their reflection in art.[202]

(2) Power versus knowledge: Francis Bacon at the beginning of the seventeenth century said that "knowledge is power",[203] and two hundred years later we find De Quincey contrasting the "Literature of Knowledge" and the "Literature of Power", where the "function of one is to teach, the other to move".[204] On the one hand, we might think of power as internal, connected with passion and emotion. For example, Edmund Burke likened the difference between Understanding and Passion to that between clear language and

strong language;[205] and similarly in this century, Ogden and Richards contrasted Descriptive or Symbolic language with Emotive language.[206] On the other hand, we might see power as external, as political power complementing ideology, as the military wing complementing the political wing, or even in such polarizations as Whig versus Tory or the later Radical versus Conservative. Locke made the distinction between making laws and enforcing them,[207] and Hegel viewed Truth as the synthesis between Will and Freedom, on the one hand, and the Universal, or Law, on the other.[208]

(3)   Originality versus imitation: Ideas of freedom and originality in the arts were developing in the seventeenth century. Dryden spoke of "Poetic Licence" as "the Liberty which poets have assumed to themselves",[209] and even Corneille said "I love to follow the rules, but far from being their slave . . . I break them without scruple".[210] Young in 1759, introduced the distinction between imitation and originality[211] although critics up to and including Coleridge approved of the imitation of nature if modified by "original genius" or a unifying passion.[212] A. W. Schlegel used the distinction to differentiate the Classical from the Romantic. The Classical consisted of "the imitation of antiquity" and resulted in "dull school exercises"; the Romantic was "modern" and founded on "independence and originality".[213] He attacked the doctrine that "art must imitate nature" and applauded instead "the bold, great, wonderful and extraordinary".[214] From this distinction between Academicism and Modernism, we see arising the Art Nouveau and Avant-Garde movements of the late nineteenth century, and the polarization between Historicism and Futurism that was to become influential in the twentieth.

PRINCIPLE OF COMBINATION (PURPLE (BLUE + RED))

The category of Will, and its typical concepts of Emotion, Sublimity and Freedom, can be seen as a combination of concepts drawn from both the category of Disjunction (e.g. perception, quantity, form) and the category of Causality (e.g. action, movement and power) (Figure 52).

(1)   Will (existence + motivation): Hobbes combined motivation with a desire for existence when he defined the will as "a bundle of desires and aversions, drives we might say, tied together by an urge for self-preservation".[215] We might note that the progession from Being to Activity in Hegel was explained through the interposition of Non-Being. This concept was of interest to Schopenhauer in two ways: first, as deficiency, "all willing comes from want, and want from deficiency, and therefore from suffering";[216] and second, as the nothingness or Nirvana whose aesthetic contemplation Schopenhauer advocated to counteract the demands of the Will.[217]

Samuel Alexander, this century, defined Will as "response to object".[218] This comprised two factors, the perception of object or situation and the activity arising from it. Between perception and activity, and in a sense governing both, was what Ryle called the "disposition of the organism",[219] and what Richards called the predetermining attitude:

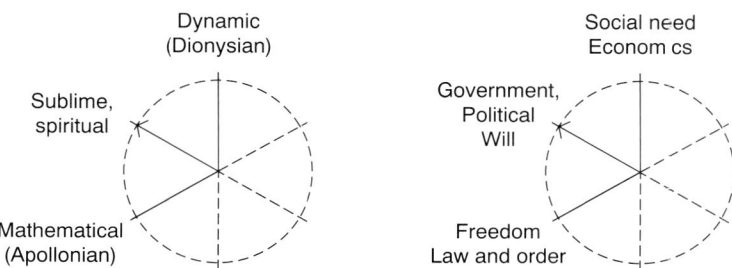

Figure 52 *Principle of combination. Two seemingly different topics, sublimity and politics, analysed through isomorphic diagrams. Kant's mathematical and dynamic sublime (left) is compared with Nietzsche's Apollonian and Dionysian spirit in art. The diagram on the right represents Bentham's twin political concerns: Liberty and Security*

"Emotions are primarily signs of attitude and owe their great prominence in the theory of artworks to this. . . . Upon the texture and form of the attitudes involved its value depends. It is not the intensity of the conscious experience, its thrill, its pleasure . . . but the organization of its impulses for freedom and fullness of life."[220]

As examples of attitude that we might encounter in art or architecture, we might contrast the attitude of Erasmus, who wrote "In Praise of Folly" in order to ridicule the pedantry of Scholasticism, with that of Giovanni Gentile who wrote, "For that lack of seriousness, that frivolity and giddiness which give birth to the whimsical – extravagant, sentimental, rhetorical and erotic art arise simply from want of feeling".[221]

(2) Sublimity (quantity + effect): Edmund Burke, in 1756, published his *Philosophical Inquiry into the Origin of our Ideas on the Sublime and the Beautiful*, and in it we see the connection made between the Will and the Sublime, ". . . a passion", he said, linked with self-preservation, and which "turns on pain and danger".[222] The first section of Kant's *Critique of Judgement* dealt with the distinction between the Sublime and the Beautiful, and we find there the division of the Sublime itself into the Mathematical and the Dynamical:[223] the Mathematical reflected the category of Disjunction and depended on quantity, size and greatness; the Dynamical in turn reflected the category of Causality and depended on the powerful effects produced. The examples he gave are the Pyramids and St Peter's in Rome where "a feeling comes home of the inadequacy of the imagination . . . which in its fruitless efforts . . . succumbs to an emotional delight".[224] In the *Will to Power*, Nietzsche similarly combined the "energy of greatness", on the one hand, with the "power of the will",[225] on the other. "Our aesthetics have hitherto been women's aesthetics", he said, "the artist has been lacking".[226] What the artist lacked was spirit, and this was of two kinds:

- Apollonian Spirit, or love of order and measure
- Dionysian Spirit, which accepts life, fully and joyfully.

"Apollonian intoxication alerts above all the eye, so that it acquires power of vision. . . . In the Dionysian state, the entire emotional system is alerted and intensified."[227]

(3) Freedom (form + power): While we might be tempted to agree with Hobbes that "liberty is the absence of external impediments to motion"[228] it is difficult to conceive of a power without form, or a motion without a place to go. Perhaps this is what Hegel meant when he said that there was no freedom without law.[229] The concept of freedom was important to the Existentialists for whom existence was likewise meaningless without activity arising from the will, a will made manifest through the power of choice. In *Roads to Freedom* Jean-Paul Sartre expressed the view that "to be is to choose",[230] and Fallico in *Art and Existentialism* argued that "art places on exhibit a way of validating existence" through the very choices that it makes. Even a piece of driftwood reflects a choice made.[231]

Regarding government and civil liberty, however, Hobbes's view was that in politics there are two different questions, one as to the best Form of the state, and the other as to its Powers.[232] Government, or indeed any kind of management, may be seen as the bringing of form to a particular set of activities, an idea reflected, for instance, in the "checks and balances" of John Locke.[233] Niccolò Machiavelli had previously said of the princes, nobles and people that "these three powers will keep each other reciprocally in check";[234] and from Charles Montesquieu's *L'Esprit de Lois* of 1748 developed "the separation of powers",[235] Judicial, Executive and Legislative, that in 1789 was adopted as a central part of the Constitution of the United States of America.

✢

Now that we have investigated possible ways of analysing the concepts included under the category of the Will, we can turn to some of its major concepts of relevance to architecture. These range from notions of emotional expression and the sublime to major developments in the realm of politics and ideology that were taking place at the time.

EMOTIONAL EXPRESSION

Both Hume and Kant distinguished between feelings and emotions, but in most accounts there is considerable overlap between the two concepts. Although both feelings and emotions draw on perception and the category of Disjunction, feelings, as we saw in the previous section, tend to borrow more from the meanings and associations of the category of Inherence; while emotions borrow more from the energy levels and motivating influences of the category of Causality.

Regarding emotions, therefore, two separate powers, belonging respectively to Cause and Effect, need to be mentioned:

- That relating to the Cause, or artist, endowed in A. W. Schlegel's words with "the power of creating what is beautiful"[236] and
- That relating to the Effect on the observer which Ross described as "the power in an object of evoking something that has value, namely the aesthetic experience".[237]

Linking the two is the work of art itself, and the question for example of how such concepts as originality and the sublime might reasonably be recognized in the work.

Emotions as Cause

The view that art was a result of blind emotion rather than wilful deliberation developed in part from the mediaeval ideas of divine inspiration and enthusiasm. We might note both the early opinion of Edmund Spenser who considered poetry to be "no arte but a divine gift . . . poured into the witte by a certain '*enthusiasmos*' and celestial inspiration",[238] and the view of François Gérard who, in the eighteenth century, linked the idea to innate genius:

> "When an ingenious track of thinking presents itself to true genius, imagination darts alongst it with great rapidity. . . . The velocity of its motion sets it on fire . . . till the mind is enraptured with its subject, and exalted into an ecstasy."[239]

"The poet is in the grip of such an emotion," he said, "that he finds almost miraculously the unity of his material". Young also thought that there was something magical or inexplicable about genius, saying that "genius differs from good understanding as a magician from a good architect". The more deliberate approach required by a "good architect"[240] was perhaps introduced by Shaftesbury when he said:

> "Every man . . . must of necessity hold his fancies under some kind of discipline and management. . . . The looser they are . . . the nearer to the madman's state. . . . Either I work upon my fancies, or they on me!"[241]

In the nineteenth century, we can discern a move towards combining deliberate choice with the force of enthusiasm, in Søren Kierkegaard, for instance, who said: "What we commit ourselves to is less important than how we commit ourselves, the energy, the earnestness, the feeling with which we choose."[242] For William Hazlitt, this input of energy was termed "gusto" or "force of style", and the concept of the "sense of power" required by the work became one of the central ideas of expressive theory.[243]

Force of style might be illustrated by Riegl who, in combating the prevailing theories of social and technological determinism current at the end of the nineteenth century, introduced the concept of a free "artistic volition" which tended to manifest itself in "stylisation . . . one-sidedly intensifying some characteristics and suppressing others".[244]

Expression of Will

The opposition of Will and Knowledge in our circle of categories is reflected in the fact that there are certain qualities in a work of art which are difficult, if not impossible, to describe. They belong to an unknown and spiritual realm. Leibniz, as we have seen, talked of a certain *"je ne sais quoi"*; Pope of the "nameless graces which no methods teach";[245] and Novalis, yet more mystically, saw that in all genuine art "a spirit is realized, produced from within . . . which is the visible product of the ego".[246] The spiritual qualities of a work were thus opposed to the known and familiar, by Shelley, for example, when he said that "Poetry . . . strips the veil of familiarity from the world and lays bare the naked and sleeping beauty which is the spirit of its forms".[247]

At the simple level, the unfamiliar expressed itself merely as novelty, a concept which had emerged from Nicolas Boileau's translation of Longinus in 1674, and which was to appear with others in the eighteenth century. "Grandeur and novelty", said Hutcheson, "are two ideas different from beauty which often recommend objects to us".[248] Novelty was "agreeable surprise" or that which stimulates "curiosity"; and the novelty of changing fashions was seen by Charles Percier in 1812, for instance, as an expression of the will.[249]

At a more complex level, the expression of the will came to be seen in the "exaggerated, animated, bold", or the "wild, visionary and extravagant" features of Romanticism as described by Lowth[250] and Foster[251] respectively. Exaggeration and distortion had been features of the Baroque, and as a manipulation of the formal or quantitative aspects of the work they compared with such concepts as the "grandeur" of size, which Hutcheson described, or the "intensity"[252] of stimulation which for J. S. Mill afforded a reason for all worthwhile poems to be short ones.[253] The idea of exaggerated size led eventually to the idea of the infinite in terms of which Hegel saw not only the soaring spires of the Gothic but also the vistas of the Classical French gardens.[254]

Emotion as Effect

Although Romantic theory in its subjectivity concerned itself mainly with the emotional expression of the artist, there were some views given on the effect of the work on the emotions of the spectator. John Dennis, in 1701, defined poetry as "an art by which a poet excites passion",[255] and Jeremy Bentham later described, more disparagingly, the poets' business which "consists in stimulating our passions and exciting our prejudices. . . . Truth, exactitude of any kind, is fatal to poetry".[256] It might be noted that Bergson took the opposite view regarding prejudice, saying that artists

> ". . . divert us from the prejudices of form and colour that come between ourselves and reality . . . they grasp something that has nothing in common with language, certain rhythms of life and breath that are closer to man than his inmost feelings, being the living law of his enthusiasm and despair, his hope and his regrets . . . they impel us to set in motion, in the depth of our being, some secret chord which was only waiting to thrill."[257]

Francis Bacon defined poetry as "accommodating the show of things to the desires of the mind",[258] and Hobbes, a little later, distinguished between pleasure of the mind and sensual pleasures, the greatest being new knowledge and new experiences respectively.[259] The connection between sensual pleasure and the "transport" or "ecstasy" of Longinus needs little elaboration, and we might note that Jules Michelet in the nineteenth century referred to the phallic imagery of Gothic spires and the "*vastes cavernes, vulves profondes*" of Indian architecture.[260] Santayana too, in the twentieth century took the view that "the whole sentimental side of our aesthetic sensibility is due to our sexual organization being remotely stirred".[261] Schopenhauer, on the contrary, saw aesthetic enjoyment as a release from desire,[262] and Wordsworth too, speaking against the "degrading thirst after outrageous stimulation" preferred the notion of poetry as "emotion recollected in tranquillity".[263]

Politics and Ideology

Another important concept belonging under the category of the Will is that of politics. Although a link with transports of delight may not be immediately obvious, we may care to think, in relation to architecture, of a Neoclassical grandeur of form, or the dreams of an architectural utopia which were often connected with political ideology.

Hobbes's *Leviathan*, subtitled *The matter, form and power of a commonwealth*, appeared in 1651, two years after the beheading of Charles I by Cromwell. John Locke's two *Treatises on Government* were written immediately after the revolution of 1688, when William of Orange was invited to accept the English throne. Both were concerned with the power of government, on the one hand, and the rights of the individual, on the other. Hobbes recognized power as the ethical good,[264] while Locke argued for a set of human rights based on a "state of nature", where "men lived together according to reason . . . in a state of perfect freedom . . . within the bounds of the law of nature, without asking leave or dependency upon the will of any man".[265]

Rousseau, like Hobbes, conceived of the state as an organic whole with human faculties, but whereas Hobbes had seen its soul as the monarch, Rousseau saw its soul as the "general will".[266] His book, *The Social Contract*, with a title borrowed from Locke, influenced the ideology of the French Revolution and, according to Russell, its "Rationalist" and "Romantic" tendencies respectively.[267] From this political turmoil, and similar political developments across Europe, emerged left- and right-wing politics, and it will be useful to look at the development of each in turn.

Left-wing Tendencies

After the French Revolution there was a natural impulse to reconsider the fabric of society. Saint-Simon in his *Du Système Industriel* of 1821 even encouraged the "artist to take his place in society as a contributor to progress and welfare";[268] and

Victor Hugo declared that "henceforth poetry shall bear the same device as politics: toleration and liberty".[269] Pierre Proudhon thought that all government was a form of oppression and became the theorist of modern anarchism.[270]

In England, Robert Owen, a textile manufacturer, believing in education and improving the conditions of the working classes, built "villages of cooperation" at New Lanark in Scotland, and New Harmony in the USA, and it is from his "social system" that the name if not the idea of socialism first developed.[271] Like Bentham, he believed that the emphasis should be on security rather than liberty. (It may be noted in passing that Bentham held Lafayette's *Declaration of the Rights of Man* of 1789 to be "nonsense, mere metaphysics".)[272]

Bentham's proposals for reform published from 1776 onwards, evolved first into the notion of "radical reform" put forward by Fox in 1797, and then into the radicalism that was to secure middle-class enfranchisement in the Reform Bill of 1832. The Chartist movement followed immediately, demanding suffrage for the working classes and that "all should have a good house to live in, with a garden back or front, just as the occupier wants".[273]

In 1848, Karl Marx and Friedrich Engels published the Communist Manifesto which urged revolution in order to break down the hierarchies of class that separated the rich from the poor.[274] It may be noted that a distinction was drawn by Marx between his own "scientific socialism" and the earlier "utopian socialism" of Saint-Simon in France and Robert Owen in England.[275]

Movements in art and architecture began to be seen in socialist terms. Hausenstein, for example, saw in Romanesque a reflection of mediaeval feudal society, and in Gothic an expression of the collectivist spirit of the mediaeval urban population;[276] William Morris advocated his own socialist views of an art "made by the people and for the people";[277] and Plekhanov in *Art and Social Life* stated that "there is no such thing as a work of art completely devoid of ideological content" and he attacked the idea that art could be separated from life.[278]

Right-wing Tendencies

The lack of a strong revolutionary government that could combine both a realistic set of policies and a single-minded will to implement them led eventually to the *coup d'état* of 1799 and the virtual domination of Napoleon Bonaparte over Europe for the next fifteen years. Interestingly, Hegel was at Jena in 1806 when the Prussian army was routed from the outskirts of town, and perhaps it was this spectacle that confirmed his unfortunate view that in peace lies ossification, while in the strife of war, moral health is preserved.[279] Tolstoy, whose most famous novel culminated in Napoleon's retreat from Moscow in 1812, maintained his own ideals of non-violence, saying that "only by the help of art can love and trust replace the vast apparatus of police, courts, war and force".[280]

Napoleon became a figurehead for those whose views of art revolved around Romantic passions, liberty and the heroic ideal. Byron was the prime example who, inspired by that "commanding art",[281] combined the writing of poetry in its most subjective form with a practical involvement in the politics of liberation of both Italy and Greece. A useful correlation might be made here between the rise of nationalism and the cult of the individual, and it is in the writings of Friedrich Nietzsche that the seeds of fascism were to find their most potent form. For Nietzsche, the task of the artist like that of the hero, lay in expressing "bravery and composure in the face of a powerful enemy":[282]

> "What does all art do? Does it not praise? Does it not glorify? Does it not select? Does it not highlight? By doing all this it strengthens certain values. . . . Art is the great stimulus to life."[283]

The aims of art to "strengthen" and to "affirm" were applied to architecture which he saw as "a mighty act of will. . . . The victory over weight and gravity and the will to power seek to render themselves visible in a building".[284] Just as Felibien had attributed an "astonishing daring of structure"[285] to the Gothic style, so we might see in Nietzsche's adulation of the "grand style"[286] a premonition of the Neoclassical monuments that were to be erected by both communist and fascist regimes alike in the twentieth century.

Evolution and Utopia

From the works of Charles Darwin published in 1859 and 1871[287] came the idea that mankind merely represented one of the more successful species of the animal kingdom. Herbert Spencer described the process of evolution as "the survival of the fittest".[288] Spencer based his own more general theories on the principle of a gradually unfolding evolution of ideas, and described the development of the social organism in terms of an internal determinism and a belief in "progress" that constituted for him the supreme law of the universe.[289] With such a one-way system, the idea of returning to a garden of Eden, as proposed by Rousseau,[290] was clearly impossible. Yet it remained a dream for a few. "All peoples who possess a history," said Schiller, "have a paradise, a state of innocence, a golden age",[291] and for many like William Morris and the pre-Raphaelites, the future lay in just such a vision of the past.

For others, the future was to be new and challenging, and the schemes proposed often included some interesting architectural content. Thomas More coined the term "Utopia" in 1518 from two Greek words meaning nowhere, and he described a world in which all property was to be shared, where there were to be no changes in fashion, and where all the buildings were to have flat roofs.[292] In such an ideal world, Shelley would have had artists assisting politicians in making the laws as they were closer to the "indestructible order" of things: "But poets, or those who imagine and express this indestructible order, are not only the authors of language, and of music, or the dance and architecture . . . they are the institutors of laws, and the founders of civil society."[293]

The idea that hope could be found in new things was prevalent at the end of the nineteenth century. In Russia, Tolstoy, for example said that "An art product is only then a genuine art product when it brings a new feeling, however insig-nificant, into the current of human life".[294] In America, William James said that "no universe is habitable which does not contain variety and novelty"[295] and condemned the ideas of Spencer and the uninspiring nature of planned utopias. In his book *The Will to Believe* he underlined the importance of the concept of free will, for only through that, he said, could we retain the hopefulness and optimism which determinism would deny.[296]

SECTION 3

CATEGORIES IN
ARCHITECTURE AND
PHILOSOPHY
A RETURN TO THE PRESENT

CHAPTER 7

NINETEENTH- AND TWENTIETH-CENTURY CATEGORIES

There were other ideas under discussion in the nineteenth century which were to be influential in the development of the categories in twentieth-century thought. With the growing complexity of philosophical method, the twin disciplines of architecture and philosophy were certainly not growing any closer, although analogies, and examples for discussion, continued to be drawn into philosophy from the field of architecture. Peirce, for example, following Kant, spoke of "architectonic" ideas, and Martin Heidegger, as we shall see, took a generalized building as an example of a subject about which many different concepts could be predicated.

This chapter will therefore look at some of the other ideas relating to classification and categorization in the arts and sciences in the nineteenth century, before focusing on particular problems relating to categories and relations in twentieth-century philosophy.

It should be said that in Britain and the USA in the twentieth century there has been virtually no discussion in philosophy on types of category. Lewis, for example, in the USA, writing in 1929 on the formal aspects of categories and relations, stated "The assumption that our categories are fixed . . . is a superstition comparable to the belief of primitive peoples. . . . If the *a priori* is something made by the mind, mind may also alter it."[1] He did, however, suggest a distinction between concepts of categories and the categories themselves when he said that "the concepts, the modes of classifying and interpreting which they represent, undergo progressive alteration with the advance of thought . . . very likely what we recognize as explicit categories are always superficial as compared with more deep-lying forms".[2]

Similar thoughts were being voiced at Oxford. Gilbert Ryle in 1938, in a paper entitled *Categories*, concluded that it was "pure myth that there exists a finite catalogue of categories or types".[3] Yet later, he suggested that the categories were certainly definite enough to allow "category mistakes" to be made, for example by allocating the term "university" to the same category as its buildings or the mind to the same category as causal mechanism.[4]

Plate 7   *Louis Sullivan, Carson Pirie Scott Building, Chicago, 1899–1903 (British Architectural Library, RIBA, London)*

"*Conversation, character were the avowed ends: wealth was good as it appeased the animal cravings, cured the smokey chimney, silenced the creaky door, brought friends together in a warm and quiet room, and kept the children and the dinner table in a different apartment. Thought, virtue, beauty were the ends*"

Emerson

Ryle's predecessor as Waynflete Professor of Metaphysical Philosophy at Oxford was R. G. Collingwood who, in 1933 in *An Essay on Philosophical Method*, suggested that there was an important distinction between classification and categorization. Classification was primarily a part of scientific methodology, while categorization was the the province of philosophy. Whereas in scientific classification, the classes, of natural history for example,[5] aimed at being mutually exclusive, in philosophy the categories tend entirely to overlap one another. (He quoted Spinoza's interpretation of the mediaeval dictum *"Omne ens est Unum, Bonum, Verum"* to illustrate that these three predicates could be assigned to every *ens* or being):[6]

> "Kind merges into kind through degree . . . certain critical points on a scale where one specific form disappears and is replaced by another. . . . This view of the relation between the terms of a philosophical series is a relation at once of distinction and opposition."[7]

In order to develop this difference between classification and categorization, or science and philosophy, we might visualize with Lewis "A sort of hierarchy or pyramid with the most comprehensive [concepts] such as those of logic at the top, and the least general, such as swans etc. at the bottom".[8] We may see that, in a sense, categorization proceeds from the top downwards and classification proceeds from the bottom upwards. We might then expect the two to meet in the middle, but given the complexities of interrelations and cross-connections in the pyramid this rarely seems to happen.

To illustrate the relevance of this we shall take two views from the nineteenth century, one from the arts (or rather literature concerning the arts), and one from the sciences: that of John Ruskin who interestingly was a neighbour of the Collingwoods in the last years of his life;[9] and that of Peter Mark Roget, physician and secretary of the Royal Society from 1827 to 1847.

LITERARY CATEGORIES

In the nineteenth century, the novelist Emile Zola was not averse in his work to the "analytical work that surgeons do",[10] but the more typical view regarding literature was expressed by the historian, Macaulay, when he said that "Analysis is not the business of the poet . . . his office is to portray, not dissect".[11] In philosophy Schopenhauer criticized Kant's table of categories saying that such analysis ". . . does open violence to truth, treating it as nature was treated by old fashioned gardeners whose works are symmetrical avenues, squares and triangles".[12]

Typical of the criticism that was given to *Roget's Thesaurus*, which we shall investigate later, was that of E. P. Whipple, who in 1872, deplored the tendency to divorce words from feelings and "to shrivel up language into a mummification of thought".[13] But perhaps one of the most influential critics of systematization in the nineteenth century was John Ruskin:

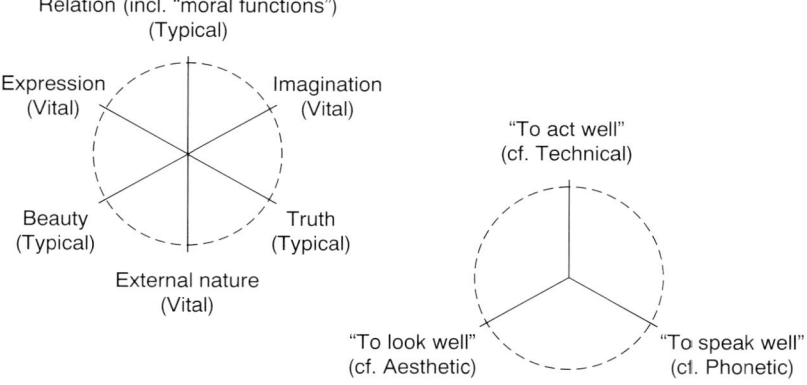

Figure 5.3 *Ruskin in* Modern Painters *described two kinds of beauty, 'typical' and "vital", the component constituents of which can be compared with our primary and secondary categories (left). In* Stones of Venice *he described three important principles of architecture which can be compared with Fergusson's categories given in parentheses (right)*

"The greatest fault of men of learning is . . . their want of perception of the connection of the branches with each other. He who holds the tree only by its extremities, can perceive nothing but the separation of its sprays."[14]

The extremities of the classificatory tree were the province of the analyst, and Ruskin distinguished between the peripheral and systematic laws that an analyst might discover, and those laws which belonged to the complexity of the whole "when the subject becomes one which no single mind can grasp":[15]

"Out of the poem or the picture once produced, men may elicit laws by the volume, and study them, with advantage, to the better understanding of the existing poem or picture; but no more write or paint another. than by discovering laws of vegetation they can make a tree to grow."[16]

The higher laws that Ruskin enumerated in the *Seven Lamps of Architecture* published in 1848 were thus not those of simple cause and effect. but instead reflected the categories or "types" that in his earlier religious phase he equated with the "divine attributes",[17] and later, with the "virtues" as personified in the stone statuettes of Venice.[18] Colours, like form, had allegorical significance and he remarked on the rainbow that it was divided "into a sevenfold, or more strictly, a threefold, order typical of the Divine Nature itself".[19] His illustration was that of Turner's painting of Apollo and the Python where "you will see rose colour and blue on the clouds as well as gold".[20] Beauty, for Ruskin, was "a reflection of God's nature in visible things" and this "Typical Beauty" of the forms was contrasted with a "Vital Beauty" of living things (Figure 5.3), a distinction which we may compare with our primary and secondary categories:

- *Typical Beauty* was concerned with form. At the beginning of *Modern Painters* Ruskin outlined his subject in terms of Beauty, Truth and Relation, the last term denoting the "moral functions and the ends of art",[21] which we may place under the category of causality.
- *Vital Beauty* was ". . . concerned not with form but expression". In Volume 3 of *Modern Painters* he argued against the Neoclassicism of Reynolds in favour of the Romantic concerns of imagination, the artist, external nature, expression and emotion.[22]

The underlying suggestion of a passive and an active grouping appeared in an appendix to *The Stones of Venice* where, in refuting "Mr Fergusson's System"[23] which stated that the Technical, Aesthetic and Phonetic (or Intellectual) aspects of architecture may be considered as mutually exclusive groups, Ruskin made alternative "suggestions as to the principles on which classification might be based". Instead of the prevailing Cartesian dualism, he proposed returning to the original threefold grouping of Body, Mind and Soul, the three natural faculties on which the laws of architecture could be based, and by subdividing each into a passive and an active aspect arrived at the formation of six categories:[24]

	Passive (typical)	*Active (vital)*	
Body:	(1) Senses	(2) Muscles	(7) Conscience
Mind:	(3) Understanding	(4) Imagination	
Soul:	(5) Feeling	(6) Resolution	

A seventh, "conscience", was added as being "inseparable from the system yet not an essential part of it". Whatever this may have meant, we might conjecture that in the *Seven Lamps* the Lamp of Sacrifice too, may have been seen as a seventh, or as introductory to the other six lamps; which may then be seen to fall into two similar groups, similar to the above if the sequence is taken vertically rather than horizontally (Figure 54):

The Seven Lamps (numbers in italic indicate Ruskin's order)[25]

	Classical (Typical)		*Romantic (Vital)*		
(1)	Beauty (4)	(4)	Life (5)	(7)	Sacrifice (1)
	(cf. Senses)		(cf. Imagination)		(cf. Conscience)
(2)	Power (3)	(5)	Memory (6)		
	(cf. Muscles)		(cf. Feeling)		
(3)	Truth (2)	(6)	Obedience (7)		
	(cf. Understanding)		(cf. Resolution)		

By a consideration of the dominant concepts found under each heading it can be seen that, except for the Lamp of Power, the pattern approximates reasonably well to that of the primary and secondary categories.

(1) Lamp of Sacrifice: As an introductory principle it discussed ideas of beauty, work, propriety and wealth, and saw architecture as both an act of devotion and a surrendering of the work to a higher will.[26]

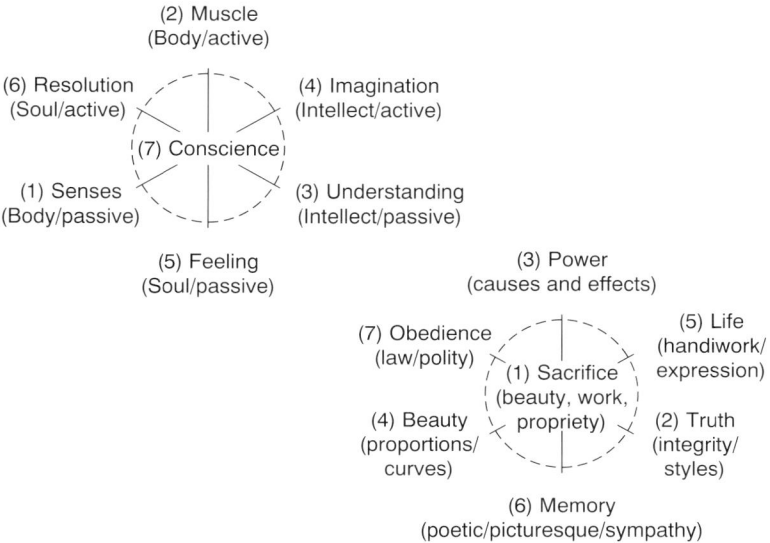

Figure 54 *Ruskin's analytical method involved dividing Body, Mind and Soul into an active and passive component (left). The resulting concepts can be compared with the* Seven Lamps of Architecture *(right) given in the order in which they appear. In the latter (1) was an introductory chapter*

(2) Lamp of Beauty: the concepts of proportion and abstraction were discussed here, and his view that although architecture is necessarily composed of straight lines, the most beautiful forms are composed of curves.[27]

(3) Lamp of Power: Much of the content of this principle falls under the category of the Sublime (or Will) or even Form in its discussion of circles and squares. The causal aspect lies in a response to powerful effects.[28]

(4) Lamp of Truth: Integrity is important as a principle, and he mentions association and historical style. Three kinds of architectural deceit are listed relating to structure, material and ornamentation.[29]

(5) Lamp of Life: The expression of vital energy and imagination were important, hence handiwork was preferable to machine work. A sense of life was reflected in variety, change and awareness of work in progress.[30]

(6) Lamp of Memory: The concept of the Picturesque and the poetic were discussed here particularly with reference to a building's age, "its voicefulness . . . and mysterious sympathy". Gothic was praised for recording past associations and memories.[31]

(7) Lamp of Obedience: The principle expressed here was not freedom of will, but law. No new style was required, but instead laws codifying for architecture "the embodiment of the polity, life, history and religious faith of a nation".[32]

If it is difficult to see the categories of Vitruvius in all this, it is because Ruskin deliberately separated architecture from building, and distinguished decoration from construction:

"The two virtues of architecture which we can justly weigh are, we said, its strength or good construction, and its beauty or good decoration . . . the intelligent part of a man being displayed in the structure of a work, his affectionate part is to be shown in its decoration . . . and when he has built his house or church, I shall ask him to ornament it."[33]

While we may note that not one of the lamps is addressed specifically to either Commodity or Firmness, we may read at the beginning of *The Stones of Venice* a formulation that, with Fergusson's system,[34] was to take Vitruvius into the twentieth century:

"We have thus . . . three great branches of architectural virtue, and we require of any building . . .
(i)   That it act well . . .
(ii)   That it speak well . . .
(iii)   That it look well . . ."[35]

In linking the second of these principles with the Intellect, the way was open for a new category of Meaning in architecture that was eventually to be added to "the new forms and functions of the art".[36] The new category naturally put pressure on the others, and while Ruskin at times placed both Commodity and Firmness under the building's ability to "act well",[37] it was clear that although three categories might still be acceptable as a core, the total number of categories was now in a position to be simply expanded.

Above all, we might note his "demand for a coherent wholeness"[38] and the need for the ultimate categories to be thoroughly integrated with one another:

"All these parts of the human system have a reciprocal bearing on one another . . . yet any one of the parts of the system may be brought into a morbid development inconsistent with the perfection of the others. . . . So that it is never so much the question, what is the solitary perfection of a given part of the man, as what is its balanced perfection in relation to the whole of him."[39]

Despite the obscurity of much of his writing, and his rejection for instance, of utility when he made the remark that "the most beautiful things in the world are the most useless, peacocks and lilies for instance",[40] he was to have a profound influence on the development of architectural criticism in the twentieth century, and we might note that both Walter Gropius[41] and Frank Lloyd Wright,[42] two of the most important founders of the Modern Movement, acknowledge Ruskin's influence on the development of their own thoughts.

SCIENTIFIC CLASSIFICATION

As an example of working from the base of the pyramid up, we might begin with Ryle's description of classification:

"Collect a range of simple, singular propositions, all similar in being about the same particular [in our case a building], then the respects in which these propositions differ from one another will be their predicates. And these predicates are classified into a finite number of families or types, the differences between which types can be indicated, though not defined."[43]

The concepts which each predicate reflects can be grouped by family resemblance which we might denote by predominant relationship type, although following Lewis and Ryle, a simple cipher or colour-coding might better reflect the idea that any name we give to these categories could itself be seen to represent a concept and therefore be subject to changing fashion:

	Relation	*(Colour)*	*Concepts*
(1)	Disjunction	(Blue)	Firmness, Form, Structure, etc.
(2)	Causality	(Red)	Commodity, Function, Utility, etc.
(3)	Inherence	(Yellow)	Delight, Meaning, Propriety, etc.

The grouping together of words of similar meaning was most notably carried out by Roget in the *Thesaurus of English Words and Phrases* published in 1852.[44] Although his notes were lost in a fire,[45] it is known that he was acquainted with the philosophers Dugald Stewart in Edinburgh and Jeremy Bentham in London, and also that he was in possession of Kant's *Critique of Pure Reason* where, in searching for headings of his own, he may well have read the following:

"This table of categories suggests some nice points and indeed is indispensable as supplying the complete plan of a whole science. . . . Since at present we are concerned not with the completeness of the system but only with the principles to be followed in its construction, I reserve this supplementary work for another occasion. It can easily be carried out with the aid of the ontological manuals."[46]

Roget's own work was carried out with the aid of manuals of synonyms (which he preferred to call "correlatives")[47] and his six main categories were not those of Kant's tables, but were similar to two other groupings found in Kant, namely Space, Time and Matter, and Intellect, Volition and Affection which corresponded to the dualistic notion of the physical world and the mental world respectively (Figure 55):

	Physical categories		*Mental categories*
(1)	Abstract Relations	(4)	Intellect
	(e.g. Time, Quantity)		(e.g. Truth, Meaning)
(2)	Space	(5)	Volition
	(e.g. Form, Motion)		(e.g. Will, Authority)
(3)	Matter	(6)	Affections
	(e.g. Organic, Inorganic)		(e.g. Feeling, Sympathy)

Although the logical basis of the *Thesaurus* has never been revised, early criticism was voiced by a younger colleague at the Royal Society, William Whewell, who said that the classification of knowledge "depended neither upon the faculties

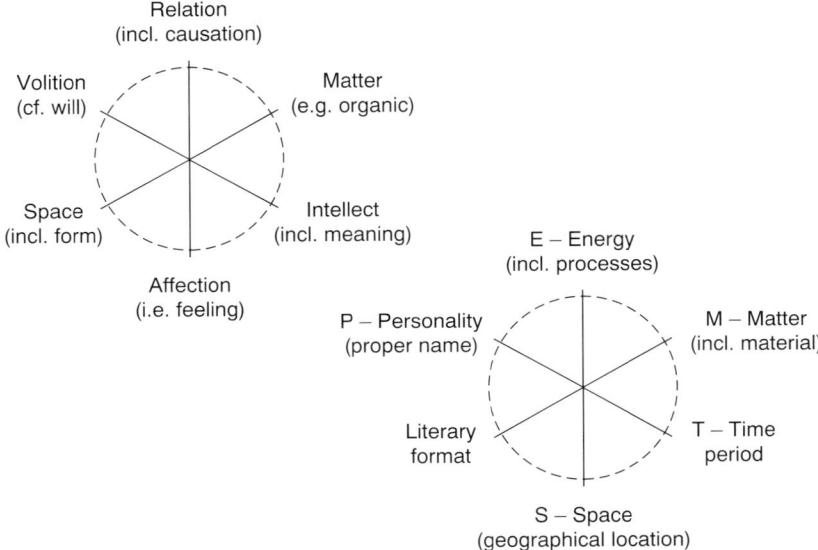

Figure 55 *Two systems of classification, Roget's (left), taken from Kant and used to structure his* Thesaurus; *and Ranganathan's (right) used as a basis for many library classification systems. "Literary format" refers to the form rather than the content of the document*

of the mind . . . nor upon the objects which each science contemplated, but upon . . . the ideas which each science involves".[48] Two examples taken from the *Thesaurus* which indicate that the initial division into Physical and Mental is questionable might include first, that "Sensation" is classified under "Matter", and second, that "Ornament" is classified under "Affections". With some minor adjustment, the *Thesaurus* might be rearranged to agree with the more rigorous system of primary and secondary categories whose development we have been following:

Primary categories	*Secondary categories*
(1) Space	(4) Matter
(e.g. Form, Quantity)	(e.g. Organic, Inorganic)
(2) Abstract relations	(5) Affection
(e.g. Causation, Motion)	(e.g. Feeling, Sympathy)
(3) Intellect	(6) Volition
(e.g. Truth, Meaning)	(e.g. Will, Authority)

Although these are not the headings that we should use, Roget's scheme has served as a useful check in collecting and arranging the simpler predicates of such propositions as "this building is X".[49] It also indicates the complexities involved, given for example that a single term like "meaning" or "to mean" has twelve separate entries depending on logical inflection.

Of more immediate use in the advancement of scientific knowledge was the development of classification systems for the arrangement and retrieval of written knowledge in the form of books, periodicals, etc. E. W. Hulme in 1911 made a clear distinction between the categories of philosophy and the classification of books, saying that the categories of the former were quite insufficient for the "welter of cross-classification and of overlapping areas of definition".[50] There was no philosophical system, for example, behind Melvil Dewey's decimal classification system,[51] first published in 1876, where building was given the number 690 and architecture 720:

100 Philosophy	600 Technology
200 Religion	700 Arts
300 Social Science	800 Literature
400 Languages	900 Geography and History
500 Pure Sciences	000 Miscellaneous

It soon began to be noticed however, that the subdivision of each category fell into similar patterns, by J. Kaiser in 1915[52] and S. R. Ranganathan in 1933. The concept of "facet analysis" was introduced by Ranganathan who determined that there were five main "facets" or "aspects" to be considered for each subject,[53] and that for each facet, time for instance, a separate "focus" could then be applied, for example, the eighteenth century. The five facets to be taken in order were:

P   Personality, the basic thing or concept
M   Matter or material
E   Energy, including operations, processes, methods
S   Space, particularly geographical location
T   Time, especially period

While Space and Time could be applied at random, each subject of the classification system was subdivided under the first three headings into its own specific pattern of "rounds" and "levels":[54]

- Rounds (P, 2P, 3P, etc.) e.g. P-Organ of body; E-disease; 2P-kind of disease; 2E-Treatment; 3P-kind of treatment; M-drug.
- Levels (P, P2, P3, etc.). In each round there may be further divisions, for example into types of organ, kinds of disease, etc.

Architecture was given the notation NA and its pattern in the system became:

$$\text{NA [P] [P2] [P3] [P4] : E}$$

Foci in [P] and [P2] denoted architecture classified by country; Foci in [P3] classified buildings by type: dwellings, castles, hotels, etc.; Foci in [P4] classified formal elements: floor, wall, roof, etc.; and Foci in [E] classified types of architectural presentation: Plan, Elevation, Section, Perspectives, Models, etc.[55]

While Ranganathan's concept of "Personality" has given some difficulty (we might compare it, for example, with Kant's thing-in-itself), his system has been used not only in compiling the CI/SfB indexing system used in the construction industry but also in compiling the RIBA's Architectural Periodicals Index. In 1953, the librarians at the RIBA, B. Mason and A. Thompson, developed a structure, since revised as part of the "Architectural Keywords" system, based on four subdivisions: Standard Subdivisions (materials, activities, services and format), Geographical Subdivisions, Date Subdivisions and Proper Names.[56] This may be displayed in terms of our primary and secondary categories as follows (Figure 55):

(1) Format of Information
(2) Activities, Services [E]
(3) Date Subdivision [T]

(4) Materials [M]
(5) Geographical Subdivision [S]
(6) Proper Names [P]

In the 1950s and 1960s, a distinction was beginning to be made in classification theory between concepts and relations. The "relational operators",[57] for instance, of J. Farradane, based on a coordination of space-factors and time-factors, included such notions as "dimensional relations", "causation or functional dependence", "association".[58] An attempt was made by Perry, Kent and Berry to break down subjects into fundamental concepts or "semantic factors", but was abandoned due to the immense complexity of relations involved even for the simplest subjects.[59] The converse of breaking down simple subjects lay in understanding how they build up into composite subjects and how the essential cross-referencing between such subjects could best be organized. With the advent of computerization, information-retrieval systems tended to shift the coordination of subjects from the indexing to the search side, and specialist vocabularies known as "thesauri" were developed to eliminate confusing synonyms by forming series of "keywords" to facilitate the search.[60]

✻

Like so many other subjects, speculation on the arts and architecture, as well as on literary classification, can only progress so far before being confronted with problems which are entirely philosophical in character. It will be necessary therefore to close this chapter with some of the most recent thoughts on the subject of categories, and the underlying concept of relationship types, so that any conclusions that we may draw can be fully and properly considered.

CATEGORIES AND RELATIONS IN TWENTIETH-CENTURY PHILOSOPHY

"The architect," Schlegel said at the beginning of the nineteenth century, "has to take into account a number of relationships",[61] giving as an example the kinds of relation involved in the construction and the purpose of a cathedral (Figure 56). While Diderot in France had discussed relations, or *rapports*, in art as early as 1751,[62] and Herbart in Germany discussed aesthetics in terms of relations in 1831,[63] it is to the United States and Britain that we shall turn to follow the concept of relation in any logical sense of the term.

Building at the centre of a
general relationship field

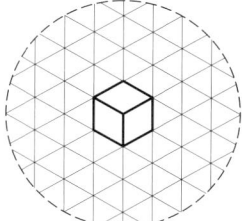

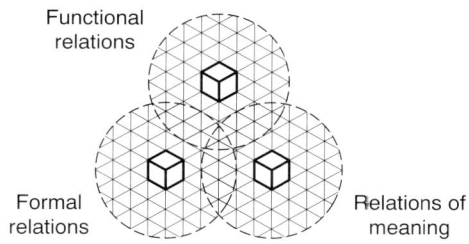

Functional
relations

Formal
relations

Relations of
meaning

Figure 56 *"The architect has to take into account a number of relationships" wrote Schlegel. We represent this concept by placing the building at the centre of a relationship field (left). More logically, we can see the building at the centre of three overlapping fields each of a different relationship type (right), namely formal relations, functional relations and relations of meaning*

Among the first fellows of the Johns Hopkins University at Baltimore, newly opened in 1876, were Charles Sanders Peirce, William James three years his junior, and Josaiah Royce, who in 1892 became professor of philosophy at Harvard. Peirce had been publishing articles on the logic of relations since 1867, and interestingly in 1890 published one entitled *The Architecture of Theories*,[64] reminiscent of Kant's view of "the architectonic character of philosophy".[65] Between 1903 and 1906, both Peirce and James lectured at the Lowell Institute in Boston, and in 1908, James travelled to England to lecture at Oxford. From there, his work influenced Bertrand Russell, who was appointed a lecturer in philosophy at Trinity College, Cambridge in 1910, and it was there that Ludwig Wittgenstein came to study a year later. Both Russell and Wittgenstein published influential books on logical analysis in 1921, by which time Wittgenstein had returned to Austria to teach, and to design a house in Vienna in the modern style.[66]

In Vienna, Wittgenstein became acquainted with the logical positivists of the Vienna Circle, and he returned to Cambridge in 1929 to rethink his earlier work and to formulate ideas which were published posthumously in 1953 as the *Philosophical Investigations*.

Meanwhile work on the categories was published in America in 1929 by C. I. Lewis who had studied at Harvard under Royce; and in England by Gilbert Ryle, professor of philosophy at Oxford, who published an essay entitled *Categories* in 1937.

CATEGORIES AND RELATIONS

In 1940, Russell, in *An Inquiry into Meaning and Truth*, asked the question:

"How far, if at all, do the logical categories of language correspond to elements in the non-linguistic world that language deals with? Or, in other words, does logic afford a basis for any metaphysical doctrine?"[67]

Objective reality
"a concatenated unity"

Subjective representation
"a colligation of concepts"

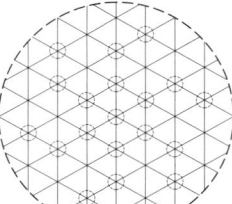
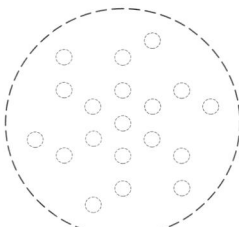

Figure 57 *If objective reality can be represented as a network of "spatial relations" and "nodes" (left), then the subjective representation of reality can be seen as a "picture" or "map" of this, emphasizing different aspects (right). Things become "colligations of concepts"; terms are likened to "centres of constellations"; and the problem becomes that of "determining the cross-bearings of a galaxy of ideas". The clear separation between mind and matter disappears, according to Russell, one emphasizing logical, and the other physical aspects respectively*

His answer, posed in slightly different words at the end of the book, was in the affirmative: "It seems that there is no escape from admitting relations as parts of the non-linguistic constitution of the world."[68]

This shift in emphasis from "categories" to "relations" reflected a development in logic which began in the nineteenth century and attempted to supplant subject/ predicate logic with a logic of relatives introduced by De Morgan in his *Formal Logic* of 1849. Its mathematical content need not concern us, but to understand the more general implications of the theory we might take from William Whewell, a contemporary of De Morgan, and another Cambridge man, the notion of a "thing" being a "colligation of concepts"[69] (Figure 57), a phrase that was to be borrowed by Peirce and Russell, and in Germany by Heidegger, who gave an architectural example. "The work of art," he said in 1935, "is a thing . . . around which its properties have assembled. . . . A building, a Greek temple, portrays nothing. It simply stands there. . . . It is the temple work that first fits together, and at the same time gathers around itself the unity of those paths and relations . . . which acquire the shape of destiny for all human beings."[70]

Elsewhere, describing categories as "modes of assertion" Heidegger compared such examples as "The house is tall . . . it is red . . . it is on the creek . . . it is an eighteenth-century one" with Kant's four categories of Quantity, Quality, Relation and Modality.[71]

The notion that the thing itself could be surrounded by a "colligation of concepts" should be distinguished carefully from, for example, Hume's associationism where it was the idea in the mind that attracted to itself other ideas through the relations of Contiguity in time and space, Causality and Resemblance. Kant clearly separated the thing-in-itself from a knowledge of the phenomenal world, and described such knowledge as "mere relations",[72] a view which underlay the Positivism of Comte and much scientific thinking of the nineteenth century. In the idealism of Hegel, however, the thing-in-itself, the symbol of the existence of the material world, was itself abandoned:

"Everything that exists stands in correlation, and this correlation is the veritable nature of every existence. The existent thing in this way has no being of its own, but only in something else."[73]

MIND AND MATTER

The idealist conclusion that if "all reality lies in relations"[74] then real existence depends on the existence of a universal mind, as Green asserted in 1874, was vigorously denied by Peirce and James. The Cartesian duality of Mind and Matter which attributed "things" to the physical world and "relations" to the mental world was no longer valid, a view which Russell reaffirmed in *Analysis of Mind* in 1921:

"Few things are more firmly established in popular philosophy than the distinction between mind and matter. . . . The stuff of which the world of our experience is composed is, in my belief, neither mind nor matter, but something more primitive than either . . . James's view that the raw material out of which the world is built up is not of two sorts, one matter and one mind, but that it is arranged in different patterns by its interrelations, and that some arrangements may be called mental, while others may be called physical."[75]

The idea that through its relations with other concepts, a clear definition of either a thing or an "object-word" could be obtained was shared initially by Wittgenstein who, writing in his *Tractatus Logico-Philosophicus*, also of 1921, began to suggest that the "primitive stuff" might be constituted out of the relations themselves:

"The world is the totality of facts, not of things . . . objects stand in a determinate relation to one another . . . a name means an object, and names are like points . . . only in the nexus of a proposition does a name have meaning."[76]
   "A proposition is a picture of reality . . . what constitutes a picture is that its elements are related to one another in a determinate way. . . . The fact that the elements of the picture are related to one another in a determinate way represents that things are related to one another in the same way. . . . Let us call this connexion of its elements the structure of the picture."[77]

He went on to differentiate between the formal relations or properties which belonged to the object and the structural relations or properties which belonged to the fact, saying that the propositions which constitute facts construct a world of objects "with the help of a logical scaffolding".[78]

VIEWS OF REALITY

The "logic of relations" as it was developed by Peirce also led to a concept of reality which he described diagrammatically in terms of "spatial relations" where a thing or term became a "node" and a relation between things became a line connecting such nodes.[79] He borrowed from Mendeleyev's table of chemical elements the notion of valency, and in order to understand his ensuing description of monads, dyads and triads, care must be taken to distinguish between the following possible interpretations:

(1) One term might be related to one, two or three others through being univalent, bivalent or trivalent.

(2) One, two or three terms might be related together to form different kinds of unity, the monads, dyads and triads, where the monad itself is an independent element of sensation.

(3) Two terms might be related in different ways through three different kinds of relation, those of firstness, secondness and thirdness which we have compared previously to relations of contiguity, causation and meaning respectively.[80]

While it is reasonably simple to picture the first two diagrammatically, we might note that in the third case, Wittgenstein introduced an arrow to depict the relation of function,[81] and both Peirce[82] and Wittgenstein[83] used the brace or bracket to depict the relation of meaning.

William James, who followed Peirce in this work, pictured the whole world as a "concatenated unity"[84] with some parts joined and other parts disjoined. There was no duality between things and thoughts, both were seen as "points of emphasis"[85] in a world of continuity. Lewis, in *Mind and the World Order* published in 1929, even queried the duality between terms and relations suggesting that we might abandon terms altogether, and look at them as being only "points of emphasis",[86] in the same way that the idealists had rejected things-in-themselves:

"Terms are analogous to points in space. A point is nothing whatever apart from its relation to other points . . . [Just as] lines may be defined by the points they connect, so points may be defined by the intersection of the lines."[87]

RELATIONSHIP FIELDS

The view that the building as a thing, and any proposition about the building, might legitimately be seen as two different areas of the same universal relationship field may be inferred from Russell. In discussing cause and effect he described how physical laws such as gravity and the mental laws of association come together in common sensation, which, he said, is subject to both kinds of law.[88] It will be recalled however, that Causality was just one among three kinds of relation which constitute the "primitive material" of the world and which could apply equally to both areas. These "overlapping fields" Collingwood compared to "different maps, in different degrees distorted, of precisely the same territory",[89] and it will be useful to see how they might be applied to both the building and the propositions which may be said to be related to it.

- *Disjunction*: The mind interprets the disjunctive relations in the world through the "scaffolding" it constructs of three-dimensional space. Part becomes oriented to part, and objects to each other according to their location relative to a larger whole. In this way, taking Heidegger's examples, the house is both "tall" and "beside a creek" through its relations within a common system of dimensions and a particular physical location.
- *Causality*: Here the building stands in a network of causes and effects where the relevant propositions relate to activity and function. The three-dimensional lattice of our first category is replaced in our understanding by something resembling a system of arrows which by their size and direction indicate input and output accordingly. Such systems may include climatic forces, cash flow or the movement of people in and around the building.
- *Inherence*: The building here finds its place among the branches of the classificatory tree by which it is differentiated from other things by its inherent qualities, and given a name, definition and meaning. The house in Heidegger's example is "red", for example, by being bracketed to other red objects; and is in the eighteenth-century style by its resemblance to other buildings of the same period.

All three relationship networks can be seen as abstractions imposed by our analytical faculties on mental representations. Their reality will only fully be able to be understood, like the realities of space and time, in terms of the complex field theories of physics and mathematics.[90]

Semantic Factors

Ferdinand de Saussure, the Swiss linguist who was developing "semiology" in France as Peirce was developing "semiotics" in the USA, likened each term of a proposition to "the centre of a constellation, the point where other coordinate terms, the sum of which is indefinite, converge".[91]

We need to turn our attention now away from the subject, the building, to "the other coordinate terms", the predicates like "tall", "functional", "eighteenth century", and consider them as terms in their own right, each standing in the middle of the same three relationship fields (Figure 58). For example, if we move from the concept of house to the concept of function we can in turn relate this idea not only to causal chains of domestic activity but through the relationships of Disjunction to the quantitative concept of efficiency, and through the relationships of Inherence to the intellectual concept of functionalism. In linguistics, as we have seen, these shades of meaning were to become known as "semantic factors",[92] and we might note that Gilbert Ryle in 1938 spoke of "sentence factors" and "proposition factors" defining them as "factors rather than parts as they cannot exist independently . . . they can only occur as factors in complexes of certain sorts".[93] Bearing in mind the different logical inflections of words when used in different sorts of contexts, we can see that it is the perceived strength or preponderance of these semantic factors that determine how each concept may be understood and classified:

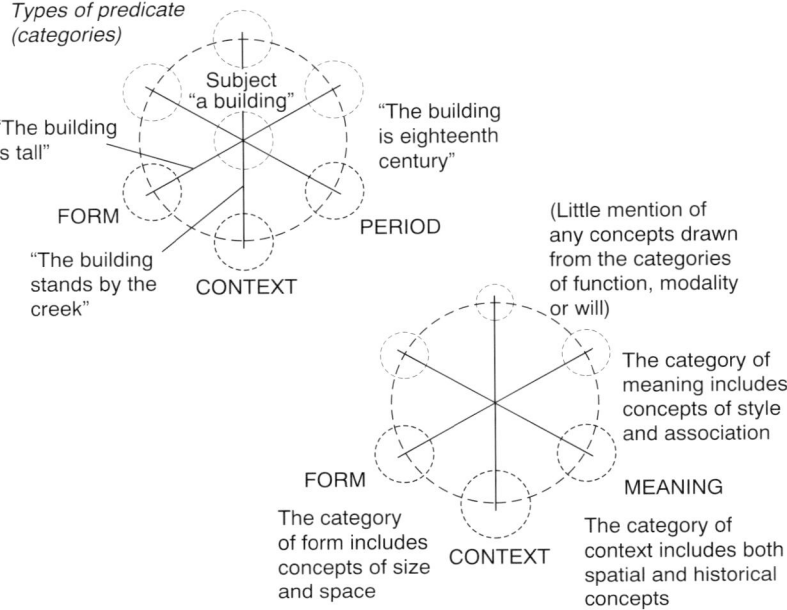

Figure 58 *Subject/predicate logic can be represented by placing the subject at the centre and the kinds of predicate (categories) around the outside. Simple propositions, such as those shown of Heidegger, link the two (left). All concepts draw their meaning from a range of categories, and the degree of emphasis on each is known as "semantic factoring" (right)*

- If a concept is strong in one field it is classified under one of the three primary categories which correspond to the three relationship fields. For instance, colour, although in one sense a quality, relates strongly to form and perception and should be classified with these concepts under the Disjunctive category.
- If a concept is strong in two fields, it should be classified under one of the secondary categories. For example, the predicate "beside the creek" is more than just one of spatial position but has strong connotations of association and meaning. The appropriate secondary category would therefore fall between Disjunction and Inherence and forms what we have called the category of Communication.

Precedent for this distinction may be found in Wittgenstein's *Tractatus* where, looking at propositions as "truth-functions", he suggested that while the predicates can be seen generally to have three kinds of value, PQR, denoting three kinds of description: Enumeration, Function and Law, combinations may occur between any two, as, for example, the "symbols that affirm both P and Q", which are thus denoted PQ.[94]

Definitions

Where the strength or preponderance of relations in two fields are unequal, a range of intermediate positions might be envisaged, and the analogy was made again by both Wittgenstein and the French linguist, Roland Barthes,[95] between the graded meaning of concepts and the colour spectrum. "And this is the position you are in," said Wittgenstein, ". . . if you look for definitions corresponding to our concepts in aesthetics or ethics . . . for all the colours merge . . . it is the field of force that is decisive".[96]

The notion that there were "object-words" which both he and Russell in the early days of logical analysis thought could be clearly defined gave way to the idea that there were no clear definitions. There is only a "halo"[97] or "corona"[98] of related meanings radiating around each term which the mind, in order to understand at all, truncates into the form of a circle.

> "Why do we call something a 'number'? Well, perhaps because it has a direct relationship with several things that have hitherto been called number. . . . And we extend our concept of number as in spinning a thread we twist fibre on fibre. And the strength of the thread does not reside in the fact that some one fibre runs through its whole length, but in the overlapping of many fibres."[99]

Ryle in *Philosophical Arguments* of 1946 similarly thought that the problem was not that of the definition of a single word:

> "The problem is not to pinpoint separately the locus of this or that single idea but to determine the cross-bearings of all of a galaxy of ideas belonging to the same or contiguous fields. The problem is not to anatomize the solitary concept, say of liberty, but to extract its logical powers as these bear on those of law, obedience, responsibility etc. . . . Like a geographical survey a philosophical survey is necessarily synoptic . . . problems cannot be solved or posed piecemeal."[100]

And so it is with architectural theory. We are not trying to pinpoint the locus of a particular idea, but to determine the cross-bearings of some of the more generalized ideas, in order to determine how their underlying logical powers may come to bear on particular works of architecture or architectural literature.

TRAITÉ SVR LA PRATIQVE DES ORDRES DE COLOMNES

DE L'ARCHITECTVRE NOMMÉE ANTIQVE.

Par A. BOSSE.

LE SOLIDE

LA AGREABLE

LA RAISON SVR TOVT.

LA THEORIE.

LA PRATIQ

LE COMMODE.

CHAPTER 8

CONCLUSION

At the beginning of the book we asked, in reference to the Vitruvian Categories, whether there might not be a natural principle behind these three, seemingly arbitrary, aspects of architecture. Are these the only three conditions for good building? How does Delight relate to Commodity and Firmness? How many kinds of delight are there and to what natural principles might they be reduced?

Our general conclusion must be that if there is a natural principle behind Firmness, Commodity and Delight then it must lie in the ultimate categories of logic that have interested philosophers since the time of the ancient Greeks (Figure 59). Not only would such categories articulate the subject of architecture, but the same categories would also serve to articulate the subjects of aesthetics or ethics when considered in their most general terms. Indeed, a more specific conclusion of the work derives from this fact and should be emphasized here before we proceed to explore it in more detail. To understand the notion of "good architecture" it is necessary to understand that the categories underlying the concept of "good" and the categories underlying the concept of "architecture" are the same.

To begin with a simple example, let us return to the two questions of how delight relates to commodity and firmness, and how many kinds of delight there are. Given that the three terms are representatives, if somewhat poor ones, of our three primary categories, we should say, in answer to the first question, that they represent the three ways in which the elements of architecture may be related to each other and to the outside world. That is, they represent the three relationship types of disjunction, causality and inherence respectively. However, the categories that structure the subject of architecture are also those that structure the different kinds of delight, for here too there is a subject that is differentiated internally only through the different ways in which the elements are related to one another. If then we have three provinces of architecture we should be able to discover three corresponding realms of delight.

Prodicus, the teacher of Socrates, distinguished between Joy, Pleasure and Delight,[1] although what the exact shades of meaning were to the ancient Greeks it would be now difficult to say (Figure 60). We should be more inclined to use the terms Beauty, Pleasure and Delight which correspond more readily to the architectural categories of Form, Function and Meaning: Beauty to the contemplation of formal relations; Pleasure to the functioning of the building particularly in terms

---

Plate 8 *Abraham Bosse, frontispiece to* Traité des manières de dessiner les ordres de l'architecture, *Paris 1664 (British Architectural Library, RIBA, London)*

"Grau, teurer Freund, ist alle Theorie
Und grün des Lebens goldner Baum" – Mephistopheles

Goethe

("All theory is grey my friend and life is golden-green")

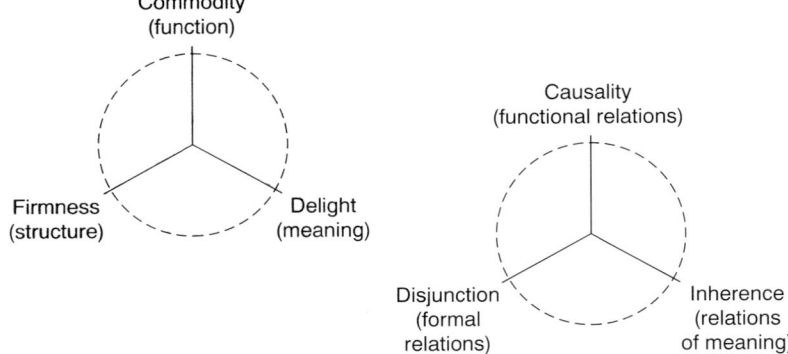

Figure 59 *The Vitruvian categories (left) are a poor representation of the primary categories and can only be seen as such if interpreted by terms similar to the ones denoted above. The primary categories of critical philosophy are shown (right) and offer a better set of "natural principles" for architectural theory*

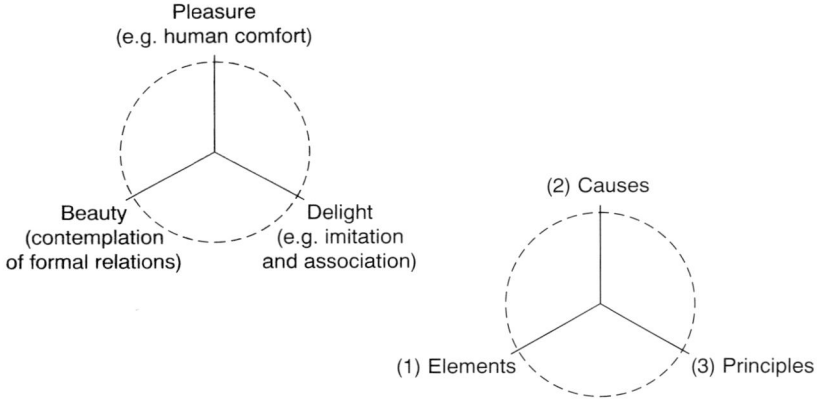

Figure 60 *Three kinds of delight described by Prodicus (left), and the distinction between elements, causes and principles described by Aristotle (right)*

of human comfort; and Delight to the recognition of meaning in a building, to the associations it arouses and the resemblances it recalls. This, of course, is an oversimplification and for a fuller discussion of the subject of aesthetics in architecture a return should be made to Chapters 5 and 6.

A more sophisticated consideration of these questions would lie in an examination of the principles by which architects and architectural writers have attempted to explain their subject. It might be supposed that these too should correspond with our primary and secondary categories, but before looking at such a correlation we should say a little more about what we mean by the notion of principles.

Aristotle distinguished between elements, causes and principles.[2] To determine the principles of good architecture the logical way forward would have been: first, to define the elements of architecture; second, to discover the causes which in some way constitute the good; and only then, as a "composite of the two"[3] bring them together as the principles of good architecture.

ELEMENTS

The initial problem of defining the elements was sidestepped by proposing a series of categories into which all possible answers to questions like "What is Architecture?" could be arranged. For Aristotle, the number of categories was ten, but by the end of the Classical era the number had been reduced to six: Substance, Relation, Quantity, Quality, Acting and being Acted upon.[4]

As we have seen, these categories correspond to the six constituent elements of architecture: Substance to construction and materials; Relation to context; Quantity to form; and Quality to meaning. The categories of Acting and being Acted upon were brought under one category by Plotinus,[5] although in the light of subsequent developments by Kant and Hegel we should prefer to maintain two separate categories: Activity relating to the functioning of the building; and Acting relating to will or spirit which provides a motive force to the subject. In accordance with similar conclusions in Volume Two we may arrange these six elements as follows:

PRIMARY CATEGORIES

Greek categories	*Architectural elements*
Quantity	Form, Pattern, Structure, Geometry, etc.
Activity	Function, Needs, Effects, Exchange, etc.
Quality	Meaning, Association, Resemblance, Style, etc.

SECONDARY CATEGORIES

Substance	Construction, Materials, Design, etc.
Relation	Context, Community, Nature, Feeling, etc.
Will	Spirit, Power, Politics, Attitudes, etc.

These are the six elements of architecture, passing under different names, around which our discussion of the subject has revolved. In themselves the elements are somewhat inert, detached and distant. They tell us little about the worth of the building as all buildings may be analysed in terms of these elements. All buildings have some sort of form. All buildings perform various functions even if in an unplanned or negative way. Whether the form may be considered good or bad, or the function valuable in any sense, is another question, and to answer it we need to turn to the notion of causes.

CAUSES AND VIRTUES

In his *Ethics* Aristotle wrote that if we want to know what a good man is, we must first decide what man himself consists of.[6] We may say the same of good

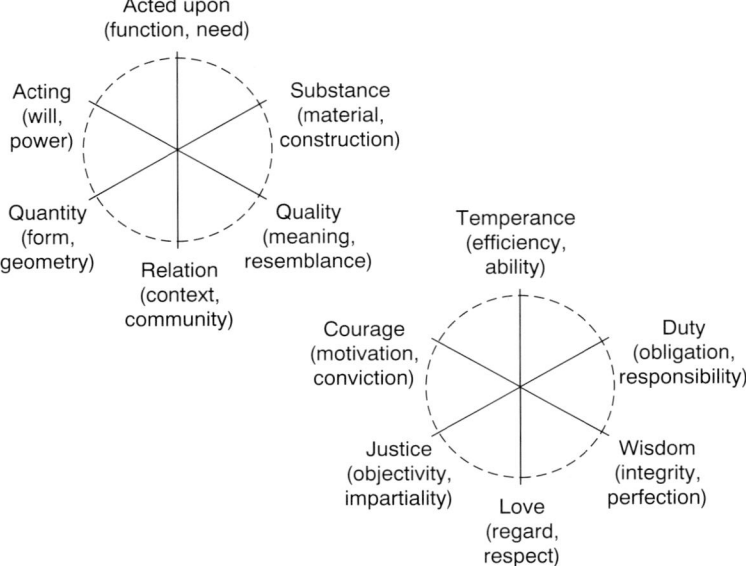

Figure 61 *The ten categories of Aristotle have been reduced to six (left) with some associated concepts noted under each. These categories may be compared with six types of good of importance to the ancient Greeks (right) and which were developed through the Middle Ages*

architecture, and to this end we have determined upon the six elements that in some way constitute architecture. The implication from Aristotle would appear to be that the various species of good will follow from this. Firmness, Commodity and Delight, for example, might be supposed to be the values following from establishing the elements of Construction, Function and Form. In fact, all it tells us is that a building should be constructed well, function well and have good form which we can see, particularly in the latter case, rather begs the question.

It may be useful instead to turn Aristotle's statement around and say that if we want to know what good architecture is we must first decide what good itself consists of. Again, because of our categorical approach, we may say that the types of good relative to a human being will correspond in a general way with the types of good relative to a building. Although Aristotle associated the idea of good with that of the final cause, "that for the sake of which everything else is done",[7] the question of definition was, once more, answered indirectly through the notion of categorization. "If we are not able to hunt the good with one idea only," wrote Plato, then "with three we may take our prey".[8]

In fact, Plato commonly listed four virtues in relation to the good man: Justice, Temperance, Wisdom and Courage.[9] In some places he realized that these were not enough, and added the virtues of honour and nobility,[10] which the Stoics elevated to Duty;[11] and Love or friendship, which were discussed by Plato and Aristotle in the *Symposium*[12] and *Nicomachean Ethics*[13] respectively (Figure 61).

Like Aristotle, we might admit that "it is hard to see how a weaver or a carpenter will be benefited in regard to his own craft by knowing this good itself".[14] Yet it is a curious fact that the RIBA Code of Professional Conduct which would regulate professional life in Britain not only reflects these Classical virtues but, like the elements of the art itself, is similarly divided into three sections each of which can be divided into two parts.[15] The first section of the Code relates to the architect's *duties* and introduces the concept of *impartiality*. The second section relates to how the architect is *motivated* and introduces the concept of *integrity*. The third section relates to an *efficient exchange* between ability and reward, and introduces the notion of *regard* for one's fellow architects and the professional body as a whole.

We may thus make a beginning with a comparison between Greek virtues, on the one hand, and these stated values of professional practice, on the other:

PRIMARY CATEGORIES

Greek virtues	*Professional values*
Justice	Impartiality, Objectivity, etc.
Temperance	Efficiency, Efficacy, Ability, Achievement, etc.
Wisdom	Integrity, Honesty, Propriety, Truth, etc.

SECONDARY CATEGORIES

Duty	Obligations, Responsibility, etc.
Love	Regard, Respect, Sympathy, Participation, etc.
Courage	Motivation, Encouragement, Conviction, etc.

In order to make a preliminary investigation, let us stay with Greek philosophy for a while and consider how each virtue relates to the categories previously listed:

- *Justice (cf. Impartiality)*: the Greek concept of justice related to the category of *quantity* in that it was seen as "a species of the proportionate",[16] distributive justice in accordance with geometrical proportion, and rectificatory justice in accordance with arithmetical proportion. Its main role lay in restoring equality (judge, *dikastis* meant one who bisected),[17] and we might think of the justice of Solomon, or the scales of justice that crown our law courts. The virtue of justice lay in its impartiality, the ability to determine questions regarding the whole of the facts, not just a part, and in "shrewdly perceiving omissions and faults".[18] Like aesthetic judgement, the attempt to achieve a balanced and unbiased picture rested on a broad contemplation of the whole, and resulted in the belief that from justice sprang the notions of order and harmony.
- *Temperance (cf. Efficiency)*: Goodness itself was seen as a "differentia of motion and activity",[19] and the final end *Eudaimonia* was defined as being, if not exactly happiness, then a very similar kind of activity.[20] The first seeds of Utilitarianism were sown when Plato said "Our object in the construction of the state is the greatest happiness of the whole".[21] Pleasure too derived from "activity",[22] from the exercising of our various faculties, the most important of which, naturally enough for such philosophers, was the faculty of reason. The notion of temperance arose from the problems encountered from dealing with conflicting pleasures, and the realization that to satisfy each part of human

nature some such regulation would be required.[23] For Aristotle, it consisted of the idea that anything in either excess or defect destroyed one's health and strength,[24] and the virtue of efficiency arose from the need for a careful exchange between expenditure and reward.

- *Wisdom (cf. Integrity)*: According to Aristotle, "Philosophic wisdom is the pleasantest of virtuous activities and consists of the contemplation of truth".[25] The category of *quality*, on the one hand, and the ideal of perfection, on the other, gave rise to two aspects of truth. In the first case, the virtue of integrity may be seen to have arisen from the coherence theory of truth where "with a true view all the data harmonize, but with a false one the facts soon clash".[26] Through integrity came a sense of honour and eventually the idea of hierarchy with which the notions of fittingness and propriety became associated. A second aspect of truth arose from the correspondence theory where the "truth of the imitation" consisted of the closeness of the rendition to the qualities of the original.[27] Perfection in art depended on the skill of the artist and his high degree of knowledge both of the attributes of the original and of the ideal form, or "heavenly pattern", of which Plato thought that the original was a copy.[28]

- *Duty (cf. Obligation)*: The nature of man himself was the question raised under the category of *substance*. Hierocles pictured "Each one of us as it were entirely encompassed by many circles, some smaller, others larger",[29] extending outwards from oneself to family, and through clothing and dwelling to all one's property and wealth. Each circle entailed certain obligations which fostered the virtues of self-respect and pride. First, there was the duty of care, to maintain one's own life through the arts of "medicine, bathing and gymnastics",[30] and that of one's possessions through proper maintenance and security. Second, there was a duty towards proper growth and development through "the arts of production and acquisition",[31] and to extend and perfect one's material being, functioning capacity and mental capacity through learning and experience.

- *Love (cf. Regard)*: One of the six elements of Empedocles was that of love or friendship which brought all things into *relation* with one another.[32] There were practical aspects mentioned by Aristotle as in the virtue of communication, "sharing in discussion and thought",[33] and when "men journey together with a view to some particular advantage whether good, pleasant or useful".[34] But also there was the concept of sympathy "which the best of us delights in", and which arises when love "fills men with affection . . . kindness . . . friendship . . . forgiveness".[35] Other feelings like empathy, important in our regard for buildings, were introduced although in a very tentative form. For instance, when age looks at youth and delights in their sports, singing and dancing because "we love to think of our former selves",[36] or in imagining ourselves elsewhere when "our soul, in ecstasy, seems to be among the persons or places of which she is speaking".[37]

- *Courage (cf. Motivation)*: Courage was one of the major virtues of the Greeks, perhaps not surprisingly when Sparta, Thebes, Athens and Macedonia were all warring with one another. Courage was seen to complement wisdom in that it implied "the knowledge of the grounds of fear and hope",[38] the two alternative attitudes we may have towards the future. It was not only to be directed against pain but also as the power of the *will* against intemperate pleasures and desires.[39] The kinds of motivation were seen by the Greeks to be various. One was directed by desire or ambition; by "strong and good opinions";[40] or by one of the animating principles of the soul – anger, emotion or passion.[41] They prided themselves on being equally spirited and wise,[42] and their art of rhetoric was highly developed to appeal to their innate "powers of command and love of freedom".[43]

✳

It would not be appropriate to discuss here the history of these moral categories much further than perhaps to draw out one or two points worth further study. Aristotle mentioned several other virtues beside the ones listed above, and later writers have concerned themselves with making various groupings of these. Thomas Aquinas, for example, developed Aristotle's notion of causes, and promoted various sets of three. We have previously discussed the importance to aesthetics of his concepts of Proportion, Clarity and Integrity, and of more importance to ethics, Faith, Hope and Charity which we analysed in terms of our secondary categories.

Henry Wotton, as we noted in Chapter 2, concluded *The Elements of Architecture* with a notice of intent to embark on a further work entitled *A Philosophical Survey of Education or Moral Architecture*.[44] The proposed work was never completed but he did draw up a plan for its division into six sections, saying "These six branches will as I conceive embrace the whole business".[45] For purposes of comparison we may order them among our categories as follows:

PRIMARY CATEGORIES
(1) Judgement/Form: ". . . the quickening and exciting of observation and judgement".
(2) Temperance/Efficiency: ". . . how to discern the natural capacities and inclinations of children".
(3) Wisdom/Integrity ". . . next must ensure the culture and furnishment of the mind".

SECONDARY CATEGORIES
(4) Duty/Obligations: ". . . the moulding of behaviour and decent forms".
(5) Love/Regard: ". . . the tempering of affections".
(6) Courage/Motivation: ". . . the timely instilling of conscientious principle and seeds of religion".

David Hume, in his *Enquiry concerning the Principles of Morals*, described a multitude of virtues, but did little in the way of analysis besides separating them into those merits that are either useful or agreeable, and into those directed towards ourselves or others.[46] Part Two of his *Treatise of Human Nature* was divided, as we have seen, into three parts which we have identified with our

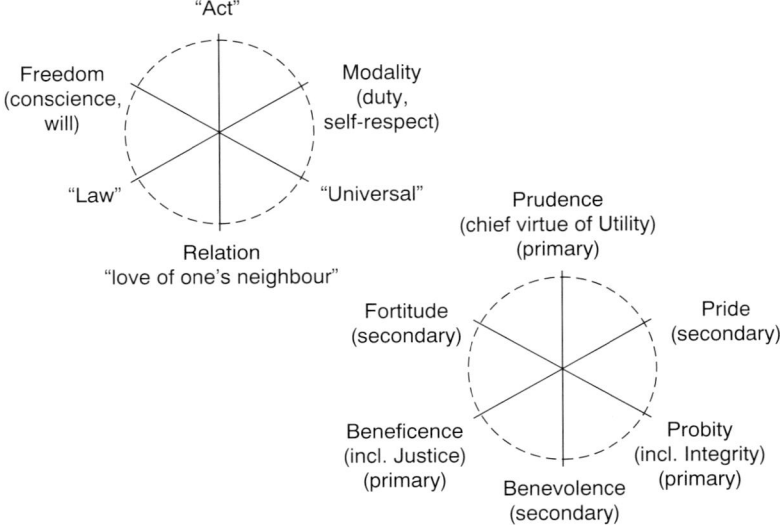

Figure 62 *Kant distinguished between objective laws and subjective virtues (left) saying "Act so that the maxim of thy action might become universal law". Jeremy Bentham discussed three primary virtues, to which all may be reduced, and a number of secondary virtues (right)*

secondary categories: Pride which with self-respect we have related to duty or obligation; Love and the important notion of sympathy which he developed; and the Direct Passions which we can identify with will and motivation.[47]

Immanuel Kant, in *The Critique of Practical Reason*, drew an interesting distinction between analytical and synthetic concepts, between logic and reality, and between laws and virtues.[48] Laws are objective, he suggested, and involve the three elements of action, universalization and law itself. "Act so that the maxim of thy action might become universal law",[49] his categorical imperative proclaims; "Act externally so that the free use of thy elective will may not interfere with the freedom of any man so far as it agrees with universal law".[50]

Virtues, on the other hand, are subjective, and while Kant wrote little on the cardinal virtues, it is worth comparing the subject matter of his *Table of the Categories of Freedom*[51] with Hume's division noted above: the category of Modality develops into a concern for duty and "respect for ourselves"; the category of relation into "love of one's neighbour"; and under the other aspects of freedom he discussed "moral feeling" and "conscientiousness" in respect of the "elective will" (Figure 62).

Jeremy Bentham, perhaps more than any other, attempted a thorough and rational division of the virtues in his *Deontology* which was published in 1829. It is a work worth mentioning here because in it he introduced the notions of "primary and secondary virtues"[52] which, while not agreeing in detail with our own primary and secondary categories, gives some vindication of the general method. His three primary virtues were:

- Benificence, under which he included Justice
- Prudence, the chief virtue in his doctrine of utility
- Probity, which we may link with integrity and propriety.

"By these three virtues", he wrote, "the whole field of morals is completely covered, to one or more of these three those others are, all of them, in some way or other resolvable".[53]

Following this statement, he analysed some secondary virtues, such as Pride, Benevolence and Fortitude, giving as an example Temperance, whose opposite, Intemperance, involved, he suggested, a combined breach of both prudence and probity.

PRINCIPLES

Returning to our division between Elements, Causes and Principles, we shall now turn our attention to the last of these terms and begin to consider what might constitute the principles of good architecture.

At the beginning of *Poetics*, Aristotle listed the typical elements that make up the arts: colour, form, rhythm, harmony, language, etc., and he described how some arts such as comedy and tragedy, "combine all the means enumerated".[54] The principles, he said, are "in a sense the same for all".[55] The art form discussed in detail is that of tragedy. Here, six essential elements common to all works of tragedy are described: melody, plot or action, thought, diction or composition, character and spectacle. In order to turn a commonplace tragedy into a good tragedy we are told to study the "internal principles"[56] of each element and learn that "that which makes things good is the proper order inhering in each thing".[57] To each element is applied the corresponding virtue appropriate to its respective category (Figure 63). There should be order and harmony in the melody; an efficiency in the handling of the action; a universality or appropriateness in the thought; a proper care in the composition of the language; a feeling of sympathy or humanity in the characterization; and a sense of awe or inspiration in the spectacle.[58] Elements and their respective causes are brought together to form a rudimentary set of principles. In a similar way we could combine the architectural elements taken from the first table above with the values taken from the second table above to arrive at the following table of architectural principles:

PRIMARY CATEGORIES
(1)   To the element of Form we should bring a requirement for Objectivity or
      Impartiality, to give:
                    IMPARTIALITY OF FORM
(2)   To the element of Function we should bring a requirement of Efficiency and
      Economy, to give:
                    EFFICIENCY OF FUNCTION
(3)   To the element of Meaning we should bring a requirement for Propriety and
      Integrity, to give:
                    INTEGRITY OF MEANING

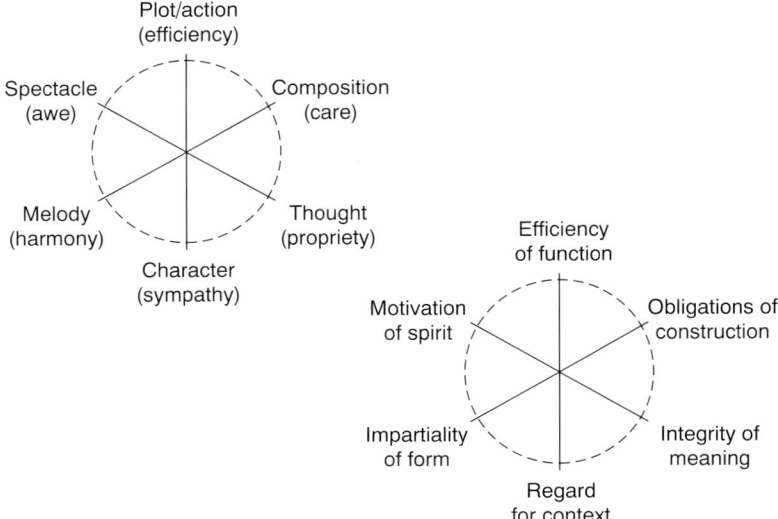

Figure 6.3 *By adding the appropriate concepts to the elements of tragedy in Greek theatre, Aristotle arrived at the six principles required for every good performance (left). By similar means we can abstract principles from codes of professional ethics and add them to the elements of architecture to arrive at a similar set of six principles (right)*

SECONDARY CATEGORIES

(4)   To the elements of Design and Construction we should bring a requirement of Responsibility and Obligation, to give:

OBLIGATIONS OF CONSTRUCTION

(5)   To the elements of Context and Community we should bring a requirement for Regard and Sympathy, to give:

REGARD FOR CONTEXT

(6)   To the elements of Will and Spirit we should bring a requirement for Motivation and Conviction, to give:

MOTIVATION OF SPIRIT

In Volume Two we shall look at how these six principles compare with the ideas and doctrines of architectural theory in the twentieth century. Here, it will be useful to summarize under each heading some of the key ideas that have been discussed in the previous chapters in order to focus more clearly on the issues involved.

PRINCIPLE 1: IMPARTIALITY OF FORM

It was Plato who first interrelated the notions of beauty, fairness and justice.[59] Although he reasserted the importance of mathematical proportions to music and the "observance of measure to the excellence or beauty of every work of art",[60] he claimed that it was the concept of symmetry that best expressed the sense of balance required. "Geometrical equality," he said, "is mighty both among Gods and men".[61] While today the balance might be achieved by considering the different visual densities of the parts, an idea owing more perhaps to Archimedes,[62] the ensuing feeling of harmony was seen as a "reconciliation of opposites"[63] or the perception of "variety in unity".[64] For Plato, aesthetic judgement required the "simplicity of a truly and nobly ordered mind",[65] and although he later ridiculed the cold impartiality of the "divine" circle and sphere,[66] he initiated the formalist notion that

> "True pleasures are those which are given by the beauty of colour and form
> . . . straight lines and circles and the plane or solid figures which are formed
> out of them. . . . There are colours too of the same character, and sounds
> when smooth and clear and utter a single pure tone."[67]

The twin principles of proportion and colour were stated most clearly by Cicero who remarked that "All bodily beauty consists in the proportion of parts together with a certain agreeableness of colour".[68]

The concept of impartiality, which is essential to the formation of a balanced judgement, was introduced into aesthetics by Kant as "disinterestedness".[69] The notion of disinterestedness entailed a setting aside of all concepts borrowed from the categories of Function ("purposiveness")[70] and Meaning ("conceptualiza-tion")[71] in order to concentrate on the form of a thing. Like Plato, Kant concentrated on the simplicity that lay at the heart of beauty, saying:

> "A mere colour, for instance the green of a lawn, or a mere tone, for
> instance that of a violin, are by most people called beautiful in themselves.
> . . . The essential thing is the design . . . what satisfies us by its form."[72]

The question that arose of whether all things may not thus be seen as beautiful was resolved by Schopenhauer who suggested that we call those things beautiful which facilitate contemplation through the ordering of their parts:

> "Since every given thing may be observed in a purely objective manner, it
> follows that everything is also beautiful. . .[73] One thing is only taken as more
> beautiful than another because it makes this pure objective contemplation
> easier."[74]

We may note the importance given to the term "objectivity" by Schopenhauer and its subsequent appearance in modern architectural theory as *Sachlichkeit*.

PRINCIPLE 2: EFFICIENCY OF FUNCTION

In a tragedy, Aristotle said "everything should arise out of the structure of the plot, each thing as a consequence of its own antecedents".[75] In a similar way, a building should develop from its own "internal principles",[76] its functions, and the activities or uses to which it is to be put. "The excellency of every structure is relative to the use for which nature or the artist has intended it,"[77] wrote Plato. The function may not be the merely practical one where "everything should have its proper place",[78] but may also be to please: "bodies are beautiful in proportion as they are useful or as the sight of them gives pleasure."[79]

The virtue of temperance served reason in requiring a certain efficiency in the arts as well as in life. Plato introduced the "principle of the mean",[80] that all arts should be on the watch against excess and defect, and Aristotle, in a passage that we have associated with Alberti, wrote "The mean is intermediate between excess and defect . . . so that we often say of a good work of art that it is not possible to either take away or add anything".[81]

Thomas Aquinas developed the idea of cause and effect, together with the principle of the "efficient cause",[82] and wrote that:

"Everything is good according to its function. . . . Austerity, in so far as it is a virtue, does not exclude all pleasure but only those which are excessive or disordered."[83]

In the eighteenth century the idea that beauty also depended in part on function was revived, and we read in Hume, for example, that "A great part of beauty . . . is derived from the idea of convenience or utility . . . the order and convenience of a palace are no less essential to its beauty than its mere figure and appearance".[84] A hundred years later the idea crossed the Atlantic where it was to develop in strength in the nineteenth century. Ralph Waldo Emerson, for example, wrote:

"Beauty rests on necessities. The line of beauty is the result of perfect economy. The cell of the bee is built at that angle which gives the most strength with the least wax."[85]

It was from ideas such as these that Louis Sullivan was to formulate his famous maxim that "form follows function",[86] which so influenced the architectural thinking of the twentieth century.

PRINCIPLE 3: INTEGRITY OF MEANING

All the arts were imitative and representational for the Greeks, and it was thought "natural for all to delight in works of imitation".[87] Commonly the delights were those of association and recollection, but there were higher pleasures in discerning meaning in the complexities of style and taste. The principle of taste was that of appropriateness, or what was "fitting in relation to the agent, the circumstances and the object".[88] Appropriateness due to the object lay, for example, in the symbolism behind the siting of a temple, "to give due elevation to virtue".[89] Appropriateness due to circumstances required a knowledge of both history and contemporary ideas, where such a taste could be measured "only in so far as it delighted the best educated".[90] Appropriateness due to the agent lay in the variety of styles open to him and that "each class or type of disposition has its own appropriate way of letting the truth appear".[91]

The concept of integrity naturally followed, and with it the coherence theory of truth whereby all aspects should fit together or harmonize. "With a true view all the data harmonize," wrote Aristotle, "but with a false one the facts soon clash".[92]

The idea that much of the meaning in art and architecture resulted from knowledge and mental association was developed in the eighteenth century by Hutcheson in Glasgow and Hume in Edinburgh. Hutcheson, for example, wrote "The association of ideas makes objects pleasant and delightful. . . . Knowledge may superadd a distinct rational pleasure."[93] Hume emphasized the comparisons that our intellectual faculties make when looking at a work of art: "It is impossible to continue in the practice of contemplating any order of beauty without being frequently obliged to form comparisons between the several species and degrees of excellence, and estimating their proportion to each other."[94]

How a work of architecture fits in with its particular culture requires knowledge of that culture, and for Ruskin this would have included a comprehensive knowledge of the various aspects of a society. "Noble architecture," he said, "is in some sort the embodiment of the Polity, Life, History and Religious Faith of a Nation".[95] Ruskin was arguing for the retention of a traditional style in architecture, saying that "if we have good laws then their age is of no importance".[96] Yet the same argument was to be applied in the twentieth century for the development of a new style to reflect developments in technology and a change in the spirit of the times, and it was here that the concept of integrity was to be put to its severest test.

PRINCIPLE 4: OBLIGATIONS OF CONSTRUCTION

The materials or substance out of which the world was made was of much interest to the Greeks, particularly in regard to the concepts of change and decomposition. "All works of art, vessels, houses, garments, when well made are least altered by time and circumstance", wrote Plato.[97] The way things were put together interested them, "whether by rivets or glue, by contact or organic unity",[98] and, indeed the birth of civilization was attributed by them to material technology, in particular "metallurgy, iron, brass, and other metals".[99] It is "part of the discipline to know the form and the matter,"[100] wrote Aristotle, "the builder has a knowledge of both the form of the house and the materials, that is bricks and beams and so forth".[101]

A duty towards care and maintenance expressed itself in a conception of structure and material, similar to the human body where "true beauty is given by gymnastics",[102] and not by "working deceitfully with lines and colours, enamels and garments".[103] In Early Christianity there was also thought to be an "inward beauty" to the body,[104] an idea which we may see reflected in the structure and limbs of the Gothic church. Duns Scotus, in words reminiscent of Aristotle, wrote of the mediaeval craftsman that "the perfect artisan has a distinct knowledge of everything to be done before he does it".[105]

Aristotle introduced the idea of the "material cause . . . that out of which a thing comes to be e.g. the bronze of a statue",[106] but he also recognized the need for material goods. Hume linked the idea of material possessions with the concept of pride, writing "Pride or self-esteem may arise from either the qualities of the mind . . . those of the body . . . or from external advantages, country, family, children, relations, riches, houses, gardens, horses, dogs, clothes".[107] Dewey, much later, developed the notion of the pride of the craftsman, and the inextricable link between the material world and the creativity of art, saying, "only where there is material employed is there expression and art".[108]

PRINCIPLE 5: REGARD FOR CONTEXT

The concept closest in meaning to that of Context in Aristotle's list of categories is that of Relation. "All excellencies depend on particular relations," he wrote "in relation to one another or to the surrounding atmosphere".[109] We may understand the concept not only in terms of how buildings relate to one another and their site but also in terms of how they relate to those who view them – the physical context and the human context respectively. The concept of relation was based on "a community of nature between the factors",[110] and this notion of community was associated with the concept of feeling by Plato: "If there were not some community of feeling among mankind, however varying in different persons – I do not see how we could ever communicate our impressions to one another."[111]

An analogy might be made between architecture and music in that "when men hear imitations their feelings move in sympathy".[112] For instance, a sense of movement was communicated, and a different character expressed, by the use of different rhythms and scales, the Lydian mode was sorrowful, the Doric warlike, the Ionian expressed softness, and the Phrygian peace.[113] Plotinus suggested the idea that beauty itself lay in the notion of something shared saying that "some things, material shapes for instance, are gracious not by anything inherent but by something communicated".[114]

The fact that fields could be seen as "smiling", was noted by Aquinas,[115] and Kant linked the idea of perceived feeling to buildings saying: "We call trees and buildings majestic or dignified, and meadows smiling or gay; even colours are called pure, chaste, tender because they arouse our feelings".[116] These ideas developed until they culminated in Tolstoy's theory of art as the communication of feeling: "Art [is] a medium for communicating feelings . . . by means of movement, lines, colours, sounds or forms expressed in words; to transmit that feeling so that others may experience the same . . . this is the activity of art."[117]

The notion that these feelings may be related in some way to bodily shape, position and movement was explored through the eighteenth and nineteenth centuries and resulted in Lipps' influential theory of Empathy, which was to pervade the literature of art in the early twentieth century.[118] There were also connections between these ideas and the Picturesque, and Townscape theory which we shall explore in Volume Two.

PRINCIPLE 6: MOTIVATION OF SPIRIT

Connected with the ability to move or stimulate was the "love of novelty which arises out of the pleasure of the new and the weariness of the old".[119] Even Plato, aware of the "restlessness of youth",[120] would have allowed new songs if not a new kind of song: "there should be every sort of change and variation to take away the effect of sameness".[121] Aristotle, in discussing political rhetoric, admitted that "people like what strikes them and are struck by what is out of the way".[122] The factor of size was important to him and he extolled both magnificence and lavishness, saying "The most valuable work of art is that which is great as well as beautiful, for the contemplation of such inspires admiration".[123]

Plato's admiration was more for the "ten thousand years" of unchanging Egyptian tradition[124] and the proposition that "if a person can only find in any way the natural melodies, he may confidently embody them in a fixed and legal form".[125] Important to either radical or conservative views of the future was the requirement for a will to motivate the spirit and to lend conviction to their generally utopian idealism.

Aristotle's concepts of power, passion and freedom reappeared in a treatise entitled *On the Sublime* attributed to Longinus in the second century AD:

"For freedom, it is said, has the power to feed the imagination of the lofty-minded and inspire hope; and where it prevails there spreads abroad the eagerness of mutual rivalry and the emulous pursuit of the foremost place."[126]

It was a work which was to influence the thinking of the eighteenth century, from Hutcheson who wrote that, "Grandeur and novelty are two ideas different from beauty which often recommend objects to us",[127] to Kant who distinguished between two types of sublime, the mathematical and the dynamical.[128]

The concept of the Will was developed early in the nineteenth century by Schopenhauer,[129] and later by Nietzsche in whose writing we may particularly note the power of motivation that should properly belong to all art:

"What does all art do? Does it not praise? Does it not glorify? Does it not select? Does it not highlight? By doing all this it strengthens certain values. . . . Art is the great stimulus to life."[130]

✣

Now that we have considered the six principles in turn, it is necessary to ask how compatible they are with one another. How does impartiality of form with its predilection for smooth surfaces relate to the obligations of construction? How does efficiency of function with its demand for economy relate to a regard for feelings and context? And how does integrity of meaning with its interest in classification and typology relate to the motivation of spirit (Figure 64)?

In ethics the problem is not an uncommon one, referred to, for example, by Kant as "a conflict of duties",[131] and it can be traced back to Plato's *Statesman*. Although the aim is to "promote not a part of virtue but the whole", Plato wrote, it is often the case that the different parts of virtue "may be at war with one another".[132]

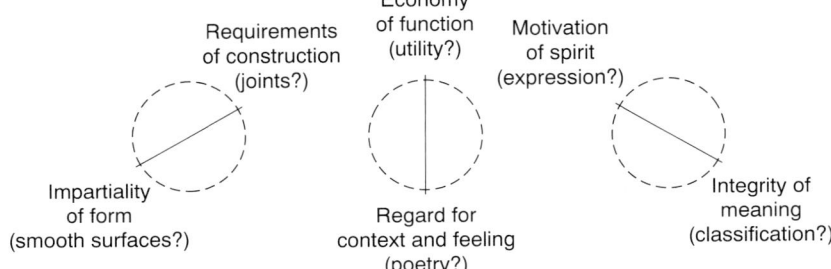

Figure 64 *One of the main problems with any set of principles is their compatibility with one another. The above diagrams show common sources of conflict, taken from each of the six categories, where either onesidedness or compromise will be required*

In some ways, for instance, decoration may be thought to be a good thing in architecture, in others it may not. Aristotle advocated that private houses should be seen as "public ornaments", and that even the town walls should be decorated.[133] Plato, on the other hand, recommended that we should "cast away pleasures and ornaments and array the soul in her proper jewels which are temperance, justice, courage, nobility and truth".[134] He deplored the "spurious beauty of dressing up",[135] preferring the simpler beauties of mathematical form and proportion where the art of architecture can be even more exacting than the art of music.[136]

Should we attempt to balance the various requirements and accept a compromise, or should we concentrate on just one or two to the probable detriment of the others? Longinus gave a clear answer to this. In asking "whether we should give preference to grandeur with some attendant faults . . . or moderation which is sound and free from error", he concluded that success in art, like success in sport, "is not estimated by the number of merits. . . . Like the pentathlete [such art] falls just below the top in every branch."[137]

The Greeks realized that "no art whatsoever can lay down a rule that will last for all time . . . although the law is always striving to make one like an obstinate and ignorant tyrant".[138] Law and order should be deemed a second best to a mind "which is true and free and in harmony with nature.[139] While they admitted that "control should be exercised over building making grace and harmony its aim"[140] they left no rules on the subject, only an all-embracing framework under which "the heads of argument tend to fall and under which the premises can be classified each according to its number".[141]

Notes and References

Note: *Op.cit.* 3.24 means work cited in Chapter 3, note 24

Chapter 1: Introduction

1. Vitruvius *The Ten Books on Architecture* (tr. Morgan M.H., 1914, Dover Publications, New York, 1960) p.284
2. *Ibid.* p.10
3. Plato *Timaeus and Critias* (tr. Taylor A., Methuen & Co., London, 1929) pp.52–56; cf. Plato *Timaeus* paras 53–56
4. Vitruvius *op.cit.*1.1, p.72
5. *Ibid.* p.73
6. Wittkower R. *Architectural Principles in the Age of Humanism* 1949 (Academy Editions, London, 1973), p.26
7. Kruft H.-W. *A History of Architectural Theory* 1985 (tr. Taylor R., Callander E. & Wood A., Zwemmer, London, 1994) p.36
8. Wittkower, *op.cit.*1.6, pp.3 & 7; cf. Alberti, note 1.10 below, BkVII, Chs4 & 5
9. *Ibid.* p.8
10. Alberti L.B. *Ten Books on Architecture* 1486 (ed. Rykwert J., tr. Bartoli 1550 & Leoni 1726, Alec Tiranti Ltd, London, 1955) p.188
11. *Leon Battista Alberti: On the Art of Building in Ten Books* 1486 (tr. Rykwert J., Leach N. & Tavernor R., MIT Press, Cambridge, Mass. (1988) 1991) p.296
12. Alberti *op.cit.*1.10, p.138; cf. *op.cit.*1.11, p.196
13. *Ibid.* p.196; cf. *op.cit.*1.11, p.305
14. Kruft *op.cit.*1.7, p.57
15. Wittkower, *op.cit.*1.6, p.23
16. *Ibid.* p.23. Wittkower writes "Attention to this passage was first drawn by Anthony Blunt in *Artistic Theory in Italy 1450–1600* Oxford, 1940, p.129"; cf. Palladio, *The Four Books on Architecture* (MIT Press, Cambridge, Mass., 1997) p.216.
17. Kruft *op.cit.*1.7, p.86
18. *Ibid.* p.100
19. *Ibid.* p.99
20. *Ibid.* p.52
21. *Ibid.* p.230; cf. Shute J., *The First and Chief Groundes of Architecture* 1563 (Gregg Press, London, 1965)
22. *Ibid.* p.126
23. *Ibid.* p.152
24. *Ibid.* p.247; cf. Mowl T. & Earnshaw B., *John Wood: Architect of Obsession* (Millstream Books, Bath, 1988) p.99
25. *Ibid.* p.249
26. Alberti, *op.cit.*1.10, p.196; cf. *op.cit.*1.11, p.302
27. *Ibid.* p.113; cf. *op.cit.*1.11, p.156
28. Aristotle *Nichomachean Ethics* (tr. Ross D., Oxford University Press, London, 1980) para.1106. Rykwert *et al.* refer not to Aristotle but to Cicero's description of the perfection of the human body. See Cicero *De Oratore* note 121 below, p.179.
29. Aristotle *Poetics* in *The Complete Works of Aristotle* (Princeton University Press, 1984) para.1451a
30. Plato *Statesman* tr. Jowett B., p.565, paras283–284

31. Alberti, *op.cit.*1.10, p.195; cf. *op.cit.*1.11, p.302
32. Rykwert, *op.cit.*1.10, footnote 241. This explanation appears to have been omitted from the later translation, *op.cit.*1.11. The specific grouping of Quantity, Quality and Relation derives more from Kant (*Critique of Pure Reason* p.127) than Aristotle. However, see Chapter 3 on "The Greek Categories."
33. Vitruvius *op.cit.*1.1, p.17
34. *Vitruvius on Architecture* (tr. Granger F., William Heinemann Ltd, London, 1931) Vol.1, p.35
35. *Ibid.* p.25. Granger's footnote suggests that Vitruvius's three terms, *taxis, diathesis, oeconomia*, seem to correspond to Democritus's *ordo, positura, figurae* given in Lucretius I, 685. Cf. Vitruvius, *op.cit.*1.1, pp.13ff
36. Kruft *op.cit.*1.7, p.30
37. *Ibid.* p.89
38. *Ibid.* p.84
39. *Ibid.* p.106; cf. Meek H.A. *Guarino Guarini and his Architecture* (Yale University Press, New Haven & London, 1988) pp.111,151
40. *Ibid.* pp.198–199
41. Wotton H. *The Elements of Architecture* 1624 (Gregg International Publishers Ltd, Farnborough, 1969) p.1; cf. Kruft, *op.cit.*1.7, pp.231–232
42. Kruft *op.cit.*1.7, p.234; cf. Bennett J.A. *The Mathematical Science of Christopher Wren* (Cambridge University Press, Cambridge, 1982) pp.3,4,92,118–122
43. *Ibid.* p.253
44. *Ibid.* p.120
45. *Ibid.* pp.133ff
46. *Ibid.* p.139. Cf. Aristotle, *op.cit.*1.28, para.1122a: "It is what is fitting then, in relation to the agent, and to the circumstances, and the object".
47. *Ibid.* p.141
48. *Ibid.* p.144
49. *Ibid.* p.283
50. *Ibid.* p.274; cf. Villari S. *J.N.L. Durand* (Rizzoli, New York, 1990) pp.58–67
51. *Ibid.* p.176; cf. Goudeau J. "Nicolaus Goldmann (1611–1665) and the practice of the study" in *Nederlandse Oudheidkundige Bond* Vol.94, No.6, pp.185–203
52. *Ibid.* p.186
53. *Ibid.* p.295; cf. Brownlee D. (ed.) *Friedrich Weinbrenner: Architect of Karlsruhe* (University of Pennsylvania Press, Philadelphia, 1986) p.37
54. *Ibid.* p.298
55. *Ibid.* p.300; cf. Snodin M. (ed.) *Karl Friedrich Schinkel: A Universal Man* (Yale University Press, New Haven & London, 1991) pp.49–50
56. Pugin A.W. *The True Principles of Pointed or Christian Architecture* 1841 (Academy Editions, London, 1973) p.1: "The two great rules for design are these: 1st, that there should be no features about a building which are not necessary for convenience, construction or propriety; 2nd, that all ornament should consist of enrichment of the essential construction of the building."
57. Ruskin J. *The Seven Lamps of Architecture* (George Allen, London, 1880)
58. Ruskin J. *The Stones of Venice* (Wiley, Chichester, 1889) p.36
59. Fergusson J. *A History of Architecture* (John Murray, London, 1893); cf. *op.cit.*1.7, p.335
60. Emerson R.W. *Essays* (Henry Altemus, Philadelphia, USA, undated), First Series, p.297. The particular essay is entitled "Intellect".
61. Scott G. *The Architecture of Humanism* (Constable & Co., London, 1914) p.1
62. Papadakis, Cooke & Benjamin (eds), *Deconstruction* (Academy Editions, London, 1989) pp.150–153
63. Scruton R. *The Aesthetics of Architecture* (Methuen & Co., London, 1979)
64. Prak N.L. *The Language of Architecture* (Mouton, The Hague, 1968)
65. St John Wilson C. "Propriety and construction", *Architectural Review* July 1985, p.19; cf. St John Wilson C., *Architectural Reflections* (Butterworth-Heinemann, Oxford, 1992)
66. Kruft *op.cit.*1.7, p.15

Chapter 2: Vitruvian Categories

1. Walton I. *Walton's Lives* (third edition) (Payne & Foss, 1817); cf. Wittkower R. *Palladio and English Palladianism* (Thames & Hudson, London, 1974) p.62; Hazlitt W.C. *The Venetian Republic* (Adam & Charles Black, London, 1915) pp.191,330 & 362; Strachan M. *The Life and Adventures of Thomas Coryate* (Oxford University Press, 1962) p.53

2. Stoye J. *English Travellers Abroad 1604–1667* (Cape, London, 1952) p 147

3. Wotton H. *The Elements of Architecture* 1624 (Gregg International Publishers, Farnborough, U.K., 1969) preface

4. Shute J. *The First and Chief Groundes of Architecture* 1563 (Gregg Press, London, 1965)

5. Wotton *op.cit.*2.3, p.1

6. *Ibid.* pp.6–7

7. *Ibid.* p.4

8. *Ibid.* p.60

9. *Ibid.* p.8

10. *Ibid.* p.7

11. *Ibid.* p.66

12. Jones I. *Inigo Jones on Palladio* (ed. Allsopp B., Oriel Press, Newcastle upon Tyne, 1970), pp.27 & 29

13. Shakespeare W. *The Life and Death of King John* Act 2, Scene 1, lines 561–598:

    "This sway of motion, this Commodity,
    Makes it head from all indifferency
    From all direction, purpose, course, intent:
    And this same bias, this Commodity,
    This bawd, this broker, this all-changing word . . ."

14. *Op.cit.*2.3, pp.22–27

15. *Ibid.* p.10

16. *Ibid.* p.29

17. *Ibid.* p.39

18. *Ibid.* p.27

19. *Ibid.* pp.7–8: "Let all the principal chambers of Delight, All Studies and Libraries be towards the East. . . . For the Morning is a friend to the Muses"

20. *Ibid.* p.12 (incorrectly numbered p.21): "[The architect's] truest ambition should be to make the form which is the nobler part (as it were) triumph over the matter: whereof I cannot but mention by the way, a foreign pattern, namely the Church of Santa Giustina in Padua: In truth a sound piece of good art, where the materials being but ordinary stone, without any garnishment of sculpture do yet ravish the beholder (and he knows not how) by a secret harmony in the proportions"

21. *Ibid.* pp.53–54 and pp.67–68

22. *Ibid.* pp.66–68

23. *Ibid.* p.34

24. *Ibid.* p.7; cf. p.63: "Art should imitate nature"

25. *Ibid.* p.17

26. *Op.cit.*2.12, p.13

27. *Ibid.* e.g. pp.4,8,12 & 37

28. Summerson J. *Architecture in Britain 1530–1830* 1953 (Penguin Books, Harmondsworth, 1970), p.118

29. *Op.cit.*2.3, pp.6–7

30. Wotton H. *Reliquiae Wottonianae* (third edition) (printed by T.Roycroft London, 1672) p.362

31. Holmes G. *The Florentine Enlightenment 1400–1450* (Weidenfeld & Nicolson, London, 1969) p.85; cf. Alberti, *op.cit.*1.10, preface p.xiii *The Life of Leone Battista Alberti by Raphael du Fresne* (Paris, 1651)

32. Alberti *op.cit.*1.10, p.196; cf. Alberti *op.cit.*1.11, p.304: "That nature is composed of threes all philosophers agree"

33. *Ibid.* p.ix; cf.1.11, p.2 which translates the last few words as "matters that are pleasant to know". In Leoni the emphasis is on knowledge; in Rykwert *et al.* the emphasis is on pleasure, or delight. The original Latin reads:

> "*Nanque artes quidem alias necessitate sectamur, alias probamus utilitate, aliae vero, quod tantum circa res cognitu gratissimas versentur, impraetio sunt*" (see note 2.58 below, Vol.1, p.2). "Necessity" relates to the Vitruvian "firmness" in as much as both relate to the physical elements, including gravity, which the building is there to deal with. In Cicero's *Academica* (see note 2.119 below) p.I.29, we read that physical force is sometimes equated with "necessity" by the Stoics (cf. note 2.67 below)

34. *Ibid.* pp.2–3; cf. 1.11, p.9 which translates *amoenitatem* as "elegance" (see also 2.57 below). The original Latin reads:

> "*Ea sunt haec: ut sint eorum singula ad certum destinatumque usum commoda et in primis saluberrima; ad firmitatem perpetuitatemque integra et solida et admodum aeterna; ad gratiam et amoenitatem compta composita et in omni parte sui, ut ita loquar, redimita*" (note 2.58 below, Vol.1, p.25)

35. *Ibid.* pp.113–115; cf. 1.11, p.159: "honed . . . to the rule of philosophy"

36. Alberti *op.cit.*1.11, p.24: "Every aspect of building . . . is borne of necessity, nourished by convenience, dignified by use"

37. Alberti *op.cit.*1.10, p.112: "the three properties required in all manner of buildings, namely, that they be accommodated to their respective purposes, stout and strong for duration, and pleasant and delightful to the sight"; cf. 1.11, p.155: "the three conditions that apply to every form of construction – that what we construct should be appropriate to its use, lasting in structure, and graceful and pleasing in appearance". The original Latin reads:

> "*Ex tribus partibus, quae ad universam aedificationem pertinebant, uti essent quidem quae adstrueremus ad usum apta, ad perpetuitatem firmissima, ad gratiam et amoenitatem paratissima*" (see note 2.58 below, Vol.2, p.445)

38. *Ibid.* e.g. pp.ix,2,13, etc.

39. *Ibid.* p.ix; cf. 1.11, pp.2 & 316 where Alberti advises us to show that "utility was the principle motive". See also quotation at note 2.36 above, and discussion of causality at note 2.68 below.

40. *Ibid.* p.13; cf. 1.11, p.24 which interprets the phrase as "unruly passion".

41. *Ibid.* p.13, cf. 1.11, p.23

42. *Ibid.* p.245, footnote 115

43. *Ibid.* p.113; cf. 1.11, p.156. Rykwert *et al.* compare the phrase with Cicero's description of the perfect body referring us to *De oratore* (William Heinemann, London, 1942) p.179. See *op.cit.*1.11, p.386, note 6

44. Holmes *op.cit.*2.31, p.111 in a passage quoting from Alberti's *On the Tranquillity of the Soul*: "The lesser comforts, wine, music, play, are not to be despised. But finally a good manner of life is a defence against all adversity" (Holmes). *Della Tranquillita dell'Animo* is modelled on Cicero and takes the form of a debate held under Brunelleschi's dome. The preliminary remarks are on the therapeutic qualities of architecture and music. Alberti then writes:

> "The Greek philosophers constructed a temple in their writings. They laid out the plan by the investigation of good and evil; set up pillars by distinguishing the effects and powers of nature; and set a roof on it to defend it from tempests, which was made up of skill in avoiding evil, desiring and pursuing good . . ."

45. Alberti *op.cit.*1.10, p.2; cf. p.112: "delight . . . the most noble of all [three] and very necessary besides"; cf. 1.11, p.155, and also p.158: "grace of form could never be separated . . . from suitability for use".

46. Alberti *op.cit.*1.11, p.9

47. Alberti *op.cit.*1.10 pp.114–115. It is the second country, Greece, where "men of learning" begin to understand the importance of the "skill of the workman". cf. 1.11, p.157. See also note 48 below.

48. Alberti *op.cit.* 1.11, p.159: ". . . by invention and the working of the intellect, or by the hand of the craftsman, or is imbued naturally in the objects themselves". cf. p.5 where Alberti places "skill" between "matter" on the one hand, and "mind" on the other.

49. Alberti *op.cit.*1.10, pp.119–128

50. *Ibid.* p.1; cf. p.xi "We consider that an edifice is a kind of body consisting like all other bodies of design and of matter"; cf. 1.11, p.5 which refers to "lineaments and matter".

51. *Ibid.* p.194: "which must be contrived in such a manner as to join and unite a certain number of parts into one body or whole, by an orderly and sure coherence and agreement of all those parts", cf. p.1: "Design consists in a right and exact adapting and joining together the lines and angles . . ."; cf. 1.11, pp.301 & 307

52. *Ibid.* pp.1–2; cf. 1.11, p.7

53. *Ibid.* p.194. Note: In the chapter following Leoni's subheading quoted, the second term becomes "finishing", e.g. "We may conclude beauty to be such a consent and agreement of the parts of a whole in which it is found as to Number, Finishing and Collocation, as Congruity, that is to say the Law of Nature requires"; cf. 1.11, p.302 where the three terms are translated "number . . . outline . . . position" (Latin *numerus . . . finitio . . . collocatio*). In fact, Alberti, later in the same chapter, discusses *finitio* as though it signified proportion. Rykwert *et al.*, following Burckhardt, think the term "Congruity" in the above passage is important, and retain instead the Latin word, *concinnitas*.

54. *Ibid.* pp.252–253, footnote 241. Rykwert compares this passage from Chapter 5 with a passage from Chapter 8: "*comparatas, coaequatas atque compactas*" which may also be compared with Quality, Quantity and Relation. This possible derivation is not mentioned in the 1988 translation.

55. *Ibid.* pp.114–115; cf. 1.11, pp.157–159

56. *Ibid.* p.ix; cf. 1.11, p.2 which, however, translates the phrases as "pleasant to know". See note 2.33 above.

57. Alberti *op.cit.*1.11, p.246: "*commoda . . . firmitatem . . . amoenitatem*". Elsewhere Alberti speaks of "*utilitatis, dignitatis, amoenitatisque*", using the masculine "*dignitas*" in place of firmness, and instead of the feminine "*venustas*" for delight. The original Latin reads:

> "*Una haec partitio utilitatis dignitatis amoenitatisque habita ratione committur*" (see note 2.58 below, Vol.1, p.65). See Cicero's distinction between masculine and feminine usage (note 2.103 below), and the related passage of Inigo Jones *op.cit.*2.28.

58. Alberti L.B. *L'architettura* Orlandi G. & Portoghesi P. (eds) (Edizioni il Polifilo, Milan, 1966), Vol.2, pp.447–449. This work includes the Latin text:

> "*Sed pulchritudo atque ornamentum per se quid sit . . . ut sit pulchritudo quidem certa cum ratione concinnitas universarum partium in eo . . . erit quidem ornamentum quasi subsidiaria quaedam lux pulchritudinis atque veluti complementum . . . ornamentum autem afficti et compacti naturam sapere magis quam innati*"

Cf. *op.cit.*1.11, pp.156 & 420. Giving the explanation that beauty is "the essential idea" and ornament is "the individual expression", Rykwert *et al.* appear to confuse the concepts of "idea" and "form". It would be better to start from the premise that ornament is indeed something "added on" and thus is merely a smaller fragment of the building, subject to the three categories of form, function and meaning just as the building is.

59. Alberti *op.cit.*1.10, p.113; cf. 1.11, p.156 "something attached or additional"

60. Alberti *op.cit.*1.11, pp.24,36,312 & 315. "The greatest glory in the art of building is to have a good sense of what is appropriate" (p.315)

61. Alberti *op.cit.*1.10, p.141, cf. p.155; cf. *op.cit.*1.11, p.200

62. *Ibid.* p.191; cf. 1.11, p.298

63. *Ibid.* p.192; cf. 1.11, p.298

64. See note 2.48 above. Compare the different interpretations of:

    (1) Mind (Form), Hand (Effect), Nature (Analogy)

    (2) Mind (Meaning), Hand (Effect), Nature (Physics)

65. See note 2.32 above

66. Alberti *op.cit.*1.10, p.196; cf. 1.11, p.305 which translates the passage "It is absolutely certain that Nature is wholly consistent"

67. From the very first page we are made aware of the importance to Alberti of the grouping: "Necessity . . . Usefulness . . . Knowledge", and he later refers to this group in terms of "the first principles of philosophy" (*op.cit.*1.11, p.94). The relation of this to the Aristotelian grouping Physics, Ethics and Theology needs a little explanation, but it is important as it is reflected in the triadic structuring of Alberti's book, and also in his restructuring of the Vitruvian categories.

    (1) Physics is dealt with in the first three chapters, from form through to material, and although only once referred to by name, physics may be equated with what Alberti termed "the Laws of Nature". (Vitruvius makes a clearer connection with Physics when he said "Nature does not admit of a truthful exploration in accordance with the doctrines of the physicists without an accurate demonstration of the primary causes of things, showing how and why they are as they are", note 2.73 below, p.41). "Necessity" is a general word that Alberti uses to reflect the requirements placed upon the architect by the physical forces of heat and light, as well as that of gravity which demands "firmness" in a building.

    (2) Ethics was a subject much discussed by the Humanists of the time. Bruni, for example, complained of the ambivalent translations of the Latin word *bonum*. Following Seneca, he proposed that a clear distinction should be made as to whether "good" in any particular passage should be translated as "virtuous" (*honestas*) or as "useful" (*utile*), a distinction made explicit in the earlier works of Cicero (note 2.102 below). We begin to see here a connection between Ethics and the Vitruvian *utilitatis*. In Books 4 and 5, Alberti discusses the functioning of a building very much in moral terms, and draws the analogy between division of labour – soldiers, farmers and priests (reflecting the Vitruvian division of buildings into defensive, utilitarian and religious kinds, q.v.) – with the moral division of the soul – Strength, Temperance and Wisdom.

    (3) Theology. In Book 6, Alberti turns to the concept of Delight, and links the work of the heavenly gods with the beauty we see around us. In Book 7, Alberti states that the temple should be the most beautiful of buildings, "the most important ornament of the city" saying "there is no doubt that a temple that delights the mind wonderfully . . . will greatly encourage piety" (cf. 1.11, p.194). There are two problems with this account. First, the subject of Physics straddles two fundamental categories which we may think of in terms of space and energy. Second, many would rather see Theology being located within the category of wisdom and truth, rather than that of beauty, although there are others who would make a claim for its location within a category that contains goodness.

68. Alberti's infusion with the Aristotelian/Scholastic doctrine of causes is manifest as early as Chapter 3, Book 1 where we find, for example, the passage, which in the Leoni translation reads: "Some of the Causes of this variety we imagine we understand; others by the obscurity of their natures are altogether hidden and unknown to us". (Rykwert *et al.* translate the word "cause" here as "reason"). The three kinds of cause, Formal, Efficient and Final, may, in a sense, be compared with the above-discussed categories of Physics, Ethics and Theology. Chapter 4 of Book 6 suggests three causes of pleasure

that we may gain from a work of architecture, namely "[the form or material] imbued naturally in the object . . . the hand of the craftsman . . . the working of the intellect" (*op.cit.*1.11, p.159). Regarding the first of these, Aristotle illustrated the concept of the Material Cause with that of a saw, for which the choice of iron was necessary. Regarding the second of these, Aristotle had illustrated the concept of Efficient Cause with that of the builder or craftsman; and it is by the intellect, and planning ahead, that the Final Cause is best exemplified.

However, this analogy too is flawed. First, all three categories are reduced to kinds of causality, quite ignoring the fact that there may be other kinds of relationship type to be taken into account. This, I suggest, has led to a certain confusion in Alberti's thinking in that sometimes "necessity" (formal cause) is placed first, and sometimes "commodity" (efficient cause) is placed first. In one place (p.315) he compounds this confusion by stating "to build conveniently is the product of both necessity and utility". We are reminded of Norberg-Schulz who divided the single category of function or "task" into two – physical control, and functional frame. Second, too often, the final cause is thought of in moral terms only, which would tend to confuse Ethics with the third category, normally, in the above system, either Theology as we have seen, or Logic. cf. note 2.117 below

69. Lotz W. *Architecture in Italy 1500–1600* 1974 (tr. Howard D., Yale University Press, London, 1995), p.157. The categories referred to are those of Palladio: "The circle mirrors God's unity, infinity, his homogeneity and justice" ("*Unita, infinita Essenza, Uniformita e Giustiza*") (p.148). Lotz does mention, however, the Vitruvian Categories in relation to Sangallo's Palazzo Farnese: "The ancient structural and ornamental forms are adequate to the function" (p.60)

70. Palladio A. *The Four Books of Architecture* (Dover Publications, New York, 1965) p.26; cf. Palladio *op.cit.*1.16, p.56

71. *Ibid.* p.1. The passage continues "That work therefore cannot be called perfect which should be useful and not durable, or durable and not useful, or having both these should be without beauty"; cf. Palladio *op.cit.*1.16, p.6

72. Kruft *op.cit.*1.7, p.84

73. Vitruvius *Vitruvius on Architecture* (tr. Granger F., William Heinemann, London, 1931), Vol. 1, p.xiv

74. *Ibid.* p.x; cf. Vitruvius, note 2.75 below, pp.11,78,82,109,198 & 199

75. Vitruvius *The Ten Books on Architecture* (tr. Morgan M.H., 1914, Dover Publications, New York, 1960), pp.5–12

76. *Ibid.* p.256

77. *Ibid.* pp.42,195,251 and *passim*

78. *Ibid.* p.73

79. *Ibid.* p.5

80. *Ibid.* pp.13–16

81. *Ibid.* pp.16–17

82. Alberti *op.cit.*1.11, pp.92–93

83. Vitruvius *op.cit.*2.75, p.17

84. Vitruvius *op.cit.*2.73, Vol 1, p.34; cf. p.35: "Now these should be so carried out that account is taken of strength, utility, grace".

85. Vitruvius *op.cit.*2.75, p.17

86. *Ibid.* p.17: "Durability will be assured when foundations are carried down to the solid ground and materials wisely and liberally selected"

87. *Ibid.* p.122

88. *Ibid.* p.86

89. *Ibid.* pp.78–86, 90–122

90. *Ibid.* pp.42–46; cf. p.41: "materials . . . and in what proportion their elementary constituents were combined"

91. *Ibid.* p.42

92. Vitruvius *op.cit.*2.73, Vol. 1, p.25: "Vitruvius's three terms seem to correspond to Democritus's "*ordo positura figurae*" given in Lucretius, I.685; see also note 2.53 above.

93. Vitruvius *op.cit.*2.75, p.10
94. *Ibid.* pp.181–182
95. *Ibid.* pp.180–181
96. *Ibid.* p.16,181–189
97. *Ibid.* p.80
98. *Ibid.* p.38; cf. Lucretius *De Rerum Natura* (tr. Rouse W., William Heinemann, London, 1947) Book 5
99. *Ibid.* pp.42–65,202–221,242–248
100. *Ibid.* pp.131–136
101. *Ibid.* p.16; cf. *op.cit.*2.73, Vol. 1: "*distributione quae graece 'oeconomia' dicitur*", and p.33, "The second stage in Economy comes when buildings are variously disposed for the use of owners".
102. Cicero *De Officiis* tr. Miller W. (William Heinemann, London, 1951); p.11, cf. pp.176–177, *honestum* (morally right) versus *utile* (expedient); cf. Cicero, note 2.117 below, p.494
103. *Ibid.* pp.130–133. "There are two orders of beauty: in the one, loveliness [*venustas*] predominates; in the other, dignity [*dignitas*]; of these, we ought to regard loveliness as the attribute of woman, and dignity as the attribute of man". The section in which this passage occurs is entitled "Propriety [*Decorum*] (1) In Outward Appearance".
104. Vitruvius *op.cit.*2.75, pp.14–16; cf. 2.73, Vol. 1, pp.26–31
105. *Ibid.* p.14
106. *Ibid.* pp.104 & 115
107. *Ibid.* pp.104 & 115
108. *Ibid.* pp.104 & 115
109. *Ibid.* pp.210–211
110. *Ibid.* p.211
111. *Ibid.* p.192; cf. note 2.73, Vol. 2, p.58: "*venustate et usu et decore*"
112. *Ibid.* p.17; cf. note 2.73, Vol. 1, pp.34–35
113. *Ibid.* p.174
114. *Ibid.* p.175
115. Lacey W.K. *Cicero and the End of the Roman Republic* (Hodder & Stoughton, 1978)
116. *Ibid.* p.136
117. Cicero *Tusculan Disputations* tr. King J.E. (William Heinemann, London, 1927) p.495: "*Physica, Ethica, Dialectica*, the three parts of philosophy according to the Stoics; cf. Alberti, *op.cit.*2.67; cf. note 3.93 below
118. Cicero *De Natura Deorum* (tr. Rackham H., William Heinemann, London, 1933) 1.45, pp.48–49
119. Cicero *op.cit.*2.102, pp.17ff; cf. pp.157 & 185; cf. Cicero *Academica* (tr. Rackham H., William Heinemann, London, 1933) pp.614–615: "Wisdom then is divided by your own school, as it is also by most philosophers into three parts", namely Physics, Ethics and Logic.
120. Cicero *op.cit.*2.102, I.138, pp.140–141: "I must discuss also what sort of house a man of rank should have. Its prime object is serviceableness [*usus*]. To this the plan of the building should be adapted; and yet careful attention should be paid to its convenience [*commoditatis*] and distinction [*dignitatisque*]".
121. Lacey *op.cit.*2.115; cf. Cicero *De Oratore op.cit.*2.43, pp.13ff.
122. Cicero *op.cit.*2.102, 1.2, pp.4–5: "*apte, distincte, ornate*"
123. *Ibid.* I.126, pp.128–129: "*formositate, ordine, ornatu ad actionem apto*"

Chapter 3: Greek Categories

1. Levey G.R. *Plato in Sicily* (Faber & Faber, London, 1956) p.22
2. Plato *Parmenides* 129 (tr. Jowett B.), *The Dialogues of Plato* (Clarendon Press, Oxford, 1875, p.162). Like/Unlike, One/Many and Motion/Rest are mentioned here. Being/Non-Being is added at 136 (p.171).

3. Cornford F.M. *Plato's Theory of Knowledge* 1935 (Routledge & Kegan Paul, London, 1960) p.274: "It has become the established practice to call these very important kinds [Existence, Motion and Rest] together with Sameness and Difference, the Platonic 'Categories'". It should be said that Cornford disagreed with this practice mainly, it would seem, because they were very different from Aristotle's categories – and Aristotle coined the term. My own opinion is that Plato's terms are closer to what we should take to be the Categories today than Aristotle's were, as Plotinus subsequently discovered.

4. Aristotle *De Generatione* 314a "Only Democritus has thought it out clearly"; cf. *Metaphysics* 983a

5. cf. Aristotle *Physics* 187b, 203a

6. *Op.cit.*3.1, p.44

7. *Ibid.* p.51

8. Plato *Lysis* 203a

9. *Op.cit.*3.1, p.66

10. Plato *Charmides* 170c

11. Plato *Menexenus* 246 (p.511) "For neither does wealth bring honour to the owner if he be a coward. . . . Nor does beauty and strength of body. . . . And all knowledge, when separated from justice and virtue, is seen to be cunning and not wisdom". cf. *Meno* 87 (p.290) which distinguishes between "goods of the body . . . health, strength, beauty and wealth", and goods of the soul . . . temperance, justice, courage . . . all under the guidance of wisdom". As does *Laws* 631 (p.200). *Gorgias* may also be referred to.

12. Plato *Republic* 601 (pp.496–497)

13. Plato *Sophist* 219 (p.428). "There is agriculture and the tending of mortal creatures, and the art of constructing or moulding vessels, and there is the art of imitation".

14. Plato *Laws* 669 (p.240)

15. *Ibid.* 655 (p.224): ". . . not to be tedious, the figures and melodies which are expressive of virtue of soul or body, or of images of virtue, are without exception good, and those which are expressive of vice are the reverse of good".

16. *Ibid.* 667 (p.238)

17. Plato *Phaedrus* 246 (p.123): "Now the divine is beauty, wisdom, goodness and the like". cf. *Republic* 505 (p.391): "Do you think that the possession of the whole world is of any value without the good? Or of all knowledge without the beautiful and good". It may be noted that the *Bhagavad Gita*, which predates Plato, referred to "words which are good and beautiful and true".

18. Plato *Phaedo* 65 (p.438); *Republic* 451 (p.330), 476 (p.360); *Parmenides* 130 (p.163); *Laws* 858 (p.427)

19. Plato *Republic* 135 (p.170). The last sentence of *Phaedo* reads "Such was the end, Echecrates, of our friend [Socrates], whom I may truly call the wisest, and justest, and best of all the men whom I have ever known".

20. Plato *Statesman* 283–284 (p.565)

21. Plato *Philebus* 55

22. Beardsley M.C. *Aesthetics from Classical Greece to the Present* (The University of Alabama Press, Tuscaloosa & London, 1966) p.27

23. Plato *Republic* 400 (p.275): "There are three principles of rhythm out of which metrical systems are framed . . . Dactylic rhythm [1/1] . . . Iambic or Trochaic rhythm [1/2 or 2/1] . . . Paeonic rhythm [3/2]"

24. Plato *Gorgias* 508

25. Plato *Philebus* 51 (p.98)

26. Plato *Republic* 400 (p.276)

27. Plato *Symposium* 187

28. Plato *Republic* 479

29. Plato *Gorgias* 464 (p.335)

30. Plato *Republic* 601 (p.497)

31. *Ibid.* 420 (p.297)

32. Plato *Gorgias* 484–486

33. Plato *Republic* 404

34. Plato *Philebus* 31 (p.73)
35. Plato *Statesman* 279 (p.559)
36. Plato *Laws* 778 (p.349)
37. Aristotle *Politics* 1328b
38. Plato *Republic* 427 (p.305); In *Laws* we find courage demoted to a "fourth rate virtue". In *Protagoras* "holiness" is added; and in *Meno*, "magnificence".
39. Plato *Statesman* 283–284 (p.565); cf. Aristotle *Ethics* 116b.
40. Plato *Laws* 688 (p.259); cf. Laches ". . . courage as a sort of wisdom"; and *Phaedo*, "wisdom as the one true coin".
41. Plato *Republic* 401 (p.277)
42. Plato *Laws* 668: "Do we not regard all music as representative and imitative?"
43. Plato *Laws* 658
44. *Ibid.* Book II *passim*; cf. Aristotle *De Poetica* 1448b
45. Plato *Philebus* e.g. 34 (p.76), 51 (p.98), 63–64 (p.113)
46. Plato *Laws* 658 (p.229)
47. Plato *Cratylus* 389 (p.210)
48. Plato *Republic* 597–599
49. *Ibid.* 597 (p.491)
50. *Ibid* 500 (p.386)
51. Plato *Laws* 713 (p.285)
52. Plato *Statesman* 309 (p.595)
53. Plato *Philebus* 65 (p.114): "Then if we are not able to hunt the good with one idea only, with three we may take our prey; beauty, symmetry and truth are the three, and these when united we may regard as the cause of the mixture, and the mixture as being good by reason of the admixture of them". Yet he starts by saying "Measure and symmetry everywhere pass into beauty and virtue".
54. Plato *Statesman* 279 (p.559); cf. Aristotle *Metaphysics* 1070a
55. Plato *Gorgias* 474 (p.347): "When you speak of beautiful things, as for example, bodies, colours, figures, sounds do you not call them beautiful in reference to some standard: bodies for example are beautiful in proportion as they are useful; or as the sight of them gives pleasure to the spectators; can you give any other account of personal beauty?"
56. Plato, e.g. *Lysis* 221: "the good is beautiful"; *Symposium* 200: "Is not the good also the beautiful?"; *Republic*: ". . . truth akin to proportion"; *Laws* 689: "How can there there be the least shadow of wisdom when there is no harmony?" Aristotle argues against this view in *Topics* 139b where he says "harmony does not contain virtue, nor virtue harmony".
57. See notes 3.2 and 3.3 above
58. Plato *Sophist* 242 (p.457)
59. Plato *Philebus* 16 (p.55)
60. *Ibid.* 18 (p.57)
61. Plato *Republic* 580–581: "There is one principle with which a man learns, another with which he is angry; the third [we] . . . have denoted by the general term 'appetitive'. . . . To these three principles three pleasures correspond".
62. Plato *Timaeus* 50 (p.633): the three natures are the process of generation (cf. Hume's causality); that in which generation takes place (cf. contiguity); and that by which the thing generated can resemble another (cf. resemblance).
63. Plato *Laws* 895 (p.465): "You would admit that we have a three-fold knowledge of things? . . . I mean that we know the essence, and that we know the definition of essence, and the name".
64. Plato *Parmenides* 144 (p.183); cf. Aristotle *De Anima* 427a: "Is it the case then that what discriminates, though both numerically one and indivisible, is at the same time divided in its being. . . . It must lose its unity by being put into activity". Note the use of the three terms, unity, activity and discrimination.
65. Plato *Timaeus* 31
66. *Ibid.* 32
67. Plato *Sophist* 249 (p.466)

68. Plato *Epistle Seven* 342 (p.95)
69. *Ibid*. 342 (p.95)
70. Plato *Laws* 778 (p.349)
71. Plato *Phaedrus* 246 (p.124); cf. *Statesman* 259 (p.536) which refers to the "sphere of knowledge": "And now we shall only be proceeding in due order if we divide the sphere of knowledge . . ."
72. Plato *Parmenides* 136
73. Plato *Symposium* 211 (p.62)
74. Plato *Philebus* 16 (p.55)
75. Hamilton J.R. *Alexander the Great* (Hutchinson University Library, London, 1973) p.112
76. *Ibid*. p.74
77. Vitruvius *op. cit*. 2.75 p.54
78. Aristotle *Politics* in *The Works of Aristotle* Ross W.D. (ed.) (Clarendon Press, Oxford, 1926) para. 1267b
79. Aristotle *Oeconomica* 1352a
80. Ross D. *Aristotle* 1923 (Routledge, London, 1995) p.2
81. Aristotle *Ethics* 1173b
82. *Op.cit*. 3.80, p.4
83. Aristotle *Metaphysics* 1075a; cf. Ross *op.cit*.3.80, pp.117–118, who noted that Aristotle was the first of the ancients to undertake a serious study of classification, referring to his *De Partibus*.
84. Aristotle *Metaphysics* 1037b; cf. *Analytica Posteriora*: "the process does not cease until the indivisible concepts, the true universals [presumably the highest categories] are established".
85. Aristotle *Metaphysics* 1043a
86. *Ibid*. 1029a: "In one sense the subject is said to be the matter; in another sense it is said to be the form; in a third it is said to be a composite of these". Cf. *Metaphysics* 1033a and 1034a, and *De Anima* 412a.
87. Aristotle *Topics* 145a; cf. *Metaphysics* 1025b: "Thus if every thought s practical or productive or theoretical"; and *Metaphysics* 1026b: "A sign of this is the fact that no science, be it practical or productive or theoretical takes the trouble to consider it. For the builder who is building a house is not producing at the same time the attributes which are accidental to the house when built, for these are infinite; for nothing prevents the house built from being pleasant to some men, harmful to others; useful to still others . . . but the art of building produces none of these attributes".
88. Aristotle *Metaphysics* 993b.
89. Aristotle *Physics* 246b; cf. 247a: "And the case is similar in regard to the states of the soul, all of which (like those of the body) exist in virtue of particular relations, the excellencies being perfections of nature, and the defects departures from it".
90. Aristotle *Physics* 246b; cf. *Rhetoric* 1361b regarding "firmness" in "young men", and Plato's *Gorgias* 474.
91. *Ibid*. 247a: "for all moral excellence is concerned with bodily pleasures and pains, which again depend on either acting or remembering or anticipating".
92. *Ibid*. 247b
93. Aristotle *Topics* 105b: "Of propositions and problems there are – to comprehend the matter in outline – three divisions: for some are ethical propositions some are on natural philosophy, while some are logical". A suggestion of this division may be found in Plato's forms, practices and notions of the *Symposium* 211, or his nature, practice and knowledge of *Phaedrus* 269.
94. Aristotle *Analytica Priora, passim*
95. Aristotle *Categories* in *Aristotle's Categories and De Interpretatione* tr. Ackrill J.L. (Clarendon Press, Oxford, 1963) Ch.4; cf. *Analytica Posteriora* 83b.
96. *Op.cit*.3.80, p.23, Ross suggests that the doctrine of ten categories was something already established. He notes that Trendelenberg held that the distinction derived from a study of grammar.

97. Plotinus *Enneads* (tr. Mackenna S. and Page B.S., The Medici Society, London, 1930) VI.3.3, VI.3.21; cf. Evangeliou C. *Aristotle's Categories and Porphyry* (E.J. Brill, Leiden, 1988) p.140; cf. Aristotle *Analytica Posteriora* 83b in which he distinguished between substance and the other categories, and referred to "predicates so related to their subjects"; and *Physics* 185a: "Substance alone is independent for everything is predicated of substance as subject".

98. Aristotle *Analytica Posteriora* 81b: "Every syllogism is effected by means of three terms. One kind of syllogism serves to prove that A inheres in C by showing that A inheres in B and B in C".

99. Long A. & Sedley D. *The Hellenistic Philosophers* (Cambridge University Press, Cambridge, 1987) p.206. Chryssipus in his *Dialectical Treatises* recognized the simple or categorical propositions of Aristotle, but added to these the "conditional" proposition, e.g. "if it is day it is light", and the "disjunctive" proposition, e.g. "either it is day or it is night". Cf. Aristotle *De Generatione* 323a: "But the disjunctive definition of 'touching' must include and distinguish (a) contact in general as the relation between two things which having position . . . and (b) reciprocal contact . . . [to do with motion]".

100. Aristotle *Metaphysics* 1055b

101. Aristotle *Ethics* 1132a

102. *Ibid*. 1131a

103. *Ibid*. 1131a

104. Aristotle *Physics* 265b

105. Aristotle *De Anima* 430b

106. Aristotle *Metaphysics* 1057a; cf. *Physics* 188a

107. A work by Aristotle on beauty and mathematics was mentioned in Roman times by Diogenes Laertius, see footnote to *Metaphysics* 1078a: "Now the most important kinds of the beautiful are order, symmetry and definiteness, and the mathematical sciences exhibit properties of these in the highest degree"; cf. *Metaphysics* 1053b where Aristotle compares colours to numbers.

108. Aristotle *Metaphysics* 1028. Aristotle uses the words "some say . . ." with a footnote referring to "the school of Xenocrates".

109. *Ibid*. 1020a

110. Aristotle *Categories* Ch.6, 4b–5a

111. *Ibid*. Ch.6, 5a

112. Aristotle *Metaphysics* 1020a

113. Long & Sedley *op.cit.* 3.99. Epictetus spoke of "hypothetical" arguments, p.226.

114. Aristotle *Topics* 100a; cf. *Physics* 195a: "The letters are the causes of the syllables . . . and the premises of the conclusion, in the sense of that from which". Cf. *Analytica Posteriora* 71b: "The premises must be the causes of the conclusion".

115. Long & Sedley *op.cit.* 3.99, p.340. Cf. Aristotle *Analytica Posteriora* 90a: "It is the cause we seek in all our enquiries".

116. Aristotle *Physics* 200a

117. Aristotle *Metaphysics* 983a. The four kinds of cause are also described in *Analytica Posteriora* 94a and *Physics* 194b.

118. *Ibid*. 982b and 1013a; cf. *Physics* 194b and 198a

119. *Ibid*. 1013a; cf. *Analytica Posteriora* 94a: "A house having being built necessitates a foundation having been laid".

120. *Ibid*. 1013a; cf. *Physics* 194b

121. *Ibid*. 996b

122. Aristotle *Ethics* 1097b

123. *Ibid*. 1176a–1176b; cf. Plato *Laws* 645: "the sacred and golden cord of reason".

124. Aristotle *Rhetoric* 1369b; cf. *Ethics* 1099b where happiness is described as "a virtuous activity of the soul", and 1153a where pleasure is described as being derived from "exercising one's faculties".

125. Aristotle *Oeconomica* 1345b: "For the ready use of household appliances the Laconian

method is a good one; for everything ought to have its own proper place and so be ready for use and not require to be searched for".

126. Aristotle *Metaphysics* 1027b
127. Long & Sedley *op.cit.* 3.99, pp.33,34,54
128. Aristotle *Categories* Ch.8, 11a. Cf. Ackrill *op.cit.* 3.95 p.108 where the close etymological connection between "similar" and "qualified" is noted.
129. Aristotle *Metaphysics* 1038b; cf. *De Interpretatione*: "Now of actual things, some are universal, others particular (I call universal that which is by nature predicated of a number of things, and particular that which is not. Man, for instance is a universal, Callias a particular).
130. *Ibid.* 1086ff.
131. Aristotle *Analytica Posteriora* 72a; cf. *Metaphysics* 1017a
132. Aristotle *De Poetica* 1447a; cf. Ross *op.cit.*3.80, p.280. Delight is seen as an outcome of the instinct to seek knowledge. The pleasure lies in recognizing what the work is meant to represent.
133. Aristotle *Ethics* 1098b
134. *Ibid.* 1122a; cf. 1165a: "Render to each class or age group what is appropriate".
135. Aristotle *Politics* 1331b
136. Plato *op.cit.*3.45; cf. Aristotle *De Poetica* 1448b: "To be learning something is the greatest of pleasures not only to philosophers. . . . The reason of the delight in seeing the picture is that one is at the same time learning and gathering the meaning of things; for if one had not seen the thing before, one's pleasure will not be in the picture as an imitation of it, but will be due to the execution or colouring or some other similar cause".
137. Aristotle *Rhetoric* 1408a. Under class he includes differences of age, sex and nationality.
138. *Ibid.* 1407a
139. *Ibid.* 1405a; cf. 1404b
140. Aristotle *Ethics* 1140a
141. Aristotle *Metaphysics* 1034b; cf. 1013a and 1029a
142. Aristotle *Politics* 1330b
143. *Ibid.* 1331a
144. *Ibid.* 1332a: "There are three things which make men good and virtuous; these are nature, habit and rational principle". Cf. *Ethics* 1179b
145. *Ibid.* 1332b
146. Aristotle *De Poetica* 1450b
147. *Ibid.* 1451a
148. Aristotle *Physics* 199b. "Organic union" is mentioned in *Physics* 213a. The "organic unity" of stories and drama is mentioned in *De Poetica* 1459a
149. Aristotle *Physics* 189b; cf. 189a "It is plausible to suppose more than two . . . for love does not gather strife together and make things out of it . . . but both act on a third thing different from both"; cf. *De Caelo* 268a "For as the Pythagoreans say, the world and all that is in it is determined by the number three since beginning and middle and end give the number of an 'all' and the number they give is the triad". Aristotle goes on to discuss the three dimensions. . . . "A magnitude if divisible one way is a line, if two ways a surface, and if three a body".
150. Aristotle *Metaphysics* 1018a; cf. 986a–986b where Aristotle discussed the ten pairs of opposites put forward by the Pythagoreans: "The principles of things are the contraries"; cf. *Physics* 188b: "Everything comes from its contrary. . . . A house comes from certain things in a state of separation instead of conjunction". One might almost say, disjunction.
151. Aristotle *De Generatione* 332a
152. *Ibid.* 330b
153. Aristotle *Metaphysics* 996b. The first cause is here called the "efficient cause". He suggests that there may be only three kinds of cause at 1044b. Form and matter are contrasted at 1029a.

154. Aristotle *De Generatione* 322b
155. *Ibid*.
156. Aristotle *De Caelo* 303b
157. Aristotle *De Generatione* 327b
158. Aristotle *Physics* 265b
159. Aristotle *De Anima* 427a.
160. Aristotle *Metaphysics* 1044b
161. Aristotle, *De Caelo* 268a
162. Aristotle *Metaphysics* 1020b; cf. *De Generatione* 333a where Aristotle supposes three categories by which different elements may be compared – by amount, by power of action, and by correspondence (or similarities in quality).
163. Aristotle *Metaphysics* 998b ff; cf. 1029a and 1070a
164. *Ibid*. 1079a; cf. 1088a: "Of all the categories a relation is least of all a nature or a substance and is posterior to quality and quantity".
165. Ex.Brit cv Speussipus
166. Long & Sedley, *op.cit.* 3.99, p.480. Cf. Plato *Theaetetus* 152: "Some say 'all things are said to be relative'".
167. *Ibid*. p.37
168. *Ibid*. p.485
169. Aristotle *De Anima* 425b
170. Aristotle *Metaphysics* 1078a: "Now the most important kinds of the beautiful are order, symmetry and definiteness, and the mathematical sciences exhibit properties of these in the highest degree".
171. *Ibid*. 1072b
172. Aristotle *Ethics* 1170a

Chapter 4: Mediaeval Categories

1. Vitruvius *On Architecture* (tr. Granger, F., Heinemann, London, 1931) p.xix
2. Eusebius *Ecclesiastical History* Vol. II (tr. Oulton, Heinemann, London, 1932)
3. Cf. Augustine *The Trinity* (tr. Mackenna S., Catholic University of America Press, 1963) p.187, "one essence and three persons"
4. Clement I; cf. Augustine *op.cit.* 4.3 p.214, "the Trinity, of which a trace '*vestigia*' appears in the creature".
5. Augustine *Confessions* (tr. Pine-Coffin, P.R., Penguin, Harmondsworth, 1961) XIII, 11, p.318; cf. Eco note 4.27 below, p.11, "he thought that the soul recognized in material objects a harmony identical with its own structure".
6. Tatarkiewicz W. *History of Aesthetics*, Vol II *Mediaeval Aesthetics*, 1962 (tr. Montgomery R.M., Polish Scientific Publishers, 1970)
7. McCallum J.R. *Abelard's Christian Theology* (Blackwell, Oxford, 1948)
8. Reese W.L. *Dictionary of Philosophy and Religion* (Harvester Press, 1980)
9. Pegis A.C. *Introduction to St. Thomas Aquinas* (Random House, 1948) p.173; cf. Duns Scotus note 4.165 below, p.94, "namely to the Good, Being and the True"
10. Thomas Aquinas *Summa Theologiae* (Blackfriars, 1967) p.30 (note); also p.189 "if by the Holy Spirit is meant the Person, it denotes a relation"; cf. Augustine *op.cit.* 4.3 p.180, "the names Father and Son do not refer to the substance but to the relation"
11. Plotinus *Enneads* (tr. Mackenna S. & Page B.S., The Medici Society, London, 1930) VI.3.3, VI.3.21; cf. VI.1.27 where even substance, or at least "matter" could be considered as a "relative".
12. *Op.cit.* 4.9 Q13v 47
13. *Ibid* S.T. Q28
14. Gilby, T. *St. Thomas Aquinas: Theological Texts* (Oxford University Press) S.T. 2a-2e
15. *Op.cit.* 4.6
16. Augustine *op.cit.* 4.3, VI, p.213

17. *Op.cit.* 4.7
18. *Op.cit.* 4.9, p.213
19. *Op.cit.* 4.5 VII.14, p.152
20. *Op.cit.* 4.11 xxv; V.1, Plotinus's predecessor, Numenius, also proposed a trinity: Father, Creator and Created, derived from Plato's *Timaeus*.
21. Theodoret *Ecclesiastical History*
22. *Op.cit.* 4.3 VI, p.212; cf. Hilary *De Trinitate* II.1
23. Exodus 3.14; John 6.35; John 14.17
24. Augustine *City of God* (tr. Healey J., Dent & Sons, London, 1931); cf. *op.cit.* 4.3 S.T. Q16.3, p.173; cf. *op.cit.* 4.9 intro. Augustine discovered twenty-two different formulations of the Trinity reflected in the world; cf. Eco note 4.27 below who derived Beauty, Goodness and Truth from a dubious passage in Aquinas's *Commentary on the Sentences* p.32
25. *Op.cit.* 4.5, I.20, p.40
26. *Op.cit.* 4.8
27. Eco U. *The Aesthetics of Thomas Aquinas* 1956 (tr. Bredin, H., Radius, 1988) p.45; Eco suggested that transcendentals "are a bit like differing visual angles from which being can be looked at"; transcendentals were introduced to the West by Philip the Chancellor in the early thirteenth century.
28. Coppleston S.J. *A History of Philosophy* Vol. II (Burns, Oates & Washbourne Ltd, 1950) p.95; cf. Augustine *op.cit.* 4.3 pp.460–461, where a list of divine names were reduced to three: eternal, wise and blessed.
29. *Op.cit.* 4.11 V.8.9
30. *Op.cit.* 4.27 p.35; also Aquinas *op.cit.* 4.10 S.T. Q5 A4
31. *Ibid.* p.198
32. *Ibid.* p.53; cf. Tatarkiewicz *op.cit.* 4.6 p.263, Witelo developed the work of Alhazen (tenth to eleventh century) on optical physics.
33. *Ibid.* p.71; cf. *op.cit.* 4.5 IV.13, pp.83–85
34. *Op.cit.* 4.11 I.6.1
35. *Ibid.* I.6.2; also VI.9.1, "It is by virtue of unity that beings are beings . . . beauty appears by this principle, unity".
36. *Op.cit.* 4.27 p.65; cf. *op.cit.* 4.10 S.T. Q39 A8
37. *Op.cit.* 4.5 II.5, p.48 and XIII.28 pp.340–341; cf. *op.cit.* 4.24 X.8: "So is the world's beauty composed of contrarieties . . . like a fair poem made gracious by antithetic figures; also X.23 "a picture shows well though it have black in diverse places"; cf. Aquinas *op.cit.* 4.14 "bright colours are edged and emphasised by shade" and "Monotony results from oneness, variety from a multitude of shifting relationships" (S.T. Ia. xviii.4ad4)
38. *Op.cit.* 4.6 p.226
39. Holt, E.G. *A Documentary History of Art*, Vol. I (Doubleday, New York, 1957); cf. Frankl note 4.74 below and the illustration of the elevation of Milan Cathedral inscribed in triangles, in Cesariano's translation of Vitruvius.
40. Panofsky E. (ed.) *Abbot Suger on the Abbey Church of St. Denis* (Princeton University Press, 1946) p.37
41. *Ibid.* p.21
42. *Op.cit.* 4.6 p.244
43. Duns Scotus *Opus Oxniense* Vol. I, 17.3.13
44. *Richard of St. Victor* (tr. Zinn G.A., SPCK, London, 1979) pp. 136, 146, 155
45. *Op.cit.* 4.27 p.50
46. *Op.cit.* 4.14 p.78 (Comp. Theol. 68)
47. The number of stages of ascent varied according to author. Richard of St Victor proposed six, as did Bonaventure who followed him.
48. Hopkins & Richardson (eds) *Anselm of Canterbury* (Harper, New York, 1970); cf. Gilby *op.cit.* 4.14 p.37
49. Gilby, *op.cit.* 4.14 p.100; cf. Pegis *op.cit.* 4.9 S.T. Q5 A4 for the order; Duns Scotus (note 4.165) p.37 reduced the types of cause to two in his "triple primacy": Pre-eminence, Efficient Cause (incl. Formal Cause as exemplar) and Final Cause; Aquinas

(note 4.9 above) compares Formal, Efficient and Final with Ambrose's Pleasant, Useful and Befitting, a grouping taken from Cicero's *De Officiis* II (S.T. Q5 A6)

50. *Op.cit.* 4.27 Aquinas's *Commentary on the Divine Names* 4.1
51. *Ibid.* p.89 (cf. pp.166–173); also Aq. *Comm. Div. Nom* IV.5); cf. Aquinas *op.cit.* (4.9) "Beauty has the aspect of a formal cause"
52. *Op.cit.* 4.5 X.34–35 pp.240–242
53. *Op.cit.* 4.6 p.248
54. I Corinthians 12.12ff.; also Romans 12.4ff
55. *Op.cit.* 4.3 p.196
56. *Op.cit.* 4.14 (Aq *Disp. VI de Potentia* 1 ad 1)
57. Lopez, R.S. *The Birth of Europe* (Phoenix House, London, 1962) p.146
58. Vitruvius *The Ten Books on Architecture* (tr. Morgan M.H., Dover, New York, 1960) I.3.1., p.17
59. *Op.cit.* 4.14 p.181ff (S.T. 1a-2ae 1xviii 8)
60. *Op.cit.* 4.5, X.33, p.239
61. *Op.cit.* 4.2
62. Gilson, E. *The Mystical Theology of St. Bernard* (tr. Downes A., Sheed & Ward, London, 1940) p.70 (*De diversis Sermo* XII.2); cf. Augustine *op.cit.* 4.5 X.34 p.240, "they make them on a far more lavish scale than required"
63. Cf. Aquinas *op.cit.* 4.14, "A good man's purposes are unified, a sinner's scattered"; also p.244, "Complete virtue makes a person good all round . . . complete virtues are all interconnected".
64. *Op.cit.* 4.14, X (Aquinas S.T. 2a-2ae i.9)
65. *Op.cit.* 4.5 X.24, p.230, "God, who is Truth itself"
66. *Op.cit.* 4.27 p.101 (S.T. I.73, Ic), also p.191 (*De Veritate* I, 2c)
67. *Op.cit.* 4.11, I.8.1, and V.3.5
68. *Op.cit.* 4.9 p.169; cf. Plotinus *op.cit.* 4.11, V.5.2, "By this inherence of ideas . . . at once truth is there"
69. Long & Sedley *op.cit.* 3.99, pp. 80, 206, 264
70. *Op.cit.* 4.9 (S.T. Q6 A2) "triple perfection", related to the "constitution of its own being", its "perfect operation", and "attaining to something else as end"
71. *Op.cit.* 4.5, XI.5, p.257
72. *Op.cit.* 4.27 p.215, a view that was introduced by Plutarch
73. Payne R. *The Christian Centuries* (W.H. Allen, London, 1967) pp.137–210
74. Frankl P. *The Gothic* (Princeton University Press, 1960). Pseudo-Raphael thought that pointed arches derived from German forests, and Wetter described the clusters of columns that "shoot up like jets of water". The fountain was an important part of mediaeval symbolism.
75. *Op.cit.* 4.5, X.7, p.214
76. *Ibid.*, e.g. X.6, p.213
77. *Op.cit.* 4.6; cf. Theodorus Studites 759–828
78. *Ibid.*
79. Cf. Honorius of Autun who said "Pictures are the literature of the laity".
80. *Op.cit.* 4.14 pp.19–34
81. Wolfson H.A. *The Philosophy of the Church Fathers* (Harvard University Press, 1956) p.65
82. *Ibid.*, pp.57ff.
83. *Op.cit.* 4.74 pp.210–222. In mediaeval symbolism each stone of the church represented a member of the congregation, and the mortar that bound them together was love.
84. Albertus Magnus *Secrets*
85. *Op.cit.* 4.27 p.24
86. Proclus *The Elements of Theology* (tr. Dodds E.R., Clarendon Press, Oxford, 1933) Prop. 103: "All things are in all things . . . in Being there is Life and Intelligence, in Life, Being and Intelligence, in Intelligence, Being and Life".
87. Panofsky E. *Gothic Architecture and Scholasticism* (Thames & Hudson, London, 1957) p.20 ". . . the spreading of a mental habit".

88. *Op.cit.* 4.74; cf. Drost who proposed that the Romanesque could be identified by the concept of "addition", and the Gothic by "division".

89. *Op.cit.* 4.74: cf. Michelet: Gothic "subdivided and again subdivided. Its process was Aristotelian, the method of Thomas Aquinas. It became a series of syllogisms in stone", cf. Semper's Gothic as "Scholasticism in stone".

90. Krautheimer R. *Early Christian and Byzantine Architecture* (Penguin, Harmondsworth, 1965)

91. *Op.cit.* 4.74

92. Morgan C. *An Investigation of the Trinity of Plato and Philo Judaeus* (1795), (Cambridge University Press, Cambridge, 1853) p.88; cf. *op.cit.* 4.74; cf. Drost who proposed that the Romanesque could be identified by the concept of "addition", and the Gothic by "division"

93. Grane L. *Peter Abelard* tr. Crowley F&C (Allen & Unwin, London, 1970) pp.82–95

94. *Op.cit.* 4.27 pp.202–209

95. *Op.cit.* 4.6

96. *Op.cit.* 4.11, VI.1.1

97. *Ibid.* VI.2.17

98. *Ibid.* V.1.4

99. *Op.cit.* 4.86 p.220

100. *Op.cit.* 4.11, III.8.5, V.1.6–8

101. *Ibid.* V.6.6

102. Rawlinson A.E.I. (ed.) *Essays on the Trinity and the Incarnation* (Longmans, London, 1928) pp.241–244

103. *Op.cit.* 4.24, X.24

104. *Op.cit.* 4.86 p.220, also Prop. 32ff; cf. Plotinus *op.cit.* 4.11 V.2, "The intellectual principle turns and contemplates the One"

105. *Op.cit.* 4.11, III.8.8

106. *Ibid.* VI.5.5; V.5.2

107. *Ibid.* III.3.7

108. Bigg C. *The Christian Platonists of Alexandria* (Clarendon Press, Oxford, 1886) p.8

109. *Op.cit.* 4.11, III 1.2 & 1.7

110. *Op.cit.* 4.8, for the "Tree of Porphyry"; cf. Plotinus *op.cit.* 4.11, V.3.10: "The intellective power must be in a state of duality . . . the intellectual act will always comport diversity as well as identity"; also V.6.1: "There can be no intellection without duality in unity"; cf. Augustine *op.cit.* 4.5, VII.1, p.134 "I thought that whatever had no dimension in space must be absolutely nothing at all . . . I did not realize that the power of thought by which I formed these images was itself something quite different from them".

111. *Op.cit.* 4.11, VI.2.4; also V.9.8: "all are one: and the resultant intellections are the idea of Being and its Shape and its Act".

112. *Ibid.* VI.5.5

113. *Ibid.* V.1.11

114. *Ibid.* VI.5.7

115. Proclus *The Platonic Theology* (tr. Taylor T. 1816, Selene Books, New York, 1985) p.178; cf. Plato's *Sophist* 248e

116. *Ibid.* p.166; cf. Plotinus *op.cit.* 4.11, 7.34: "here is no longer a duality but a two-in-one"; Augustine also suggested combining transcendentals: "Eternal Truth, true Love, beloved Eternity". *Op.cit.* 4.5, VII.10.

117. *Ibid.* p.291

118. *Ibid.* p.81

119. I Corinthians 13.13; cf. Aquinas *op.cit.* 4.9 (De Doct. Christ. I.37) who disputes Augustine's order that "Faith precedes Charity and Charity, Hope".

120. *Op.cit.* 4.10 pp.568–594 (S.T. Q62. A1)

121. Matthew 28.19; cf. *op.cit.* 4.79 which states that critical scholarship rejects the attribution of the formula to Jesus. However, it was in existence before the end of the

first century and occurs in apostolic work *Didache* VII, 1 & 3; cf. also I Corinthians 6.11 and II Corinthians 13.14

122. *Op.cit.* 4.86 p.297: the Second Person as "self-communicating" and p.298 the "Holy Ghost as the Power of God"; cf. Tillich, note 4.297 below, Vol III p.301: "the threefold manifestation of God as Creative Power, Saving Love and Ecstatic Transformation".

123. *Op.cit.* 4.7 (preface)

124. Dante Alighieri *Il Convito* tr. Sayer E.P. (Routledge & Son, London, 1887) p.62

125. *Op.cit.* 4.14 p.184; cf. Augustine *op.cit.* 4.24 VIII who introduced passion and feeling as instruments of virtue against Roman stoicism; also Aquinas *op.cit.* 4.14 pp.219–223: "Formal elements come from reason, material elements from the emotions"

126. *Op.cit.* 4.27 pp.166ff; cf. Coppleston *op.cit.* 4.28 re Duns Scotus

127. Hesiod *Theogony* tr. Banks J. (Bell & Sons, London, 1879) v.116–120, p.7

128. Aristotle *De Generatione et Corruptione* 330bff.

129. Inge, W.R. *The Philosophy of Plotinus* (Longmans, London, 1929); cf. Augustine *op.cit.* 4.24, IV.10: "Let Jupiter alone be all these . . . let all these be but as parts and virtues of him"; cf. also Proclus *op.cit.* 4.119, Vol II p.66: "the twelve gods convolve every mundane genus"

130. *Op.cit.* 4.115 p.88, also Vol II, p.290; cf. Plotinus *op.cit.* 4.11, III.5.8: "Male gods represent the intellectual powers and the female gods their souls"; also Aquinas *op.cit.* 4.14 p.314: ". . . divine nature from the Father and human nature from the Mother."

131. Cf. Augustine *op.cit.* 4.24, IV.10 who lists the attributes of the Roman deities; cf. *op.cit.* 4.86; Varro said of the *Penates*, which Macrobius translated "the gods", that the Tuscans thought that there were six male and six female, although unnamed. He also mentions the Capitoline triad, Jupiter, Juno and Minerva.

132. *Op.cit.* 4.81

133. *Op.cit.* 4.7. Abelard studied Old Testament sources; cf. Book of Wisdom of Solomon 11.20 from which Augustine translated "Measure and number and weight" as "limit, species and order", order being constituted of "rest and stability". Abelard also introduced the thoughts of Hindu philosophy, as had Cicero (Tusc. V.25), Strabo (Bk. XV), and Plutarch (Alex. 69). In the *Bhagavad Gita* (c.500 BC) we read about the "good and beautiful and true" (17.15), and the *Trimurti*, Brahma, Vishnu and Shiva have had attributed to them the concepts of Creation, Love and Strife respectively.

134. *Op.cit.* 4.86; for the various attributes of the Logos in Philo see Bigg *op.cit.* 4.108; cf. Augustine *op.cit.* 4.3 p.266: "love . . . which binds or seeks to bind some two together"

135. *Op.cit.* 4.81 pp.233–251; cf. *op.cit.* 4.86

136. *Op.cit.* 4.86. Creative Power belonged to the Second Person.

137. *Op.cit.* 4.3 VI, cf. I Corinthians 1.24; cf. Origen's divine perfections "perfectly wise, perfectly just, perfectly mighty"

138. *Op.cit.* 4.93. Pope Innocent II condemned Abelard as a heretic; cf. Tillich note 4.297 below.

139. Dante Alighieri *The Divine Comedy* tr. Sinclair J.D. (John Lane, London, 1939) Vol. I, *The Inferno*, Canto I, line 104; however, cf. Canto 3: "Divine Power made me and supreme Wisdom and primal Love."

140. Bonaventure *The Soul's Journey into God* (tr. Cousins E., Paulist Press, New York, 1978) p.54. Bonaventure records that a vision of the six-winged seraph had appeared to Francis, that God completed the world in six days, and that there were six steps up to the throne of Solomon (I Kings 10.19); cf. Aquinas *op.cit.* 4.14; "frequently what is stated as primary is in reality secondary" (*Disp. IV de Veritate* I).

141. Richard of St Victor *op.cit.* 4.44 p.161: six ascending levels of contemplation, two based in the imagination, two in the reason and two in the understanding.

142. *Op.cit.* 4.140 p.64

143. *Ibid.* p.61

144. *Op.cit.* 4.115 pp.178ff

145. Bonner, A. (tr. & ed.) *Selected Works of Ramon Lull* (Princeton University Press, 1985). His earlier *Ars Demonstrativa* described sixteen attributes to God. These were subsequently reduced to nine in the *Ars Brevis* of 1308.

146. Basil, Epistle 38 to Gregory of Nyssa; cf. Philo who described the *Logos* crowned with a rainbow, *op.cit.* 4.104; Clement I who suggested that Joseph's coat of many colours symbolized his many attributes; and even the west window at Chartres that depicts Mary in a rainbow coloured dress and crowned with a yellow halo.

147. *"Entia praeter necessitatem non sunt multiplicanda"* Ex. Brit. (1947) s.v. "Occam"

148. *Op.cit.* 4.24, X.30; also *op.cit.* 4.3 p.139

149. Exodus 24.10

150. Isaiah 1.18

151. Psalms 68.11–13

152. Revelation 4.2–3; cf. Ezekiel 1.4 "a radiance like brass"

153. *Ibid.*: "burning before the throne were seven flaming torches, the seven spirits of God"

154. Judges 8.26

155. *Op.cit.* 4.139 Vol II *Purgatorio* Canto 24

156. Hope & Walch *The Colour Compendium* (Van Nostrand Reinhold, New York, 1990) p.287: "purple symbolizes the power of the Spirit in Christianity". Church dogma permitted only three colours to be seen in the rainbow, red, yellow (or green), and blue.

157. *Ibid.* However, see the section on Heraldry and the meanings of its colours, or tinctures.

158. *Op.cit.* 4.14 pp.184–192

159. *Op.cit.* 4.11 VI.1.26–27

160. *Ibid.* VI.3.22

161. *Ibid.* I.6.3: "the house before him . . . is the inner idea stamped upon exterior matter"

162. *Op.cit.* 4.129 p.99

163. I Corinthians 12.8

164. *Op.cit.* 4.14 (*I Sent.* prologue)

165. Duns Scotus *Philosophical Writings* (tr & ed. Wolter A., Nelson, Edinburgh, 1962) p.61

166. *Op.cit.* 4.129 Vol 2, p.216

167. *Op.cit.* 4.27 pp.166–173

168. *Ibid.*

169. *Op.cit.* 4.11, V.8.5; cf. V.9.6

170. *Op.cit.* 4.129, Vol 2, pp.132–143 (Plotinus V.3.17)

171. *The Works of Dionysius the Areopagite* (tr. Parker J., Parker, J. & Co, 1897) p.42 (D.N. IV.9 (705B)); cf. note 4.196 below; cf. also Plotinus *op.cit.* 4.11, IV.4.16: "soul as a circle in motion . . . widening towards . . . coiling about"

172. *Op.cit.* 4.165 p.128: ". . . something with only an incidental unity in the faculty of imagination, which represents the thing according to its quantity, colour and other sensible accidents."

173. *Ibid.* p.129

174. *Op.cit.* 4.11, I.6.9

175. *Ibid.* I.6.5

176. *Ibid.* I.6.7: "the upward path . . . appointed purifications . . . to behold that solitary dwelling, existence, the unmingled, the pure"

177. Gilson, E. *The Christian Philosophy of St. Augustine* (tr. Lynch, Gollancz, London, 1961) p.61 (*De Gen. ad Litt* VII. 27–38); cf. Augustine *op.cit.* 4.3, VIII, p.247

178. *Op.cit.* 4.9 p.281 (Q75 A1): "Life is shown principally by two activities, knowledge and movement"

179. *Op.cit.* 4.14; cf. "When the Queen of Sheba had seen all Solomon's wisdom, and the house that he had built . . . there was no more spirit in her" (I Kings 10.2–5).

180. *Op.cit.* 4.73

181. Eco *op.cit.* 4.27 p.97 (*Comm. in Psalmos* XLIV.2)

182. *Op.cit.* 4.14 p.118 (Comp. Theol. 145)

213

183. *Op.cit.* 4.11, V.2
184. *Ibid.* VI.8.17
185. *Op.cit.* 4.129, p.216
186. Gilby *op.cit.* 4.14 pp.86–95 (*Disp. de spirit. creaturis* 4)
187. *Op.cit.* 4.14 (*Disp. IV de Veritate* I)
188. *Op.cit.* 4.5, II.3; IV. 12, also *op.cit.* 4.3 p.214 (cf. Romans 1.20); cf. Plotinus *op.cit.* 4.11, I.9.17: "forms whose beauty must fill us with veneration for their creator"
189. *Op.cit.* 4.14 pp.74–75
190. *Op.cit.* 4.5, XI.5, p.257; cf. Aquinas *op.cit.* 4.14 pp.100–112 who relates it to Final, Formal and Efficient causes (cf. Plato's *Republic*)
191. *Op.cit.* 4.11, I.6.1
192. Jordan, M. *Ordering Wisdom in Aquinas* (University of Notre Dame Press, Indiana, 1986) p.12
193. John I.14
194. Hebrews 4.12
195. Eco *op.cit.* 4.27 pp.53–56
196. Cf. Augustine *op.cit.* 4.5: As a baby "I would toss my arms and legs about and make noises, hoping that such few signs as I could make would show my meaning" Unfortunately there was no common language.
197. *Op.cit.* 4.11 IV.4.
198. Hathaway R.F. *Hierarchy and the Definition of Order in the Letters of Pseudo-Dionysius* (University of California Press, 1969) pp.117–140
199. Gilby *op.cit.* 4.14 (S.T. 1a xxxvii.1)
200. *Ibid.* p.208
201. *Op.cit.* 4.198
202. *Op.cit.* 4.27 p.51
203. *Op.cit.* 3.99 p.80; cf. William of Auvergne who said that beauty arises "where knowledge and feeling coincide", *op.cit.* 4.27 p.236.
204. *Op.cit.* 4.11, III.5.1
205. *Ibid.* IV.4.25–26
206. *Ibid.* IV.5.2
207. *Ibid.* VI.7.22
208. *Op.cit.* 4.14 pp.86–95 (*Comm. Hebrews* iv Lect. 2)
209. Bonaventure *Life of St. Francis*; cf. *op.cit.* 4.140. In Francis's *Canticle of the Sun* attributes are distributed among the natural elements: Brother Wind (Fair), Sister Water (Useful), Brother Sun (significance), Mother Earth (sustains), Sister Moon (lovely), Brother Fire (strong)
210. *Op.cit.* 4.2
211. *Op.cit.* 4.9 p.110 (S.T. Q13.6)
212. *Op.cit.* 4.11, IV.4.41
213. *Ibid.* p.76
214. Augustine *De Musica* in Tillman & Cahn (eds), *Philosophy of Art and Aesthetics* (Harper & Row, New York, 1969)
215. *Op.cit.* 3.99
216. *Op.cit.* 4.177 p.132; cf. Augustine *op.cit.* 4.24,12.6
217. *Op.cit.* 4.74 p.70; cf. Augustine *op.cit.* 4.24, X.28: "Weight is to the body as love is to the soul."
218. *Op.cit.* 3.99 p.288
219. *Op.cit.* 4.27 p.35
220. Longinus *On the Sublime* tr. Roberts W.R. (Cambridge University Press, Cambridge, 1899) pp.103–127
221. *Ibid.* p.103; cf. Augustine on subtlety *op.cit.* 4.24, X.22: "shave his eyebrows, a very nothing to his body, yet how much does it deform him."
222. *Ibid.* p.97
223. *Ibid.* pp.103–127
224. *Ibid.* pp.103–127

225. *Ibid*. pp.97–101
226. *Ibid*. pp.103–127
227. *Op.cit*. 4.73
228. *Op.cit*. 4.5 p.261, XI.10; cf. *op.cit*. 4.24, X.32; cf. *op.cit*. 4.5 XIII.5 p.314: "When I read that your spirit moved over the waters, I catch a faint glimpse of the Trinity."
229. *Op.cit*. 4.11, VI.8.12–13; IV.4.35
230. *Op.cit*. 4.14 (S.T. Ia. xxxvi.1 and *De Rationibus Fidei* 4)
231. *Op.cit*. 4.11 III.8.9; cf. Augustine *op.cit*. 4.5, X.6, p.213: "the soul . . . animates the whole body. It gives it life"; cf. also William of Auvergne who maintained that the "power" of the soul is its essence (Aquinas S.T. Q77 A1).
232. *Op.cit*. 4.9 (S.T. Q19.A2)
233. *Op.cit*. 4.220 p.53
234. *Ibid*. p.155
235. *Op.cit*. 4.93
236. *Op.cit*. 4.14 pp.144–165 (S.T. 1a-2ae xci 2–3)
237. *Ibid*. pp.78–84 (S.T. Ia.x1v.6)
238. *Op.cit*. 4.81 p.464
239. *Op.cit*. 4.9 p.46
240. *Op.cit*. 4.11, V.5.2
241. *Op.cit*. 4.9 p.226; cf. *op.cit*. 4.14 p.318
242. *Op.cit*. 4.220 pp.57–59
243. *Op.cit*. 4.5, X.33, p.239; cf. IX.7 p.191: "hymns and psalms were introduced . . . to revive their flagging spirits"; cf. also IX.4, p.187: "the Paraclete, the truthgiving Spirit".
244. *Op.cit*. 4.177 p.160
245. *Op.cit*. 4.73. Justinian's words were "Oh Solomon, I have outdone thee": cf. Augustine *op.cit*. 4.5 X.36, p.244: "you condemn the ambitions of this world".
246. *Op.cit*. 4.90
247. Folz R. *The Coronation of Charlemagne* (tr. Anderson J.E., Routledge & Kegan Paul, London, 1974) p.181. Alcuin of York wrote to Charlemagne in 799 saying "If many people became imbued with your ideas a new Athens would be established in *Francia* . . . ennobled by the teachings of Christ": cf. also the phrase "three *Francia's*, one *Francorum*"; cf. Augustine *op.cit*. 4.24 p.21: "that which is harmony in music is unity in a city".
248. *Op.cit*. 4.24 (intro). The idea of Cosmopolis is recorded in Posidonius. Marcus Aurelius refers to "City of God".
249. *Op.cit*. 4.129
250. *Op.cit*. 4.220 p.43, 135
251. *Ibid*. p.79. Longinus compares the method of Demosthenes which was like "a flash of lightning" with that of Cicero which was more like "a wide-spread conflagration."
252. *Ibid*. pp.101ff.
253. *Op.cit*. 4.11, V.5.12
254. *Op.cit*. 4.177
255. *Ibid*. Note 29; cf. Augustine *op.cit*. 4.3, XV.21.41
256. *Op.cit*. 4.11, VI.9.9
257. *Ibid*. I.6.2
258. *Ibid*. IV.4.35
259. *Op.cit*. 4.14 (Comp. Theol.49) "*ex Patre Filioque*". The Spirit was seen as arising partly from the Father seen as Power, and partly from the Son seen as Awareness.
260. For Augustine, Aristotle's categories "yielded only thorns and thistles", *op.cit*. 4.5, IV.16 p.87.
261. *Op.cit*. 4.11, VI.3.21
262. *Ibid*. VI.3.3
263. Cf. *op.cit*. 4.8. Porphyry added "Species" to Aristotle's four predicables, Avicenna amended "Special Difference" to "Essence."
264. Aristotle *De Interpretatione* (tr. Ackrill J., Clarendon Press, Oxford, 1963) 17a.38, p.47

265. Moody E. *The Logic of William of Ockham*, (Sheed and Ward, London, 1935) p.75

266. *Op.cit.* 4.14 pp.19–34: "consider God from many points of view . . . diversity represented by the plurality of predicate and subject."

267. Eriugena *Periphyseon* (*Division of Nature*) (tr. O'Meara J., Bellarmin, Dumbarton Oaks, 1987) p.53

268. *Op.cit.* 4.14 p.52; also pp.52ff.: "In created things relation is an accident, but in God it is his substance."

269. *Op.cit.* 4.9 (S.T. Q13.A7)

270. *Op.cit.* 4.11 VI.2.4

271. *Op.cit.* 4.165 p.25

272. Novatian *On the Trinity* (tr. Moore H., Macmillan & Co., London, 1919) p.30

273. *Op.cit.* 4.267 p.53; cf. *op.cit.* 4.28 p.119

274. *Op.cit.* 4.14 pp.52ff. (*Disp. VIII de Pot.* I)

275. *Op.cit.* 4.102 pp.214–227 (*Athen. Leg.* 10.24). Athenagoras is reputed to have founded the Catechismic School at Alexandria from where his teachings influenced Victorinus and in turn Augustine.

276. *Op.cit.* 4.3 p.207, p.266: "so then there are three, the lover, the beloved and the love".

277. *Op.cit.* 4.3 (intro). It was Tertullian who emphasized that the Spirit was a Person co-equal with the Father and the Son; cf. *op.cit.* 4.81 pp.317ff, p.330. The Greeks first used the formula three "*hypostases*" in one "*ousia*" (substance) occasionally substituting "*prosopon*" (person) for "*hypostasis*", *op.cit.* 4.267 note p.40 and p.112, "*prosopon*" also meaning a "mask" or "character in a play"; cf. *op.cit.* 4.102 p.159: One substance in three persons received official recognition at the Synod of Constantinople in AD 382.

278. *Op.cit.* 4.102 pp.291–297

279. *Op.cit.* 4.7 (*Christ. Theol.* 1275c)

280. *Op.cit.* 4.81 p.342

281. *Op.cit.* 4.165 p.121

282. *Op.cit.* 4.102, Kirk K.E. *Evolution of the Doctrine of the Trinity*; cf. Augustine *op.cit.* 4.24, IV.26: "But these were fictions of Homer", quoth Cicero, "transferring human effects unto the gods."

283. Ockham, G. de *Opera Theologica* Vol IV (St Bonaventure University, New York, 1979) p.153: "*et tamen quod una essentia sit realiter illae tres relationes*"; cf. note 4.307 below, p.146, also p.144 where Aquinas "equated substance with relation . . . Occam enquired why in that case there should not be more than one substance since there is more than one relation".

284. *Op.cit.* 4.81 p.251

285. *Op.cit.* 4.7

286. *Op.cit.* 4.102

287. *Ibid.*

288. *Op.cit.* 4.11, V.6.8

289. *Ibid.* VI.8.18

290. Demaray J.G. *Dante and the Book of the Cosmos* (The American Philosophical Society, 1987); cf. p.99. Mentioned in regard to rose windows is the "trinitarian geometry of a kind made famous by Chancellor Thierry of Chartres" cf. James J., "Mediaeval Geometry" in *AA Quarterly* **5**, No. 2, 1973

291. *Op.cit.* 4.139

292. *Op.cit.* 4.108 p.64

293. *Ibid.* p.68

294. Baynes N.H. *Constantine the Great and the Christian Church* (Oxford University Press, Oxford, 1931) pp.60ff., cf. p.97. The sun symbolized the resurrection. In Tertullian's day some thought that the sun was the Christian's God. For the six principles represented by the six spokes we might turn to Augustine *op.cit.* 4.177 p.90 (*De Vera Religione* 30.56). Notions which depended on "divine illumination" included "Justice, Chastity, Faith, Truth, Charity, Goodness and the like".

295. Dante *op.cit.* 4.139, Vol II *Purgatorio* Canto 30: Beatrice "girt with olive over a white veil clothed under a green mantle with the colour of living flame"; cf. Canto 9 and the colour symbolism of the three steps leading to the gate of St Peter, white, purple and red.
296. Loeschen J.R. *The Divine Community* (16thC. Journal Publishers, Missouri) p.15
297. Tillich P. *Systematic Theology* Vol I, p.276, cf. p.74 where the First Person can be seen as a correlation of Being and Creation, and the Second Person, resolution through Love re-uniting us with the world. Also p.278, "the classical term, logos, is most adequate for the Second Principle, that of meaning and structure".
298. *Op.cit.* 4.156
299. Exodus 28.15–21
300. Richard of St Victor *Benjamin Minor* tr Yankowski S.V. (Wiefeld & Mehl, Ansbach). From Genesis 29.32–30.24 and 49.1–27, the following rows can be deduced:

Ruben (First-Born/Strength)	Simeon (Strife)	Levi (Law)
Judah (First among Nations)	Zebulun (Commerce)	Issachar (Reward)
Dan (Judgement)	Gad (Good Fortune)	Asher (Happiness)
Naphtali (Beauty)	Joseph (Fruitfulness)	Benjamin (Ecstasy of Mind)

301. *Op.cit.* 4.74 pp.222–223, p.233
302. *Ibid.* p.233
303. *Op.cit.* 4.283 pp.84ff.
304. *Ibid.* (introduction)
305. *Ibid.* p.76
306. *Ibid.* pp.297ff.
307. Bainton R.H. *Early and Mediaeval Christianity* (Hodder & Stoughton, London, 1962) p.152. For example, Servetus ridiculed the views of Henry de Gad (died 1293) whose view was that Creation was the work of Intelligence and Will acting as Wisdom and Love. To act in this way, he said, they must be Persons and not just Qualities. Servetus likened this to the speculative and practical intellects copulating together and begetting. Servetus was burned at the stake in 1553.

CHAPTER 5: MODERN CATEGORIES I

1. Gerbier B. *A Brief Discourse concerning the Three Chief Principles of Magnificent Buildings vis Solidity, Conveniency and Ornament* 1662 (Gregg International Publishing, 1969)
2. Frankl P. *The Gothic* (Princeton University Press, 1960) p.864; cf. p.861, Evelyn's "Proportion, Use or Beauty"; cf. Evelyn's translation of Freart's *A Parallel of Architecture*.
3. Abrams M.H. *The Mirror and the Lamp* (Oxford University Press, Oxford, 1953) p.14
4. Beardsley M.C. *Aesthetics from Classical Greece to the Present* 1966 (University of Alabama Press, Tuscaloosa & London, 1975) p.142; cf. p.141, Boileau N. *L'art poétique* 1674, Cantos I & IV: "Love reason then: and let what e'er you Write Borrow from her its Beauty, Force and Light".
5. Carritt E. *Philosophies of Beauty* (Clarendon Press, Oxford, 1931) p.56; cf. Hobbes T. *Leviathan* (Blackwell, Oxford, 1946).
6. *Op.cit.* 5.4 pp.172–173; cf. Hobbes T., *Answer to Davenant's Preface to Gondibert*, IV, 449–450
7. *Op.cit.* 5.4 pp.134–135; cf. Scaliger J.C. *Poetices Libri Septem* 1561
8. Harrington K. *Changing Ideas on Architecture in the Encyclopédie 1750–1776* (UMI Research Press, 1985) pp.16ff.
9. Ficino M. *The Philebus Commentary* (tr. Allen M., University of California Press, 1975) pp.78, 110, 238; cf. Allen M., *The Platonism of Marsilio Ficino* (University of California Press, 1984) pp.107, 185ff.

10. *Op.cit.* 5.8 pp.124ff, 132; cf. Shaftesbury note 5.49 below who linked Beauty, Goodness and Truth in such passages as "all beauty is truth" (p.94), "beauty and good are still the same" (p.138), and "beauty and truth are plainly joined with the notion of utility and convenience" (p.267).

11. Muratori *op.cit.* 5.5 p.61; Shelley *op.cit.* 5.3 p.127; for Diderot see Crocker L.G. *Two Diderot Studies* (Johns Hopkins University Press, 1952) pp.99–101 where Diderot compares "*Le vrai, le bon et le beau*" to Father, Son and Holy Ghost.

12. *Op.cit.* 5.4 p.278; cf. Nietzsche F., *Will to Power*, p.264

13. Cousin V. *The True, the Beautiful and the Good* 1818 (tr. Wight O.W., T & T Clark, Edinburgh, 1854)

14. Descartes R. *Discourse on Method* in *The Philosophical Works of Descartes* Vol. I (tr. Haldane E. & Ross G., Dover, New York, 1911) p.126

15. Locke J. *Essay Concerning Human Understanding* (J.F. Dove, London, 1828) p.274 where association is connected with the "wrong connexion of ideas".

16. Compare this with "the celebrated Locke's" division into Intuitive Knowledge, Rational Knowledge and Judgement, *op.cit.* 5.15, 4.17.17 following a threefold knowledge of existence through Intuition, Demonstration and Sensation, 4.9.2.

17. *Op.cit.* 5.14 *Meditations* p.153; cf. *Discourse on Method* p.101

18. *Op.cit.* 5.15 p.61: "Let's then suppose the mind to be, as we say, white paper, void of all characters; p.367 "Knowledge is the perception of the agreement or disagreement of ideas" of which there are four sorts: Identity, Relation, Co-existence and Real Existence. Identity and Coexistence were then admitted to be "truly nothing but relations" (pp.369–372; 4.1.2–4.1.7); cf. 2.21.3.

19. Hobbes T. *Leviathan* (Blackwell, Oxford, 1946) p.13: "By consequence, or train of thought, I understand that succession of one thought to another which is called . . . mental discourse"; cf. p.15 two kinds based on whether we seek the cause or effect.

20. Aristotle *De Natura* (*Parva Naturalia*) 451, 10–20; cf. Coleridge S.T. *Biographia Literaria* (Dent, London, 1965) p.59 who distinguished five kinds of association in Aristotle: time, space, causation, likeness and contrast.

21. Hume D. *An Enquiry Concerning Human Understanding* in *Essential Works of David Hume* Cohen R. (ed.) (Bantam, London 1965) p.57

22. Kant I. *Critique of Pure Reason* (tr. Smith N.K., Macmillan, London, 1968) p.87

23. *Ibid.* pp.107, 113

24. *Ibid.* p.109

25. *Ibid.* p.116

26. *Ibid.* p.116

27. Stace W.T. *The Philosophy of Hegel* (Macmillan & Co, London, 1924) p.222

28. *Ibid.* See fold-out diagram showing Hegel's system.

29. *Ibid.* p.70

30. *Ibid.* pp.63, 65

31. Hegel G.W.F. *Logic* (tr. Wallace W., Clarendon Press, Oxford, 1975) pp.124ff.

32. *Op.cit.* 5.27 p.123

33. *Ibid.* p.129

34. *Op.cit.* 5.31 p.128

35. *Op.cit.* 5.27 p.129; cf. *op.cit.* 5.31 pp.166ff.

36. *Ibid.* pp.222ff.; cf. *op.cit.* 5.31 pp.134, 221, 225

37. *Op.cit.* 5.31 pp.275ff., cf. *Cognitio* – the True, Volition – the Good, and the Absolute – the Beautiful

38. Schopenhauer A. *The World as Will and Representation* (tr. Payne E., Dover Publications, New York, 1966) p.459

39. Peirce C.S. *Collected Papers of Charles Sanders Peirce* Hartshorne C. & Weiss P. (eds) (Harvard University Press, 1931), Vol. I, p.200

40. *Ibid.* p.200; cf. Locke *op.cit.* 5.15, 2.9.15: "Perception . . . the first operation of our intellectual faculties", 2.4.1 our idea of solidity arises from "resistance", 4.21.5 semiotics as the third part of our knowledge.

41. *Op.cit.* 5.39 pp.148–179

42. *Ibid.*

43. *Ibid.* p.179

44. *Ibid.* pp.149–159

45. *Ibid.* pp.159–163

46. *Ibid.* pp. 170–176

47. *Ibid.* p.176

48. Passmore J. *A Hundred Years of Philosophy* 1957 (Penguin, Harmondsworth, 1968) p.301; cf. Peirce *op.cit.* 5.39 Vol II: Logic follows Ethics and both follow Aesthetics, "Esthetics therefore . . . appears to be possibly the first indispensable propedeutic to logic".

49. Shaftesbury, 3rd Earl of, *Characteristics* (Bobbs Merrill, New York, 1964), p.132: "The beautiful, the fair, the comely were never in the matter, but in the art and design, never in body itself, but in the form".

50. Hutcheson F. *An Inquiry into the Original of Our Ideas of Beauty and Virtue* in *Eighteenth Century Critical Essays* Elledge S. (ed.) (Cornell University Press, 1961) p.354

51. *Op.cit.* 5.4 p.156; cf. Baumgarten A.G., *Reflections on Poetry* 1735 which differentiated Logic, which was concerned with thought, from Aesthetics, which was concerned with perception.

52. Kant I. *The Critique of Judgement* (tr. Meredith J.C., Clarendon Press, Oxford, 1952) pp.57–60

53. *Op.cit.* 5.4 p.215; cf. *op.cit.* 5.52 pp.57–60

54. *Op.cit.* 5.52 pp.69ff.

55. *Op.cit.* 5.50 pp.355ff.

56. *Op.cit.* 5.52 p.66

57. *Op.cit.* 5.48 p.495

58. *Op.cit.* 5.21 *Of the Standard of Taste* p.451

59. *Ibid.* pp.52ff.

60. *Op.cit.* 5.15 pp.61–62: "All ideas come from sensation or reflection", the former e.g. "light and colour . . . force an entrance to the mind", the latter "might properly enough be called internal sense".

61. *Op.cit.* 5.22 p.34

62. *Ibid.* p.314

63. Hazlitt W. *Hazlitt on English Literature* Zeitlin J. (ed.) (Oxford University Press, Oxford, 1913) in the essay "On Poetry in General" (1818) p.254

64. *Op.cit.* 5.4 p.268; cf. *op.cit.* 5.38 34; I.231

65. *Ibid.* p.270; cf. *op.cit.* 5.38 I, 271–272

66. *Op.cit.* 5.48 pp.468ff.

67. *Op.cit.* 5.4 p.279; cf. Nietzsche *Birth of Tragedy* pp.263, 290

68. *Ibid.* p.332; cf. Dewey J. *Experience and Nature* p.389

69. *Ibid.* p.326; cf. Bergson H. *Laughter* p.157

70. Hampshire S. "Logic & Appreciation" in Elton W. (ed.) *Aesthetics & Language* (Blackwell, Oxford, 1954); and Collingwood R.G., *Outlines of a Philosophy of Art* (Oxford University Press, Oxford, 1925) pp.28,88

71. *Op.cit.* 5.15 pp. 104, 117–118; cf. Berkeley G., *The Works of George Berkeley* Luce A. & Jesop T. (eds) (Nelson & Sons, Edinburgh, 1949) Vol IV *De Motu* p.47: "all place is relative . . . for up, down, left and right and all places and regions are founded in some relation, and necessarily connote and suppose a body different from the body moved"; cf. Comte's three relations of Coexistence, Succession and Resemblance.

72. *Op.cit.* 5.21 p.57

73. Bertalanffy L. von *General System Theory* (Penguin, Harmondsworth, 1968)

74. *Op.cit.* 5.2 p.821

75. *Op.cit.* 5.48 p.464: Waismann F.: "Language makes cuts through reality . . . it does not merely picture facts. . . . How we make our cuts depends on the structure of language"; cf. Saussure note 6.128 below, p.111: "language might also be compared to a sheet of paper" which we cut through with a pair of scissors.

76. *Op.cit.* 5.27 p.32; cf. *op.cit.* 5.31 p.135
77. *Ibid.* pp.440–486
78. *Op.cit.* 5.5 p.174; cf. note 6.13 below
79. *Op.cit.* 5.4 p.202; cf. Diderot's *Encyclopédie* article on Beauty
80. *Ibid.* Cf. Crocker *op.cit.* 5.11 p.55 where Diderot defines beauty as "the perception of relationships"
81. *Op.cit.* 5.4 p.331; *Reasons in Art* pp.15–16
82. *Ibid.* p.285
83. *Ibid.* p.288
84. *Op.cit.* 5.5 p.223; cf. Bradley A.C. *Poetry for Poetry's Sake* 1901
85. *Op.cit.* 5.4 pp.302–303
86. *Ibid.* Cf. Ruskin J. *Modern Painters* Vol II, 3.1.2
87. *Op.cit.* 5.5 pp.307–308; cf. Dewey J., *Experience and Nature* 1929
88. *Op.cit.* 5.39 p.162
89. *Ibid.* p.311
90. *Op.cit.* 5.4 p.310; cf. Tolstoy L.N. *What is Art?* pp.165–166
91. *Ibid.* p.310; cf. p.170
92. *Ibid.* p.313; cf. pp.278,331
93. *Ibid.* p.303; cf. Ruskin J. *Stones of Venice* Vol II, Ch. 6
94. *Op.cit.* 5.19 pp.31–32; cf. Locke *op.cit.* 5.15, 2.20.2: "Things are good and evil only in reference to pleasure and pain"
95. *Op.cit.* 5.3 p.77; cf. Lowth
96. Russell B. *History of Western Philosophy* (George Allen & Unwin Ltd, London, 1946) p.706
97. *Ibid.* p.568; cf. Leibniz
98. *Op.cit.* 5.5 p.198; cf. Santayana G., *The Sense of Beauty* 1896
99. *Op.cit.* 5.48 p.310; cf. Stout
100. *Op.cit.* 5.3 p.266; cf. Spratt
101. The first two of Newton's Laws of Motion have been attributed to Galileo.
102. *Op.cit.* 5.3 p.74; cf. Dennis J. *The Grounds of Criticism in Poetry* 1704
103. *Op.cit.* 5.49 p.158
104. *Op.cit.* 5.4 p.149; cf. Reynolds J. *Discourses on Art* (XIII, Wark (ed.), p.231); p.150 cf. *ibid.* (VI, pp.97–98)
105. *Op.cit.* 5.48 p.321
106. Copleston F. *A History of Philosophy* Vol 9, Part I (Doubleday, New York, 1974) pp.97ff.
107. *Op.cit.* 5.48 p.29; cf. Mill J.S.
108. *Op.cit.* 5.3 p.17
109. *Op.cit.* 5.49 p.267
110. *Op.cit.* 5.5 pp.80–81; cf. Berkeley G. *The New Alciphron* 1732; Hutcheson disagreed with Berkeley asking whether "a coffin-shape for a door would bear a more manifest aptitude to the human shape", *op.cit.* 5.50 p.553.
111. *Op.cit.* 5.5 p.85; cf. note 5.180 below, II.i.8
112. *Op.cit.* 5.2 p.555; cf. Pugin A.W. *The True Principles of Pointed or Christian Architecture* p.52
113. *Op.cit.* 5.2 p.571; cf. Viollet-le-Duc *Annales Archéologiques* 1846 pp.266, 348; "*L'architecture a pour but l'expression d'un besoin . . . Cette charmant construction, si simple, si claire . . .*"
114. *Op.cit.* 5.4 pp.307–308
115. *Op.cit.* 5.4 p.308; cf. Emerson R.W.'s essay "Conduct of Life" 1860
116. *Op.cit.* 5.4 p.379; cf. Spencer H. *Principles of Psychology* 1872
117. *Op.cit.* 5.52 pp.34, 61–63, 80
118. *Op.cit.* 5.2 p.806. Pol Abrahams saw the Gothic as "romanticized mechanics" as opposed to the "narrow utilitarianism" of Viollet-le-Duc (1934).
119. *Op.cit.* 5.3 p.301
120. Mill J.S. *Utilitarianism* Warnock M. (ed.) (Collins, Glasgow, 1962) p.265: see also

Wordsworth's influence on Mill (p.10), and the essay on Bentham in the same work (p.123).

121. *Op.cit.* 5.4 p.287, where Gautier asks "Are people to prefer the bread of the body to the bread of the soul? . . . I would rather do without potatoes than roses."

122. *Op.cit.* 5.48 p.214

123. *Op.cit.* 5.15 pp.82ff.

124. *Op.cit.* 5.5 pp.272, 284; cf. Alexander S. *Space, Time & Deity* 1920: "Beauty belongs to the complex of mind and its object [and] is in this sense a 'tertiary' quality of the beautiful object."

125. *Op.cit.* 5.4 p.333: "Empirically, things are poignant, tragic, beautiful, humorous . . . these traits stand in themselves on precisely the same level as colours, sounds, qualities of contact, taste and smell."

126. *Op.cit.* 5.96 p.585

127. *Op.cit.* 5.3 p.263

128. Addison J. *Essays of Joseph Addison* Frazer J.G. (ed.) (Macmillan & Co, London, 1915): "Fine Taste of Writing" p.173

129. *Op.cit.* 5.49 p.257

130. *Op.cit.* 5.50 pp.350, 354

131. *Op.cit.* 5.21 p.457

132. *Ibid.* pp.462, 463

133. *Op.cit.* 5.50 pp.351, 367

134. *Op.cit.* 5.4 p.203ff; cf. Alison A. *Essays on the Nature and Principles of Taste* 1770

135. *Op.cit.* 5.4 p.204

136. *Op.cit.* 5.3 p.14; cf. Kames, Henry Home, Lord *Elements of Criticism* 1762

137. *Ibid.* p.12; cf. Young E. *Conjectures on Original Composition* 1759

138. *Ibid.* p.231

139. *Ibid.* p.291; De Quincey credited the view to Wordsworth whose analogy was ". . . not what the garb is to the body but what the body is to the soul."

140. *Op.cit.* 5.15 p.367

141. Hume D. *A Treatise of Human Nature* Selby-Bigge L.A. (ed.) 1896, pp.20–21; cf. Locke *op.cit.* 5.15, 3.3.1ff.

142. *Op.cit.* 5.2 p.506; cf. Banister Fletcher, *A History of Architecture* (17th edition), p.389

143. *Ibid.* p.289: re Serlio's stage settings appropriate to each class

144. *Op.cit.* 5.48 p.17

145. *Ibid.* p.324

146. *Op.cit.* 5.106 Vol 8, Part I, p.147; cf. Spencer H., *First Principles* (6th edition) p.127

147. *Op.cit.* 5.3 p.38, cf. p.45

148. *Ibid.* p.56

149. *Ibid.* p.345

150. *Ibid.* p.56

151. Mention should be made of Locke *op.cit.* 5.15, 2.21.5 where one aspect of understanding is the "signification of signs".

152. *Op.cit.* 5.4 p.161; cf. Lessing G.E. *Laokoon* 1766

153. *Ibid.* p.263

154. Goethe J.W. von *The Theory of Colours* (tr. Eastlake C.L., MIT Press, Cambridge, Mass., 1970) p.350

155. *Op.cit.* 5.39 Vol. I., pp.170, 284, 287ff.; Vol. II, pp.51, 135ff.

156. *Op.cit.* 6.128 pp.66, 113

157. Ogden C.K. & Richards I.A. *The Meaning of Meaning* 1923 (Kegan Paul, Trench, Trubner & Co Ltd, London, 1994)

158. *Op.cit.* 5.39 Vol. II, p.51

159. *Ibid.* Vol. I. p.195

160. Morris C.W. *Signs, Language and Behaviour* (Prentice-Hall, New York, 1946), p.217; cf. Locke *op.cit.* 5.15, 4.21, the division of sciences into *Physica* (things), *Practica* (actions) and *Semiotica* (signs).

161. *Op.cit.* 5.4 p.354

162. *Op.cit.* 5.48 p.460
163. *Op.cit.* 5.49 p.94
164. *Ibid.* p.97
165. Bradley F.B. *Essays on Truth & Reality* (Clarendon Press, Oxford, 1914); cf. White A.R., *Truth* (Macmillan, London, 1970) Ch.6, "Three Traditional Theories"
166. *Op.cit.* 5.106 Vol 8, Part 2, p.61: "Peirce did not approve of the way in which James was developing the theory of pragmatism and, in 1905, he changed the name of his own theory from pragmatism to pragmaticism"; for definition see *op.cit.* 5.39 Vol. V.9
167. *Op.cit.* 5.3 p.263
168. *Ibid.* pp.314–315: in Abrams's words: "Poetry is true in that poems exist, are very valuable, and are the product and cause of actual emotional and imaginative experiences".
169. *Ibid.* p.318
170. *Op.cit.* 5.49 p.94
171. *Ibid.* p.94
172. *Op.cit.* 5.3 p.278
173. Dryden J. *Apologie for Heroique Poetry and Poetique Licence* 1677
174. *Op.cit.* 5.96 p.704
175. *Op.cit.* 5.3 pp.204–205, 219
176. Ruskin J. *The Seven Lamps of Architecture* (2nd edition) (George Allen, London, 1880) pp.199–203
177. *Ibid.* p.39: "Abstractedly, there appears no reason why iron should not be used as well as wood; and the time is probably near when a new system of architectural laws will be developed, adapted entirely to metallic construction."
178. *Op.cit.* 5.52 p.39, cf. p.15: Theoretical concepts "rest . . . upon the legislative authority of the Understanding", Practical precepts rest "upon that of Reason"; cf. *op.cit.* 5.22 pp.176ff.
179. *Op.cit.* 5.15 p.153
180. *Op.cit.* 5.141 Vol. II, cf. 3 parts of Book 2: "Of Pride & Humility", "Of Love & Hatred", and "Of the Will and the Direct Passions"
181. *Op.cit.* 5.96 p. 590; cf. Locke *op.cit.* 5.15 pp.313–314: "the several species are linked together and differ but in almost insensible degrees", and p.321: "these boundaries of species are as men, and not as nature, makes them."
182. Newton I. *Optics* 1704 (G. Bell & Sons, London, 1931) see p.155
183. *Op.cit.* 5.4 p.157; cf. Leibniz G.W. *Discourse on Metaphysics* 1686
184. *Ibid.* pp.157–159; cf. Baumgarten A.G. *Aesthetica* 1750
185. *Op.cit.* 5.52 p.39, the intellectual faculties are termed by Kant "Cognitive faculties" and appear in the order: Understanding, Judgement, Reason; the intuitive faculties are an interpretation of Kant's general "mental faculties", namely the Cognitive faculties, Feelings of pleasure and displeasure, and the faculty of Desire, where we may see Imagination underlying the cognitive faculties in its "bringing together the manifold of intuition" (p.58); cf. *op.cit.* 5.22 p.87.
186. *Op.cit.* 5.182; cf. Hobbes T. *Elements of Philosophy* (1656) in *The English Works of Thomas Hobbes* Vol. 1, Molesworth, W. (ed.) (John Bohn, London, 1839) p.79: "In the meantime it is manifest that in the searching out of causes, there is need partly of the analytical and partly of the synthetical method"; see also the use of the terms in the scientists, Boyle (1667) and Hooke (1702).
187. *Op.cit.* 5.22 p.108: "All relations of thought in judgements are (a) of the predicate to the subject, (b) of the ground to its consequence, (c) of the divided knowledge and of the members of the division taken together, to each other"; cf. p.176, the correlation of Understanding, Judgement, Reason with concepts, judgements and inferences; cf. Hegel *op.cit.* 5.27 p.368, (a) Understanding concerned with genus, species, law of Quality, (b) Judgement concerned with separating, partition, division or Quantity, (c) Reason concerned with syllogisms or the categories "alive with movement . . . flowing into one another" or Measure.
188. *Op.cit.* 5.22 p.111

189. *Ibid.*
190. Bergson H. *An Introduction to Metaphysics* (tr. Hulme T., Macmillan, London, 1913) pp.1ff.
191. *Op.cit.* 5.22 p.87
192. *Op.cit.* 5.38 pp.42, 99
193. *Op.cit.* 5.22 pp.106–107
194. *Ibid.* p.280, cf. p.66
195. *Ibid.* p.114
196. *Op.cit.* 5.27 pp.81, 222
197. *Op.cit.* 5.22 p.116
198. *Ibid.*
199. *Op.cit.* 5.31
200. *Op.cit.* 5.27, Hegel's highest triad under the Absolute consisted of (a) Logical Idea (Idea in itself), (b) Nature (Idea outside itself) and (c) Spirit (Idea in and for itself).
201. Schopenhauer A. *On the Four-Fold Root of the Principle of Sufficient Reason* 1813, tr. Payne E. (La Salle, Illinois, 1974)
202. *Op.cit.* 5.154 p.350: "When we find the two separate principles producing green on the one hand and red in their intenser state, we can hardly refrain thinking in the first case on the earthly, in the last on the heavenly, generation of the *Elohim*".
203. *Ibid.* p.224
204. *Ibid.* p.28
205. *Op.cit.* 5.31 p.174

CHAPTER 6: MODERN CATEGORIES II

1. *Op.cit.* 5.3 p.141, cf. p.140; also *op.cit.* 5.63 pp.252, 261, 274
2. *Op.cit.* 5.2 p.467: "Everything impels us to venerate the creator, where the spirit soars freely aloft, and with love and longing aspires towards the infinite" (1820).
3. *Op.cit.* 5.4 Ch.10, "Romanticism"
4. Lovejoy A.O. *On the Discrimination of Romanticisms* in Abrams M.H. (ed.) *English Romantic Poets* (Oxford University Press, Oxford, 1960)
5. *Sturm und Drang*, a play by F.M. von Klinger (1776)
6. *Op.cit.* 5.3 p.90
7. *Op.cit.* 5.2 p.417; cf. Goethe J.W., *Von Deutscher Baukunst* 1772
8. Nisbet H.B. (ed.), *German Aesthetic and Literary Criticism* (Cambridge University Press, Cambridge, 1985) Vol. I, p.193, Schiller: "The poet either is nature or he will seek her. The former is the naive [ancient], the latter the sentimental [modern] poet."
9. Fichte J.G. *Science of Knowledge* (tr. Kroeger A.E., Lippincott, Philadelphia, 1868) pp.331ff.
10. *Op.cit.* 5.4 p.233; cf. Schelling F.W. von, *Lectures on the Philosophy of Art* (1802–1803) (see *Werke V*, 593: cf. 577)
11. Schlegel F. *Athenaüm Fragments* in *op.cit.* 6.8 Vol. II, p.47
12. Schlegel A.W. *Lectures on Dramatic Art & Literature* (tr. Black J., G. Bell & Sons, London, 1883) p.23
13. Bosanquet B. *Introduction to Hegel's Philosophy of Fine Art* (Kegan Paul, London, 1905) p.206: Sculpture as Classical: Painting, Music and Poetry as increasingly Romantic.
14. *Op.cit.* 5.4 p.161: the signs are contiguously placed in painting, and placed in succession in poetry.
15. *Op.cit.* 5.201
16. *Op.cit.* 5.38
17. *Op.cit.* 5.49 pp.97, 270
18. Gilpin W. *Three Essays: on Picturesque Beauty; on Picturesque Travel; and on Sketching Landscape* (R. Blamire, London, 1794)
19. *Op.cit.* 5.3 p.100

20. Wordsworth W. *The Prose Works of William Wordsworth* Owen W. & Smyser J. (eds) (Clarendon Press, Oxford, 1974) Vol. I pp.144, 126, 122, 148, 126, 124, 144
21. *Ibid.* p.148
22. *Ibid.* pp.126, 148
23. *Op.cit.* 5.8 p.94
24. *Op.cit.* 5.96 p.662
25. *The Oxford Dictionary of Quotations* (2nd edition, 1953), p.12: "a phrase of unknown origin dating from before the French Revolution"; cf. p.11 the American Declaration of Independence of 4 July 1776: "We hold these truths to be self-evident, that all men are created equal, that they are endowed by their Creator with certain unalienable rights, that among these are life, liberty and the pursuit of happiness" from an initial text drafted by Thomas Jefferson.
26. *Op.cit.* 5.2 p.524
27. *Encyclopaedia Britannica* (1947 edition), s.v. "Chateaubriand"
28. *Ibid.* s.v. "French Literature, 19th Century"
29. *Op.cit.* 6.4
30. *Op.cit.* 5.4 p.294
31. *Op.cit.* 6.27 s.v. "French Literature"
32. *Op.cit.* 5.4 p.296
33. *Op.cit.* 5.22 p.115
34. *Ibid.* pp.107, 109, 239
35. *Op.cit.* 5.96 p.574
36. *Op.cit.* 5.22 p.215
37. *Op.cit.* 6.27 s.v. "Smith A."
38. Marx K, *Essential Works of Marxism* Mendel P.A. (ed.) (Bantam Books, London, 1961); cf. *op.cit.* 5.96 p.749 to Marx K., *Eleven Theses on Feuerbach* 1845
39. *Op.cit.* 5.27. Under the category of "Nature", subcategory "Mechanics", Space and Time proceed to Motion, and then to "Matter and Motion"; cf. Kant *op.cit.* 5.22 p.82 "Space and Time are its pure forms, and sensation in general its matter."
40. Bertalanffy *op.cit.* 5.73 p.239: "In the theory of relativity, space and time fuse in the Minkowski union, where time is another coordinate of a four-dimensional continuum."
41. *Op.cit.* 5.22 pp.65, 280
42. *Op.cit.* 5.4 p.227; cf. Schiller J.C.F. von *Letters on the Aesthetic Education of Man* 1793–1795, Letter 12
43. *Op.cit.* 5.2 p.460
44. *Op.cit.* 5.3 p.212
45. *Op.cit.* 5.31 pp.127, 132–134
46. *Op.cit.* 5.8 p.47
47. *Op.cit.* 5.22 p.76
48. *Op.cit.* 5.48 p.105
49. *Op.cit.* 5.3 pp.181–183; cf. Locke *op.cit.* 5.15, 2.8.23 and 2.23.9: "Three sorts of ideas make our complex one of substances: Primary Qualities, Secondary Qualities and Powers."
50. *Op.cit.* 5.39 p.228
51. *Op.cit.* 5.3 p.205
52. *Op.cit.* 5.31 pp. 177–178
53. *Op.cit.* 5.5 p.135; cf. Schelling's Lecture "The Relation of the Arts of Form to Nature" 1807
54. *Op.cit.* 6.40 p.42
55. Foster J. *Application of the Epithet Romantic* 1805, mentioned in Babbitt I., *Rousseau and Romanticism* (Constable, London, 1919)
56. *Op.cit.* 5.19 p.43, cf. p.44 "In a good poem . . . both judgement and fancy are required"
57. *Op.cit.* 5.15 p.97: "wit lying most in the assemblage of ideas . . . judgement in separating carefully one from another"
58. *Op.cit.* 5.22 p.112; cf. Diderot *op.cit.* 5.11: "Imagination . . . is the power to see links and relationships"; cf. Shelley *op.cit.* 5.3 p.130: Imagination as "the principle of synthesis"

59. *Op.cit.* 5.21 p.58
60. *Op.cit.* 5.3 pp. 192, 217: Carlyle: ". . . the artificial is the conscious, mechanical; the natural is the unconscious, dynamical"
61. *Op.cit.* 5.3 p.170
62. Coleridge S.T. *Biographia Literaria* (Dent, London, 1965)
63. *Ibid.* p.174
64. *Op.cit.* 5.48 p.302
65. *Op.cit.* 5.3 p.182
66. *Op.cit.* 5.5 p.280; cf. Richards I.A. *Principles of Literary Criticism* (Routledge & Kegan Paul, London, 1924)
67. *Op.cit.* 5.39 Vol. II p.495
68. *Ibid.* p.499
69. *Op.cit.* 5.3 p.140
70. *Op.cit.* 5.4 pp.172–173; cf. *op.cit.* 5.6
71. *Op.cit.* 5.3 p.187
72. *Op.cit.* 5.8 pp. 5, 7, 21–22, 24
73. *Ibid.* p.38
74. *Op.cit.* 5.3 p.188
75. Summerson J. *Architecture in Britain 1530–1830* (Penguin, Harmondsworth, 1953) p.264
76. *Op.cit.* 5.3 p.192
77. *Ibid.* p.49
78. *Ibid.* p.48
79. *Ibid.* The fine arts, all "like poetry, are to express their intellectual purposes, thoughts, conceptions, sentiments that have their origin in the human mind".
80. *Ibid.* pp.227–228
81. *Ibid.* pp.256ff
82. *Ibid.* p.119
83. *Op.cit.* 5.4 p.130; cf. Dürer A., *Four Books on Human Proportion* (1528) pp.177, 247
84. *Op.cit.* 5.4 p.300
85. *Ibid.* p.333; cf. Dewey J., *Art as Experience* (1934) p.48
86. *Op.cit.* 5.141 pp.78, 85
87. *Op.cit.* 5.21 p.545; cf. *op.cit.* 5.141 pp. 78–79
88. *Op.cit.* 6.8 p.180
89. *Op.cit.* 5.3 p.192
90. *Op.cit.* 5.141 pp.78–79
91. *Op.cit.* 5.4 p.338; cf. *op.cit.* 6.85 p.63
92. *Op.cit.* 5.49 p.136
93. Pugin A.W. *The True Principles of Pointed or Christian Architecture* (Academy Editions, London, 1973) p.1: "The two great rules for design are these: 1st that there should be no features about the building which are not necessary for convenience, construction or propriety; 2nd that all ornament should consist of enrichment of the essential construction of the building. . . . In pure architecture the smallest detail should have a meaning or serve a purpose . . ."
94. *Op.cit.* 5.2 pp.344–345
95. *Ibid.* p.405; cf. Chambers W. *Treatise on Civil Architecture* 1759, p.128
96. *Op.cit.* 5.141 p.180
97. *Op.cit.* 5.22 pp.116–117
98. *Ibid.* p.235; cf. p.105: "all intuitions rest on affections, concepts rest on functions"
99. *Ibid.* p.235: "The word community is in the German language ambiguous. It may mean either 'communio' or 'commercium'"
100. *Op.cit.* 5.52 pp.226–227
101. *Op.cit.* 5.5 p.158; cf. Herbart J.F. *Encyclopaedia of Philosophy* 1831
102. *Op.cit.* 5.4 pp.310–313; cf. Tolstoy L.N. *What is Art?* 1898: "Art is a medium for communicating feelings . . . communication involves two parties and can fail at either

226

end . . . communicated feelings should be such that a healthy peasant can share" (cf Wordsworth's Cumbrian Dalesman).

103. Jaspers K. *Philosophy* Vol. II (1932) (tr. Ashton E.B., University of Chicago Press, 1970) pp.17ff.; cf. *The Philosophy of Karl Jaspers* Schilpp P.A. (ed.) (Tudor Publications, 1957); cf. Hegel *op.cit.* 5.31 pp.213–222, Substance as thesis, Causality as antithesis, Reciprocity as synthesis – compare this with Kant's order of Inherence, Causality and Disjunction.

104. *Op.cit.* 5.2 p.447, attributed to Seillière E.A. *Le Mal Romantique* (Paris 1908)

105. Rousseau J.-J. *Emile* (1762) (tr. Foxley B., Dent, London, 1911)

106. *Op.cit.* 5.2 p.63; cf. *op.cit.* 5.141 p.114

107. *Op.cit.* 5.31 pp. 107, 317, and p.218: "Reciprocal action realizes the causal relation in its complete development"; cf. *op.cit.* 5.27 "Reason is the more developed phase, rather than feeling which lacks universality"

108. Emerson R.W. *Essays, New England Reformers*, xiii "The Poet"; (Henry Altemus, Philadelphia) 2nd Series, p.11

109. *Op.cit.* 5.3 p.303

110. *Ibid.* p.49; cf. *op.cit.* 5.4 p.249; cf. Mill J.S., *What is Poetry?* 1833, pp.197–198

111. *Ibid.* p.332

112. *Op.cit.* 5.176 p.178

113. *Op.cit.* 5.128 Vol. I. pp.48–49

114. *Op.cit.* 5.3 p.65

115. *Ibid.*

116. *Op.cit.* 5.4 p.300: Art "stengthens those sympathies with one another, those bonds of affection and mutual love, that are the true basis of social order"

117. *Op.cit.* 5.4 p.306; cf. Morris W., *Art and the Beauty of the Earth* 1881

118. *Op.cit.* 5.22 p.233

119. *Ibid.* p.236

120. *Op.cit.* 5.160 p.118

121. *Op.cit.* 5.141 p.112

122. *Op.cit.* 5.3 p.135

123. *Op.cit.* 5.96 p.704

124. *Op.cit.* 5.52 p.38

125. *Op.cit.* 5.39 pp.149, 200

126. *Op.cit.* 5.5 p.187; cf. Pater W., *Appreciations, Style* 1888

127. *Op.cit.* 5.4 p.128; cf. *op.cit.* 6.83, cf. p.129 where Dürer suggests also that "Use is a part of beauty"

128. Saussure F. de *Course in General Linguistics* (1916) (tr. Harris R., Duckworth, London, 1983) pp.121ff., cf. p.122 where Saussure draws the analogy with a column – the syntagmic relation is that between column and architrave, and the associative relation is that between Doric, Ionic and Corinthian.

129. *Op.cit.* 5.48 p.377

130. *Op.cit.* 5.5 p.223; cf. Bradley A.C. *Poetry for Poetry's Sake* 1901

131. *Op.cit.* 5.5 p.264; cf. Bell C. *Art* 1913

132. *Op.cit.* 5.4 p.248

133. *Op.cit.* 5.3 p.90 for Herder, p.48 for J.S. Mill

134. *Ibid.* p.50

135. *Ibid.* pp. 149–150

136. *Ibid.* p.94

137. *Op.cit.* 5.4, see *op.cit.* 6.10

138. *Op.cit.* 5.5 p.156; cf. *op.cit.* 6.101

139. *Op.cit.* 5.3 p.25

140. *Ibid.*

141. *Op.cit.* 5.5 p.181; cf. Hanslick E. *The Beautiful in Music* 1854

142. *Op.cit.* 5.4 pp. 272–274

143. *Op.cit.* 5.5 p.258; cf. Mitchell W. *Structure and Growth of the Mind* 1907. Mitchell in distinguishing the two "mental acts" referred both to "*Einfühlung*, a word coined

expressly to mean (a) our reading a spirit into others and into things, and (b) our having fellow feeling with them". Later on the same page, the latter becomes distinguished from the former by being termed "*Einsfühlung*".

144. *Op.cit.* 5.141 p.112

145. *Op.cit.* 5.3 p.330; cf. *op.cit.* 6.20 p.141

146. Austen J. *Pride and Prejudice* 1813 (Pan Books, London 1967) pp.177, 180

147. *Op.cit.* 5.3 p.49; cf. Scott W. *Essays on the Drama* (1819): "It is the artist's object . . . to communicate, as well as colours and words can do, the same sublime sensations . . ."

148. *Op.cit.* 5.5 pp. 178–179; cf. Ruskin J. *Modern Painters* IV.x.8

149. *Op.cit.* 5.4 p.310, *op.cit.* 5.5 p.191; cf. Tolstoy L.N. *What is Art?*

150. *Op.cit.* 5.5 pp. 191–194

151. *Op.cit.* 5.4 p.380

152. *Op.cit.* 5.2 p.588

153. *Op.cit.* 5.4 p.199

154. *Op.cit.* 5.2 p.344

155. *Op.cit.* 5.2 p.413 cf. Avril L. *Temples anciennes et modernes* (London 1774), p.157 ". . . especially when the piers imitating the Greek fluting, are composed of spindles or round shafts"

156. *Ibid.* p.476

157. *Ibid.* p.475

158. *Ibid.* p.706

159. *Ibid.* p.541, in an essay on the Picturesque in Architecture 1852

160. Ruskin J. *The Stones of Venice* (Wiley, Chichester, 1889) Vol. II p.178

161. *Op.cit.* 5.5 p.254; cf. Lipps T. *Empathy, Inward Imitation and Sense Feelings* 1903

162. *Ibid.* p.253

163. *Op.cit.* 5.4 p.291

164. *Ibid.*

165. *Op.cit.* 5.3 p.62, from Wordsworth's "Lines Composed a Few Miles above Tintern Abbey" 1778

166. *Op.cit.* 5.5 p.124

167. *Op.cit.* 5.2 p.428: used to differentiate cartoons painted in chiaroscuro from those drawn in outline.

168. *Op.cit.* 6.75

169. *Ibid.* pp.425–426

170. *Op.cit.* 5.2 p.454: "There are as many styles as arts: a plastic, a picturesque, a musical, a poetic . . . an architectural and a choreographic"

171. *Op.cit.* 5.176 pp.186–187

172. *Op.cit.* 5.5 p.199; cf. Santayana G. *The Sense of Beauty* 1896

173. *Op.cit.* 5.5 p.276; cf. Hulme T.E. *Speculations* 1924

174. *Op.cit.* 5.128 Vol. II, pp. 193–194

175. *Ibid.* p.192

176. *Op.cit.* 6.8 p.180

177. *Op.cit.* 5.2 p.460. Schlegel repeats Forster's comparison with "the jets of water from a mighty fountain" regarding the vaulting.

178. *Op.cit.* 5.176 p.104

179. Collingwood R.G. *The Principles of Art* (Clarendon Press, Oxford, 1938); cf. *Outlines of a Philosophy of Art* (Oxford University Press, Oxford, 1925) pp.64–65

180. *Op.cit.* 5.3 p.65

181. *Ibid.* p.53

182. *Ibid.* p.52

183. *Op.cit.* 5.52 p.225

184. *Op.cit.* 6.13 pp.185–186

185. *Op.cit.* 5.39 Vol. I, p.158

186. Hatje G. (ed.) *Encyclopaedia of Modern Architecture* (Thames & Hudson, London, 1963) p.97; cf. Biesantz H. & Klingborg A. *The Goetheanum* (Rudolf Steiner Press, London, 1979)

228

187. Scott G. *The Architecture of Humanism* (Constable, London, 1914)
188. *Op.cit.* 5.19 pp.37–38: "Will therefore is the last appetite in deliberating . . . it is called deliberating because it is a putting an end to the liberty we had of doing."
189. *Op.cit.* 5.141 p.197
190. *Op.cit.* 5.52 p.39
191. *Op.cit.* 5.22 p.464
192. *Op.cit.* 5.52 p.39, p.124: "There is a specific distinction between affections and passions. Affections are merely related to feelings; passions belong to the faculty of desire"
193. *Op.cit.* 5.4 p.173; cf. *op.cit.* 5.19 pp.31ff., Ch.6 "Of the interior beginnings of voluntary motions, commonly called the passions"
194. *Op.cit.* 5.201
195. Carritt E.F. *The Theory of Beauty* (Methuen & Co, London, 1914) p.122, ". . . the aesthetic experience as a release and a forgetting, a brief enfranchisement from the Danaid task of knowledge and the Sisyphean struggle with desire. We are eased of the heavy and weary weight of a world not only unintelligible but impracticable; and the bliss which cradles us in its divinely tranquil arms is the bliss not of passion but of a lifted yoke and riven fetters."
196. *Op.cit.* 5.27 p.440: "Spirit and Absolute are synonymous terms" as a combination of reason and being, cf. pp.103ff. "the last category is also the first".
197. *Op.cit.* 5.52 p.39
198. *Op.cit.* 6.105 p.235; cf. Locke *op.cit.* 5.15 2.6.2: "The two great and principle actions of the mind are . . . perception, or thinking; and volition, or willing", also 2.21.5: "Will and Understanding, two powers."
199. *Op.cit.* 6.9 pp.331–332
200. *Op.cit* 6.62 p.68
201. *Op.cit.* 5.38
202. *Op.cit.* 5.4 p.347; cf. Jung C.G. *Contributions to Analytical Psychology* tr. Baynes & Baynes, pp.245–248
203. *Op.cit.* 5.96 p.527
204. *Op.cit.* 5.3 p.143
205. *Op.cit.* 5.3 p.151; cf. p.77: Lowth (1753) "reason speaks literally, the passions poetically"
206. *Op.cit.* 5.3 p.151
207. *Op.cit.* 5.96 p.607; cf. *op.cit.* 5.15 p.244
208. *Ibid.* p.707
209. *Op.cit.* 5.173
210. *Op.cit.* 5.4 p.145, said in connection with the three unities.
211. *Op.cit.* 5.3 p.12
212. *Ibid.* p.55
213. *Op.cit.* 6.12 pp.20–21
214. *Op.cit.* 5.3 p.281
215. *Op.cit.* 5.4 p.173
216. *Op.cit.* 5.5 p.141
217. *Op.cit.* 5.38
218. *Op.cit.* 5.48 pp.267–268
219. Ryle G. *The Concept of Mind* 1949 (Penguin, Harmondsworth, 1963) see Ch. 3, the "Myth of Volition", and Ch. 4, "Emotions as Propensities"
220. Richards I.A. *Principles of Literary Criticism* 1924 (Routledge and Kegan Paul, London, 1960) p.101
221. *Op.cit.* 5.5 p.330; cf. Gentile G. *The Philosophy of Art* 1931
222. *Op.cit.* 5.4 p.194; cf. Burke E. *A Philosophical Enquiry into the Origin of Our Ideas of the Sublime and the Beautiful* 1757, p.52
223. *Op.cit.* 5.52 pp.94ff.; cf. *op.cit.* 5.22 p.116
224. *Op.cit.* 5.52 pp.99–100
225. *Op.cit.* 5.96 p.731

226. *Op.cit.* 5.4 p.276; cf. Nietzsche *Will to Power* tr. Levy, p.256
227. Nietzsche F. *Twilight of the Idols* tr. Hollingdale R. (Penguin, Harmondsworth, 1968) p.73; cf. Nietzsche *The Birth of Tragedy*
228. *Op.cit.* 5.19 pp.84, 136: "Liberty of freedom, signifieth the absence of opposition; by opposition I mean external impediments of motion"
229. *Op.cit.* 5.96 p.707
230. *Op.cit.* 5.4 p.492; cf. Sartre: "I am free . . . bare capacity for action, a being whose very nature is not to be anything in particular . . . a man exists as nothing, if he were anything he would not be free."
231. *Op.cit.* 5.4 p.375
232. *Op.cit.* 5.96 p.539; cf. *op.cit.* 5.19 *Leviathan, or the Matter, Forme and Power of a Commonwealth*
233. *Ibid.* pp.613ff.
234. *Ibid.* pp.494–495
235. *Ibid.* pp.615–616
236. *Op.cit.* 6.12 p.18
237. *Op.cit.* 5.5 p.316; cf. Ross W.D. *The Right and the Good* 1930
238. *Op.cit.* 5.3 p.188
239. *Ibid.* p.191
240. *Op.cit.* 5.4 p.168
241. *Op.cit.* 5.49 p.208
242. *Op.cit.* 5.48 p.469
243. *Op.cit.* 5.3 p.134
244. *Op.cit.* 5.2 p.631 "Artistic Volition" a translation of "*Kuntswollen*" or Art Will.
245. *Op.cit.* 5.3 p.194; cf. Pope A. *Essay on Criticism*, where the "*je ne sais quoi*" is discussed
246. *Ibid.* p.90
247. *Ibid.* p.127
248. *Op.cit.* 5.50 p.372
249. *Op.cit.* 5.2 p.629
250. *Op.cit.* 5.3 pp. 76–77: Lowth (1753), "For the passions are naturally inclined to amplifications; they wonderfully magnify and exaggerate whatever dwells upon the mind, and labour to express it in animated, bold and magnificent terms."
251. *Op.cit.* 6.55
252. *Op.cit.* 5.50 p.372
253. *Op.cit.* 5.3 p.136; E.A. Poe defined poetry in terms of intensity saying that a long poem is "simply a flat contradiction in terms".
254. *Op.cit.* 5.2 pp. 476–477
255. *Op.cit.* 5.3 p.74
256. *Ibid.* p.301
257. *Op.cit.* 5.5 pp.206–207; cf. Bergson H. *Laughter* 1900
258. *Op.cit.* 5.3 p.139, the desires of man for a "more ample Greatness, a more exact Goodnesse, and a more absolute varietie than can be found in the Nature of Things"
259. *Op.cit.* 5.4 p.173
260. *Op.cit.* 5.2 p.287, cf. Michelet J. *Histoire de France* (1833–1860). Art possesses masculine and feminine aspects . . . reason and nature respectively.
261. *Op.cit.* 5.5 p.198; cf. Santayana G. *The Sense of Beauty* 1896
262. *Op.cit.* 6.195
263. *Op.cit.* 6.20 p.148; Wordsworth tempers the production of excitement with propriety in recognizing the "danger that the excitement may be carried beyond its proper bounds".
264. *Op.cit.* 5.96 p.620; cf. *op.cit.* 5.19 pp.56ff.
265. *Ibid.* pp.602–603
266. *Ibid.* p.672
267. *Ibid.* p.691: "The romantic revolt passes from Byron, Schopenhauer and Nietzsche to Mussolini and Hitler; the rationalistic revolt begins with the French philosophers of

230

the revolution, passes on . . . to the philosophical radicals in England, then acquires a deeper form in Marx and issues in Soviet Russia."

268. *Op.cit.* 6.38: Engels F. *Socialism: Utopian and Scientific* pp.45ff.

269. *Op.cit.* 5.4 p.299

270. *Ibid.* pp.288, 300

271. *Op.cit.* 5.96 p.747; cf. *op.cit.* 6.27 s.v. "Owen R."

272. *Ibid.* p.742

273. *Op.cit.* 6.38, p.300

274. *Ibid.* Marx K. & Engels F. *The Communist Manifesto* p.13: "The history of all hitherto existing society is the history of class struggles . . ."

275. *Ibid.* p.62

276. *Op.cit.* 5.2 p.688

277. *Op.cit.* 5.4 p.305; cf. Morris W. *The Art of the People* 1879, in Works XXII, pp.42–46

278. *Op.cit.* 5.4 p.357; cf. Plekhanov G.V. *Art and Social Life* 1912, p.65

279. *Op.cit.* 5.96 p.711; cf. Kant *op.cit.* 5.52 pp.112–113: "War itself . . . has something sublime about it. . . . On the other hand a prolonged peace favours the predominance of a mere commercial spirit . . . self-interest, cowardice and effeminacy"; cf. Hobbes *op.cit.* 5.19 p.82, regarding the evils of war. "In such condition, there is no place for industry . . . no culture of the earth . . . no commodious building . . . no arts, no letters, no society . . . and the life of man solitary, poor, nasty, brutish and short."

280. *Op.cit.* 5.4 p.313

281. *Op.cit.* 5.96 p.719, lines from "The Corsair": "Still sway their souls with that commanding art/That dazzles, leads, yet chills the vulgar heart"

282. *Op.cit.* 6.227 p.82

283. *Ibid.* p.81: "*L'art pour l'art* means: the devil take morality"

284. *Ibid.* p.74

285. *Op.cit.* 5.2 p.344

286. *Op.cit.* 6.227 p.74: "The highest feeling of power and security finds expression in that which possesses grand style"

287. Darwin C. *On the Origin of Species* 1859, and *The Descent of Man* 1871

288. *Op.cit.* 5.106 Vol. 8, Part 1, p.157; cf. *op.cit.* 5.4 p.379 and Spencer H. *Principles of Psychology* 1855, where artistic activity was seen as a form of play. Humans develop a surplus of energy in their struggle to survive.

289. *Ibid.* p.149

290. *Op.cit.* 5.96 p.663; cf. Rousseau J.J. *Discourse on Inequality* 1754; "Man is naturally good and only by institutions is he made bad"

291. *Op.cit.* 6.8 p.211

292. *Op.cit.* 5.96 p.505

293. *Op.cit.* 5.3 p.138

294. *Op.cit.* 5.5 p.192; cf. Tolstoy L.N. *What is Art?* 1896

295. *Op.cit.* 5.48 p.102, James stood for "romantic spontaneity" against the "hurdy-gurdy monotony" of Spencer.

296. *Ibid.* p.111

Chapter 7: Nineteenth- and Twentieth-century Categories

1. Lewis C.I. 'Mind and the World Order' 1929, pp.233–234: "Certain fundamental categories are doubtless very ancient and permanent: thing and property, cause and effect, mind and body and the relation of valid inference. . ."

2. *Ibid.* p.236; cf. p.239 "Confirmation of this conception . . . could only come from detailed examination of at least the major categories. . . . Such a task cannot be undertaken here."

3. Ryle G. *Collected Papers* Vol II, (Hutchinson, London, 1971): *Categories* 1938

pp.178ff.; cf. p.170 "Doctrines of categories and theories of types are explorations in the same field . . . and the field is still largely unexplored."

4. Ryle G. *The Concept of Mind* (Penguin, Harmondsworth, 1949) pp.17ff.; Descartes' myth as a "category mistake. . . . It represents the facts of mental life as if they belonged to one logical type or category . . . when they actually belong to another."

5. Collingwood R.G. *An Essay on Philosophical Method* (Clarendon Press, Oxford, 1933) pp.31–33; cf. p.117: "Philosophy as categorical thinking"

6. *Ibid.* p.30

7. *Ibid.* p.57

8. *Op.cit.* 7.1 p.305

9. Collingwood's father, W.G. Collingwood, friend and biographer of Ruskin, lived at "Lanehead" a few miles north of Ruskin's "Brantwood" on the east shore of Coniston Water.

10. *Op.cit.* 5.4 p.293

11. *Op.cit.* 5.3 p.306

12. *Op.cit.* 5.38 p.430

13. *Op.cit.* 7.45 p.275

14. *Op.cit.* 6.160 Vol. I p.394

15. *Ibid.* p.392

16. *Op.cit.* 6.160 Vol. III, p.98

17. Landow G.P. *The Aesthetic and Critical Theories of John Ruskin* (Princeton University Press, 1971) p.114; Ruskin J. *Modern Painters* Vol. II

18. *Op.cit.* 6.160 Vol. II. p.329

19. *Ibid.* Vol. II p.146; cf. *op.cit.* 5.176 p.427: "And as the sunlight undivided is the 'type' of the wisdom and righteousness of God, so divided and softened into colour by means of the firmamental ministry is the type of the wisdom of God becoming sanctification and redemption."

20. *Op.cit.* 7.17 p.427; cf. pp.91, 159, having divorced Beauty from Utility and Truth, Ruskin then proceeds to associate it with Morals and Theory.

21. *Ibid.* pp.23, 26, 114; cf. *op.cit.* 7.17 and Ruskin J. *Modern Painters* Vol. II: Six "types" – Symmetry, Moderation, Unity, Purity, Repose, Infinity (my order)

22. *Ibid.* pp.29, 148ff.

23. *Op.cit.* 6.160 Vol. I, Appendix 13, "Mr Fergusson's System", p.388: "There is no connection between the two systems; mine indeed does not profess to be a system, it is a mere arrangement". However, compare Ruskin's Beauty, Action and Voice with Fergusson's Aesthetic, Technical and Phonetic divisions.

24. *Ibid.* Vol. I, Appendix 14 "Division of Humanity", p.394

25. *Op.cit.* 5.176 p.4: "Both arrangement and nomenclature are those of convenience rather than of system; the one is arbitrary and the other illogical; nor is it pretended that all or even the greater number of the principles necessary to the well-being of the art are included in the inquiry."

26. *Ibid.* pp.8ff.; cf. pp.9–10

27. *Ibid.* pp.103ff.; cf. pp.108, 124

28. *Ibid.* pp.70ff., Ruskin sees Beauty as imitative compared with the Sublime which is original, an "expression of power"; cf. p.79, "the square and circle are pre-eminently the areas of power."

29. *Ibid.* pp.29ff.; cf. pp.30, 35, 40, 55: "We may not be able to command good, or beautiful, or inventive architecture, but we can command an honest architecture" (p.35).

30. *Ibid.* pp.148ff.; cf. pp.149, 165, 169; p.171: "how precious the intelligence must become which renders incompletion itself a means of additional expression"

31. *Ibid.* pp.177ff.; cf. pp.178, 183, 188

32. *Ibid.* pp.199ff.; cf. p.204 where he recommends the four styles to be adopted: Pisan Romanesque, early Western Italian Gothic, Venetian Gothic and Early English Decorated.

33. *Op.cit.* 6.160 Vol. I pp.38, 39, 46

34. Fergusson J. *A History of Architecture* (John Murray, London, 1893); cf. pp.4–6, all the

232

arts can be categorized according to three aspects, Technical, Aesthetic and Phonetic: Joinery is strong in the technical aspect, drama in the phonetic, while "architecture . . . combines all the three classes in nearly equal proportions".

35. *Op.cit.* 6.160 Vol. I, p.36, to "speak well" involved "talking, as the duty of monuments or tombs to record facts and express feelings"

36. *Op.cit.* 5.176 p.3

37. *Op.cit.* 6.160 Vol. I, p.36: "that it act well and do the thing it was intended to do in the best way"; and p.38, where he links "action" with "strength" and "construction".

38. *Op.cit.* 7.17 p.307; cf. *op.cit.* 6.160 p.392: "Every man of science knows the difficulty of arranging a reasonable system of classificiation . . . the best are convenient rather than reasonable". Four kinds of classificatory system are then discussed.

39. *Op.cit.* 6.160 Vol. I, pp.395–396

40. *Ibid.* p.46

41. *Op.cit.* 7.17 p.218

42. *Ibid.*

43. *Op.cit.* 7.3 p.171

44. Roget P. *Roget's Thesaurus: The Everyman Edition* (1952) (Pan Books, London, 1972): see Roget's original introduction, pp.559ff.

45. Emblen D.L. *Peter Mark Roget: The Word and the Man* (Longmans, London, 1970)

46. *Op.cit.* 5.22 pp.114–115; cf. p.116: "The table contains all the elementary concepts of the understanding . . . and accordingly indicates all the momenta of a projected speculative science and even their order, as I have elsewhere shown".

47. *Op.cit.* 7.45 p.262: "Roget offered something new . . . the converse of a dictionary. Instead of presenting words to find ideas, here we start with ideas to find words".

48. Vickery B.C. *Classification and Indexing in Science* (Butterworth, Oxford, 1958) p.124

49. Broadbent G., Bunt R. & Llorens T. (eds) *Meaning and Behaviour in the Built Environment* (Wiley, Chichester, 1980): Hershberger R. "Semantic Scales" where descriptive adjectives were checked against *Roget's Thesaurus*

50. *Op.cit.* 7.48 p.132

51. Foskett A.C. *The Subject Approach to Information* (Clive Bingley, London, 1971); cf. Hobbes *op.cit.* 5.19 pp.54–55 who attempted the classification of subjects as they concerned themselves with Quantity, Motion and Quality respectively (note order), i.e. from Geometry and Arithmetic through Architecture and Engineering to Poetry and Logic.

52. *Ibid.* Cf. Kaiser J. *Systematic Indexing* 1911, where three factors were utilized in classification: the concrete, process and place.

53. *Ibid.* Cf. Ranganathan S.R. *Dictionary Catalogue Code* 1945, and the various editions of his *Colon Classification*

54. *Ibid.* p.271

55. Ranganathan S.R. *Colon Classification*

56. *Op.cit.* 7.51 pp.57ff.

57. *Ibid.* p.26: "Knowledge is multi-dimensional, that is to say subjects are related to one another in many different ways . . . we cannot display multiple relationships", cf. p.43.

58. *Ibid.* Cf. Farradane J.E.L., various papers from 1966; Farradane's Table showing nine "relational operators":

		TIME		
		non-time relation	temporary	fixed
SPACE	concurrent	/θconcurrence	/* comparison	/; association
	not distinct	/= equivalence	/+ dimensional state	/(appurtenances
	distinct	/) distinctness	/- reaction	/: causation or functional dependence

Examples include "Authors/:Books" meaning books by English Authors
"/θ Nationality/=English"

The "problem is that the generality of operators makes it difficult to see which is the right one to choose"

59. *Ibid*. pp.368–369

60. *Ibid*. pp.26ff., 49

61. *Op.cit*. 5.2 pp.455–6; cf. Fry R. *Transformations* 1926: "Our reaction to works of art is a reaction to relations and not to sensations or objects or persons or events", *op.cit*. 5.5 p.267

62. *Op.cit*. 5.79

63. *Op.cit*. 5.5 p.155; cf. Herbart J.F. "Introduction to Philosophy" Lectures 1813–1837, II.89: "All the single elements which general aesthetic has to indicate are relations".

64. *Op.cit*. 5.39 cf. p.75, "The Architectonic Character of Philosophy" where he notes that Kant first drew the analogy between "a philosophical doctrine and a piece of architecture".

65. *Op.cit*. 5.22 pp.60, 429, 653ff.: *The Architectonic of Pure Reason*; cf. p.654 where Kant distinguished a "technical unity" from an "architectonic unity . . . the unity of the end to which all the parts relate and in the idea of which they all stand in relation to one another" (p.653).

66. Wright G.H. von, quoted in Pears D., *Wittgenstein* (Fontana/Collins, London, 1971) p.15; cf. Bartley W.W. *Wittgenstein* (Quartet Books, London, 1974) which names the co-architect as Paul Engelmann, a disciple of Adolf Loos whose Steiner House is comparable (p.95).

67. Russell B. *An Inquiry into Meaning and Truth* 1940 (Pelican, London. 1962) p.19

68. *Ibid*. p.325

69. *Op.cit*. 5.39 Vol. 2, p.267; cf. Russell *op.cit*. 7.67 pp.92–93; cf. Locke *op.cit*. 5.15 on the "coexistence" of qualities (p.371).

70. Heidegger M. "The Origin of the Work of Art" 1935, in *Basic Writings* Krell D.F. (ed.) (Routledge & Kegan Paul, London, 1978) pp.153, 168

71. Heidegger M. *What is a Thing?* (1935) tr. Barton W. & Deutsch V. (Henry Regnery, Chicago, 1967) pp.62, 187

72. *Op.cit*. 5.22 p.87

73. *Op.cit*. 5.31 p.191

74. *Op.cit*. 5.48 p.58: "The least we can experience, he argues, is already a set of relations . . . to talk at all, Green concludes, is to relate"; cf. p.60 where Bradley "rejects Green's main thesis that the real consists in relations", ". . . diversity is prior to relations . . .", the experience of something is a "feeling which is a unity and yet contains diversity" Relating is a subsequent abstraction (p.63).

75. Russell B. *Analysis of Mind* (George Allen & Unwin, London, 1921) pp.10, 23

76. Wittgenstein L. *Tractatus Logico-Philosophicus* (1921) (tr. Pears D. & McGuiness B., Routledge & Kegan Paul, London, 1961) pp.1, 13, 23, 25

77. *Ibid*. pp.37, 15

78. *Ibid*. pp.51, 41

79. *Op.cit*. 5.39 Vol. I, p.176, 159

80. *Ibid*. pp.142ff, 149ff, 159ff, 170ff

81. *Op.cit*. 7.76 p.23: "Names are like points; propositions like arrows'; p.61, "I write elementary propositions as functions of names".

82. *Op.cit*. 5.39 Vol. II, p.159: "We may show the relation between the different kinds of sign by a brace thus:

cf. p.282

83. *Op.cit*. 7.76 p.123: "Truth combinations I express by means of brackets."

84. *Op.cit*. 5.48 p.108, James argues for pluralism against Bradley's monism – see 7.74 above.

85. *Op.cit*. 5.48 p.106

86. *Op. cit.* 7.1 p.52
87. *Ibid.* pp.82, 106
88. *Op.cit.* 7.75 pp.25–26
89. *Op.cit.* 5.48 p.303; cf. *op.cit.* 7.5 p.31: "The specific classes of a philosophical genus do not exclude one another, they overlap one another."
90. *Op.cit.* 5.73 p.99
91. *Op.cit.* 6.128 p.124
92. *Op.cit.* 7.51 pp.368–369: Perry J.W. & Kent A. *Semantic Factoring* (WRU, Cleveland, Ohio)
93. *Op.cit.* 7.3 pp.173–174
94. *Op.cit.* 7.76 p.101
95. Barthes R. *Elements of Semiology* (tr. Lavers A. & Smith C., Cape Editions 4, London, 1967)
96. Wittgenstein L. *Philosophical Investigations* 1953 (tr. Anscombe G., Blackwell, Oxford, 1978) p.36; cf. p.152 ". . . that belief is a particular colouring to thoughts"
97. *Ibid.* p.44: "Thought is surrounded by a halo – its essence, logic, presents an order, in fact the *a priori* order of the world"; cf. Kant's "penumbra".
98. *Ibid.* p.181: "Suppose someone said: every familiar word, in a book for example, actually carries an atmosphere with it in our minds, a 'corona' of lightly indicated uses".
99. *Ibid.* p.32
100. *Op.cit.* 7.3: *Philosophical Arguments* (1945) pp.201–202

Chapter 8: Conclusion

1. Plato *Protagoras* 358; cf. Aristotle *Topics* 112b
2. Aristotle *Metaphysics* 1025b, 1069a. Ross noted that the three terms, principles, causes and elements were used indiscriminately by Aristotle, notwithstanding his careful definition; cf. *Physics* 184a where the term "condition" is substituted for "cause", leading to the subsequent identification of conditional propositions with the category of causality. Aristotle *Physics* 184a: cf. *Metaphysics* 1025b–1026a where we may compare the sequence element/cause/principle with the sequences productive/practical/theoretical and mathematics/physics/theology.
3. *Ibid.* 1043a; cf. *Physics* 192a
4. *Op.cit.* 4.11, V.3.3; cf. V.2.4, V.3.21
5. *Ibid.* VI.1.16, VI.3.21
6. Aristotle *Ethics* 1097b: "To say that happiness is the chief good seems a platitude, and a clearer account of what it is is still desired. This might perhaps be given, if we could first ascertain the function of man. For just as for a flute player, a sculptor, or any artist, and, in general, for all things that have a function or activity, the good and the 'well' is thought to reside in the function, so it would seem to be for a man, if he has a function".
7. *Ibid.* 1097a
8. Plato *Philebus* 65: "Then if we are not able to hunt the good with one idea only, with three we may take our prey; Beauty, Symmetry and Truth are the three, and these when united we may regard as the cause of the mixture, and the mixture as being good by reason of the admixture of them".
9. Plato *Republic* 427 & 504; cf. *Laws* 906, where they are reduced to three "justice and temperance and wisdom". Note order.
10. Plato *Laws* 697, & *Phaedo* 114–115. In *Protagoras* 349, holiness, is added, and in *Meno* 74, magnificence.
11. Cicero *De Officiis* tr Miller W. (William Heinemann, London, 1951)
12. Plato *Symposium*. In the *Symposium*, Plato discussed six kinds of love through the views of six characters. Jowett noted that "the speeches have been said to follow in pairs". One interpretation might be the following:

Ethical pair – Phaedrus (love in action) and Pausanius (heavenly and earthly love)
Physical pair – Eryximachus (opposites and harmony) and Aristophanes (modality)
Philosophical pair – Agathon (imagery) and Socrates (desire).

Of love, Plato writes (*Symposium* 178) that it is "the principle which ought to be the guide of men".

13. Aristotle *Ethics* 1160. Cf 1126b where Aristotle writes under the heading of "virtues of social intercourse" that "no name has been assigned to it, though it most resembles friendship".

14. *Ibid.* 1097a

15. Royal Institute of British Architects *Code of Professional Conduct* 1991 (Riba Publications, London, 1997) pp.5, 6, 8

16. Aristotle *Ethics* 1131a; cf. Plato *Republic* 401 and *Laws* 934

17. *Ibid.* 1132a; cf. Plato *Cratylus* 416

18. Plato *Republic* 401

19. Aristotle *Metaphysics* 1020a; cf. *Ethics* 1099b and *Rhetoric* 1369b

20. Aristotle *Ethics* 1169a: "happiness is an activity . . . happiness lies in living and being active". Cf. *Politics* 1325a.

21. Plato *Republic* 420

22. Aristotle *Ethics* 1153a, 1177a; cf. Plato *Laws* 645: "the sacred and golden cord of reason".

23. Aristotle *Ethics* 1098a & 1118a. cf. Plato *Republic* 389

24. *Ibid.* 1104a: "It is the nature of such things to be destroyed by defect and excess, as we see in the case of strength and of health."

25. *Ibid.* 1177a

26. *Ibid.* 1098b

27. Plato *Laws* 638–639

28. Plato *Republic* 500: "The state can only be happy which is planned by artists who make use of the heavenly patterns . . . [they will make the ways of men] as far as possible, in agreement with the ways of God . . . selecting from and mingling the various elements of life."

29. Long and Sedley *op.cit.* 3.99

30. Plato *Sophist* 437. cf. Aristotle *Ethics* 1120a: "nor will he neglect his own property"

31. *Ibid.* 219

32. Aristotle *De Generatione* 314a. The word "relation" is not used in regard to Empedocles "but only a mingling and a divorce". Cf. *Metaphysics* 984b where both Parmenides and Hesiod were noted as having love as a first principle "a cause which will move things and bring them together". Cf. *Physics* 250b–252a: "Love . . . its essential function being to unite."

33. Aristotle *Ethics* 1170a

34. *Ibid.* 1160a

35. Plato *Republic* 605. "Sympathy" is mentioned by Aristotle in *Politics* 1340; cf. Plato *Symposium* 197

36. Plato *Laws* 657

37. Plato *Ion* 535.

38. Plato *Laches* 196. Cf. *Laws* 644–647

39. *Ibid.* 191. The term "endurance" is used rather than "will".

40. Plato *Republic* 427

41. *Ibid.* 435

42. Aristotle *Politics* 1327b

43. *Ibid.* 1328a

44. Wotton H. *Reliquiae Wottonianae* (3rd edition) (printed by T.Roycroft. London, 1672)

45. *Ibid.*

46. Hume D. *Enquiry concerning the Principles of Morals* [1751]. According to the editor, Hume "wished to discover the foundations on which the principles rest".

47. *Op.cit.* 5.141

48. Kant I. *Critique of Practical Reason* 1788 tr. Abbott T.K. (Longmans, Green & Co, London, 1883); pp.207–212; cf. *ibid. Fundamental Principles of the Metaphysics of Morals* [1785] pp.30–38

49. *Ibid. Introduction to the Metaphysics of Morals* [1792] p.296

50. *Ibid.* p.307

51. *Ibid. Critique of Practical Reason* pp.158–180; cf. *Introduction to the Metaphysics of Morals* p.309

52. Bentham J. *Deontology* (Clarendon Press, Oxford, 1983) p.178

53. *Ibid.* p.190

54. Aristotle *Poetics* (tr. Warrington J., J.M.Dent & Sons Ltd, London, 1963); 1447a–1447b: "Just as some . . . use form and colour in order to imitate and portray many things, while others use the voice, so also in the above-mentioned arts the means employed as a whole are rhythm, language and harmony. . . . Finally there are certain other arts – e.g. Dithyramb and Nomic poetry, Tragedy and Comedy – which employ every one of the means enumerated."

55. Aristotle *Metaphysics* 1070a

56. Aristotle *Physics* 199b: "In plants too we find the relation of means to end. . . . For those things are natural which, by a continuous movement originated from an internal principle, arrive at some completion."

57. Plato *Gorgias* 506

58. Aristotle *Poetics* 1450a: "Every tragedy, therefore, must contain six (and only six) parts which determine its quality. They are Spectacle, Melody, Diction, Character, Thought and Plot."

   (a) Order and harmony in the melody? 1449b: "A tragedy is the imitation of an action (1) that is serious . . . (2) in language with pleasurable accessories . . . [i.e.] with rhythm and harmony or song superadded"

   (b) Efficiency in the handling of the action? 1449b: "A tragedy is the imitation of an action (1) that is serious . . . and is complete in itself". At 1451a Aristotle discusses the necessary "unity" of the plot with nothing superfluous but "fixed by the nature of the thing"

   (c) Universality or appropriateness in the thought? 1450b: "Thought, by which I mean . . . what befits the occasion. . . . Thought is shown in all that is said by way of . . . enunciating some universal proposition"

   (d) Proper care in the handling of the composition? 1449b: "By 'Diction' I mean the metrical composition". 1450a: ". . . well constructed from the viewpoint of Diction".

   (e) A feeling of sympathy or humanity in the characterization? 1450a: "Character is what makes us ascribe certain moral qualities to the agent". 1454a–1454b: "All the characters should be good. . . . Tragedy is an imitation of persons better than the average man". The idea follows from Plato in that sympathy with the character is necessary to promote our education, and the instillation of the principle of the good within us, through imitation or emulation.

   (f) Sense of awe or inspiration in the spectacle? 1449b: "A tragedy is the imitation of an action (1) that is serious . . . (4) with incidents arousing pity and fear, whereby to provide an outlet for such emotions". 1453b: "Fear and pity may be aroused by the Spectacle". However, Aristotle adds that to "produce this effect by Spectacle is less artistic" than by using the plot, and demotes the art of Spectacle to that of the costumier, the stage designer and the make-up artist.

59. Plato *Laws* 859: "We are agreed that justice and just men and things and actions are all fair and if a person were to maintain that just men, even when deformed in body, are still perfectly beautiful in respect of the justice of their minds, no one would say that there was any inconsistency in this."

60. Plato *Statesman* 284

61. Plato *Gorgias* 508
62. Cf. Klee P. *Pedagogical Sketchbook* (Faber & Faber, London, 1925) p.23 where Klee describes a "non-symmetrical balance" in painting caused by the different "weights" of light and dark colours.
63. Plato *Symposium* 187
64. Plato *Phaedo* 110d
65. Plato *Republic* 400
66. Plato *Philebus* 62
67. *Ibid.* 51
68. *Op.cit.* 4.27 p.71; cf. *op.cit.* 4.5, IV.13, pp.83–85
69. *Op.cit.* 5.52 pp.57–60
70. *Ibid.* pp.69ff.
71. *Ibid.*
72. *Ibid.* 5.52 p.66
73. *Op.cit.* 5.4 p.270; cf. *op.cit.* 5.38 I. pp. 271–272
74. *Ibid.*
75. Aristotle *Poetics* 1452a
76. Aristotle *Physics* 199b
77. Plato *Republic* 601
78. Aristotle *Oeconomica*
79. Plato *Gorgias* 474
80. Plato *Statesman* 283–284
81. Aristotle *Ethics* 1106b
82. *Op.cit.* 4.49
83. *Op.cit.* 4.27 Aquinas's *Commentary on the Divine Names* 4.1
84. *Op.cit.* 5.5 pp.80–81
85. *Op.cit.* 5.4 pp.307–308
86. Sullivan L. *The Autobiography of an Idea* 1924 (Dover Publications, New York, 1956) pp.257–258
87. Aristotle *Poetics* 1448b
88. Aristotle *Ethics* 1122a
89. Aristotle *Politics* 1331a
90. Plato *Laws* 658; cf. 654
91. Aristotle *Rhetorica* 1407a; cf. *Ethics* 1165a; cf. Plato *Laws* 657–658
92. Aristotle *Ethics* 1098b
93. *Op.cit.* 5.50 pp.350, 354
94. *Op.cit.* 5.21 pp.462, 463
95. *Op.cit.* 5.176 pp.199ff.
96. *Ibid.*
97. Plato *Republic* 381
98. Aristotle *Physics* 227a
99. Plato *Laws* 672–688
100. Aristotle *Physics* 194a
101. *Ibid.*
102. Plato *Gorgias* 465
103. *Ibid.*
104. *Op.cit.* 4.14
105. *Op.cit.* 4.165
106. Aristotle *Metaphysics* 1013a; cf. 1029a and *Physics* 194b; cf. Aristotle *Ethics* 1099a; cf. Plato *Laws* 743: "There are three things about which every man has an interest . . . money . . . body . . . soul."
107. *Op.cit.* 5.21 p.545
108. *Op.cit.* 5.4 p.338
109. Aristotle *Physics* 246b: ". . . all excellencies depend upon particular relations. Thus bodily excellences such as health and a good state of body we regard as consisting in a blending of hot and cold elements within the body in due proportion, in relation either

238

to one another or to the surrounding atmosphere: and in like manner we regard beauty, strength and all the other bodily excellencies and defects."

110. Aristotle *De Anima* 430a
111. Plato *Gorgias* 481: "O Callicles, if there were not some community of feelings among mankind, however varying in different persons – I do not see how we could ever communicate our impressions to one another."
112. Aristotle *Politics* 1340
113. Plato *Republic* 398
114. *Op.cit.* 4.11 I.6.1.
115. *Op.cit.* 4.9 p.110 (S.T. Q13.6)
116. *Op.cit.* 5.52 p.225
117. *Op.cit.* 5.4 pp.310, *op.cit.* 5.5 p.191; cf. Tolstoy L.N. *What is Art?*
118. *Ibid.* p.380
119. Plato *Laws* 657
120. *Ibid.* 653: "the young of all creatures cannot be quiet in their bodies or in their voices; they are always wanting to move or to cry out."
121. *Ibid.* 665; cf. *Republic* 424: "musical innovation is full of danger to the state".
122. Aristotle *Rhetoric* 1404b
123. Aristotle *Ethics* 1122b
124. Plato *Laws* 656
125. *Ibid.* 657
126. *Op.cit.* 4.220 pp.57–59
127. *Op.cit.* 5.50 p.372
128. *Op.cit.* 5.52 pp.94ff.
129. *Op.cit.* 5.201
130. *Op.cit.* 6.227 p.81
131. *Op.cit.* 8.48, *Introduction to the Metaphysics of Morals*, p.280
132. Plato *Statesman* 306, *Laws* 705; cf. *Republic* 443
133. Aristotle *Ethics* 1123a, *Politics* 1331a
134. Plato *Phaedo* 114–115
135. Plato *Gorgias* 465
136. Plato *Philebus* 56: "The art of the builder which has a number of measures and instruments attains from them a greater degree of accuracy than the other arts."
137. *Op.cit.* 4.220, pp.127,131; cf. Vitruvius *op.cit.* 1.1 pp.10–11: "For, in the midst of all the great variety of subjects, an individual cannot attain to perfection in each."
138. Plato *Statesman* 294
139. Plato *Laws* 875
140. Plato *Republic* 400–401
141. Aristotle *Topics* 163a; From hereon the imagination takes over: "Not by wisdom but by a sort of genius and divine inspiration"; by being "able to make a unity out of several images"; "Can anyone have a more exacting way of considering anything than being able to look at one idea gathered from many different things" (Plato *Apology* 22; Aristotle *De Anima* 434a; and Plato *Laws* 965 respectively).

BIBLIOGRAPHY

ARCHITECTURE

Alberti L.B. *Leon Battista Alberti: On the Art of Building in Ten Books* 1486 (tr.Rykwert J., Leach N., & Tavernor R., MIT Press, Cambridge, Mass., 1991)

Alberti L.B. *Ten Books on Architecture* 1486 (tr. Bartoli 1550, tr.Leoni 1726, Rykwert J. (ed), Alec Tiranti Ltd, London, 1955)

Fergusson J. *A History of Architecture* (John Murray, London 1893)

Jones I. *Inigo Jones on Palladio* (Allsopp B. (ed.), Oriel Press, Newcastle upon Tyne, 1970)

Krautheimer R. *Early Christian and Byzantine Architecture* (Penguin, Harmondsworth, 1965)

Kruft H.-W. *A History of Architectural Theory* 1985 (tr. Taylor, Callander & Wood, Zwemmer, London, 1994)

Lotz W. *Architecture in Italy 1500-1600* 1974 (tr. Howard D., Yale University Press, London, 1995)

Palladio A. *Andrea Palladio: The Four Books on Architecture* (tr. Tavernor R. & Schofield R., MIT Press, Cambridge, Mass., 1997)

Panofsky E. (ed.) *Abbot Suger on the Abbey Church of St. Denis* (Princeton University Press. New York, 1946)

Panofsky E. *Gothic Architecture and Scholasticism* (Thames & Hudson, London, 1957)

Pugin A.W. *The True Principles of Pointed or Christian Architecture* (Academy Editions, London, 1973)

Ruskin J. *The Seven Lamps of Architecture* (George Allen, London, 1880)

Ruskin J. *The Stones of Venice* (Wiley, Chichester, UK, 1889)

Scott G. *The Architecture of Humanism* (Constable & Co., London, 1914)

Scruton R. *The Aesthetics of Architecture* (Methuen, London, 1979)

Summerson J. *Architecture in Britain 1530–1830* 1953 (Penguin Books, Harmondsworth, 1970)

Vitruvius *The Ten Books on Architecture* (tr. Morgan M.H., 1914, Dover Publications Inc., New York, 1960)

Vitruvius *Vitruvius on Architecture* (tr. Granger F., William Heinemann, London, 1931)

Wittkower R. *Architectural Principles in the Age of Humanism* 1949, (Academy Editions, London, 1973)

Wotton H. *The Elements of Architecture* 1624 (Gregg International Publishers, Farnborough, 1969)

PHILOSOPHY AND LITERATURE

Abrams M.H. *The Mirror and the Lamp: Romantic Theory and the Critical Tradition* (Oxford University Press, Oxford, 1953)

Addison J. *Essays of Joseph Addison* (Frazer J.G. (ed.) Macmillan & Co., London, 1915)

Beardsley M.C. *Aesthetics from Classical Greece to the Present* (University of Alabama Press, 1966)

Bosanquet B. *Introduction to Hegel's Philosophy of Fine Art* (Kegan Paul, London, 1905)

Burke E. *A Philosophical Enquiry into the Origin of Our Ideas of the Sublime and the Beautiful* 1757

Carritt E.F. *Philosophies of Beauty* (Clarendon Press, Oxford, 1931)

Carritt E.F. *The Theory of Beauty* (Methuen & Co., London, 1914)

Coleridge S.T. *Biographia Literaria* (Dent, London 1965)

Collingwood R.G. *Outlines of a Philosophy of Art* (Oxford University Press, Oxford, 1925)

Dickie G. *Aesthetics: An Introduction* (Pegasus, New York, 1971)

Elledge S. (ed.) *Eighteenth Century Critical Essays* (Cornell University Press, New York, 1961)

Elton W. (ed.) *Aesthetics & Language* (Blackwell, Oxford, 1954)

Emerson R.W. *Essays* (Henry Altemus, Philadelphia, USA, undated)

Frankl P. *The Gothic* (Princeton University Press, New York, 1960)

Gilpin W. *Three Essays: on Picturesque Beauty; on Picturesque Travel; and on Sketching Landscape* (R. Blamire, London, 1794)

Goethe J.W. von *The Theory of Colours* (tr. Eastlake C.L., MIT Press, Cambridge, Mass., 1970)

Harrington K. *Changing Ideas on Architecture in the Encyclopédie 1750–1776* (UMI Research Press, 1985)

Hazlitt W. *Hazlitt on English Literature* (Zeitlin J. (ed.) Oxford University Press, Oxford, 1913)

Holt, E.G. *A Documentary History of Art* (Doubleday, New York, 1957)

Landow G.P. *The Aesthetic and Critical Theories of John Ruskin* (Princeton University Press, New York, 1971)

Longinus *On the Sublime* (tr. Roberts W.R., Cambridge University Press, Cambridge, 1899)

Morris C.W. *Signs, Language and Behaviour* (Prentice-Hall, New York, 1946)

Newton I. *Optics* 1704 (G. Bell & Sons, London, 1931)

Nisbet H.B. (ed.) *German Aesthetic and Literary Criticism* (Cambridge University Press, Cambridge, 1985)

Ogden C.K. & Richards I.A. *The Meaning of Meaning* 1923 (Kegan Paul, Trench, Trubner & Co Ltd, London, 1994)

Richards I.A. *Principles of Literary Criticism* 1924 (Routledge and Kegan Paul, London, 1960)

Roget P. *Roget's Thesaurus: The Everyman Edition* 1952 (Pan Books, London, 1972)

Saussure F. de *Course in General Linguistics* 1916 (tr. Harris R., Duckworth, New York, 1960)

Schlegel A.W. *Lectures on Dramatic Art & Literature* (tr. Black J., G. Bell & Sons, London, 1883)

Shaftesbury, Third Earl of *Characteristics* (Bobbs Merrill, New York, 1964)

Tatarkiewicz W. *History of Aesthetics, Vol II Mediaeval Aesthetics* 1962 (tr. Montgomery R.M., Polish Scientific Publishers, 1970)

Tillman F.A. & Cahn S.M. (eds) *Philosophy of Art and Aesthetics* (Harper & Row, New York, 1969)

Vickery B.C. *Classification and Indexing in Science* (Butterworths, London, 1958)

Wordsworth W. *The Prose Works of William Wordsworth* (Owen W. & Smyser J. (eds), Clarendon Press, Oxford, 1974)

CLASSICAL PHILOSOPHY

Aristotle, *Analytica Posteriora, Analytica Priora, De Anima, Categories, De Caelo, De Generatione, De Interpretatione, Metaphysics, Nichomachean Ethics, Oeconomia, Physics, Poetics, Politics, Rhetoric, Topics*

Cicero *Academica, De Natura Deorum, De Officiis, Tusculan Disputations*

Cornford F.M. *Plato's Theory of Knowledge* 1935 (Routledge & Kegan Paul, London, 1960)

Evangeliou C. *Aristotle's Categories and Porphyry* (E.J. Brill, Leiden, 1988)

Lacey W.K. *Cicero and the End of the Roman Republic* (Hodder & Stoughton, London, 1978)

Long A. & Sedley D. *The Hellenistic Philosophers* (Cambridge University Press, Cambridge, 1987)

Lucretius *De Rerum Natura* (tr. Rouse W., William Heinemann, London, 1947)

Plato *Charmides, Cratylus, Epistle Seven, Gorgias, Laws, Lysis, Menexenus, Meno, Parmenides, Phaedo, Phaedrus, Philebus, Republic, Sophist, Statesman, Symposium, Timaeus*

Ross D. *Aristotle* 1923 (Routledge, London, 1995)

MEDIAEVAL PHILOSOPHY

Aquinas T. *Summa Theologiae* (Blackfriars. London, 1967)

Augustine *City of God* (tr. Healey J., Dent & Sons, London, 1931)

Augustine *Confessions* (tr. Pine-Coffin P.R., Penguin, Harmondsworth, 1961)

Augustine *The Trinity* (tr. MacKenna S., Catholic University of America Press. 1963)

Bainton R.H. *Early and Mediaeval Christianity* (Hodder & Stoughton, London, 1962)

Baynes N.H. *Constantine the Great and the Christian Church* (Oxford University Press, 1931)

Bigg C. *The Christian Platonists of Alexandria* (Clarendon Press, Oxford, 1886)

Bonaventure *The Soul's Journey into God* (tr. Cousins E., Paulist Press, New York, 1978)

Bonner A. (tr. & ed.) *Selected Works of Ramon Lull* (Princeton University Press, New York, 1985)

Coppleston S.J. *A History of Philosophy* Vol I (Burns, Oates & Washbourne Ltd, 1950)

Dante Alighieri *The Divine Comedy* (tr. Sinclair J.D., John Lane, London, 1939)

Demaray J.G. *Dante and the Book of the Cosmos* (The American Philosophical Society, 1987)

Dionysius the Areopagite *The Works of Dionysius the Areopagite* (tr. Parker J., Parker J. & Co., 1897)

Duns Scotus *Philosophical Writings* (Wolter A. (tr. & ed), Nelson, Edinburgh, 1962)

Eco U. *The Aesthetics of Thomas Aquinas* 1956 (tr. Bredin H., Radius, 1988)

Eriugena *Periphyseon* (tr. O'Meara J., Bellarmin, Dumbarton Oaks, 1987)

Eusebius *Ecclesiastical History* (tr. Oulton, Heinemann, London, 1932)

Gilby T. *St. Thomas Aquinas: Theological Texts* (Oxford University Press, Oxford, 1955)

Gilson E. *The Mystical Theology of St. Bernard* (tr. Downes A., Sheed & Ward, London, 1940)

Gilson E. *The Christian Philosophy of St. Augustine* (tr. Lynch, Gollancz, London, 1961)

Grane L. *Peter Abelard* (tr. Crowley F. & C., Allen & Unwin, London, 1970)

Hathaway R.F. *Hierarchy and the Definition of Order in the Letters of Pseudo-Dionysius* (University of California Press, 1969)

Hesiod *Theogony* (tr. Banks J., Bell & Sons, London, 1879)

Inge W.R. *The Philosophy of Plotinus* (Longmans, London, 1929)

Jordan M. *Ordering Wisdom in Aquinas* (University of Notre Dame Press, Indiana, 1986)

Kirk K.E. *Evolution of the Doctrine of the Trinity*

Loeschen J.R. *The Divine Community* (16thC. Journal Publishers, Missouri)

McCallum J.R. *Abelard's Christian Theology* (Blackwell, Oxford, 1948)

Moody E. *The Logic of William of Ockham* (Sheed and Ward, London, 1935)

Morgan C. *An Investigation of the Trinity of Plato and Philo Judaeus* 1795 (Cambridge University Press, Cambridge, 1853)

Novatian *On the Trinity* (tr. Moore H., Macmillan & Co., London, 1919)

Ockham G. de *Opera Theologica* Vol IV (St Bonaventure University, New York 1979)

Payne R. *The Christian Centuries* (W.H. Allen, London, 1967)

Pegis A.C. *Introduction to St. Thomas Aquinas* (Random House, New York, 1948)

Plotinus *Enneads* (tr. Mackenna S. & Page B.S., The Medici Society, London, 1930)

Proclus *The Elements of Theology* (tr. Dodds E.R., Clarendon Press, Oxford, 1933)

Proclus *The Platonic Theology* (tr. Taylor T. (1816), Selene Books, New York 1985)

Rawlinson A.E.I. (ed.) *Essays on the Trinity and the Incarnation* (Longmans, London, 1928)

Richard of St. Victor (tr. Zinn, G.A., SPCK, London, 1979)

Richard of St Victor *Benjamin Minor* (tr. Yankowski S.V., Wiefeld & Mehl, Ansbach)

Tillich P. *Systematic Theology* (Nisbet, 1951)

Wolfson H.A. *The Philosophy of the Church Fathers* (Harvard University Press, New York, 1956)

MODERN PHILOSOPHY

Babbitt I. *Rousseau and Romanticism* (Constable, London, 1919)

Bentham B. *Deontology* (Clarendon Press, Oxford, 1983)

Bergson H. *An Introduction to Metaphysics* (tr. Hulme T., Macmillan, London, 1913)

Berkeley G. *The Works of George Berkeley* (Luce A. & Jesop T. (eds), Nelson & Sons, Edinburgh, 1949)

Bradley F.B. *Essays on Truth & Reality* (Clarendon Press, Oxford, 1914)

Collingwood R.G. *An Essay on Philosophical Method* (Clarendon Press, Oxford, 1933)

Collingwood, R.G. *The Principles of Art* (Clarendon Press, Oxford, 1938)

Copleston F. *A History of Philosophy* (Doubleday, New York, 1974)

Descartes R. *Discourse on Method* in *The Philosophical Works of Descartes* Vol. I (tr. Haldane E. & Ross G., Dover, New York, 1911)

Feibleman J.K. *An Introduction to Peirce's Philosophy* (George Allen & Unwin, London, 1960)

Fichte J.G. *Science of Knowledge* (tr. Kroeger A.E., Lippincott, Philadelphia, 1868)

Ficino M. *The Philebus Commentary* (tr. Allen M, University of California Press, 1975)

Hegel G.W.F. *Logic* (tr. Wallace W., Clarendon Press, Oxford, 1975)

Heidegger M. *Basic Writings* (Krell D.F. (ed.), Routledge & Kegan Paul, London, 1978)

Heidegger M. *What is a Thing?* (1935) (tr. Barton W. & Deutsch V., Henry Regnery, Chicago, 1967)

Hobbes T. *The English Works of Thomas Hobbes* (Molesworth W. (ed.), John Bohn, London, 1839)

Hobbes T. *Leviathan* (Blackwell, Oxford, 1946)

Holmes G. *The Florentine Enlightenment 1400–1450* (Weidenfeld & Nicolson, London, 1969)

Hume D. *A Treatise of Human Nature* (Selby-Bigge L.A. (ed.), Clarendon Press, Oxford, 1888)

Hume D. *An Enquiry Concerning Human Understanding* in *Essential Works of David Hume* (Cohen R. (ed.) Bantam, London, 1965)

Hume D. *Enquiry concerning the Principles of Morals* 1751

Jaspers K. *The Philosophy of Karl Jaspers* (Schilpp P.A (ed.), Tudor Publications, 1957)

Jaspers K. *Philosophy* Vol. II 1932 (tr. Ashton E.B., University of Chicago Press, 1970)

Kant I. *Critique of Practical Reason* 1788 (tr. Abbott T.K., Longmans, Green & Co, London, 1883)

Kant I. *Critique of Pure Reason* (tr. Smith N.K., Macmillan, London, 1968)

Kant I. *The Critique of Judgement* (tr. Meredith J.C., Clarendon Press, Oxford, 1952)

Kant I. *Introduction to the Metaphysics of Morals* 1792 (tr. Abbott T.K., Longmans, Green & Co., London, 1883)

Locke J. *Essay Concerning Human Understanding* (J.F. Dove, London, 1828)

Mill J.S. *Utilitarianism* (Warnock M. (ed.), Collins, London, 1962)

Nietzsche F. *Twilight of the Idols* (tr. Hollingdale R., Penguin, Harmondsworth, 1968)

Passmore J. *A Hundred Years of Philosophy* 1957 (Penguin, Harmondsworth, 1968)

Pears D. *Wittgenstein* (Fontana/Collins, London, 1971)

Peirce C.S. *Collected Papers of Charles Sanders Peirce* (Hartshorne C. & Weiss P. (eds), Harvard University Press, New York, 1931)

Russell B. *An Inquiry into Meaning and Truth* 1940 (Pelican, London, 1962)

Russell B. *Analysis of Mind* (George Allen & Unwin, London, 1921)

Russell B. *History of Western Philosophy* (George Allen & Unwin, London, 1946)

Ryle G. *The Concept of Mind* 1949 (Penguin, Harmondsworth, 1963)

Schopenhauer A. *The World as Will and Representation* (tr. Payne E., Dover Publications, New York, 1966)

Schopenhauer A. *On the Four-Fold Root of the Principle of Sufficient Reason* (tr. Payne E., La Salle, Illinois, 1974)

Stace W.T. *The Philosophy of Hegel* (Macmillan & Co, London, 1924)

Wittgenstein L. *Philosophical Investigations* (tr. Anscombe G.E.M., Blackwell, Oxford, 1978)

Wittgenstein L. *Tractatus Logico-Philosophicus* 1921 (tr. Pears D. & McGuiness B., Routledge & Kegan Paul, London, 1961)

INDEX

NOTE: This is an index of names and concepts only. Pages indicating main sections are in **bold** type. Pages where plates are to be found are in *italics*.